'A GREAT AND NOBLE OCCUPATION!'

The Society of Legal Scholars, originally the Society of Public Teachers of Law, was created in 1909, but was fortunate to survive its first half-century. It had few members, lacked financial resources and was weak in influence. In comparison with other university disciplines, law enjoyed a fragile status, and was often held in low esteem by barristers and solicitors. At times the SPTL was caught up in problems of its own making, for instance refusing to admit women until the late 1940s. But there were also moments of excitement and achievement: the years between 1909 and the start of the First World War were full of hope and new ideas, and the establishment of the *Journal of the Society of Public Teachers of Law* in the 1920s was an important achievement for legal scholars.

During the social revolution of the 1960s the SPTL continued to function as a rather sedate gentleman's club, gathering at its annual conference to socialise, rather than to engage in academic debate. The 1970s saw a sustained drive from its Young Members' Group to create a new, more serious organisation, with better conferences and more effective decision-making processes. The Society evolved slowly, but the process accelerated in the 1990s, with members encouraged to reinforce their intellectual contribution to the discipline and act as a central point for policy debate within the legal academic community. As we stand at the beginning of the twenty-first century, the Society, with nearly 3,000 members, has come a long way from its small beginnings.

'A Great and Noble Occupation!'

The History of the Society of Legal Scholars

Fiona Cownie
and
Raymond Cocks

·HART·
PUBLISHING

OXFORD AND PORTLAND, OREGON
2009

Published in North America (US and Canada) by
Hart Publishing
c/o International Specialized Book Services
920 NE 58th Avenue, Suite 300
Portland, OR 97213-3786
USA
Tel: +1 503 287 3093 or toll-free: (1) 800 944 6190
Fax: +1 503 280 8832
E-mail: orders@isbs.com
Website: http://www.isbs.com

Hart Publishing Ltd, 16C Worcester Place, Oxford OX1 2JW
Telephone: +44 (0)1865 517530 Fax: +44 (0)1865 510710
E-mail: mail@hartpub.co.uk
Website: http://www.hartpub.co.uk

British Library Cataloguing in Publication Data
Data Available

ISBN: 978-1-84113-678-3

Typeset by Forewords Ltd, Oxford
Printed and bound in Great Britain by
TJ International Ltd, Padstow, Cornwall

PREFACE

2009 was originally chosen as the year in which to publish the history of the Society of Legal Scholars because it is the year in which the Society becomes 100 years old. However, we hope that the resulting publication does not merely fulfil a wish on the part of the Society to commemorate its centenary, but will also provide a substantial contribution to the history of legal education in the UK, about which far too little is known.

During its first 100 years, the Society has grown enormously. About 60 law teachers expressed interest in joining the Society when it was first formed. In 2009 the Society is welcoming its 3,000th member. Over the years, the Society has changed its name from the Society of Public Teachers of Law to the Society of Legal Scholars, it has established a scholarly journal (originally the *Journal of the Society of Public Teachers of Law*, now *Legal Studies*) and it has provided annual meetings where, over the years, thousands of participants have considered issues of interest to academic lawyers. In recounting the story of these, and other significant events in the Society's history, we have benefited from free access to the Society's rich archive. However, the archive is by no means complete, and we have suffered the usual frustrations of historians, bemoaning those who in earlier years thought fit to destroy potentially fascinating documents.

Our approach throughout has been to try to allow those involved in the Society's history to speak for themselves through the documents we have unearthed. The Society's archive has never before been subjected to systematic examination, and we have taken the decision therefore to focus closely on the history of the Society itself, touching on general matters, including current affairs, legal education and higher education policy only where those were relevant to events that were significant for the Society. Like any research, this is a work in progress, in the sense that we hope it will inspire others to build on the basis we have provided and take further the project of charting the history of legal academics in the UK and Ireland.

We should like to draw the attention of readers to the fact that from 1990 onwards the Society's archives are not yet open to the general public. We were granted access to records from that date onwards by the Society on the understanding that we would use our discretion in what we made public. During the 1990s we have only omitted material not otherwise publicly available which, were it to have been included, would have constituted a breach of privacy relating to living individuals. As regards the 2000s, we have decided to include an epilogue which covers those years, as it is not possible, without the benefit of some distance of time, to properly evaluate events so close to our own time, quite apart from the Society's need to keep confidential some recent documents which relate to matters still under negotiation or discussion with various third parties.

Finally, readers should note that both the authors have been involved with the Society in various capacities in the 1990s/2000s. In writing about the Society we have therefore attempted to meet Delamont's challenge to 'make the familiar strange'.[1] It will be up to the reader to make up their own minds to what extent we have succeeded.

We hope that readers will find the history of this learned society of academic lawyers as fascinating as we do, and that, by analysing some of the less glorious aspects of the Society's history we have not undermined too much the opinion of the Society's founder, Henry Goudy, that 'We are teachers of Law—a great and noble occupation!'

Ray Cocks and Fiona Cownie
Keele, May 2009

---

[1] S Delamont, 'Just Like the Novels? Researching the Occupational Culture(s) of Higher Education', in R Cuthbert (ed), *Working in Higher Education* (Buckingham, SRHE & Open University Press, 1996) 147.

ACKNOWLEDGEMENTS

Writing the history of the Society of Legal Scholars has been a fascinating task, carried out as a joint venture between a legal historian and a legal education specialist. We hope that readers will agree that we have pooled our respective expertise to good effect. Readers should know that Professor Ray Cocks has been primarily responsible for writing the material relating to the first 50 years of the Society's existence, and Professor Fiona Cownie has taken primary responsibility for material from 1960 to the present day.

In carrying out the research for this book, we have been greatly helped by a number of people, to whom we would like to express our thanks. Professor William Twining, a Past President of the Society, was most helpful, both in discussing this project and in making available large numbers of his private documents relating to the Society, which augmented those he had already deposited in the Society's archive. We are most grateful for his continuing interest in, and support of, this project. Professor David Sugarman was also most generous with his time in discussing the project in its early stages. Jules Winterton, Associate Director and Librarian of the Institute of Advanced Studies, welcomed us and greatly facilitated our research. We would also like to thank the staff of the Institute, including in particular the Archivist, Elizabeth Dawson, who not only helped us to access the archive, but also shared her office with us for several years. Lesley Young, Information Services Manager at the Institute, was equally helpful. Eliza Boudier, Secretary to the Director, and Monica Humble, Finance Assistant, helped us to master the intricacies of the photocopying machine and rescued us when necessary. All of these people generously provided assistance which made our task much easier. Deborah Parry (formerly of the University of Hull) responded to requests for material for the archive and provided documents which filled in some of the frustrating gaps that would otherwise have existed. Sally Thomson, current SLS Administrator, and Professor Nick Wikeley, former Honorary Secretary of the Society, deposited in the Archive large numbers of documents relating to the year 2000 onwards, all beautifully organised—saving us an enormous sorting job, for which we are extremely grateful. Others who have sent useful material include John Woodliffe (formerly of Leicester University), Hannah Quirk of Manchester University and Professor Geoffrey Samuels of Kent University. Many thanks to you all. Our joint thanks also go to Richard Hart and his team, whose patience and professionalism has been outstanding.

Ray Cocks would like to thank Andrew Francis and Phil Handler for their comments on a nearly final draft of his part of this project. Fiona Cownie would like to express her thanks to Kate Malleson and Maurice Mitchell, whose generous hospitality over the past few years has enabled her to stay in London to access the archives. Also to Sam, Peter and Ellie—thank you for sharing your house with me for so long! Also to Elaine Morton, of the Flower Corner, in Leicester, whose blooms have cheered up my office as I worked on this project; equally to Anne and Mel Empsall, for their interest in legal academics of times past. My thanks would not be complete without acknowledging, as always, my heartfelt gratitude for the continuing support of my fellow-academic and husband, Tony Bradney.

CONTENTS

Preface   v

Acknowledgements   vii

Chronological List of the Society's Office Holders   xi

1   New Questions Affecting the Teaching of Law: 1908–1909   1

2   Hope Followed by Dismay: 1910–1918   15

3   Defiance and Debate: 1919–1930   37

4   Research, Dissent and the Possible Admission of Women: 1930–1939   49

5   War, Respectability, the Admission of Women, Legal Education with
    'Vituperative Epithets' and Increasing Self-confidence: 1940–1960   59

6   The First Fifty Years: A Summary   79

7   The Swinging Sixties   85

8   The 1970s: Reform Begins   121

9   The 1980s: A Difficult Decade   163

10 The 1990s: A Decade of Change   207

11 The New Millennium: 2000 and Beyond   245

Index   265

CHRONOLOGICAL LIST OF THE SOCIETY'S OFFICE HOLDERS

Presidents of the Society

1909–10	The late Professor H Goudy
1910–11	The late Sir Alfred Hopkinson Jenks, FBA KC
1911–12	The late Dr Blake Odgers, KC
1912–13	The late Sir John Macdonnell,
1913–14	The late Dr Henry Bond
1914–15	The late Professor Sir William Holdsworth OM, KC, FBA
1915–16	The late Sir Ernest Trevelyan
1916–17	The late Professor AF Murison, CBE KC
1917–18	The late Professor A Pearce Buckland, FBA Higgins, CBE, KC, FBA
1918–19	The late Professor H Goudy Burgin, MP
1919–20	The late Professor Edward
1920–21	The late Professor Geldart, CBE
1921–22	The late Mr GH Hurst
1922–23	The late Professor HD KCB, FBA Hazeltine, FBA
1923–24	The late Professor Sir William
1924–25	The late Professor JL Brierly,
1925–26	The late Professor WW Buckland, FBA
1926–27	The late Right Hon E Leslie
1927–28	The late Professor HC Gutteridge, QC
1928–29	The late Judge HC Dowdall, QC
1929–30	The late Professor Sir Percy Winfield, QC, FBA
1930–31	The late Dr AEW Hazel, CBE, KC
1931–32	The late Professor JDI Hughes
1932–33	The late Professor F de Zulueta, FBA
1933–34	The late Right Hon Lord McNair, CBE, QC, FBA
1934–35	The late Professor RA Eastwood, OBE
1935–36	The late Professor RW Lee, FBA
1936–37	The late Professor HF Jolowicz
1937–38	The late Professor HA Hollond, DSO, OBE
1938–39	The late Dr GRY Radcliffe
1939–46	The late Judge Raleigh Batt
1946–47	The late Dean CE Smalley-Baker, QC

1947–48   The late Dr WT Stallybrass, OBE
1948–49   The late Professor Sir David Hughes Parry, QC
1949–50   The late Professor AL Goodhart, KBE, QC, FBA
1950–51   The late Professor ECS Wade, QC, FBA
1951–52   The late Mr PA Landon, MC
1952–53   The late Professor Denis Browne
1953–54   The late Professor TFT Plucknett, FBA
1954–55   The late Right Hon Lord Chorley, QC
1955–56   The late Professor DJLl Davies
1956–57   The late Professor JL Montrose
1957–58   The late Professor PW Duff
1958–59   The late Professor HG Hanbury, QC
1959–60   The late Professor FH Lawson, FBA
1960–61   The late Professor D Seaborne Davies
1961–62   The late Professor GW Keeton, FBA
1962–63   The late Professor AH Campbell
1963–64   The late Professor O Hood Phillips, QC
1964–65   The late Professor BA Wortley, OBE, QC, CMG
1965–66   The late Rt Hon Sir Robert Megarry, FBA
1966–67   The late Professor JA Coutts
1967–68   The late Sir Arthur Ll Armitage
1968–69   The late Professor Sir Norman Anderson, OBE, QC, FBA
1969–70   The late Professor Sir Rupert Cross FBA
1970–71   The late Professor Sir Thomas Smith QC, FBA
1971–72   The late Professor PS James
1972–73   The late Professor RH Graveson QC
1973–74   The late Professor Glanville Williams QC, FBA
1974–75   The late Professor CF Parker
1975–76   The late Professor FR Crane
1976–77   The late Professor LCB Gower, FBA
1977–78   The late Professor H Street, CBE, FBA
1978–79   Professor WL Twining, FBA
1979–80   The late Professor Sir John Smith, CBE, QC, FBA
1980–81   Professor PG Stein, QC, FBA
1981–82   The late Professor JK Grodecki, OBE
1982–83   Professor PH Pettit
1983–84   The late Professor Sir Neil MacCormick, QC, MEP, FBA
1984–85   Professor L Neville Brown, OBE
1985–86   The late Professor AL Diamond, QC
1986–87   Professor JA Jolowicz, QC
1987–88   Professor HK Bevan
1988–89   Professor JA Andrews CBE
1989–90   Professor JF Wilson
1990–91   Professor MC Meston

1991–92   Professor RM Goode, CBE, QC, FBA
1992–93   The Hon Sir Ross Cranston
1993–94   Professor JG Miller
1994–95   Professor JCW Wylie
1995–96   Professor J Tiley CBE
1996–97   Professor H Beale QC
1997–98   Professor M Brazier, OBE
1998–99   Professor JS Bell QC, FBA, FRSA
1999–00   Professor Dame Hazel Genn CBE
2000–01   Professor JM Thomson
2001–02   Professor RIE Card
2002–03   The late Professor PBH Birks, QC, FBA
2003–04   Professor JR Birds
2004–05   Professor A Paterson
2005–06   Professor AM Dugdale
2006–07   Professor Celia Wells, OBE
2007–08   Professor Sarah Worthington
2008–09   Professor Fiona Cownie

Honorary Treasurers

1909–15   The late Professor HD Hazeltine, FBA
1915–21   The late Right Hon Lord McNair, CBE, QC, FBA
1921–28   The late Professor Sir Percy OBE Winfield, QC, FBA
1928–51   The late Mr PA Landon, MC
1951–60   The late Trevor C Thomas Hazeltine, FBA
1960–63   John F Wilson
1963–71   The late Professor FR Crane McNair, CBE, QC, FBA
1971–83   Professor L Neville Brown,
1983–00   Clive A Weston
2000–05   Professor KM Stanton
2005–   Professor D Miers

Honorary Secretaries

1909–19   The late Professor Edward Jenks, FBA
1919–24   The late Right Hon E Leslie Burgin, MP
1924–38   The late Professor ECS Wade, QC, FBA
1938–50   The late Professor DJLl Davies

1950–60   The late Professor LCB Gower, MBE, FBA
1960–63   The late Professor ER Hardy Ivamy
1963–72   Professor JF Wilson
1972–75   Professor JS Read
1975–81   Professor PB Fairest
1981–89   Professor DB Casson
1989–96   The late Professor P B H Birks, QC, FBA
1996–01   Professor DJ Hayton
2001–06   Professor NJ Wikeley
2006–   Professor SJ Bailey

Subject Section Secretaries

1991–96   Professor FD Rose
1996–99   Professor DJ Feldman
1999–2006 Professor P Sparkes
2006–   Professor L Vickers

Honorary Editors of *Legal Studies*

1924–55   The late Professor HF Jolowicz
1955–62   The late Professor FH Lawson,
1962–80   Professor JA Jolowicz, QC
1981–93   Professor JA Andrews CBE
1994–98   Professor J Bell FBA
1998–2005 Professor Derek Morgan and Professor Celia Wells
2005–08   Professor Nick Wikeley
2009–   Professor R Merkin, Professor J Poole, Professor J Steele

We are *teachers of Law*—a great and noble occupation!
(Professor Goudy, first President of the Society of Public Teachers of Law, in his Introductory Address to the Society, 1909)

The objects of the Society shall be the furtherance of the cause of legal education in England and Wales, and the work and interests of public teachers of law therein, by holding discussions and enquiries, by publishing documents, and by taking such other steps as may from time to time be deemed desirable.
(Preliminary draft of the Society's objects, 1909)

1

New Questions Affecting the Teaching of Law: 1908–1909

I am anxious to enlist your support in a scheme which has been in my mind for some little time, and which seems now to have a fair chance of being realised.

The ranks of the teachers of law throughout the kingdom have increased substantially in the last few years, and are likely, with the growth of provincial Universities, to increase still more in the future. The work of these new teachers is different from that of older established teachers at Oxford and Cambridge; but it is equally important, and likely to become still more important in the future. Moreover, new questions effecting the teaching of law, and particularly in relation to the professional side of study, are continually presenting themselves.

Would it not be in the natural order of things, and for the benefit of all concerned, that a society or association of teachers of law be formed, to meet occasionally (say once a year) in London or some other convenient centre, to discuss questions of general interest connected with legal education? It would be, I think a mistake to limit the usefulness of the contemplated Society by constitutional restrictions, but personally I can think of more than one direction in which it might usefully employ itself.[1]

These words were written on 19 June 1908 by Edward Jenks, a law teacher in London, in a letter to Walter Copinger, then one of the Professors of Law in Manchester. It was carefully phrased with a view to eliciting support from a law teacher who, along with all other law teachers in England and Wales at that time,

---

[1] General Correspondence Files, 1908–50, 19 June 1908, A.SPTL 2/1–2. Unless otherwise stated, references to manuscripts are to the archives at the Institute of Advanced Legal Studies, Russell Square, London. The archive presents numerous challenges because SPTL officers used different systems of referencing at different times and the records were periodically weeded. Anyone working with the records soon has cause to be grateful to the modern archivists at the Institute and the system of referencing they have developed. In some respects the system is intricate because of the need to relate the new references to inconsistent practice in the original records: we have used our judgement in this regard. Also, in what follows we often do not use page numbers because the original pagination is sometimes inconsistent. Instead we refer to the relevant committee or meeting or person and give the date used in the records. The Class is given for all archive texts but the full archive description is only used where it would assist the understanding of the reader. Note that the full class, dates and description for A.SPTL 1, which is extensively used below, is 1909–77, Minute Books of Council, General Committee and Special Committee but for the sake of brevity it is referred to as Minutes of General Meetings, followed, where appropriate, by a reference to a specific meeting or committee and the class reference.

had no experience of a professional organisation for academic lawyers. The letter from Jenks went on in a practical way.

> Of course, what one thinks of immediately on hearing such proposals is, the question of time; but I suggest something on the model of the Association of International Law, which does most useful work without trespassing much upon the time of its members. One annual meeting, with a certain amount of work done in the interval by special committees, would, I think, be all that was needed, at any rate at first. The more personal meetings at the general gathering would itself be a gain to all concerned.
>
> I have broached the matter to my former colleague, Professor Goudy, of Oxford, to Dr Blake Odgers, the head of the teaching staff at the Council of Legal Education and to Sir John Macdonell, Professor of Comparative Jurisprudence in the University of London; and, without committing themselves to details, these gentlemen are inclined to regard the proposal with favour. I am addressing a letter also to Professor Kenny, of Cambridge, Professor Maitland's successor in the Chair of English Law.
>
> My proposal is, that, before separating for the holidays, we six (if I am so fortunate as to secure all) should put our names to a carefully worded circular, which I would undertake to see through the Press, and dispatch to every Public teacher of law in England at the beginning of the October term, inviting him to attend a constituent meeting in London in the middle of December. . . . There would be little difficulty about securing a suitable and dignified meeting place.

The remainder of the letter made it clear that Jenks wanted a small constituent committee, and the inference was that it would be followed by the first meeting of the new society at some time in 1909. The further communications inviting law teachers to attend this meeting had a purposeful tone.

> The mere fact of an occasional meeting of legal teachers would itself be no small incentive to enthusiasm and improvement in work admittedly difficult. But it may well be that it would be desirable, from time to time, to utter, on behalf of what has really become a special profession, some organised expression of opinion on subjects affecting the teaching of law; and this can only be done through a definite and permanent body representing legal teachers. We do not desire to prejudge or limit in any way the scope of an organisation which we hope to see come into existence; but we may instance, as subjects well worthy [for] the consideration of such an organisation the relation of academic to professional teaching of law, and the proper contents and sequence of legal curricula.[2]

Copinger and other recipients responded in a positive way and a general invitation to a constituent meeting was sent out in October. The invitation produced at least one significant note of doubt. Arthur Chapman of Leeds University wrote back on 27 October 1908, saying 'I suppose there is no danger of such an organisation in the end imposing upon the various Schools of Law one rigid pattern of abstraction or one inflexible list of subjects.'[3] Jenks replied the next day, arguing:

---

[2] Ibid.
[3] Ibid.

I think you need have no fear whatever as to the result of the Society's work being to stereotype any general scheme of education; and, indeed, it seems to me that there is a far greater danger of such an event happening through force of circumstances whilst there is no organ which can utter a protest on behalf of the only persons who are really competent to speak on the question. On the other hand, it seems to me desirable that, if they are so agreed, public teachers of law should be able to recommend the adoption of certain general principles in teaching.[4]

Jenks's argument was convincing in that representatives from Leeds (including Chapman) participated in the early years of the Society's work without raising this again as an issue. Jenks had given an early indication that in so far as he had a say in the matter he would support flexible but informed ideas for educational change. In his view, the expression of a unified opinion on the part of law teachers need not threaten institutional autonomy.

In any event, there were enough supportive responses for a constituent committee to meet on 15 December at 4.30 pm in the Law Society Council Room. AD Bowers, who was to give half a century of administrative service to the Society, has shown that the result, in the form of providing for the setting up a new organisation, was a foregone conclusion.[5] Professor Dicey proposed the motion for 'The formation of the Society of Public Teachers of Law in England and Wales, consisting of teachers of law in England and Wales appointed by any public body.'[6] The proposal was accepted unanimously.

With almost perpetual energy in the following months Jenks was communicating with others and claiming support from about 60 teachers of law, including, for example, Henry Bond from Cambridge, Edward Bramley from Sheffield, Chaloner Dowdall from Liverpool, William Holdsworth from Oxford, Professor Levi from Aberystwyth, Professor Morgan from University College London, W Blake Odgers KC from the Council of Legal Education, Professor Phillips from Leeds, and Sir Alfred Hopkinson from Manchester. There is doubt about the precise number of law teachers in the country at this time but one list in the SPTL archives suggests 20 at Oxford, 20 at Cambridge, 18 at London, 9 at the Law Society, 11 at the Inns of Court, 1 at Birmingham, 2 at Bristol, 3 at Leeds, 9 at Liverpool, 9 at Manchester, 3 at Nottingham, 5 at Sheffield, 2 from the county of

---

[4] Ibid. The records reveal more favourable reactions from other teachers such as that of A Aston of Downing College, Cambridge who wrote on 13 October 1908 that 'such a meeting can hardly fail to be of use to the profession'.

[5] AD Bowers, 'The Founding of the Society' (1959–1960) 5(NS) *JSPTL* 1, 3–5. Bowers was the first honorary assistant secretary of the Society and over the decades he was to make a notable administrative contribution to its work. On his 100th birthday on 25 February 1982 the Society sent a number of its members to visit him at home. Amongst other things, Bowers was remembered by people in the Society as someone who had survived service in the Boer War and later in the battles of the Somme and Passchendaele. See A.SPTL 10/8.

[6] The official record of this meeting is at A.SPTL 2/2 which is not complete and is frustratingly described as 'Chiefly regarding constituent meeting unimportant stuff destroyed by Dr Radcliffe, March 1937 under Committee resolution of December 1935.' Dr Radcliffe was acting as 'Hon Sec'. The problems caused by Society officials destroying what they thought was unimportant are a constant issue for anyone writing a history of the Society. The significance of periodical 'weeding' is assessed in ch 2, below. The records do also contain a brief printed summary of the meeting.

Sussex and 2 from Wales.[7] In other words it seems there was a membership of approximately 60 from a pool of over 100. An annual general meeting had become a possibility but this did nothing to stop Jenks from continuing with his efforts to increase membership in May and June. On 26 May he wrote to Chaloner Dowdall at Liverpool, saying

> I wish you would get Emmott and one or two of the other members of your Faculty to join the Society. There is really now a chance of doing something for legal education, if the people most interested will only buck up. With the exception of your own letter, the only one yet received from Liverpool is that of Sparrow—a refusal.[8]

Later, on 2 June he pointed out to Goudy that 'We must try to get Kenny, who is really the best known Cambridge teacher at present.'[9] In respect of both these initiatives he was successful.

The first Annual General Meeting was held at precisely 4.00 pm on Thursday, 1 July 1909 in the Council Room of the Law Society.[10] The Chair was taken by Professor Goudy, a well-known Oxford professor with a reputation for radical views and a long-term friend and supporter of Jenks. There is every reason to believe that Goudy and Jenks had been discussing the formation of the Society for some time, although these informal discussions were not recorded. AD Bowers and Professor Pettit are surely correct in concluding that the founding of the Society should be seen as the work of these two law teachers with their precise respective roles not being entirely clear. Bowers concludes that 'both should be credited with the idea of the Society's foundation'.[11] Certainly, Jenks could not have done it by himself. He needed well-established professorial support and at the start the Society was founded on Goudy's eminence and Jenks's energy. But it has to be said that it was not long before the energy of the latter was of primary importance. As Professor Pettit put it 'Jenks was the one who really got things moving.'[12] Born in 1861, Jenks was a Cambridge graduate in law and history and had wide experience of teaching. Professor of Law at Melbourne (1889–1891) and at Liverpool (1892–96) and Reader in Law at Oxford (1896–1903), he became Principal and Director in Legal Studies at the Law Society in 1903 and began a phase of deep involvement with law teaching in the capital. He transformed teaching at the Law Society and he went on to work

---

[7] A.SPTL 3/1.

[8] A.SPTL 2/2, Part I.

[9] Ibid.

[10] Minutes of General Meetings, Annual General Meeting, 1 July 1909: A.SPTL 1/1. (For the general use of this source, see above n 1.) See too A.SPTL 3/3: 'The Society was formally inaugurated, and its first general meeting held, at the Law Society Hall on 1st July, 1909.'

[11] On Goudy, see TB Smith, (1972–73) 12(NS) *JSPTL* 3. Goudy was educated at Glasgow, Edinburgh and Königsberg; he was elected to the Edinburgh Chair of Civil Law in 1889 and appointed to the Regius Chair of Civil Law at Oxford in 1893 by Gladstone after the latter had consulted with Bryce. More generally, see AD Bowers, 'The Founding of the Society' (1959–60) 5(NS) *JSPTL* 1, 2. PH Pettit, 'The Society of Public Teachers of Law—The First Seventy-Five Years' (1983) 3 *Legal Studies* 231.

[12] Ibid, 231.

with the Webbs in setting up a Law Department at the London School of Economics (LSE). He combined a knowledge of international developments in legal education with personal experience of teaching law in both academic and professional contexts. Having played a major role in creating it, he was not the sort of person who would allow a new organisation to falter.[13]

Forty-two people attended the Annual General Meeting, including Professor EC Clark from Cambridge, WM Geldart and WS Holdsworth from Oxford, W Blake Odgers KC (who was linked, as we have seen, with the Inns of Court School of Law), and younger academics such as PH Winfield, later an authority on the law of tort. It was agreed that:

> The objects of the Society shall be the furtherance of the cause of legal education in England and Wales, and the work and interests of public teachers of law therein, by holding discussions and enquiries, by publishing documents, and by taking such other steps as may from time to time be deemed desirable.[14]

Professor Goudy spoke at some length, declaring amongst other things that:

> Our posts as teachers, it is true, do not bring us any great emoluments or honours, such as await success at the Bar and in other fields. . . . But the dignity of our office we must hold and assert to be inferior to none.[15]

On this determined note a Vice-President for the coming year was elected. Professor Alfred Hopkinson KC, Vice-Chancellor of the University of Manchester was, like Walter Copinger, a law professor and a committed supporter of the idea that legal academics should organise themselves.[16] A new society of lawyers had come into existence.

---

13 On Jenks, see Lord Chorley's article in (1947–51) 1(NS) *JSPTL* 114 and the entry by Tony Honore in the *Oxford Dictionary of National Biography* (Oxford, 2004), where he points out that Jenks was 'By nature pugnacious'. This is corroborated in a note by Sir Harold Dankwerts in (1959–60) 9(NS) *JSPTL* 9. The latter points out at p 9 that Jenks had a 'combative nature' and that 'Meetings conducted by Jenks were always a joy, though somewhat exhausting.' But Dankwerts adds at p 10 that 'There is no doubt that he was a most profound lawyer, with the greatest powers of industry.' Jenks married in 1890 and his wife died soon after childbirth in 1891. Later, Jenks remarried. The child of the first marriage, a son, survived but was killed in the First World War in 1917. Jenks died in 1939. For Jenks's views on legal education prior to the formation of the Society, see (1907) 23 *Law Quarterly Review* 266. Obviously, at the Law Society he was very much involved with professional education. Soon after the creation of the SPTL he wanted someone to put forward a motion for an investigation into 'a general scheme of legal education for articled clerks': see 15 June 1909, A.SPTL 2/2 Part I.

14 Minutes of General Meetings, Annual General Meeting, 1 July 1909, A.SPTL 1/1.

15 Introductory Address to the Society of Public Teachers of Law in England and Wales by the President, Henry Goudy, DCL, delivered at the First Annual General Meeting, printed copy dated 1 July 1909 with A.SPTL 3/1. Also summarised in the records at A.SPTL 1/1 A2.

16 On Manchester Law Faculty, see M Mulholland, *The Faculty of Law of Manchester University: A Brief History, 1855–2000* (Manchester, Manchester University Press, 2000). I am grateful to the author for pointing out that the Faculty records are not a useful source of information on the SPTL. Sir Alfred Hopkinson was also a Unionist Member of Parliament and had many years of experience at the University and its predecessors in Manchester. We will see in ch 2 that his chief interest was in the education of articled clerks seeking to become solicitors.

Problematical Professions

What were the 'new questions affecting the teaching of law' to which Jenks referred? In particular, why was there a sense of a need for a new Society for academic lawyers? What was it about developments at Oxford and Cambridge, the growth of provincial universities and new professional courses in London that produced a desire for organisation amongst law teachers? The answer lies partly in the history of legal education for England and Wales, partly in the role of the legal professions, and partly in a related attempt in effect to answer the question: what is it to be a law teacher?

The new organisation was operating in a distinctive historical context. The conventional view—often expressed with the benefit of hindsight—is that legal education from, say, 1750 to 1900 looks like a series of missed opportunities. In the 1760s Blackstone's *Commentaries on the Laws of England* had reflected his lectures at Oxford and had thereafter provided a reference point for anyone seeking to teach English law to undergraduates. But little was made of this and Blackstone's temporary success merely highlights the uncertain history of what happened in respect of the teaching of English law at the universities in the years which followed. Lectures on common law topics did not, by and large, find a university audience. As in previous centuries, there were opportunities in respect of Roman law and international law at Oxford and Cambridge but topics in English law were seen as being predominantly professional and best understood in the context of practice in the courts.[17]

There was an important attempt to expose this as a failing and to remedy the shortcoming with the foundation of University College London in 1826. It was hoped that distinguished professors such as John Austin would anchor the teaching of English law in a metropolitan university. As is well known, the attempt had some successes. Austin's lectures were inaudible but in later years, in

---

[17] W Blackstone, *Commentaries on the Laws of England* (Oxford, Oxford University Press, 1765). Studies in 18th- and 19th-century legal education include JH Baker, *An Introduction to English Legal History*, 4th edn (London, Butterworths, 1999) ch 10, 'Legal Education in the Universities'; DJ Ibbetson, C Viner and his Chair in JA Bush and A Wijffels (eds), *Learning the Law: Teaching and the Transmission of the Law in England, 1150–1900* (London, Hambledon Press, 1999) 315–29; CW Brooks and M Lobban, 'Apprenticeship or Academy? The Idea of a Law University, 1830–1860', in Bush and Wijffels, *Learning the Law*, 353–83; D Sugarman, 'Legal Theory, the Common Law Mind and the Making of the Textbook Tradition', in W Twining (ed), *Legal Theory and the Common Law* (Oxford, Oxford University Press, 1986) 26–61; W Twining, *Blackstone's Tower: The English Law School* (London, Stevens & Sons/Sweet & Maxwell, 1994); RL Abel, *The Legal Profession in England and Wales* (Blackwell, Oxford, 1988) part IV; N Duxbury, *Frederick Pollock and the English Juristic Tradition* (Oxford, Oxford University Press, 2004); HG Hanbury, *The Vinerian Chair and Legal Education* (Oxford, Oxford University Press, 1958); FH Lawson, *The Oxford Law School, 1850–1965* (Oxford, Oxford University Press, 1968); WR Cornish and G de N Clark, *Law and Society in England, 1750–1950* (London, Sweet & Maxwell, 1989) 105–7; B Abel-Smith and RB Stevens, *Lawyers and the Courts: A Sociological Study of the English Legal System, 1750-1965* (London, Heinemann, 1967); JH Baker, 'University College and Legal Education, 1826–1976' (1977) 30 *Current Legal Problems* 1; W Twining, '1836 and All That: Laws in the University of London, 1836–1986' (1987) 40 *Current Legal Problems* 261.

book form, they served as the foundation for important parts of his influential writing on jurisprudence. Professor Amos secured an audience for a while in respect of topics related to professional practice. Intellectually, there were interesting links between the law teachers and the reform of law in India. But at this time undergraduates never appeared in sufficiently large numbers to establish a sustained presence. At King's College another metropolitan attempt was made with the provision of undergraduate law degrees, and the lectures of Professor Park in particular were successful for a while. There was also a remarkable and more sustained development of comparative study in Hindu and Islamic law. But, again, these were exceptions, and by the middle of the nineteenth century the failure to provide an effective programme of study in English law was seen by some as being scandalous. In fact, by this time there was nothing anachronistic in seeing legal education as a series of missed opportunities because a number of contemporaries saw it in precisely this way and were embarrassed by it. The teaching of solicitors was minimal despite the creation of the Law Society. More generally, the situation invited unfavourable comparisons with the law schools of France, Germany and the United States. Within England and Wales it frustrated those who saw clear theoretical analysis as a foundation for much-needed reforms in substantive law. Again and again, reformers felt thwarted by the uncritical assumption that the ideas of practitioners should be the central or even exclusive approach to any appreciation of the subject.[18]

With little to justify optimism for what might happen at the universities, attention turned to the Inns of Court. In the mid-1840s a small group of reformers managed to secure the appointment of a Parliamentary Select Committee on legal education, and in the early 1850s this was followed by an investigation into the role of the Inns of Court. The failure of the Inns of that time to provide useful instruction was revealed in full, and the proposed remedy lay in the creation of a new School of Law supported financially by the four Inns. In the early 1850s there were radical hopes for this enterprise. It had strong support from leading lawyers such as Lord Brougham and Richard Bethell, later Lord Westbury. It attracted talented teachers. The lectures on jurisprudence were given by Henry Maine and became influential when many of their themes appeared in Maine's 'best-selling' book *Ancient Law*. Others such as Broome lectured on more practical subjects. It was during these years that Charles Dickens published the articles which were to become his major novel of legal life, *Bleak House*, and it was as if the new teaching initiative offered an antidote to the idea that lawyers were always introverted and more concerned with procedures and profit than with what the law could do for people.[19]

---

[18] Amongst the sources mentioned in n 17, Brooks and Lobban, 'Apprenticeship or Academy?' is particularly useful on this phase.

[19] Ibid, and C Dickens, *Bleak House* (London, 1853); H Maine, *Ancient Law* (London, John Murray, 1861); RCJ Cocks, 'That Exalted and Noble Science of Jurisprudence: The Recruitment of Jurists with "Superior Qualifications" by the Middle Temple in the Mid-Nineteenth Century' (1999) 20 *Journal of Legal History* 62; RCJ Cocks, *Foundations of the Modern Bar* (London, Sweet & Maxwell, 1982) ch 4.

But the hopes for radical change in legal education were not realised. By the end of the 1850s sceptics saw unresolved problems. It was not undergraduates who were being taught but prospective barristers on a one-year course. Even more striking to contemporaries, the examinations at the end of the course were voluntary! In other words, it was still possible to be called to the Bar without having taken an examination because the Inns ensured that the papers were a voluntary 'extra'. Examinations for the Bar eventually became compulsory in 1872.[20]

Fortunately for the reformers of the day there was a revival of interest in the 1860s in the teaching of English law at the ancient universities. Oxford established a combined degree in Law and History. Cambridge developed an undergraduate programme containing both theoretical and substantive elements. Teachers and writers such as Maine, Bryce, Pollock and Clark worked on the creation of new degree programmes and found an undergraduate audience. But it was as if legal education still lacked an identity that would enable it to withstand comparison with other subjects.[21]

The issue was not merely rhetorical. Law was trying to claim a place in advanced education both in relation to the legal professions and as against other university disciplines. At a time when other programmes were being established in, say, economics or political science, the place of the law teacher remained in many ways ambiguous. Was he (invariably at this time he was a he) part of a liberal arts movement designed to secure a training of the mind? Or was he someone with a significant duty to the legal profession; and, if so, what was this responsibility? For example, was it to teach certain law subjects which the profession viewed as being of practical relevance?[22]

The hopes of those seeking to resolve these issues reached their nadir as the Inns of Court continued to fail to acknowledge honours degrees in law as sufficient evidence of some competence, however slight and incomplete. It was as if the ancient universities and the Bar inhabited different worlds of legal education. The legal author and teacher Frederick Pollock was not impressed: in addition to his other academic roles, he had been Professor of Common Law at the Inns of Court between 1884 and 1900 and he recorded his frustration in the *Law Quarterly Review* and elsewhere. He thought the system of law teaching at the Inns was 'absurd'.[23] For Pollock, the Inns reflected the views of practitioners: 'the bulk of the legal profession in England remains in its usual and deplorable state of profound indifference and ignorance on the whole matter'.[24] In reality, neither the legal professions nor the older academic disciplines treated the claim that undergraduate law degrees had merit with much respect. Behind these issues lay

[20] Cocks, *Foundations of the Modern Bar*, above n 19, 177.

[21] D Sugarman, 'Legal Theory, the Common Law Mind and the Making of the Textbook Tradition', in Twining, *Legal Theory and the Common Law*, above n 17, eg 56.

[22] For explorations of these themes, see S Collini, *Public Moralists: Political Thought and Intellectual Life in Britain: 1850–1930* (Oxford, Clarendon Press, 1991) esp ch 7.

[23] (1898) 14 *Law Quarterly Review* 127 and see Duxbury, above n 17, 51.

[24] (1892) 8 *Law Quarterly Review* 20.

an additional problem with money. The law teachers lacked the funding available to legal education at Harvard or Yale and they were unable to take advantage of the political and social changes which were opening up an increasingly significant role for law schools generally in American society.[25] They also lacked the professionally recognised place for the law teacher in continental civilian systems. It was as if the roles allotted to them were parochial and secondary. Their uncertain status in the universities sometimes made them look to the professions. Conversely, the indifference or hostility of practitioners made them sometimes look to the universities. It seemed as if they had no home.

Despite this unpromising setting, a small number of late-Victorian lawyers had ideas about new forms of legal education. At various times in the last three decades of the nineteenth century there were grand plans for an Imperial Law School in the capital and there were hopes for new forms of legal education within the framework of the University of London. Abel-Smith and Stevens explored what then happened in some detail in their book, *Lawyers and the Courts*.[26] It was an entangled story of grand ideas colliding with an incapacity at any one time to bring together the views of people at the Inns of Court, the Law Society, Oxford and Cambridge, and the University of London. The Bar (as distinct from some distinguished judges) opposed proposals for the reform of London University in 1884 and 1891. On the latter occasion the Inns of Court actually ignored a request from a Privy Council Committee to attend and discuss the issues. Later, a Royal Commission encountered similar professional obstacles but there was, at least, legislative reform for the University and a further opportunity for linking its educational work in law to the four Inns. Despite generous provision for representation of the Inns, in January 1900 yet again the Inns refused to participate in a reform which would have transformed law teaching.

The Victorian reformers never gave up, but the extent of their difficulties sometimes led them to reflect on the underlying cause of their problems. James Bryce, the jurist and statesman, pointed as early as 1871 to the assumptions which characterised many professional opinions and in doing so revealed the full extent of the problem.

> [T]he tendency of an English practitioner is by no means towards a search for principles: indeed he becomes absolutely averse to them; and the characteristic excellence which the profession has delighted to honour is the so-called 'case-lawyer' . . . Such a practitioner may acquire a sort of instinct which will usually keep him right, but may be unable to state the general doctrines on which the solution of a class of cases depends.

For Bryce the educational consequences were all too clear.

> The result of all this is to make the process of learning English law very slow and somewhat distasteful. Certain persons indeed there are who, having no feeling for symmetry,

---

[25] RB Stevens, *Law School: Legal Education in America from the 1850s to the 1980s* (Chapel Hill, University of North Carolina Press, 1983).

[26] Abel-Smith and Stevens, above n 17, ch 7.

are willing to pick up their knowledge by scraps and morsels, and who, so to speak, role themselves about in cases in the hope that bits of legal knowledge will stick.[27]

Given this sort of intellectual context it is hardly surprising that years later in a valedictory lecture Bryce railed against 'the short-sighted and perhaps somewhat perverse unwillingness of the authorities who control admission . . . to practice to give full recognition to Oxford degrees'. [28]

To make matters more difficult what was *not* said about legal education was often as significant as what was asserted. Lord Halsbury of *Halsbury's Laws* had obvious opportunities as Lord Chancellor to explore the role of legal education in law making but conspicuously failed to take them. The professional exemplar of the day was not, say, the law reformer or analyst of law but rather the 'Great Advocate' such as Marshall Hall or Sir Edward Clarke. Lawyers such as these did not attribute their professional success to their legal education but rather to their practical apprenticeship in courts of law. Beyond these views lay the knowledge that the lawyers could rely for support on a powerful mixture of interests across politics and government, not least from an increasingly influential Lord Chancellor's Department.[29] To many lawyers it was as if legal education was hardly necessary for either the understanding of law or the advancement of their careers. In the words of a modern study of the Bar, the professions had 'ensured the subservience of academic law to professional demands'.[30]

But, again, reformers refused to acknowledge defeat. The setback of 1900 was followed by a project to establish a school of law which would stand outside the University of London. Funds were available from the sale of certain properties and there was support from the Attorney-General, Sir Robert Finlay. By May of 1903 there were proposals for a Legal Education Authority with its own buildings. Now the Inns were divided, but this did more to produce inaction than anything else. The opponents of change were supported by some lawyers working in an individual capacity. The Inner Temple was particularly opposed and Lord Halsbury fortified its dissent. Once again the reformers experienced difficulties. By 1907 the pages of the *Law Quarterly Review* could be scathing in their criticisms of the Inns. 'The Inns which ought to give us a lead in this matter, have never been able to take a large and liberal view of their duty to learning.'[31] With obvious frustration it was pointed out that 'There must, ultimately, be some understanding, some division of labour, between the Universities and the Inns.'[32]

In the course of these years the Law Society was determined to bring about some sort of change for the sake of improving the education of articled clerks.

---

[27] J Bryce, *Studies in History and Jurisprudence* (Oxford, Clarendon Press, 1901) vol II, 490–91. The 'Inaugural Lecture' was given in 1871.

[28] Ibid, 519.

[29] See generally R Stevens, *The Independence of the Judiciary* (Oxford, Oxford University Press, 1993).

[30] RCJ Cocks, *Foundations of the Modern Bar* (London, Sweet & Maxwell, 1982) 231.

[31] (1907) 23 *Law Quarterly Review* 260 (T Raleigh).

[32] Ibid, 264.

After his arrival at the Law Society Edward Jenks succeeded in establishing a Law School. It was hardly a grand achievement in international terms, but its creation took imagination and effort and it did at least signal a new departure. In future, the Inns of Court would not be allowed a stranglehold on all developments in professional legal education. There was the prospect of progress in the education of solicitors. For Jenks it brought the additional satisfaction of offering an alternative to the private and unregulated 'coach' for whom he had little or no respect, and in the years following 1903 he greatly improved the Law Society's educational provision.[33]

In this regard there was also the prospect of change outside London. At the same time as the Law Society developed teaching in Chancery Lane it also fostered the teaching of law for articled clerks at provincial universities such as Birmingham and Sheffield and, more generally, through local Law Societies. These provincial developments had just begun to intrude on metropolitan awareness. To take one example, 'Edward Bramley, a young Sheffield solicitor and, at the time, secretary to the Sheffield and District Law Society, presented to the University College, Sheffield, a scheme for the instruction of articled clerks.'[34] Enough money was found to support an experimental course of lectures and teaching began in 1899. After some initial difficulties the numbers attending settled to about 12–15 a year. Sheffield University was given its Charter in 1905 and soon thereafter proposals were put up for permanent law teaching with funding coming half from the University and half from the Law Society. Bramley and others working with him, such as WF Trotter, wanted a Faculty of Law which could go beyond the professional courses and award degrees in law. At this point Jenks played an important role and provided support for linkage between national and local Law Societies. As a result an organisation called the Yorkshire Board of Legal Studies and the national Law Society guaranteed more than half the costs of a possible Faculty. Formal approval from the Privy Council arrived in 1909 but the Faculty was functioning from 1908 with a professor and a small number of lecturers.

> For many years, the character of the Sheffield Law Faculty was essentially local. In this respect the Faculty was reflecting the pre-war pattern both of the University itself and the provincial law schools throughout the country. Moreover, of those who came to read law, nearly all intended to enter the legal profession, usually to become solicitors.[35]

Despite the small number of students, in many ways these reforming efforts were

---

[33] For a valuable study of tensions within the Law Society at this time, see D Sugarman, 'Bourgeois Collectivism, Professional Power and the Boundaries of the State. The Private and Public Life of the Law Society, 1825 to 1914' (1996) 3(1/2) *International Journal of the Legal Profession* 81. For an account of Jenks's work at the Law Society, see AD Bowers, 'The Founding of the Society' (1959–60) 5(NS) *JSPTL* 1.

[34] OR Marshall, *The Jubilee Lectures of the Faculty of Law University of Sheffield* (London, Stevens and Sons, 1960) vii.

[35] Ibid, ix.

striking achievements and they were the more remarkable for the way they plainly went against the grain of expectations on the part of many practising lawyers, particularly barristers.

Provincial initiatives and the support of the Law Society for the work of law departments beyond London, Oxford and Cambridge obviously pointed in the direction of change. But, again and again, anyone thinking of organising law teachers had to come to terms with the legal professions. In respect of solicitors the 'precedents' for this sort of arrangement were mixed in terms of what they could do for teachers of law. There was nothing in the arrangements of the Law Society to encourage the formation of an organisation of law teachers. There was nothing that would enhance the status of law teachers. There were certain *potential* links with an organisation for academic lawyers but they were not such as to engender enthusiasm. For example, the Law Society had the dismal task of being partly responsible for the regulation of the professional conduct of solicitors, and in serious cases of alleged malpractice the Law Society was one of the parties involved in removal of the right to practice. But even if a capacity to exclude certain people from the opportunity to teach was in the minds of some law teachers, at the time it was a topic that would have to be approached with caution. Exclusionary or even disciplinary roles for a new academic society of any sort were likely to be contentious. The structure of the Law Society was an unlikely precedent for an organisation for teachers of law and in the long run might offer only equivocal support. This unpromising setting makes the work of Jenks as a teacher at the Law Society and an academic reformer all the more remarkable.

Just as important as administrative issues was the need to consider the status of solicitors as against that of barristers. If the new society identified closely with solicitors it would be associated with what was then indisputably the junior branch of the legal profession. At the time, both the social and professional supremacy of the Bar was beyond question. A close link with the Law Society might be looked at with scepticism by prospective members of an academic organisation at the older universities.

The Bar of the day had a potential attraction to someone such as Jenks in that it offered a clear example of a structure which could provide a precedent for law teachers. The Bar Committee had been established in 1883 in response to the belief of a few reforming barristers that the Inns of Court were not capable of organising the profession in an efficient way which could protect the needs of modern practitioners. It was not just educational issues on which the Inns were sometimes divided amongst themselves. It was also thought that they had become conservative after the judges returned to them in the years which followed the abolition of the Serjeants' Inn. It seems likely that a teacher of law thinking of a professional association for teachers in the early 1900s would have had this in mind. But, as with the Law Society, it would also have been obvious that this possible model for a new organisation came with problems. The status and role of the Bar Committee was open to question for the obvious reasons that the Inns of Court remained and frequently eclipsed the power of the Bar Committee. The Inns had survived radical attempts at reform in the mid-Victorian years and, if anything, were now more fashionable than they had been. Their social and professional influence was undeniable and the Bar Committee could only offer limited prospects as a precedent for a professional organisation. In fact, after a lively start, the Committee became respectable, irrelevant and little interested in legal education.[36]

Beyond the issues of structure there were important points of social friction which would have been of real concern to anyone founding an organisation for law teachers at this time. It was well known that in previous decades there had been numerous difficulties in the self-regulation of the Bar in respect of finding a satisfactory boundary between social and professional roles. In particular, there were problems outside London on the Circuits. In many respects the latter were self-regulating and some of the Circuit organisations—known as Messes—were caught up in debates as to whether they were social clubs or guardians of professional standards or both. Could someone be excluded from a Mess on the grounds that he was a disagreeable companion? If so, could the Mess then use its authority to prevent the person concerned from practising? Those who argued for the relevance of social acceptability were to some extent out-manoeuvred by the end of the century but the issue had not been fully resolved.[37] In short, the dominant profession of the day presented something of a muddled example of self-regulation. There was no one administrative structure with conclusive powers and there was no general agreement on the professional significance of social roles.

Faced with this unpromising context an academic group had to come to terms with both professional power and professions which, in modern terminology, offered no useful role model for academic lawyers. In many respects, the professions were a significant source of opposition to possible reforms and, in themselves, they offered no clear route for a new organisation to take. It was likely that relations between teachers of law and the professions would be both unavoidable and difficult. The reluctance of the Inns of Court in particular to respond to major educational initiatives was obvious. The lack of any clear social setting for law teachers within the professions, and the lack of professional respect for legal education, pointed to both the weakness of law teachers in influencing legal events and the likelihood that some at least of the teachers would find their position sufficiently irritating—or even humiliating—to want to do something about it. At the same time anyone seeking change would be well advised to act with a combination of caution and determination in their dealings with practitioners. Power lay with the professions.

In short, the assumptions produced by the history of legal education, and the

---

[36] Cocks, above n 30, 215–18.
[37] Ibid, ch 6.

professional context facing the Society, presented a major challenge to its creators. In the words of Peter Birks, writing in 1996,

> At the beginning of this century the common law had barely begun to acknowledge the existence, much less the importance, of jurists, and the notion that university law schools might be essential to the education of lawyers was still novel.[38]

From the start, the organisation would require a clear intellectual justification for its existence. Beyond this, it would have to develop an independent and distinctive administrative structure which could sustain it across decades. Without both of these it was likely to appear to be no more than an educational anomaly which was subservient to the work and status of solicitors and barristers.

Two events in particular reveal that Jenks was fully aware of these problems. On the evening before the first Annual General Meeting he arranged a social event not for law teachers in general but for the founders of the Society and senior judges.[39] He saw the importance of having the sort of judicial support which would command respect in the professions. For the moment, judges outside the Society were more important for its future than teachers within the Society.

Later in the same year he entered into dismal but realistic correspondence with Alfred Topham of 3 New Square, Lincoln's Inn, barrister, teacher of law and author in subsequent years of popular works for students on property law. In response to an invitation to join the Society, Topham replied:

> I doubt whether it would be advantageous for me to associate myself publically with the Society as I have found that it is not at all helpful to one's practice at the Bar to be too notoriously connected with teaching work.[40]

Jenks responded by saying: 'I am sorry to learn that you do not see your way to join our Society; but can quite understand your reasons.'[41]

Jenks knew very well the extent of the difficulties which faced the new organisation.

---

[38] PBH Birks (ed), 'What Are Law Schools For?', *Pressing Problems in the Law*, Vol 2 (Oxford, Oxford University Press, 1996) Editor's Preface, v.

[39] General Correspondence Files, 1908–50, A.SPTL 2/2 Part 2: these records also reveal that on 7 June he had described this as 'a most distinguished gathering'.

[40] General Correspondence Files, 1908–50, 15 September 1909, A.SPTL 2/11.

[41] 20 September 1909, A.SPTL 2/11.

2

Hope Followed by Dismay: 1910–1918

Every professional teacher ought to be able, and to be required to do, (whatever else he may do) a 'day's work everyday' at his proper subject. This implies a need for a reasonable supplement to the present very insufficient endowments. Whether this is to be got, and how, is a contingency of the future; but, unless teachers are put in a position to 'make a business' of their work, it is absurd to expect them to cope with the appalling amount of research that is waiting to be done, or to enter the lists with foreign scholars.

(Professor Murison, President of the SPTL, 6 July 1917)

Given the professional and academic tensions they were faced with at this time, the initial statements of the people creating the new organisation were going to be of particular importance. As we have seen, at the first Annual General Meeting, the President, Professor Goudy gave an Introductory Address expressed in optimistic terms. In its detail it went beyond polite social greetings. He wanted law teachers to be ambitious. In his full address he pointed to Rome as an example of a civilisation that gave a high status to teachers of law. 'It is our duty and our privilege to teach to the aspiring youth of this country the Law in all its manifold departments.'[1] He specified Roman law, 'the Law of England in all its various, great departments (Common Law, Equity, Real Property etc)', legal history, international law, conflict of laws, 'the Laws of India and our Colonies', constitutional law and comparative law.[2] Further, he gave a distinctive tilt as to how these duties could be taken forward.

We must honestly endeavour to do what we can for our students, both by word and writing, but especially by word. Because upon us undoubtedly rests, in considerable measure, responsibility for the future competency of our judges and barristers and solicitors, and to some extent also of our legislators, statesmen, and administrators. We must, too, remember that the future reform of the laws, and consequent amelioration of the social and political conditions in this country, may largely depend upon the knowledge we impart to, and the ideas we instil into, the minds of our pupils.[3]

[1] Minutes of General Meetings, First Annual General Meeting, 1 July 1909, A.SPTL 1/1. The Address was also printed and a copy may be found in A.SPTL 3/3. Page references are to the printed version. The sentence quoted above is at p 3.

[2] Ibid.

[3] Ibid, 4.

In order to illustrate the points he was making, and with a view to responding to the difficulties presented by professional assumptions about education, he turned to the place he knew best, Oxford. In reality he was using educational history as an argument for change. He now saw progress after years of difficulty. Reflecting the events mentioned in the previous chapter, he argued that between the Civil War of the seventeenth century and the middle of the nineteenth century the study of law at Oxford was, in his view, little more than nominal. As he put it in a striking sentence, 'It was considered to lie outside University culture altogether.'[4]

For Goudy, in the course of the second half of the nineteenth century this had been transformed. The President pointed out that, half a century ago, the only provision made by the University for legal teaching consisted of two inadequately endowed professorships, one of the civil law, and one of the common law, the holders of which did not systematically teach, and were not infrequently non-resident. But, he added, there were now four professors, four readers, one University lecturer, and a large number of college lecturers and tutors engaged in the teaching of law.[5] Similar progress had taken place at Cambridge, while the growth of the new provincial universities, as well as the organisation of law studies in the metropolis during the last two or three decades, had also been significant . Furthermore standards had improved.

> Despite its severe and testing character, the examination for BCL in particular has gone on slowly but steadily increasing in favour; and this year no less than thirty-one candidates entered their names for it—the largest number, I believe, on record. Alas! I must admit that only seven of these passed successfully through the ordeal.[6]

In effect this, and other early pronouncements, set an agenda. Old assumptions would now be challenged. Pay was and would remain a difficult issue where there would have to be compromise. But dignity was not negotiable. The teacher of law had a duty which went beyond passing over a knowledge of the law. In the course of 'honest endeavour' the teacher had to ensure that those who were trained in the law were competent in discharging its many roles. In doing this the teacher had critically to consider the ideas he imparted so that the future reform of the laws was taken forward in a way that would ameliorate social and political conditions. In other words, the teacher of law had broad and demanding duties that were both legal and public. Professor Goudy was providing a radical answer to the question: what is a law teacher? Such a person was neither an adjunct to the legal professions nor someone confined to conventional academic roles. Instead he discharged duties that were both highly intellectual and public. The Society of Public Teachers of Law had the potential to do more than draw a line, as it were, between private instruction and those who taught in institutions such as universities and the Law Society. The use of the word 'Public' could have a dual role. It served to exclude private tutors and it pointed to major responsibilities. Given the

---

[4] Ibid, 4.
[5] Ibid, 6.
[6] Ibid.

professional context within which law teachers were working, Goudy was setting a very ambitious agenda.

A Society without a Home

Professor Goudy had discussed values in unequivocal terms and had taken further the debate on what it is to be a law teacher. But he had not provided an administrative structure for the new organisation. Work on this was likely to be unexciting and at times exasperating and would called for steady effort on the part of Honorary Secretaries and Treasurers. Under the proposals of the constit-uent meeting Presidents were appointed for one year only; they could promote lively initiatives and there was some limited sense of continuity through would-be Presidents usually serving for a preliminary year as Vice-Presidents and some-times also as members of various committees. But for obvious reasons in the early years the Presidents and Vice-Presidents had little experience of everyday work and left large amounts of routine activity to the Secretary and Treasurer. It followed that there was the potential for people in these positions, such as Jenks, to make decisions of fundamental importance to the long-term future of the Society.

Certainly, the Secretaries and Treasurers were to work hard on behalf of the Society when it was establishing itself. They were helped by Assistant Secretaries, particularly, as we have seen, by AD Bowers who served in one way of another for the first half of the century. In the course of its early years the Society was kept financially viable with (for most years) the original annual subscription of half a guinea.[7] There were repeated problems of non-payment from certain members, and there were never lavish reserves, but the Society's financial arrangements proved to be viable. Admittedly Annual Dinners could cause problems. In many early years the Annual Dinner was funded by the institution which was the host for the occasion. When this changed (in part because the growth in membership increased the cost of these meetings) there was an obvious need for special payments to be made and this was sometimes unpopular and difficult to achieve in full. General financial stability was an achievement but there were limits to what had been done. A lack of any substantial reserves would restrict special educational initiatives to projects that either did not require money or could be

---

[7] Rule 4 of 1910 allowed for the charging of a subscription, but did not specify the sum. In practice for many years it was half a guinea. These rules may be found most conveniently in the printed records for 1910 of the List of Members: they are printed at the end of the List, but they were voted on and accepted at the First Annual General Meeting: see Minutes of General Meetings, Annual General Meeting, 1 July 1909, A.SPTL 1/1. The Special Committee on rules met three times: see references to their work in Meeting of the General Committee, 15 December 1909, A.SPTL, 1/3–4. For the full Rules see A.SPTL 6.

developed in partnership with wealthier institutions. It was clear that from the start the SPTL was not going to be rich.[8]

The Secretary and Treasurer did more than arrange the Annual Meeting and collect fees. They organised the activities of the General Committee which met at least once a year and sometimes much more often. Many important decisions were made by the Society's General Committee attended by the President, Vice-Presidents and (at this time) by a fluctuating number of others selected for membership from the Society as a whole.[9] The Committee was at the heart of the evolution of policy and over the years probably had as much impact on events as the Annual Meeting. Beyond the General Committee, the Secretary and Treasurer had an influence on the way in which ad hoc subcommittees were set up for special purposes. Most of all, of course, the Secretary did the everyday work which involved answering letters and co-ordinating meetings. In the course of doing this there were occasional expressions of exasperation. 'It is curious how difficult it is to arrange anything with Manchester. . . . The Manchester people seem invariably to have peculiar arrangements.'[10]

Implicit in all this was the fact that the Society had no fixed office and permanent location for files. In psychological terms this was likely to be important. It was to be a Society associated with its dispersed membership rather than with one permanently fixed centre of power. It was not the most efficient arrangement, but it was possible that some degree of inefficiency would be offset by an increased sense of collegiality: the Society was its members rather than a 'fixed' administration in a particular building. In the early years this was asserted in clear terms with Sir Alfred Hopkinson responding to the idea of a permanent link with one institution saying that 'It seems to me quite important that, as a catholic and comprehensive Society, we should not be supposed to be tied to any outside body.'[11] Jenks shared this view but he was cautious about meetings beyond London during the early years. When Goudy suggested one in Oxford, Jenks replied that

> The suggestion of a General Meeting at Oxford is extremely pleasant, but do you not think that, for the first two or three years, it might be better to hold the meeting in London, on account of its central position? When the Society has taken firm root, we might then confidently expect a full meeting at Oxford or Cambridge.[12]

---

[8] There were personal links with organisations and universities in the USA and the rules of the Association of American Law Schools were considered when the SPTL drafted its own regulations, but they were not followed as a 'precedent'. See the following section of this chapter.

[9] For the rules of election to the Committee, see Rules 10–12 of 1910 and n 7 above. They were designed to ensure broad representation. We will see below in ch 4 that it was sometimes felt that they failed to do this and in practice gave disproportionate influence to London, Oxford and Cambridge.

[10] Jenks in a letter to Goudy, 21 April 1910, A.SPTL 2/3. During these months Jenks was disappointed with the 'take up' at Manchester despite the best efforts of Profs Copinger and Hopkinson: letter from Jenks to Copinger on 26 May 1909, A.SPTL 2/3.

[11] No date, A.SPTL 2/3.

[12] 5 March 1910, A.SPTL 2/3.

These arrangements were to have an impact on how members of the Society came to see their own history and, further, on how the present history is written. For members there was a likelihood that the Society's past would come to be seen in the way that successive Secretaries saw its past because it was the Secretaries who kept the records and could unearth 'precedents' and make claims as to what was established practice and the like. The everyday control that Secretaries had over the records of the Society poses a challenge for historians such as the present authors. Given that the records had no fixed home and could be found in different parts of the country at different times it was likely that many records would vanish over the years. To some extent this even became an official policy. As we have seen, successive Secretaries were given authority to 'weed' the records and unfortunately proved highly efficient at this task.[13] Usually the criterion for saving documents was simply what was regarded as important at the time. The practical consequence is a set of records that has to be used with considerable caution. For the first four decades we have a good set of files for the General Committee meetings, a fairly good set of records for the ad hoc subcommittees, a variety of types of documents for the Annual Meetings, and highly selective groups of letters and incidental papers. Together, these make for a compilation of documents that fail to give a full overview of the Society's activities and are weak in revealing personal disputes which only surface incidentally (but sometimes, as we will see, brutally) in the course of records relating to major issues of policy. So, for example, it is only through incidental luck that we learn, say, that at one time in the 1930s Professor Hughes of Leeds was seen—perhaps unfairly—by some in the north of England as a mere agent of people with vested interests at Oxford, Cambridge and London.[14] Most difficult of all, we will see that the information relating to debates about the admission of women suggest radical distortions of the record in the late 1930s.[15]

Of course, the apparently random documents that were retained tell us something of what was regarded as important, and this in itself is revealing. The early years record eating in restaurants. Later, with meetings usually at academic institutions, we can learn what was eaten at, say, the LSE in 1946.[16] In other words, food and collegiality were seen as significant. For the modern legal historian there is the need constantly to guard against writing the history of the SPTL as seen by its successive Secretaries. At the same time it has to be recognised that these were the people who sustained the Society as an organisation and, over time, did much to shape it. As a matter of impression, their cumulative influence was greater than that of most Presidents.

[13] For an example of weeding, see A.SPTL 2/2 where a past General Committee was assumed to have authorised an Honorary Secretary to destroy records and the latter had done so in March 1937. This has an impact on our understanding of very early meetings: see ch 1, n 5. The General Committee did, in fact, authorise the destruction in question: see 7 December 1935, A.SPTL 1/4/A5.

[14] See ch 4.

[15] See chs 4 and 5.

[16] At a time of rationing it managed to go as far as 'Roast Chicken, New Potatoes, Green Peas, Fresh Fruit Flan and Coffee', 12 July 1946, A.SPTL 4/4.

The Early Use of Rules

The task of linking Goudy's ambitious ideals to the everyday work of the new Society was demanding. There were likely to be times when there was a gap between ideal and reality. From the start there was the problem of developing and using rules. We have seen that the purposes of the Society could be expressed succinctly:

> The objects of the Society shall be the furtherance of the cause of legal education in England and Wales, and the work and interests of public teachers of law therein, by holding discussions and enquiries, by publishing documents, and by taking such other steps as may from time to time be deemed desirable.[17]

But creating detailed rules to realise this objective was a different matter. Drafts for the rules were being considered from an early stage by a committee set up after the Constituent meeting of December 1908. There was initial interest in following the rules for the Association of American Law Schools; Jenks wrote to Goudy about this on 15 February 1909, saying that he had not yet had time to consider the American example in any detail. He followed this up with a letter on 17 February, saying

> Please do not trouble to return the copy of the American rules; as I have a copy for each member of the Committee. But perhaps you would kindly bring it with you to the meeting. I am not sure that it will be much of a help to us; for I fancy that the American problems are rather different from ours.[18]

In the early years of the Society there was sustained interest in American forms of legal education but little enthusiasm for following the rules of American organisations.

The rules which were produced and which were published in an accessible form by November 1910 reflected the tensions inherent in the 'world' of the Edwardian law teacher. Who was a *public* teacher of law? Could someone join simply by reason of having a professional qualification? Would an academic qualification in the form of a law degree be a prerequisite? Could someone be excluded simply on the ground that they were uncollegial and not liked as a social companion? Or because his political views were regarded as outrageous? Could someone be excluded for scandalous conduct? Given the long history of Bar Messes being uncertain of the extent to which they could use social sanctions which might blight a professional career (considered in the previous chapter),

---

[17] Minutes of General Meetings, First Annual General Meeting, 1 July 1909, A.SPTL 1/1.

[18] At Minutes of General Meetings, Second Annual General Meeting, 15 July 1910, A.SPTL 1/1, there is a reference to 'the kindred Association of American Law Schools'. Copies of the 'constitution' of the American Law Schools Association were supplied by HD Hazeltine, an American at Cambridge: 10 February 1909, A.SPTL 2/2, Part I. On Hazeltine, see his piece on 'The Present State of Legal Education in England' (1910) 26 *Law Quarterly Review* 17, and N Duxbury, *Frederick Pollock and the English Juristic Tradition* (Oxford, Oxford University Press, 2004) 2, 63, 188.

there was an obvious potential for major arguments within the new society. Rules that appeared dry could prove to be highly prescriptive.

Two of the rules which were produced in the course of 1909 were of central importance. Under Rule 4:

> Ordinary members of the Society shall be such public teachers of law in England and Wales as shall signify to the Honorary Secretary of the Society their wish to become members, shall duly pay their subscriptions, and shall conform to the rules of the Society. Provided, that no one shall become an ordinary member until his acceptance as such has been formally notified to him by the Honorary Secretary, and that, before such notification, the General Committee may, if it thinks fit, after giving the candidate an opportunity of explanation, refer the question of the acceptance of any member to the next or any general meeting of the Society, whose decision shall be final.

This left undefined the definition of public teacher of law. The first sentence appears to grant a conditional right under which someone who was a public teacher of law could, subject to conditions such as paying his subscription, become a member of the Society through signifying his wish to do so to the Honorary Secretary. However, the second sentence creates a proviso giving any general meeting of the Society the capacity to consider 'the question of . . . acceptance' after the candidate has had an 'opportunity of explanation'. Subject to what might be relevant elsewhere in the rules, and subject to the general law on associations of this type, this would appear to confer broad discretion on any general committee which might justify rejection on professional, social or even political grounds. In this context Rule 5 was of assistance. The side note to Rule 5 refers to 'Definition of public teachers'. The substance of the Rule states:

> For the purposes of Rule 4, the expression 'public teachers of law in England or Wales' shall include all gentlemen engaged in teaching law in England or Wales in virtue of appointment or official recognition by any university, college, incorporated society, council, board of studies, or other body, not being a body established or existing for the purpose of making pecuniary profit divisible among its members. The General Committee may require evidence of such qualifications if it think fit; and on any question that may arise as to the interpretation and application of this rule the decision of the Committee shall, unless and until reversed by a general meeting of the Society, be conclusive. Provided that a member ceasing for one year to be engaged in the teaching of law shall, ipso facto, cease to be an ordinary member of the Society.[19]

Plainly this would exclude from the Society individual private tutors not working for a university, and also individual tutors working within an organisation creating profits divisible among the membership. Further the reference to 'gentlemen' might be successful in excluding women should the issue be contested.[20] In

---

[19] To repeat n 7 above, these rules may be found most conveniently in the printed records for 1910 of the List of Members: they are printed at the end of the List.
[20] Note that *Bebb v Law Society*, [1914] 1 Ch 286 revealed that women would be unable to qualify as solicitors even where a statute did not expressly exclude them.

short, personal tutors and teachers at organised 'crammers' and women would probably have no role in the new Society.

Perhaps less plain than this was the reference in Rule 5 to 'such qualifications'. Did this merely refer back to qualification by reason of a particular type of appointment or official recognition or might it include other qualifications? Further, whatever the precise scope of Rule Five, when taken in conjunction with Rule 4 it remained the case that any general meeting of the Society could exclude an applicant on grounds not set out in express terms within the rules.

Subject to the national law of associations, this left open numerous possibilities of social and political discrimination, including of course the exclusion of women. (The admission of women to the SPTL is considered below in chapters 4 and 5). In strict educational terms there was the latent issue of legal qualifications. There was no requirement for a university degree in law or, for that matter, in any other subject as a prerequisite for membership. Presumably the simple reason for this was that there were far too many successful practitioners without degrees for this course to be taken; the Society would have excluded from its ranks solicitors and barristers who wished to teach and who had only professional qualifications. Nor, in fact, was a professional qualification required. There was not even a restriction to people who had either an academic or a professional qualification of any sort. Note, however, that this could be turned on its head in that there was no express prohibition preventing such a test being used. Nor was there any rule requiring or preventing an investigation into character with the use of, say, references. Nor was there a rule requiring that applicants worked at one type of public institution rather than another, so it would be possible in ways that might never be recorded to discriminate at some future time against, say, law teachers in commercial colleges or (to consider a future issue) law teachers in polytechnics. In effect the rules provided that anyone who was a 'Public Teacher of Law' could apply to join, and subject to the properly exercised (but in reality unrecorded) discretion of any General Committee, they could be excluded on a number of grounds.

Certain early discussions within the Society provide glimpses of how the Rules were interpreted, but it seems likely that contentious records, particularly any which might have related to issues of character, have long since been destroyed. When the Rules were being drafted there was considerable stress on the importance of ordinary members being active teachers. In Jenks's words,

> It has, I think, been the general view of the drafting committee that a man who ceases to be a public teacher of law would naturally drop out of the ranks of ordinary members of the Society, which is, amongst other things, undoubtedly a trade union. It seems possible that active members of the profession might, if the Society becomes an organ of professional opinion, object to have their views controlled by those who had ceased to be practically interested in such questions.[21]

---

[21] Jenks to WR Bisschop (*sic*) at 3 Temple Gardens, EC, 11 June 1909, A.SPTL 2/3.

Later, in July, Jenks was in correspondence with W A Evans, a barrister and Secretary to the Headmasters' Conference. Jenks had to tell him that the Rules which had just been adopted at the first Annual General Meeting would exclude him because he was not teaching law.[22]

In the following year there was worry about an applicant's standard of work. On 19 February 1910 Jenks expressed concern to Goudy about a Mr Costello. Costello was a barrister who did some teaching in the Midlands. On a visit to Nottingham Jenks 'found that he was regarded there as an able lecturer, but . . . they thought that he treated his work somewhat casually'.[23] However, by 4 March Costello had come to be regarded as a satisfactory applicant for membership by the General Committee and it is difficult to resist the conclusion that it had been sensed that grave problems would arise for the Society if it enquired into someone's assiduity as a teacher when this was rumoured to be in doubt. It looks as if this early confidential exchange subsequently ensured that there were no further discussions of this nature when someone applied for membership. Alternatively, to stress the point again, any documents relating to applications which revealed such discussions of a personal nature and which might have been defamatory have long since vanished from the records, weeded out by successive Secretaries. We cannot be sure of what was happening, but it is interesting that Costello went on to be an active member of the Society and, after a successful career at the Bar, became a judge. The records (correctly or otherwise) suggest that the process of election was largely uncontentious to the extent that *personal* qualities were not openly discussed.

In general terms this simple approach to membership was of the utmost importance to the Society. It saved it from what would have been explicit and unending and unedifying disputes about the significance of personal forms of behaviour. In particular, it saved it from the type of dispute which occasionally convulsed a Bar Mess. The clear understanding as to what made for membership, or at least the avoidance of public disputes about membership, was also of assistance in enabling Jenks to attempt to exert influence on behalf of the Society, which implicitly raised questions about who could qualify for membership. In other words, it saved him from having to worry about problems in his own 'back yard'.

With happy inconsistency, this did nothing to stop Jenks from asserting a need for qualifications in law teachers when corresponding with others. For example, in 1910 the following resolution was debated at some length:

> That the Committee be . . . hereby authorised to take such steps as it shall think fit to urge upon the Education Committee of the London County Council that it is desir-

[22] 5 July 1909 and 6 July 1909, A.SPTL 2/3.

[23] 19 February 1910, A.SPTL 2/3. Other issues arose in connection with Costello: see letters 21 October 1909 and 22 October 1909, A.SPTL 2/2, Part I. For a case involving another applicant, see Meeting of the General Committee, 15 December 1915, A.SPTL 1/3–4. Mr Meadmore would be made a member on proof 'of his being at present actively engaged in the performance of his duties as County Council Instructor in legal subjects'.

able, in the interests of public instruction and of those engaged in legal tuition, that only persons with legal qualifications should be appointed as Lecturers in Commercial Law and in Municipal Law under the Education Committee; and further strongly to represent to the Education Committee that a fee of at least one guinea for each evening's attendance should be paid for such lecturers.[24]

In seeking to assert the need for legal qualifications, the new Society was cautiously edging towards an understanding as to the prerequisites for the effective teaching of law anywhere in England and Wales.

Somewhat self-consciously, Jenks followed this up and wrote to the relevant official at the London County Council (LCC), saying 'I write on behalf of the Society of Public Teachers of Law (whose membership comprises the great majority of official teachers of law throughout England) to bring to your notice a matter effecting the action of the London County Council.' In substance he went on to argue that anyone teaching law on their courses should be qualified, but he did not say what counted as a qualification.

> My Committee is led to believe that this truth is realised by your Council in the parallel case of sanitation and other subjects requiring a training in physical science, and would venture to suggest that neither a good teacher of law nor a good teacher of sanitation or public health can be produced by the mere reading of text-books.[25]

It may have been this episode that led some contemporaries to go as far as calling the SPTL 'Jenks's trade union'. If so, it was not a notably successful trade union in this instance. The dispute caused the Society initial frustration as when, on 14 July 1911, a distinguished member of the SPTL, Sir Earnest Trevelyan, 'called attention to the indecisive character of the correspondence with the London County Council'.[26] By July 1912 the Society was satisfied at the response of the LCC in terms of the Council requiring appropriate qualifications for law teachers but not content in respect of what it saw as being the proper remuneration for those with qualifications.[27] These arguments about qualifications and money in connection with LCC courses persisted for years with inconsistent results.[28] In short, it became obvious from the early years of the organisation that there were real limits to the powers of the Society. In particular, the experience of these years was likely to make it wary of disputes about working practices with outside bodies.

---

[24] Minutes of General Meetings, Second Annual General Meeting, 15 July 1910, A.SPTL 1/1.

[25] October 1910, A SPTL 2/4.

[26] Minutes of General Meetings, Third Annual General Meeting, 14 July 1911, A.SPTL 1/1. Sir Ernest Trevelyan, President SPTL 1915–16, Born 1850, Judge of the High Court in Calcutta, 1885–98, Vice-Chancellor of Calcutta University, 1897–98, Reader in Indian Law at Oxford, 1900–23, Lecturer at the Council of Legal Education.

[27] Minutes of General Meetings, Fourth Annual General Meeting, 5 July 1912, A.SPTL 1/1.

[28] For example, they were discussed at the Sixth Annual General Meeting. Minutes of General Meetings, Sixth Annual General Meeting, 1914, A.SPTL 1/1.

Educational Reform

The Society was on firmer ground in seeking reforms in legal education. In his term as President between 1910 and 1911 the Vice-Chancellor of Manchester University, Sir Alfred Hopkinson, wanted changes to the education of articled clerks. Amongst other things, he thought their general education would be improved by making Latin compulsory.[29] Others, too, were interested in professional education. There was a variety of degree courses available at universities around the country but it was believed that many students were interested in purely professional qualifications achieved without taking degrees. The result, nationally, was an intricate array of different types of course.

Grasping this requires some attention to academic detail. For example, at Leeds for the Bachelor of Laws there was an 'Intermediate' course of one year consisting of (i) Roman law (Institutes of Justinian and general history); (ii) elements of English law (Stephen's *Commentaries*, vols I–III); (iii) law and custom of the English Constitution; (iv) any subject included in the course for the Intermediate examination for the ordinary BA or BCom (subject (iv) was not compulsory for candidates who were graduates of any university within the UK). The final course of two years involved either (i) Roman law (general history, Institutes of Gaius and Justinian, selected title of digest), (ii) jurisprudence (historical and analytical), and (iii) public or private international law; or (i) real and personal property (including conveyancing), (ii) equity (including company law), (iii) common law (including criminal law and bankruptcy), (iv) evidence and procedure, and (v) jurisprudence. There was also provision for a one-year Master of Laws.[30]

As with other provincial universities at this time, what was likely to enhance student numbers during these years was the opportunity for 'professional qualifications'. At Leeds 'The University provides systematic instruction for students preparing for the examinations of The Council of Legal Education and the Law Society.' In respect of, say, the Law Society, this involved at least one year of study for the 'Solicitor of the Supreme Court Intermediate', which under the generic heading 'Elementary English Law' required real and personal property and conveyancing, the law of contract, succession and bankruptcy, family law, public law, civil procedure, crimes and criminal procedure, accounts and book-keeping. For the 'Final' (Pass and Honours) a course of at least two years concentrated exclusively on real and personal property and conveyancing (presumably to a much higher standard than the 'Intermediate') and on 'Matters usually determined or administered in the Chancery Division.'[31]

Roughly comparable arrangements to those at Leeds could be found at, say,

---

[29] Minutes of General Meetings, Second Annual General Meeting, 15 July 1910, A.SPTL 1/1.
[30] 'Handbook of the Legal Curricula Pursued at the Various Centres of Public Legal Education in England and Wales', A.SPTL 5/12.
[31] Ibid, and 19–20 and 20–21.

the University College of Wales at Aberystwyth, the University of Liverpool, the University of Manchester or the University of Sheffield.[32] In places the arrangements were not so extensive. In Birmingham under the local Board of Legal Studies 'Four courses of lectures or classes are held each Term in the subjects of the qualifying examinations of the Law Society. Classes are also held (one a term) in the subjects of the London LLB curriculum.'[33] In Hull under the Yorkshire Board of Legal Studies

> One course of classes is held weekly during the six winter months on one or more of the of the subjects of the qualifying examinations of the Law Society. The classes rank as Extension Lectures of the University of Leeds, but are held by a Lecturer specially appointed and maintained by the Yorkshire Board of Legal Studies.[34]

At Sussex 'Classes in connection with the qualifying examinations of the Law Society are held at Brighton during nine months of the year and there are generally three courses running concurrently.'[35] Similar arrangements could be found for example at Bristol where, additionally, 'Candidates for the London LLB degree are also advised by one of the local Board's Lecturers.'[36]

Boards of Studies took different forms in different places; for instance some were incorporated and some were not. They usually included representative of local Law Societies, universities and colleges as well as local practitioners. The last page of an SPTL Handbook stressed that they were 'public' organisations, thereby emphasising the fact that those who taught at them would be eligible to join the new Society.[37]

In so far as part of their funding came from the Law Society, it might be said that the university faculties which grew out of them owe a major early debt to the national Law Society working under Jenks's influence.

Given these arrangements, it is not surprising that Hopkinson and other members of the Society responded by talking about the education of articled clerks and sought to broaden it. Sir Alfred Hopkinson wanted more than Latin. 'The teacher and the student should be in personal touch and cross-examination of each other, and the practice of distinguishing between relevant and irrelevant matters, were points which should be kept in mind.'[38] It soon became clear that there was a general interest in the topic amongst members of the Society. The Committee which investigated the matter consisted of people such as Edward Bramley (Sheffield), Professor Emmott (Liverpool), Professor Goudy (Oxford), Pearce Higgins (Cambridge), Edward Jenks (Law Society), Professor Levi (Wales), Professor Phillips (Leeds), and AM Wilshere (Birmingham and Bristol). Nationally, law teachers were coming to know each other.[39]

---

[32] Ibid, at, respectively, 18, 12, 10 and 17.
[33] Ibid, 21–2.
[34] Ibid, 22.
[35] Ibid, 23.
[36] Ibid, 22.
[37] Ibid.
[38] Minutes of General Meetings, Second Annual General Meeting, 15 July 1910, A.SPTL 1/1.
[39] Ibid.

Students of 'Grit'

In an active Presidency between 1911 and 1912 Blake Odgers from the Inns of Courts' Council of Legal Education—a man noted for his cheerfulness and energy—was particularly determined to stress the potential public role of the Society.[40] Obviously aware of the widespread view that the Inns wanted nothing new in the training of barristers, he set out to discuss ideas. He saw no inconsistency in using his position at the Council of Legal Education to praise law teachers whether they were working on professional or university courses. In fact he was emotional about professional study. In a book published in 1901 he had written

> Remember this, students of the four Inns, and wherever you may practice hereafter, whether in England or in India or in any of our distant colonies, remember ever to maintain the traditions, and to observe the unwritten laws, of a learned, a fearless, and an honourable profession.[41]

Beyond the Inns he now stressed that members of the SPTL should seek 'the making of the law of England clear, not only to the professions, but to the English people'. In linking professional and university law teaching

> He drew a distinction between the teaching of law which was necessary and proper at a University, and that which was required before the student could commence to practice professionally. The former would naturally be more scientific, more academic, and more historical; while the latter would have to deal with procedure and other practical matters, and would mainly treat the law as it stands at the present day. . . . The theoretical study should precede the practical.[42]

These views reflected national debate arising out of the work of a Royal Commission on University Education in London which issued its first, provisional, report in 1910.[43] In 1909 Gaudy and Jenks had agreed between themselves that the SPTL was not yet in a position to make representations to such a body.[44] But there was an obvious possibility of it recommending reform given the fact that it was chaired by Lord Haldane, an adventurous lawyer and future Lord Chancellor. It is, of course, necessary to recall that the context of these arguments was radically

---

[40] '[A] delightful man—so full of life and energy': Copinger to Jenks, 9 November 1908, A.SPTL 2/1–2.

[41] *A Century of Law Reform: Twelve Lectures on the Changes in the Law of England During the Nineteenth Century* (London, Macmillan, 1901), 42.

[42] Ibid. See, too, Minutes of General Meetings, Fourth Annual General Meeting, 5 July 1912, A.SPTL 1/1.

[43] Royal Commission on University Education in London, 1910, HMSO, First Report, Cmd 5166.

[44] Letter, 4 June 1909, A.SPTL 2/2 Part I. Note, too the letter from Jenks to Sir John Macdonell suggesting that the Society did not get involved with the Royal Commission on the ground that 'our walls are not yet fire-proof': letter 4 June 1909, A.SPTL 2/2 Part 2. Presumably, he meant by this that there were as yet still too many open questions about the potential roles of the Society; he may also have feared direct opposition from the Inns of Court and thought it was best to work indirectly with the Inns through the Council of Legal Education.

different from that with which a modern law teacher is familiar. There were very many fewer students: in 1909–10 there were 32 at University College, 11 at King's College and 5 at LSE. They paid 10 guineas a year. Only a minority of students had an opportunity even to contemplate a rounded programme of legal studies at degree level.[45] Sidney Webb, giving evidence to the Commission in an early phase of its work, and speaking in his capacity as someone involved with the foundation of the LSE and interested in the general progress of higher education, pointed out that the Commissioners were faced with 'essentially a University for the sons and daughters of householders of limited means and strenuous lives'. In reality they were working with students of 'grit' for whom intellectual adventure was a luxury.[46]

Sidney Webb hoped to link the demands of economy, motivation for professional qualification and academic merit: for him there should be specialised knowledge and professional training. As he put it:

> This involves the revival of an older conception of a University course deliberately framed so as to prepare the undergraduate from the outset for the practical pursuit of his profession, but in such a way as to turn him out equipped, not only as a trained professional but also as a cultivated citizen.[47]

At an abstract level there was no shortage of thought about how professional and university roles should be developed.

In respect of law, the Royal Commission encountered many of the old arguments about the roles of the Inns, the Law Society and university schools. But now, as the debates within the SPTL suggested, some of the lines were more clearly drawn. There was sufficient confidence to suggest that the professional bodies were not suited to having a decisive influence over a university law school. This raised once more the question of which place should teach which subjects? At this point the Law Society became conservative and claimed in its representations to the Commission that it should have exclusive powers over the process of assessing prospective solicitors. In other words there was no question of granting exemptions in respect of courses taken at a university. Instead it was a simple matter of theory being a university preserve and all practical requirements being tested by the profession. It was for this reason that the Law Society was less satisfied with education in Manchester, where it was in university hands, than it was in places such as Liverpool and Bristol, where it was heavily influenced by the professions.[48]

In respect of the Bar and the judiciary, Sir Herbert Cozens-Hardy had already been reported as telling the Royal Commission that the 'prevalent view among

---

[45] For the numbers of law students, see Royal Commission on University Education in London, above n 43, 41: evidence of Sidney Webb.

[46] Ibid, 22, para 11.

[47] Ibid, 22, para 17.

[48] B Abel-Smith and R Stevens, *Lawyers and the Courts: A Sociological Study of the English Legal System, 1750–1965* (London, Heinemann, 1970) 179. Note that by the 1930s Manchester's Prof Eastwood was recommending professional links for Law Schools: see ch 4.

the benchers' was that the Council of Legal Education should not become part of the University of London.[49] From the start he was blunt. When asked by the Commissioners:

> You do not think we shall get to the day, at all events yet a while, when the University Degree in Law, even with lawyers having a large voice in framing the Course of Study for it, should count as a qualification for being called to the Bar.

He replied simply: 'No.'[50]

Working within the context of ideas such as these, Blake Odgers did not see himself as being in any way anti-intellectual. In fact on one occasion when he made observations on the respective roles of the professions and universities he did it by way of setting the scene for a paper given to the Society on the same afternoon by Professor Girard of the University of Paris. The latter's topic was Roman law and its current educational roles.

> After dwelling on the various causes which had combined to diminish the importance of Roman Law as a practical or professional study, Professor Girard pointed out the apparently inconsistent fact, that the interest in Roman law throughout Europe, remained as great as ever. This fact he attributed to the value of Roman Law (a) as an essential preliminary to the understanding of modern systems (b) as the best foundation for the teaching of modern law (c) as a rich field of historical and textual speculation.[51]

The discussions made for a lively mix of ideas.

For the Society the debates of these years raised again and again the question of how it could go beyond interesting generalisations and influence the practice of legal education around the country at a time when there were few students to teach. The Fifth Annual General Meeting, held on 4 July 1913, at the LSE, produced exasperated Presidential observations from Sir John Macdonell, Professor of Comparative Law at University College London. He spoke with reference to certain 'men of eminence who had given utterance to hard sayings as to the worthlessness of jurisprudence' and, in contrast, the much more incisive proposals for further work on educational projects and the need for the teacher of law 'to put life into what often seemed to others dead matter'.[52] Professor Macdonell's concern is all the easier to understand when it is placed in the context of the Final Report of the Royal Commission on University Education in London which appeared in 1913.[53] For example, the Commission stated that:

> We have no doubt there ought to be a Faculty of Laws in the University of London, but at present there does not exist a body of teachers in this Faculty to whom the title, status and salary of University Professors or Readers have been assigned, or who have yet been recommended by Boards of Advisors for those titles. The absence of endowment

[49] Royal Commission on University Education in London, above n 43, 74.
[50] Ibid.
[51] Minutes of General Meetings, Fourth Annual General Meeting, 5 July 1912, A.SPTL 1/1.
[52] Minutes of General Meetings, Fifth Annual General Meeting, 4 July 1913, A.SPTL 1/1.
[53] Royal Commission on University Education in London, Final Report, 1913, HMSO, Cmd 6717.

is chiefly responsible for this, as men of learning and distinction are not wanting among the teachers. The only member of the Faculty who is a University Professor is Sir John Macdonell, the Quain Professor of Comparative Law at University College, and even in this case the salary is quite inadequate and the professorship is only a part-time appointment.[54]

Set against this lack of metropolitan provision there was still the hope for something better and the belief that there could be constructive linkage between university work and professional courses. The Report went on to emphasise the view that

> The large and increasing number of men who ought to study some branch of law as the best preparation for their future work in life should not be deprived of the scientific training which they can obtain only in a university.[55]

Clearly, the new Society was operating in an intellectual and financial context that produced alternating expressions of frustration and hope for the future. It is noticeable that some members of the Society were involved in the work of the Royal Commission but it is easy to see why Jenks and Gaudy had hesitations about getting the Society itself caught up in these controversies at this stage of its life.[56] To emphasise the point again, the Society had divisions within its ranks, with some of those connected with the Inns of Court School of Law looking over their shoulders to the Benchers of the Inns. Members of the Commission were self-consciously attempting to find a way forward for legal education which would provide both resources and an intellectually satisfying role for the law teacher. But it was equally obvious that declarations of intent were a long way from being implemented and teachers of law were not agreed amongst themselves.

It may be that Jenks sensed that major change was not a practical possibility at this time and that the Society would benefit from a focus on something achievable. Here he used his links with Australia. He referred his colleagues to a letter from 'Professor Harrison Moore of Melbourne, suggesting the suitability of publication by the Society of case books, on lines similar to those adopted in the United States.' He pointed out that the letter spoke generally of publishing books 'somewhat on the American lines' and stressed that 'This of course goes far beyond the books of leading cases published in England hitherto.' Harrison wanted such books because 'The assiduity of our students is knocking the library Reports to pieces.' The Honorary Secretary (Jenks) mentioned that he had asked Professor Moore to furnish further details of his proposals, but even before a reply was received the Society decided to set up a special committee to look into the matter. When the reply did come Harrison Moore pointed out that the cases in such books are presented in the order in which they might be found in a textbook and this type of book could be used in conjunction with the American

---

[54] Ibid, para 330.
[55] Ibid, para 330.
[56] See n 44 above.

'case-method', but could also be used quite independently of it.[57] Jenks had arranged for the meeting to take place at the LSE and at the end of discussion he adjourned the session for a meal at the Worshipful Company of Saddlers at Cheapside.

As a matter of impression, the more focused debates about rules and case-books, etc, gave the Society's members a sense of coming together. The new organisation had not instantly resolved the major problems of law teachers, but, within three or four years, the SPTL had gone through a threshold in terms of social cohesion and achieved everyday recognition amongst a significant number law teachers. The Sixth Annual General Meeting was held in the Codrington Library at All Souls College, Oxford in the summer of 1914.[58] The President, Dr Henry Bond, a Cambridge don, was joined by Professor Phillips of Leeds as Vice-President, and by others such as Edward Bramley, Sir Frederick Pollock, AD McNair, Professor Vinogradoff and WS Holdsworth. The meeting had an air of optimism. Membership of the Society was increasing and its financial position was 'healthy'. The special committee on the production of case-books reported in positive terms, but amongst the members there was some dispute about the merits of the project. Eventually there was a compromise and it was decided that 'the General Committee be authorised to sanction the publication, on behalf of (but without expense to) the Society a Collection of Leading Cases on Real Property Law'.[59] More adventurously Mr Bramley from Sheffield 'raised the question of the extension of the scope of the Society to Scotland; and Dr Blake Odgers, in supporting the suggestion, alluded also to a possible extension to Ireland'.[60] The session finished with an academic paper from Sir Frederick Pollock, after which everyone met for dinner.

The meeting is also interesting for what it did not discuss. The Royal Commission on University Education in London had at last reported in full and final form at the end of 1913. But there is no record of it being discussed; presumably the silence arose in part because the Society had not made representations and in part because there was no formal debate on its views for the reasons given above: it could have been too divisive. But it must, surely, have been considered informally and it is likely that it met with approval in some quarters. The Chair of the Commission had been made an Honorary Member of the Society. The Report argued that

> the most scientific study of (law) which a university can provide will be the best foundation for professional work, and will alone fit a man to deal with intellectual freedom, and from a wide point of view, with the questions he will have to answer from day to day in his professional practice.[61]

---

[57] These letters are mentioned at Minutes of General Meetings, Fifth Annual General Meeting, 4 July 1913, A SPTL 1/1. See too 10 December 1921, A.SPTL 1/3–4 and the end of the Minute Volume: letters 21 April 1913 and 25 November 1913. A.SPTL 1/3–4 reveals meetings on 12 March 1914 and 22 April 1914. For the fate of the discussions about case-books, see the next chapter.

[58] Minutes of General Meetings, Sixth Annual General Meeting, A.SPTL, 1/1.

[59] Ibid.

[60] Ibid.

[61] Royal Commission on University Education in London, Final Report, above n 53, para 337.

Abel-Smith and Stevens rightly stress the importance of this.[62] It was being suggested that a university and a profession had different objectives, but a university could put on courses of long-term value to practising lawyers. As they point out, it is possible that the sustained conservatism of some within the Inns of Court had made it impossible for the professions to develop direct representation in the universities. This had unintentionally done something to protect the autonomy of the universities and their capacity to innovate in legal education. But for the moment, those directing the SPTL were steering it away from such controversial topics.

The 'Great War' and Pessimism

In August 1914 the First World War began and by the time of the next Annual General Meeting in 1915 many of the pre-conditions for the Society's enthusiasm for meeting socially in its early years had vanished. There was a low attendance of twenty-five. The gathering was at the Law Society and the retiring President, Professor Phillips from Leeds, referred 'to the international crisis, and more particularly to the effects, present and future, which it exerted and would exert upon law schools throughout the country. He contrasted the position on the occasion of the last General Meeting with that prevailing at the present time . . . and he expressed a fervent hope that it would be possible to avoid a breach in the continuity of any Law School.[63]

In this climate of uncertainty the admission of lawyers who might apply from Scotland or Ireland was put over to a later date.[64] As if this was not sufficiently discouraging the Society then pitched itself into a debate on the expulsion of certain Honorary Members. From the early days of the Society there had been distinguished appointments. These included well-known 'names' of the day such as James Ames of Harvard and the judge and jurist Oliver Wendell Holmes. The link, incidentally, remained chiefly social but it was also a part of the sustained interest in American legal education. Alongside this there were interesting initiatives in respect of British Honorary Members. Apart from Lord Haldane, mentioned above the Prime Minister of the day, HH Asquith accepted, as did a number of judges. The appointment of Graham Harrison, then at the Board of Customs and Excise and subsequently a distinguished Parliamentary Counsel, reveals an interest in the civil service. The Society plainly wished to be seen as respectable and wanted to be known in government and 'Whitehall' and even internationally. Inevitably, in making these appointments, it had also turned to the distinguished law schools in Germany. As a result the Honorary Membership

---

[62] Abel-Smith and Stevens, above n 48, 180.
[63] Minutes of General Meetings, Seventh Annual General Meeting, 2 July 1915, A.SPTL 1/1.
[64] Ibid.

now included a number of eminent German lawyers and Jenks proposed 'That the names of Professor Heinrich Brunner and Professor von Gierke, representatives of Germany, be removed from the list of Honorary Members of the Society'.[65] The motion was seconded by Holdsworth. In the ensuing debate Sir Frederick Pollock, Professor Goudy, Dr Blake Odgers and others opposed the proposition but it was supported by a substantial majority and at the end the motion was carried by 18 votes to 7.[66] The Honorary members in question were struck out.

By the Annual General Meeting of 1916 the gloom had intensified and there was a self-conscious search for observations which would give the little group a sense of purpose. In the presence of distinguished Honorary Members such as Viscount Bryce, Lord Parker of Waddington and the draftsman and authority on Parliament Sir Courteney Ilbert the mood was sombre. The President, Sir Ernest Trevelyan, admitted that he was being speculative but he:

> foresaw a great diminution in the number of law students, due to the losses in the war, unwillingness of soldiers to return to civil routine, and diminution in prospects of professional work, especially for barristers. Never-the-less, he thought that the necessity for the reconstruction of International Law, the changes foreshadowed in Constitutional Law, and the increased interest taken in the old country by colonials, might, to a certain extent, compensate for the losses. He suggested that, in the inevitable reorganisation of education after the war, an opportunity might be found for incorporating certain branches of law in the general scheme of a liberal education.[67]

In an after-dinner speech which was not fully recorded Bryce appears to have argued that there was reason for optimism in respect of German thought on legal issues.[68] This was entirely consistent with his lifelong belief in the merits of seeing virtue in the legal thought of other countries. As early as 1871 Bryce had written critically saying that 'Narrow as is the sea that parts England from the continent of Europe, it has cut her off as effectually from many continental influences as if she lay far out in mid-Atlantic'.[69] Bryce had been a strong 'Germanophile' since his early days when he was known internationally for his essay on the Holy Roman Empire. Later, in 1880, when he was elected as the Liberal Member of Parliament for Tower Hamlets, he had made a point of addressing newly arrived immigrants from Germany in fluent German.[70]

But whatever was said about German law in 1916 it was remarked at the next meeting held at the LSE in 1917 that the hopes had not been realised. Any

[65] Ibid.

[66] Ibid. It seems that Bryce was not present. In many other contexts Pollock had been strongly anti-German: see N Duxbury, *Frederick Pollock and the English Juristic Tradition* (Oxford, Oxford University Press, 2004) 2.

[67] Minutes of General Meetings, Eighth Annual General Meeting, 7 July 1916, A.SPTL 1/1.

[68] Ibid, and later reference in Minutes of General Meetings, Ninth Annual General Meeting, 6 July 1917, A.SPTL 1/1.

[69] J Bryce, *Studies in History and Jurisprudence* (Oxford, Clarendon Press, 1901) vol II, 475, lecture given in 1871.

[70] HAL Fisher, *James Bryce* (New York, Macmillan, 1927) vol I, 171.

reconsideration of what had happened in respect of Honorary Members must, surely, have become even less likely when the only child of Jenks's first marriage was killed in action. In some respects the tone of pessimism was reinforced as when it was announced that the project for a book on cases in real property would not be taken any further. It seems the chief problem was finance, but there may have been other issues, not least of copyright.[71]

Attempting to confront this pessimism the then President, Professor Murison (of University College London) was almost defiant in his determination to continue debates about central issues in legal education. 'While emphasising the requirement of adequate teaching, he insisted that the most important duty of the teacher is original work; nothing else would give the English school any sort of standing in the world of legal learning. But both objects – as the two run into each other – demand a continuum and undistracted labour. Every professional teacher ought to be able, and to be required to do, (whatever else he may do) a 'day's work everyday' at his proper subject. This implies a need for a reasonable supplement to the present very insufficient endowments. Whether this is to be got, and how, is a contingency of the future; but, unless teachers are put in a position to 'make a business' of their work, it is absurd to expect them to cope with the appalling amount of research that is waiting to be done, or to enter the lists with foreign scholars'.[72] Appropriately enough this was followed up by a paper from Dr Hazeltine, (who, as we have seen, was an American then teaching at Cambridge) on 'Law Schools and Legal Practitioners in the United States'. This generated some dispute and, as on other occasions, there was obvious interest in 'the peculiar and far-reaching influence of Langdell, to which America owed its characteristic 'case-book' system'.[73]

The Annual General Meeting for 1918 was a mixed experience. Only 18 members could attend. The deaths in battle of two members (Aston and Livingstone) were recorded and the President spent his address remarking on the impact of war. He was not entirely gloomy. Strikingly he was interested in the role of legal skills in programmes of reconstruction.

> The state had made much use of academically trained experts in all departments during the war; it was possible that some teachers in the Law Schools might, when peace was restored, be needed for a time to assist in the reconstruction; peace when it came would open up wide fields of usefulness to Members of the Society, especially in spreading a wider knowledge of English law, the history of British Institutions, and International Law, among the people of the kingdom.[74]

This unusual comment (in the sense that it was not representative of previous Society debates) on the role of lawyers in what a later age might call social engineering was all the more significant because it was followed by an address from

---

[71] Minutes of General Meetings, Ninth Annual General Meeting, 9 July 1917, A.SPTL 1/1.
[72] Ibid.
[73] Ibid.
[74] Minutes of General Meetings, Tenth Annual General Meeting, 1918, A.SPTL 1/1.

the President of the Law Society on 'A Proposed Ministry of Justice' with the Lord Chancellor being seen purely as a judicial officer.[75]

These occasional radical thoughts could not conceal the transformation in the Society brought about by the War. With war came the exclusion of German honorary members, delay in considering possible applications from lawyers in Scotland and Ireland, increasing concern about the decline in the number of law students and a reassessment of professional roles, albeit at an abstract level. A few of the more reflective members were beginning to wonder if at the end of four years of horror and grief there might be a new way of thinking about legal roles in the future, but no-one knew how this might be resourced. There was almost complete uncertainty.

[75] Ibid.

3

Defiance and Debate: 1919–1930

[L]egal teachers have duties and responsibilities which bind them very closely to legal scholarship and authorship; and they are also intimately concerned, together with other elements of the community, with the progressive development of the substance and form of the system of justice.

(Professor HD Hazeltine, writing in the first issue of the *Journal of the Society of Public Teachers of Law*, 1924)

Only 13 members were present when the Society met at Gray's Inn in July 1919. Professor Goudy stood in for a further term as President, presumably for want of another suitable candidate. Jenks was ill and the absence of his guiding hand was noticed and remarked upon.[1]

The response to these difficult circumstances was strikingly idealistic and even hopeful. Dr Pearce Higgins from Cambridge revealed that there were some grounds for optimism in legal education. He

recalled the lean years for educational institutions for which the War had been responsible, and expressed the universal gratification felt at the present revival, which had, however, brought its difficulties, in as much as students were returning in large numbers, ill-prepared for their legal studies, but, happily, with the keen desire to make good the leeway.[2]

It appears that Higgins was thinking of people attending courses both in London and the provinces and this hint of optimism was enough to direct Professor Goudy as retiring President into a further set of grand generalisations.

In his view the Society ought not to be content merely with guiding successive generations of students, but should take a leading part in the reform of the law. It seemed to him that there were three great objects demanding the Society's attention and efforts . . . (1) the establishment of an Imperial School of Law, (2) the formation of a Ministry of Justice, and (3) Codification of the Law.[3]

As before, Jenks was unequivocal in saying that lawyers had public duties.

---

[1] Minutes of General Meetings, Eleventh Annual General Meeting, 3 July 1919, A.SPTL 1/1.
[2] Ibid, and see (1920) 36 *Law Quarterly Review* 429.
[3] Minutes of General Meetings, Eleventh Annual General Meeting, 3 July 1919, A.SPTL 1/1.

The possibility of an Imperial School of Law had never entirely vanished from the late-Victorian and Edwardian debates about the role of the University of London and it was now showing some resilience as an idea. Certainly, in Goudy's view, it should be in London where it would be

> working in conjunction with such bodies as the Selden Society and the Society of Comparative Legislation, the Grotius Society, and others, and should receive the support and recognition of all those educational institutions which at present existed, in different localities and without co-ordination or co-operation.

It should be near the Law Courts (by which he presumably meant the Law Courts in the Strand). It should teach all the Imperial legal systems. It should redress the shaming fact that there was 'not one good Roman Law library in London'.[4] He congratulated Jenks on the recently published edition of his *Digest of the Law* and pointed out that it could be a useful instrument for later programmes of codification.[5] Goudy, now on the verge of retiring from academic life, was at his most ambitious and not in the least deterred by the difficulties of the Society.

A capacity to combine strategic grandeur with a small attendance was carried into the next Annual General Meeting. The gathering of July 1920 was held at the Inner Temple and only 16 were present. Jenks was now President and he had an effective Vice-President in Professor Geldart of Oxford. Jenks's secretarial work was carried out effectively by Dr Burgin, who already had more than ten years' experience of the Society. There was discussion about the need to increase membership, which then stood at a total of 105. The role of the Case Book Committee was debated once again.[6] Most of all, Jenks was adventurous in his analysis of the need for a new type of legal education. As so often with Jenks, the best method of defence was attack.

> He called attention to the new type of law which had been one of the many outcomes of the war, and suggested new methods which law teachers would find it necessary to adopt in order to deal with the changed conditions, and the ample opportunity which existed for law teachers at the present time, showing how such opportunities might be met by improved organisation and new methods of teaching. [There were] . . . ways in which their military work had effected changes in the outlook of law students and their manner of approaching their legal studies, and the changes in the law itself which the altered conditions brought about by the war had necessitated.[7]

Jenks approached these pedagogical issues in individual rather than structural terms. Writing in the *Law Quarterly Review* in 1920, he said, with obvious feeling, that:

> While improvement in organisation involves long and often fruitless discussions, conciliation of conflicting interests or supposed interests, and generally a good deal of

---

[4] Ibid.
[5] E Jenks, *Digest of English Civil Law* (London, Butterworth, 1921).
[6] Minutes of General Meetings, Twelfth Annual General Meeting, 9 July 1920, A.SPTL 1/1.
[7] Ibid.

creaking machinery, the adoption of new methods of teaching is—at any rate, in this country—largely open to the individual teacher.[8]

So it was predictable that Jenks did not provide more analysis on 'the new methods'. This 'individualistic' attitude to teaching was important. It obviously allowed for local initiatives, but it also restricted the role of the Society in developing national debate on methods of legal teaching. It was another reminder that the Society had limited powers and that sometimes these limitations were happily self-imposed by the members of the Society. The members could give their personal views on teaching and, by agreement, share ideas in an ad hoc manner. But, for the moment, it would be difficult to go beyond this.

Beneath the level of the Annual General Meetings Jenks was faced with some personal feuding. At the General Committee held on 10 December 1921 a simmering issue came into the open when there was 'a proposal by Mr Crew that the Lord Chancellor (Lord Birkenhead) be invited . . . to accept Honorary membership'.[9] This motion was not seconded. In reality it seems that the proposal was designed to embarrass Jenks. The problem went back to Jenks's time at Oxford when, according to an anecdote, in a viva he had asked the undergraduate FE Smith (the future Lord Birkenhead) about one of the rules in Shelley's case. Smith failed to answer and, it is alleged, went on to say that whatever the rule was he would ensure that it was changed when he became Lord Chancellor. The practical result, it was further alleged, was that the candidate did not get a First in the BCL and held a grievance against Jenks for the rest of his life, and was possibly determined to see that Jenks never became a King's Counsel. The issue was raised again at later meetings which Jenks may have deliberately avoided. It soured the atmosphere.[10]

More serious for Jenks was the loss of Professor Goudy, who had retired in 1920. The absence of Goudy, with his emphasis on long-term strategies, may have led Jenks to concentrate on a number of practical initiatives. There were further dealings with the LCC and after investigation one of the law teachers at the latter was accepted for membership subject to evidence of qualifications. The evidence was not recorded but it seems that it was unsatisfactory.[11] There was active planning for an Annual General Meeting at UCL with, amongst other things, hopes for tea and an invitation or subscription dinner. Strikingly, those attending the meal would be required to wear morning dress. The fact that this was an express prerequisite at an early stage of planning suggests that it may have been contentious to some members. Surely it points to a frail concern for social status. (It was not, it seems repeated, and when the economy was in serious difficulty in 1931 there was, in fact, no formal dinner.)[12]

---

[8] E Jenks (1920) 36 *Law Quarterly Review* 431.

[9] 10 December 1921, A.SPTL 1/3–4.

[10] PH Pettit, 'The Society of Public Teachers of Law—The First Seventy-Five Years' (1983) 3 *Legal Studies* 231.

[11] Minute Book, 10 December 1921, A.SPTL 1/3–4, and Minute Book, 21 April 1922, A.SPTL 1/4.

[12] Minute Book, 21 April, 1922 and 12 December, 1931, A.SPTL 1/4.

Jenks also pushed forward with a number of programmes through using the work of sub-committees of the General Committee. For example, a group was set up to consider life insurance 'and the provision for old age by policies'. The full-time staff of the universities had the advantage of using the 'Federated Super-annuation Scheme', but others, such as part-time law teachers, faced difficulties when trying to obtain some sort of pension. The possible use of 'life insurance' was explored and it was resolved to carry out research in each 'centre of legal education'. By July 1922 there was a desire to put pressure on 'the governing bodies of the various centres of legal education in favour of assisting the scheme by adequate contributions towards premiums paid by members of the Society'.[13]

The idea of publishing a case book was further considered. There were problems, openly discussed, with the Incorporated Council of Law Reporting which was reported as simply refusing permission for the reproduction of its reports as a system of looseleaf cases. This was not enough to bring the initiative to an end and some members began to consider using other series of law reports. The project was considered again over a number of years.[14] Taken as a whole, the Society was determined that something would be done but there was still no certainty about the outcome.

Jenks was now over 60 years old and was something of a person in a hurry for practical results. He had a major achievement to his credit in the legislative programme for Parliament in 1922. In the words of Lord Chorley, writing in later years, he 'inspired the passing of the Solicitors Act, 1922 under which legal education for certified clerks became compulsory, and which led to the development of many Red Brick University Law Schools'.[15] This move also, incidentally, further enhanced the power of the Law Society because any university putting on such courses required its approval. The achievement of this statutory reform belongs more to Jenks than to the Society: the Society appears to have done nothing to support or oppose the initiative. We have seen that important developments were already taking place in 'Red Brick University Law Schools' with support from the Law Society, but the previous efforts now had the significant boost of statutory endorsement.[16] Years later, when Lord Chorley wrote an obituary of Jenks, he wryly observed that 'In 1924 at the age of 63 Jenks took the first step towards retirement when he accepted the newly founded Chair of English Law in the University of London.'[17]

---

[13] Minute Book, 1 July 1922, A.SPTL 1/4.

[14] Minute Book, 27 November 1922, 13 December 1922, 13 January 1923, A.SPTL 1/4.

[15] Lord Chorley (1947–51) 1(NS) *JSPTL* 114.

[16] The Solicitors Act 1922 (12 and 13 Geo 5 c 57) ss 1–10. For lively discussion of this reform, see Parliamentary Debates, Fifth Series (1922) Vol 152, cols 767–98.

[17] Chorley, above n 15, 115.

Teaching Legal History

With the deaths of Dicey and Geldart in 1922 it was all the more necessary to look to new initiatives which would enhance the Society's reputation. Soon there were two further undertakings, both of which which, in different ways, were to give the Society new dimensions. On 13 January 1923 the General Committee decided that 'the attention of centres of learning should be called to the importance of Year Book study'. It was felt that 'the practical importance of the subject should be emphasised', although one member thought that this was possibly best left to postgraduates.[18]

The 'Year Book Project' was of considerable importance because for the first time the Society was seeking to advance and (in some way yet to be determined by the Society) to subsidise the teaching of a particular law subject. The drive for this innovation was surely in part the achievement of Maitland's reputation (the great legal historian had died in 1906). This was not only of interest in itself but it gave English studies in law a reputable position which could in a very small way withstand international comparison with what was happening at, say, Harvard. It was also a way of enhancing such studies domestically at a time when teachers in universities were too readily identified with an exclusive concern for Law Society qualifications. It had the potential to give the Society a sense of self-confidence as *the* forum for debates about legal education in England and Wales. As Jenks had argued in 1920, legal history could 'appeal to the intelligence rather than the memory of the student'.[19]

A modern legal historian has explained the year books in the following way:

The first surviving reports of arguments or remarks attributed to named judges are from the 1250s. They are little more than collections of dicta; some are apparently intended to illustrate accounts of procedure; some are found in collections arranged by forms of action; and some, from the 1280s onwards, are the reports of particular eyre sessions or terms at Westminster. The last format was the one that prevailed. Eyres were becoming infrequent, though the last sessions were reported in full. From 1291, however, there is a continuous stream of reports of arguments in the Common Pleas. The reports were written in the Anglo-French dialect spoken in court. The arguments are given in abridged form, often impenetrably brief, but with the names of the speakers and occasional comments. Their authorship is unknown, and they are referred to by the generic name 'year-books'.[20]

This initiative turned into a mixed achievement for the Society. After some years of trying to take the project forward, there were peripatetic lectures at various universities by the legal historian William Craddock Bolland, formerly Sanders Reader at Cambridge. At the meeting of 15 December 1926 Bolland is recorded as giving the Year Book lectures at Sheffield, Leeds and Manchester and being

---

[18] Minute Book, 13 January 1923, A.SPTL 1/4.
[19] Jenks, above n 8.
[20] AJH Baker, *An Introduction to English Legal History*, 4th edn (London, Butterworths, 2002) 179.

paid £109 12s and 5d.[21] Unfortunately, Bolland was to die in 1927. (After something of a struggle the Society managed to marshal enough support to obtain a civil list pension for his widow which must have served as a further reminder of the dangers of part-time law teachers having no conventional annuity.)[22] Bolland was replaced by GJ Turner, and, again, there was some financial support from the Selden Society.[23] When the General Committee met in Manchester in 1929 it was told that a special committee of Winfield, Holdsworth and Wade had proposed a lectureship on medieval English law and had discussed the possibility of supporting it through a gift from a benefactor or subscriptions from members.[24] The episode was both sad and revealing. In the course of trying to take forward this initiative it was becoming clear that the Society simply lacked the funds to have a direct impact on legal education through the provision of courses. It also highlighted the Society's particular difficulties in developing studies that were not of immediate professional relevance.

The Creation of a Journal

At a meeting in 1923 the General Committee resolved 'that a sub-committee be appointed to consider the whole question of the possible issue of a journal, and to report'.[25] This sub-committee included the President, Jenks and the young Cambridge academic Gutteridge. Before long, those on the sub-committee had met and decided that subject to the need for an editor the scheme was 'both feasible and desirable, and that it need not be unduly costly'.[26] The project injected an air of confidence into the work of the Society and this was bolstered by the arrival of new members such as Hanbury from Oxford, Haggen from Leeds and Hughes Parry from Aberystwyth. JR Atkin, later Lord Atkin, was given Honorary Membership.[27] It is true that the optimism was slightly eclipsed by Mr Crew once more raising issues that others found awkward. But it was now clear that the Society as a whole was engaged in a serious project. When the General Committee met on 20 October 1923 it decided to proceed with the journal, and to the delight and, in all probability, surprise of those present, a case book on real property had been published. A further round of new membership applications revealed a strengthening of provincial representation with, for example, WGH Cook from University College Southampton, Griffith Morgan from University

---

[21] Minute Book, 15 December 1926, A.SPTL 1/4. And see Minute Book, 21 April 1923, 18 October 1924, 18 March 1925, A.SPTL 1/4. On Bolland, see A.SPTL 2/21.
[22] Minute Book, 10 December 1927, A.SPTL 1/4.
[23] Ibid.
[24] Ibid, Minute Book, 13 July 1929, A.SPTL 1/4.
[25] Ibid, 13 January 1923.
[26] Ibid, 21 April 1923.
[27] Ibid, 13 January 1923.

College Exeter, Harold Potter from Birmingham and JW Van Druten from Bangor.[28]

By March 1924 the General Committee was attending to details in respect of the plans for a journal. It would be issued free to all members and Honorary Members of the Society (although the arrangement for Honorary Members was changed in later years). It was also decided that it would be withheld from members whose subscriptions were in arrears. Non-members of the Society could purchase the *Journal* for 3s 6d.[29] In July the significance of the contemporary appearance of the *Cambridge Law Journal* was recognised, and Jolowicz, as one of its editors, was invited to come to a meeting of the General Committee at the LSE and give the Society the benefit of his experience in the creation of that periodical. He openly said that he supported the idea of an SPTL publication and, speaking personally, felt he could say that the two publications would not be in competition. He thought that the objects should be 'definitely educational' and that the cost would be '£50 per annum at most'. Despite this endorsement, some members had doubts and now Crew objected to this and almost everything.[30]

In any event, these doubts were brushed aside and the Journal appeared in 1924.[31] Its content accurately reflected the Society's concerns during recent years. The first article in the *Journal* had the optimistic title of 'Forward Tendencies in English Legal Education' and was by the American scholar based in Cambridge, HD Hazeltine, who has been mentioned in a previous chapter.[32] Its argument was more cautious than the title might have suggested but it called for significant reforms and set out parameters for debate within the Society. The author wanted 'a permanent committee charged with the duty of making enquiries from time to time as to the state of legal education and of reporting the results to the General Committee and, ultimately, to the Society'. English arrangements for legal education were put in an unfavourable light by way of contrast to what had been achieved in Canada, the United States, Australia and Europe. But there had been some progress. Unaware at that time of the long-term fate of the attempt to intervene in the teaching of legal history Hazeltine noted that 'the important subject of English Legal History is at last receiving its due place of prominence in the *curricula* of several of our schools'. More generally, a fair number of universities had now been given Law Society approval for courses under the Solicitors Act of 1922: Oxford, Cambridge, London, Leeds, Liverpool, Manchester, Sheffield, Birmingham, Bristol, Armstrong (Newcastle-upon-Tyne), and the university colleges of Exeter, Aberystwyth, Bangor, Cardiff, Swansea and Southampton. Hazeltine hoped for co-operation between the universities and the two legal

---

[28] Ibid, 20 October 1923.

[29] Ibid, 22 March 1924.

[30] Ibid, 12 July 1924. HF Jolowicz accepted the editorship of the *JSPTL*: see (1924) 1 *JSPTL* 65 and (1925) 2 *JSPTL* 71.

[31] (1924) 1 *JSPTL*.

[32] (1924) 1 *JSPTL* 1. On Hazeltine, see ch 2, n 18.

professions and he was unequivocal in saying that the objectives of the society should be to further legal education and justice.[33]

For Hazletine, learning law required intellectual engagement: 'contact of mind on mind is the essence of all teaching, formal or informal'. For him the chief objectives of members should be furthering legal education and justice, and neither of these could 'be attained in the fullest measure, however, without the sympathetic and practical co-operation of the universities and of both branches of the profession'.[34] He was optimistic about professional co-operation at this time. Presumably in response to the recent admission of women to the legal professions, he spoke of educating young men *and women* for the professions. Given the acute importance of the admission of women to how the SPTL saw itself, this remark had great potential. But he went on to blur the issue by returning to exclusive references to men with no hint of the possibility that this might be interpreted so as to include women. In this regard he argued:

> [L]egal teachers have duties and responsibilities which bind them very closely to legal scholarship and authorship; and they are also intimately concerned, together with other elements of the community, with the progressive development of the substance and form of the system of justice. In lieu of the right word one might perhaps describe him as a 'jurist', if this much used and much abused word be interpreted aright. It is clearly the duty of the teacher-jurist to edit and to write books of the law, to make his contribution to legal scholarship and literature, but it is equally his duty to take an active and effective part in the moulding of the law's traditional body of principles and practice into a closer conformity with the ever-changing needs of the community.[35]

To emphasise the importance of the Bar he added that:

> The active assistance of the Bar Council is greatly to be desired. In the USA the various Bar Associations take a very prominent part in solving the problems of legal education; and they work in close co-operation with the Association of American Law Schools.[36]

The new *Journal* also emphasised the importance of what was happening at provincial universities. For instance, C Grant Robertson, Principal of the University of Birmingham, gave an analysis of the task involved in establishing 'A Birmingham School of Law'. He pointed out that there was an increasing number of provincial universities in England, and if progress was to be made in legal education, there had to be both students and a capacity to teach to university standard. Inevitably, provincial progress had been slow, in part because universities had not yielded to 'an uninstructed demand for cheap and quick returns'.[37] Accordingly, law had had to wait, but there was no doubting the commitment to it as a subject of high-level study. The local professions were supportive and, generally,

---

[33] (1924) 1 *JSPTL* 4, 8, 9.
[34] Ibid, 11, 15.
[35] Ibid, 12, 13.
[36] Ibid, 16.
[37] Ibid, 22.

the reasons for regarding the study and teaching of law as an indispensable function of a university are so obvious and so irrefutably based on human experience and the aims of any society claiming to be civilized that they need not be explained or emphasised here.[38]

Finally, the new *Journal* provided a source of information about law teaching and research that would have otherwise been completely lacking. For example, Professor Eastwood gave information on developments at Manchester University. An outline of the work of the Society's General Committee was provided. The death of Courtney Ilbert was recorded. There was a list of works published by members during the last year.[39] And so on.

In substance the new *Journal* was both a way of sharing information amongst law teachers and a manifesto for the Society with its ambitions and its critical view of the problems which confronted the teacher of law. In his Presidential Address given at Oxford on 12 July 1924, WS Holdsworth reflected the themes to be found in the first volume of the Society's *Journal*.[40] There was the same strenuous assertion of potential educational progress combined with self-conscious incidental references to the professions.

> We are all members of the legal profession, but just as the Bar is organised in the four Inns of Court, just as solicitors are organised by the Law Society, so the public teachers of law need an organisation of their own.

He explored some of the details of educational provision, stressing, for example, the desirability of putting on formal lectures. But it was not only teaching which mattered. 'All Public Teachers of Law, and more especially those who devote their whole time to the teaching of law, should undertake some piece of research.[41]

The *Journal* gives an impression of a group of people looking with hesitant optimism to the future and exploring a wide range of educational issues. Apart from publishing Holdsworth's Presidential Address of the previous year, it had Atkin LJ discussing the 'Future Development of English Law' and Henry L Levy-Ullmann considering comparative law in the University of Paris.[42] It gave an opportunity to put forward and develop distinctive views of legal education.

A wide-ranging argument was put forward by JDI Hughes, Professor of Law at the University of Leeds. Like many others he sought a balance between, in his words, 'apprenticeship' and 'liberal study'. But in other respects he was different. He expressed himself in a style which some might find both elliptical and flowery. In an article entitled 'From a Modern Law School' he wrote that 'Education is a process, not the mortgage of information by dictation of lectures, subject to redemption by examination, when the transaction is closed.' Further

---

[38] Ibid, 22–3.
[39] Ibid, 39–40, 23–4.
[40] WS Holdsworth, 'The Vocation of a Public Teacher of Law' (1925) 2 *JSPTL* 1.
[41] Ibid, 4, 9.
[42] Ibid, 12–6.

the problem of a type of legal culture which can be related in content and treatment with co-ordinate activities in the profession served, without surrendering anything vital in the English university tradition, is one of progressive interest making considerable demands upon the teachers involved.[43]

When 'unpacked', the convoluted second statement is of real interest. It sees the problems confronting members in terms of culture, and the culture of the world in which they worked could be related to that of the professions without the teaching of law losing its identity and merit. Moreover, in furthering a new type of education there was an opportunity for progress, but this was making notable demands on law teachers. In other words, the new Society had to change social expectations as well as introduce reforms in legal education. In more modern terminology, teaching law was a cultural event.

The first and second editions of the *Journal* set the tone for the remainder of the 1920s. Presidential addresses at the Annual General Meetings, initiatives during the year on the part of officers (ECS Wade had been made Honorary Secretary in 1925) and further papers in later editions looked at the educational and professional issues which had always concerned the Society. But there were also some new focal points. In 1926 the Society held a meeting outside Oxford, Cambridge and London. In going to Liverpool it responded in part to recognition of the existence of Law Schools in the north and in part to the efforts of H Chaloner Dowdall, a local practitioner, teacher and politician (Mayor of Liverpool) as well as Professor GH Emmott at the University.[44]

There was a sense of freedom in Society debates at this time, with some unusual ideas coming through. At a meeting in December 1927 Professor de Montmorency argued,

> That this Society regards it as most desirable that some teaching in the principles of law should be given in the upper forms of all secondary schools; that the Society believes that this reform would have a great influence for good in national education generally, as well in its effect as in the training for both branches of the profession; that it cannot be carried out unless all English Universities introduce a compulsory paper on legal principles in the final examination in Arts; that the Society therefore directs that this resolution should be communicated to the appropriate officers of the various English Universities.[45]

This adventurous idea did not find support and at the meeting of the General Committee in April 1928 it was resolved that the suggestions would be taken no further.[46]

In 1927 and 1928 the General Committee contemplated changing the name of the Society on the grounds that the name 'suggests the protection of professional interests rather than the promotion of studies and other public ends'.[47] In part

---

43 Ibid, 22, 28 and 29.
44 (1927) 4 *JSPTL* 62.
45 Minute Book, 15 November 1927, A.SPTL 1/4.
46 Minute Book, 21 April 1928, A.SPTL 1/4.
47 Minute Book, 10 December 1927, A.SPTL 1/4.

this may have been a response to the fear of it being described as a 'trade union'. In any event, no one much liked the existing name and it was pointed out that 'The increasing importance of the society renders an appropriate name increasingly important. Law Schools are everywhere increasing not only in numbers, thoroughness [*sic*] and scope but also in public and professional esteem.' At the same time 'The greatest difficulty is as to an alternative.' Possible new titles included 'The Association of Law Schools', 'The Law Schools Club', 'The Law School's Society' and 'The English Law Schools Association'. None of these was regarded as satisfactory although the last suggestion was felt to be the best of them. At the meeting of the General Committee in 1928 it was decided to recommend a change of name to 'The Law Schools Association'. But at this time the debate led nowhere.[48]

When the General Committee met on 15 December of the same year it was pointed out that: 'There is no society affording a point of corporate contact between law teachers throughout the empire.' This may be the explanation for the undated paper on 'The Imperial Professoriate' mentioned above. It is worth re-emphasising its range in its references to people at, say, Johannesburg, Winnepeg, Melbourne, Otago, Bombay, Calcutta, Lucknow, Madras, Rangoon, Colombo, etc. In any event, at the General Committee for December 1929 there was a debate about allowing people at these places to become corresponding members and some were elected on 15 March 1930. They included, for example, Dr Walton of McGill and Dean RG McKerion of Witwatersrand.[49]

By the end of the 1920s the pessimism of the immediate post-war years had been left behind and the Society was more outward-looking. Certain obvious difficulties remained. The Society was solvent but it lacked resources to take direct initiatives in legal education. It was prepared to discuss the relationship between law teachers and professional expectations in critical terms, but it was still the case that the power and status of the professional bodies could hardly be rivalled by the Society. It was as if much of the future 'agenda' for legal education was still unclear. But despite these sources of uncertainty, the Society had survived the Great War and was increasing in self-confidence.

[48] Minute Book, 21 April, 1928, A.SPTL 1/4. The most probable reason for nothing happening was a lack of enthusiasm for change on the part of Jenks. See also (1927–28) 4 *JSPTL* 62.
[49] A.SPTL 1/4.

4

Research, Dissent and the Possible Admission of Women: 1930–1939

[T]he SPTL pays more attention to Oxford, Cambridge and London—where legal education is already developed—than to the smaller places where there are some really good men struggling to develop it, and of whose existence some official appreciation would be of considerable assistance.

(Professor Eastwood, to the Honorary Secretary ECS Wade, 10 July 1932)

In 1929 HC Gutteridge gave the Presidential Address in Cambridge and raised the question of research for law teachers. Whereas some previous Presidents had spoken in general terms about the desirability of research, Gutteridge was more pointed in his argument. For him, the professions made people too utilitarian in their choice of interests and, as an alternative, he began to explore the best way of providing for what contemporaries were sometimes calling 'Advanced Legal Studies'.[1] In the following year the Annual General Meeting was at the LSE and it looked at first as if the new President, PH Winfield, was intent on returning to the usual concerns of the Society with their focus on teaching. Speaking under the title 'Reforms in the Teaching of Law', he in fact considered the work of members in the broadest context and with an eye to brutal reality. After beginning by exploring improvements in opportunities for law teaching, he pointed to the nature of the teacher's existence. 'In some of the law schools he is allowed to practice, and, for financial reasons, could scarcely teach at all if the rule were otherwise.' In addition, there were administrative responsibilities, which were 'often highly necessary'. On top of this there was examining and, as he put it, 'Finally there is research.' In other words, he revealed the weakness of the provision for research: it was likely to be following on behind not only teaching but also professional practice, administration and examining. At the same time, research was necessary. 'No teacher worth the name can afford to neglect this, for it is part of his equipment for his profession.'[2]

---

[1] HC Gutteridge, 'Advanced Legal Studies', a Presidential Address delivered to the Society at its Annual Meeting of 8 July 1928, at Cambridge, printed in (1929) 6 *JSPTL* 1.

[2] PH Winfield, 'Reforms in the Teaching of Law', A Presidential Address delivered to the Society at its Annual Meeting of 12 July 1930, at LSE, printed in (1930) 7 *JSPTL* 1. Winfield took research 'to

A similar theme was explored by F de Zulueta when he spoke in 1932 about 'The Recruitment of Public Teachers of Law'. He compared the national arrangements in France and Germany with the lack of any system in England. 'The sum of my argument is just this, that though our methods of recruitment secure able men and efficient teachers, they do not give sufficient weight to research.' De Zulueta saw various assumptions underlying this approach. 'The opinion that law is not the best first University course may be a prejudice, but it is deeply rooted, and I must confess to believing that in regard to abler men it is often sound.'[3] For him, as with Gutteridge, an important part of the way forward lay in the need to develop an organisation for advanced studies.

These ideas were of a piece with current debates about the Lord Chancellor's Committee on Legal Education. This had been set up as a result of pressure from Laski at the LSE and others elsewhere who hoped to see some equivalent of the Harvard Law School emerge in Britain. From the start the idea was controversial, not least because it was likely to involve using funds from the Inns of Court and also because, of course, it brought with it the idea that current provision was inadequate. According to Laski, at least one prominent member of the Society, Holdsworth, had opposed the creation of the Committee from the start by telling Sankey, the Lord Chancellor in the Labour Administration of 1929, that no inquiry was needed, since English legal education could hardly be improved.[4] In other words it appears that whatever Holdsworth might be doing to defend the role of the SPTL when he spoke to fellow members of the Society, he was not at this precise time going to see the Society being used as an instrument of reform. It would be easy with the academic assumptions of the twenty-first century to associate something like the SPTL with an interest in reform, but this would not be a good guide to the inter-war years. It was possible for academic 'conservatives' to support the existence of the organisation without wanting it to be used to advance radical change.

The setting up of the new Committee cannot, then, be seen as an achievement for the SPTL, which appears to have taken no action at this stage. But, strikingly, after the Committee came into existence interest increased. In July 1932 the General Committee decided that the Officers of the Society would make representations to the Lord Chancellor's Committee on Legal Education.[5] In formal terms, the latter's function was to consider the organisation of legal education in England with a view to providing close co-ordination between the work done by the universities and the professional bodies and also to consider the provision of advanced research in legal studies. Under Lord Atkin as Chair it reported in 1934 after eight meetings in respect of which much of the evidence came from the

include also the independent investigation of any subject whether the conclusions arrived at are published to the world or not'.

  [3] F de Zulueta (1933) 10 *JSPTL* 9 and 6 (address delivered in 1932).
  [4] B Abel-Smith and R Stevens, *Lawyers and the Courts: A Sociological Study of the English Legal System, 1750–1965* (London, Heinemann, 1970) 184–5.
  [5] Minute Book, 16 July 1932, A.SPTL 1/4.

senior ranks of the professions and could be described as less than revolutionary. Moderate suggestions on the part of those seeking change had some slight impact.[6] In the words of Abel-Smith and Stevens: 'The only two recommendations worthy of note were that a standing advisory committee should be established to co-ordinate examination and teaching requirements, and that an Institute of Advanced Legal Studies should be established in London.'[7] The latter should be a focus for research in all branches of law with an emphasis on comparative law and it should also be of use to people coming from the dominions and colonies.

In respect of the first recommendation, the Society was invited to play a part and responded with enthusiasm and something like embarrassed self-consciousness as to the role of academics. A draft memorandum revealed a desire to show an awareness of professional issues in explaining the importance of the Society. 'By far the greater number of members either are or have been engaged in the practice of the law, in the case of the younger members (apart from those at Oxford and Cambridge) almost without exception.'[8] In respect of institutional affiliation they fell into one of three categories: 51 were at Oxford or Cambridge; 65 were at other universities and colleges; and 21 were at the Inns of Court or the Law Society. Given the opportunity to have Society representatives on the Committee, there was some lobbying for nominations, with Professor Eastwood of Manchester writing to Wade on 27 June 1935 and seeking collective representation for 'the northern group, ie Manchester, Liverpool, Birmingham, Leeds and Sheffield'.[9] The Society nominated six and succeeded in getting four appointed.

In reality the Society's new-found enthusiasm had been misplaced. As Professor Pettit has pointed out in his article in *Legal Studies*, the committee never came into existence.[10] It is easy to think of possible explanations for this, not least the desire of those in the professions to be able to discuss the topic of 'exemptions' from professional examinations with individual institutions rather than a united professional body.

The second recommendation had a more sustained and, as is well known, ultimately more fruitful history. In 1936 a paper for the General Committee was completed by Lee, Jolowicz and Radcliffe on 'The Projected Institute of Legal Research'. It pointed out that such an Institute had been 'mooted over and over again during the last half century without having emerged from the region of aspiration'.[11] Now there was hope for an Institute of Legal Research and the idea was seen as moving out of mere aspiration and towards reality. There would be links (as yet undefined) with London University and the new organisation might

---

[6] Report of the Legal Education Committee, Cmd 4663, 1934. For Lord Atkin's role, see G Lewis, *Lord Atkin* (Oxford, Hart Publishing, 1999) 164, and for his thoughts on education see (1932) 9 *JSPTL* 28.

[7] Abel-Smith and Stevens, above n 4, 185.

[8] A.SPTL 2/28 and see Minute Book, 29 September 1934, A.SPTL 1/4.

[9] Letter, 27 June 1935, Eastwood to Wade, A.SPTL 2/28.

[10] PH Pettit, 'The Society of Public Teachers of Law—The First Seventy-Five Years' (1983) 3 *Legal Studies* 231, 238.

[11] Minute Book, 21 March 1936, A.SPTL 1/4.

follow the precedent of the Institute of Historical Research. Also, it could be related to the 'movement towards law reform'. Already there was interest abroad in what was being proposed. Some, such as Professor Lee of Oxford, were euphoric:

> If I may add my personal testimony, I have conversed with foreigners (not to be dismissed as mere visionaries), who believe that London has a mission to perform as a centre of legal research for the whole world. The idea is inspiring.[12]

But in practice matters moved slowly. Two years later *The Times* revealed that the Lord Chancellor had set up a committee containing a majority of SPTL representatives specifically to consider Branch B of the Report of the Committee on Legal Education. It was 'to advise as to the best practicable means of carrying into effect the recommendations . . . with regard to the establishment in London of an Institute for the promotion of advanced studies in the history and principles of law.'[13] A constitution for the new body was subsequently debated on various occasions, including the General Committee Meeting of 13 July 1938,[14] but nothing was done until after the Second World War. It was as if the idea failed to find the requisite political constituency during the 1930s and the efforts of the SPTL had been frustrated.

Another attempt to challenge existing arrangements had been developing for some years. In 1934 Professor Hughes Parry gave a paper on 'Modern Problems and Methods of Law Reform'. He pointed to the recent creation of the Law Revision Committee, and added, with a hint of regret, that it has to have matters submitted to it by the Lord Chancellor. 'It is, indeed, quite clear that it is not the function of any particular person or body to make a general survey of the field of law and to suggest subjects ripe for reform.' More generally, he was less than happy 'with our present method of drafting statutes'.

> Until there is set up some official or public body charged with the task of systematically preparing the field for reform, we as a Society, would be well advised to undertake thorough and systematic preparatory surveys—historical and comparative—of the problems and methods of law reform.[15]

At first the work of the Law Revision Committee was promising and might have allayed Parry's early fears. The Committee had been set up by Lord Sankey, the Lord Chancellor, and Professor Pettit noted that the Committee contained two ordinary members of the Society in Lord McNair and Professor Gutteridge (as they became), and an honorary member in Lord Wright.[16] The Committee produced eight reports in five years, and all but one of them was implemented. However, it ceased to function by the end of the 1930s and was not revived until

---

[12] 1 May 1936, A.SPTL 2/28.

[13] *The Times*, 6 May 1938.

[14] General Committee Minutes, 13 July 1938, A.SPTL 1/5.

[15] A paper read to University College of South Wales and Monmouthshire at Cardiff, 13 July 1934, printed in (1934) 10 *JSPTL* 10.

[16] Pettit, above n 10, 242.

the establishment of the more adventurously named Law Reform Committee of 1952.[17] It was as if it lacked political momentum at this time.

The combined experiences of the committee to co-ordinate examinations and teaching, the committee to explore the setting up of a centre for advanced research and the Law Revision Committee all highlight clear tensions in legal thought in the 1930s. It is beyond dispute that there were would-be reformers in legal education who wanted new relations with the professions and who saw an important role for law teachers in research and legal change. Equally, it is obvious that they faced inertia and even opposition and the Society could not be used as a force for radical change.

Despite this unpromising context for reformers some members of the Society continued to sustain educational debates. JDI Hughes, Professor of Law at Leeds, was President in 1931–32 and in further developing his ideas of the 1920s (considered in the previous chapter) he spoke of 'Culture and Anarchy in Legal Education', revealing a concern for how the work of universities related to professional expectations. He pointed to increasing links with the professions, asking: '[C]an we in any way strengthen the bridge between academic life and practice without sacrificing the fundamentals for which we stand?' In his view matters had been simpler in the past when the focus had often been on empire. 'From this outlook came the reliance of the man of affairs upon natural aptitude and a certain scorn of organised knowledge.' In the context of law this could produce the problem of a divergence between cultural and vocational forms of study, with the latter being seen as 'practical'. It was now necessary to unite them, and he argued as to how this might be done:

> [I]f we could evolve a specific legal culture, there is not a single demand which is at present made by the faculties and by the professional examining bodies which could not be brought into a unified system of education, and there is no reason why a unified system of examination should not be the result instead of the anarchy of the present system.[18]

In 1933 this was taken further by GL Haggen, also of Leeds who considered 'The Training of the Practical Man'.

> Much has been said at our meetings about the practical man, but I hardly think we need make any apology for referring to him again. He represents perhaps the most disturbing problems that members of this Society as a body have to face. . . . Unfortunately, or fortunately, these problems are not the same for all of us. Oxford and Cambridge may regard practical people with that equanimity which only age and independent means give. For the Law Society's School and the Council of Legal Education, the problem is simplified, since they are mainly concerned, I take it, to see that men are equipped, so far as they can be equipped in a School, for the practice of their profession. For those of us who labour in the newer Universities and University Colleges the problem is most difficult, because we are bound to meet professional requirements

---

[17] Ibid, p. 243.
[18] JDI Hughes (1932) 9 *JSPTL* 1 and note debate at 10–11.

without sacrificing University standards and the University tradition which it is our paramount duty to maintain.[19]

In his view people should go to university because 'life is so much more important than practice'. The well-educated lawyer met professional demands at the same time as he reached university standards.

Speculative analysis such as this could produce adverse responses from those who felt they had more pressing concerns. In July, 1932 Professor Eastwood in Manchester wrote to the Honorary Secretary, ECS Wade, and argued

> that the SPTL pays more attention to Oxford, Cambridge and London—where legal education is already developed—than to the smaller places where there are some really good men struggling to develop it, and of whose existence some official appreciation would be of considerable assistance.[20]

The Annual General Meeting in Liverpool in 1926 was the first held outside Oxford, Cambridge and London, and officers of the Society had not been appointed from other universities. Indeed Eastwood more or less suggested that the appointments were 'a put up job' in response to advance discussions in respect of which the provincial universities could not participate for geographical reasons. Some behaviour had been objectionable, as when it was suggested that 'Cardiff is inaccessible', whereas from Manchester it is easier to get to Cardiff than to Oxford or Cambridge. Professor Eastwood wrote further that:

> Hughes' Presidency has given dissatisfaction to a number. That is not because people do not like Hughes. We all do. But more than any other among the provincial teachers he represents the Oxford point of view, and not the point of view held by many of us that legal education in a city should be the result of the cooperative efforts of the local legal profession and the teachers; and some people did in fact regard his office as an attempt to gain provincial sympathies whilst still having at our head the older university man with the older university tradition.[21]

No doubt it was partly in response to these divisions within the Society that Annual General Meetings (and sometimes other meetings) were held in a variety of cities during the 1930s. These included Oxford in 1931, Leeds in 1933, Cardiff in 1934, Exeter in 1935, and Bristol in 1936. As if to make the point that Cardiff was not inaccessible, the Society went out of its way to supply members with appropriate train timetables from Paddington—though it should be noted that nothing was said about getting to Cardiff from the north of England.[22]

On a more positive note the General Committee decided on 9 December 1933 to set up a new sub-committee to reconsider the admission of members from Scotland and Northern Ireland. In substance it was responding to the 'enlargement' debates of 1914 which had been put to one side with the start of the First

---

[19] GL Haggen (1933) 10 *JSPTL* 14.
[20] 10 July 1932, A.SPTL 2/28.
[21] Ibid. Eastwood was President 1934–5.
[22] A.SPTL 3/11, and letter, Eastwood to Wade, 10 July 1932, A.SPTL 2/28.

World War. The sub-committee recommended change and this was endorsed in debates during 1934.[23] Obviously this reform was to the lasting benefit of the organisation.

Jenks, writing from retirement, used the *Law Quarterly Review* of 1935 to provide a sense of context for these developments and, as always in his case, he emphasised optimism rather than problems. Since the reforms in the 1922 Act the pre-existing Law Schools had increased their student numbers and enlarged their staffs. He was delighted at the fact that there were 'Law Schools, at Bristol, Newcastle-upon-Tyne, Exeter, Southampton, and Swansea'.[24] In London there had been progress in the creation of professorships. For Jenks, the Society's recovery from the War was all but complete. 'Struck, in its early years, by the devastating shock of the Great War, it survived the blow with almost unimpaired strength; and since that date, its progress has been rapid and its energies ever increasing.' He was sensitive to the problems of representation caused by expansion and pointed out that the 'normal activities' of the society 'are carried out by a Committee which comprises a representative of each of the larger Law Schools, and two joint representatives of the smaller'. At the time the Society had about 200 members with 138 engaged in teaching. There were four types of member: the active; the honorary, the corresponding; and the formerly active. It was difficult to assess the number of students being taught, but Jenks's private research pointed to a substantial increase. He concluded that there were 1,879 students on academic courses and 1,825 on professional courses, giving a total of 3,704. In respect of the academic students 1,010 were divided between Oxford and Cambridge, and 307 were in London. Elsewhere there was an uneven distribution with, say, Manchester having 90 students (with an additional 49 on professional courses) and Southampton having 8 (with an additional 54 on professional courses). These figures are a stark reminder of the extent to which numbers had been increasing and also of the heavy preponderance of Oxford and Cambridge. Provincial developments were important but comparatively small.[25]

The everyday work of the Society continued. For example, there was concern about the role of law in government. In September 1934 the General Committee expressed its belief that the Civil Service Commission should set higher standards in legal analysis for the Civil Service Examinations, particularly for the most senior administrators.[26] Later a Standing Committee on Curricula sought to make representations to the Law Society on, amongst other things, the need for local government law and administrative law to be a part of the Solicitors' Honours Examination.[27] In response to a different concern, the last remnants of the money for the teaching of legal history were to be transferred to the Selden

[23] General Committee Meeting, 9 December 1933, setting up a sub-committee to consider the issue, and see reports back at 17 March 1934 and 14 July 1934, A.SPTL 1/4.

[24] Jenks (1935) 51 *Law Quarterly Review* 169. Solicitors Act 1922, 12 and 13 Geo 5 ch 57: the Act is considered in ch 3, n 16.

[25] Jenks, above n 24, 174.

[26] General Committee Minutes, 29 September 1934, A.SPTL 1/4.

[27] Date not given, but after 1934, A.SPTL 1/4.

Society in 1938.[28] There were occasional difficulties with applications for admission as when 'An application by Dr EJ Cohn (Birkbeck College) was considered. In view of the fact that teaching in law at that college had now ceased, the committee was unable to admit Dr Cohn on his existing qualification.'[29] There was uncertainty as to certain categories of membership. In 1939 it was decided that thenceforth emeritus membership should exist for those who had ceased public teaching of law and who had been prominent as ordinary members for a long period and who have been elected as such by the Committee. Associate members would be either ordinary members who had ceased to teach and wished to be associates, or teachers of law who held or had held appointments at certain universities. The latter included

> such Universities, University Colleges and public law teaching bodies of the Empire (together with its Protectorates and Mandated Territories) other than those of Great Britain and Northern Ireland, or in such Universities of the United States of America as the General Committee may approve for the purpose provided they have been elected associate members by the General Committee.[30]

Towards the end of the decade there were some financial difficulties and in 1939 there was an increase in the annual subscription. But any suggested increase became irrelevant during the war years when it was not enforced. Despite financial problems there was a proposal for a wine fund. 'The Committee considered a memorandum by Mr Holland to the effect that a wine fund should be instituted with Dr Radcliffe as chairman and contributions invited from members, so that better wines could be provided at Annual Dinners at less expense.' But the meeting regarded the proposal as impractical.[31] There was an interest in a wide variety of new topics. The Honorary Secretary was authorised to nominate a member to attend a conference with the Howard League for Penal Reform which was making representations in respect of legislative proposals. As these random examples suggest, there was a lot of regular work being done in this way and over the years it surely did something to increase awareness of the Society's existence amongst law teachers and, in a much more limited way, in the legal professions.

Within the Society, the social life at the Annual General Meetings varied in its intensity over the 1930s. On 12 December 1931, at a time of very difficult national economic conditions, the General Committee decided that at the next Conference dinner 'no formal dinner should be held, in view of the national economy campaign, but that arrangements should be made for members to dine together informally'.[32] In contrast, on 10 July 1937 there was the 'University of London Dinner for the Society of Public Teachers of Law', and the 'Plan of Table'

---

[28] General Committee Minutes, 3 July 1938, A.SPTL 1/5.

[29] Ibid.

[30] General Committee Minutes, 23 March 1939, A.SPTL 1/5. See too General Committee Minutes, 16 December 1938, A.SPTL 1/5.

[31] General Committee Minutes, 16 December 1938, A.SPTL 1/5.

[32] 12 December 1931, A.SPTL 1/4. By way of dramatic contrast, morning dress had been suggested for the dinner at UCL in 1922: see ch 3, n 12.

points to a grand occasion with distinguished guests including Professor Roscoe Pound, Lord Atkin, Sir Maurice Gwyer and Professor Goodhart. Elsewhere a young Glanville Williams was sitting next to Mr Crow, the man who had caused difficulties for Jenks in earlier years. There were well over 100 guests, not one of them a woman. The formal record suggests that the Annual General Meeting at Edinburgh in 1939 was also a smoothly run social occasion, not least because it was celebrating the role of the Society in Scotland. Dinner jackets were to be worn at the dinner and the menu included 'Tay salmon mayonnaise' and Scotch woodcock.[33]

Beneath this social activity there was conflict over the possible admission of women to the Society. The admission of women as a topic for discussion is notably absent from the official record of the Society's work during the 1920s and most of the 1930s. This is suggestive given that access to the legal professions for women had received national attention in the first two decades of the century. For example, the Court of Appeal in England rejected Gwyneth Bebb's attempt to become a solicitor in 1913.[34] It took sustained national demands and the impact of the First World War on the perception of female roles to produce statutory change. This arrived in the Sex Disqualification (Removal) Act of 1919, after which women could become barristers or solicitors.[35] Legislative change for the professions appears to have had no impact on the SPTL. The Society did not state, say, that it would consider changing the rule which required all members to be 'gentlemen' if there was an application from one of the women engaged in law teaching during these decades. It is difficult to account for this without there having been some element of outright hostility to women as prospective colleagues.

From correspondence, and some records of later years giving retrospective information, we know that the admission of women did in fact engage attention after the mid-1930s. In a letter of 16 February 1949 Professor Eastwood wrote from Manchester to professor DJ Ll Davies of Aberystwyth (at that time the Society's Honorary Secretary) about Miss Edith Hesling who, by 1949, had been on the staff at Manchester for 15 years. Eastwood pointed out that

> She was the first woman to be called by Gray's Inn and the first woman to join the northern circuit. I think that she was the second woman to be appointed to a law teaching post in a University, the first being, I think, Ivy Williams at Oxford.

He added: 'I took soundings about 15 years ago: [it was] clear then [that a] majority of the Committee were not in favour.'[36] We also know that at the General Committee on 13 July 1938 'A letter from Miss Colwill (a lecturer in law at the Goldsmith's College, University of London) applying for membership, was considered. The Committee resolved that the wording of Rule 5 limited

---

[33] General Committee Minutes, 25 March, 1939, A.SPTL 1/5 and A.SPTL 4/4.
[34] *Bebb v The Law Society* [1914] 1 Ch 286. See ch 2, n 20.
[35] 9 and 10 Geo 5 c 71.
[36] A.SPTL 2/42. Edith Hesling is sometimes referred to by her married name, Mrs Bradbury.

membership to all male persons.'[37] Presumably, it was this rejection which was enough to trigger a debate in Edinburgh which is unrecorded but in which we know (again from retrospective information) that Professor Lee of Oxford proposed that women should be admitted. It looks very much as if significant opposition to women as members was voiced on this occasion. Certainly, there was no agreement in principle. It may be that the outcome of the debate was that the General Committee was required to *consider* opening membership to women.[38] The start of the Second World War came soon after the Edinburgh meeting and the conflict was to delay further work on this until the late 1940s. It was not as if large numbers of the Society were demanding change. In any event, the official records point to a greater interest in food such as 'Tay salmon mayonnaise'. The reality was that women could enter the legal professions, but not the SPTL.

---

[37] General Committee Minutes, 13 July 1938, A.SPTL 1/5.

[38] We do know that the matter was at least discussed in Edinburgh: see A.SPTL 2/42, letter, DJ Ll Davies to Eastwood, 21 February 1949. We also know from the letter that nothing was done in response to the debate. For the (retrospective) printed record (perhaps to be viewed with some scepticism) see (1947–51) 1(NS) *JSPTL* 285.

5

War, Respectability, the Admission of Women, Legal Education with 'Vituperative Epithets' and Increasing Self-confidence: 1940–1960

In the past some members strongly opposed any suggestion that women should be admitted to the Society, but that opposition now appears to have died down.
(Professor DJ Ll Davies, Honorary Secretary, writing on 21 February 1949)

[T]hat the only necessary amendment in the Rules to admit duly qualified women to membership would be the substitution of the word 'persons' for the word 'gentlemen' in Rule 5 . . . and it was resolved to recommend the General Meeting to amend the Rule accordingly.
(General Committee Minutes, 24 March 1949)

The Second World War

As early as 25 March 1939, almost six months before the declaration of war, the General Committee was considering the impact of international conflict on its work. 'Professor Browne raised the question of the effect which would be produced on the problems of legal education by the possible adoption of a compulsory system of national service.' It was thought it would be premature at that stage to explore the issue 'but the officers (of the Committee) were instructed to bear the matter in mind'.[1] They were well advised to do so. By 20 March 1940, when the General Committee met in London at the Law Society, all involved were agreed that there would have to be 'Emergency Measures'. The subscription was taken back to the old rate of half a guinea. Publication of the journal was postponed: in fact it did not appear until well after the end of the

---

[1] General Committee Minutes, 25 March 1939, A.SPTL 1/5.

war. The period of office for the existing committee was extended until further notice. F Rayleigh Batt, the current President, was, in fact, to remain as President until 1946 (after 1942 he combined some teaching at Liverpool University with being a county court judge). Annual Meetings would last only one day and would be in London. In respect of other matters it was hoped 'that the normal activities of the Society should be carried on so far as practicable'.[2]

The Committee was soon trying to explore positive responses to wartime conditions. Dr Radcliffe put forward a proposal to provide legal literature and tuition through correspondence with the setting, correction and return of test papers for people serving in the Army and possibly in the Air Force and Navy. In response, a sub-committee on 'Education in the Forces' was set up.

> The Meeting felt that the scheme would be the most use to invalids, prisoners of war, and wounded men, and that troops in field training would have little opportunity for study. Dr Wade stated that men in such branches as Anti-Aircraft Brigades would be glad to take part in the scheme at any time of the year in order to relieve the monotony.[3]

Under the chairmanship of Dr Radcliffe the Committee set to work and members of the Society were asked whether they would be able to assist by setting and correcting papers for students in all the services. Dr Radcliffe also liaised with the Council of Legal Education and the Legal Education Committee of the Law Society. The latter agreed to take over the administration of the scheme and this was put into the hands of its secretary, Mr AD Bowers (who we have seen already had considerable administrative experience within the SPTL) and his assistant Miss Rice. After further discussion the War Office handled correspondence courses for all the services, with the Law Society administering legal studies.

The remarkable programme that grew out of this arrangement was described in retrospect in the Society's *Journal* for 1947 and it is particularly fortunate that this is so because the period 1940–60 has depleted archives: for some years they are almost non-existent. As a result, the *Journal* is often the best source of information.

> The intending student paid a fee of 10s and his entry form was sent by the War Office to the Law Society, which registered him and sent him a detailed syllabus on the subject he had selected, together with a set of test papers, instructions, advice and information, and the name and address of the tutor to whom he had been allotted. Thereafter tutor and student corresponded direct. The tutors, who were law teachers, barristers and solicitors, acted voluntarily, and (except in a few cases after the war was over) without any remuneration, their out-of-pocket expenses only being refunded if necessary. Local assistance was also obtainable in a few cases, eg in Canada and West Africa. The object of the scheme was not primarily to prepare men for any particular examinations, but to enable them to begin, or continue, their education in some field

---

[2] General Committee Minutes 20 March 1940, A.SPTL 1/5.
[3] Ibid.

of their choice, and the legal subjects (only one of which could be taken at a time) were at first limited to eight: Contract, Torts, English Legal System, Criminal Law, Bankruptcy, Company Law, Negotiable Instruments and Sale of goods, to which Constitutional Law, Equity, Real Property, and Conveyancing were subsequently added.[4]

During the war, there was a strong response with over 5,000 participants by June 1945. Of course, a large number of these did not follow through. Servicemen taking the courses were in some cases killed in action, or suddenly sent to new locations with imperfect postal arrangements or they simply found it difficult to study. The Society's post-war *Journal* noted that if everyone had sent in work the voluntary tutors could hardly have coped. But for all the difficulties, this was a striking achievement by the triangular relationship of the SPTL, the War Office and the Law Society. In terms of student numbers, was there any comparable achievement before the teaching of law began at the Open University?

A more concentrated scheme involved soldiers taking professional examinations in prisoner-of-war camps. Again this work was recorded in the post-war *Journal* of the Society:

> The German authorities would not permit the passage to and fro of correspondence papers and answers, but text-books, syllabuses and test questions were sent in the hope that 'mutual aid groups' would be formed. The Council of Legal Education helped prisoners to be admitted in absentia to Inns of Court, and both it and The Law Society, as well as some Universities (London and Birmingham), were able to arrange for their examinations to be held in POW Camps. The Germans only, it should be noted—not the Italians or Japanese—allowed this to be done.[5]

The result was an impressive array of passes, some at a high level. In a few instances the arrangements went even further with the provision of classes. A detailed account of what this sort of study involved was given by the academic lawyer CJ Hamson of Trinity College, Cambridge who found himself stuck in Oflag VIIB where he started to put on courses in law. Hamson praised the work of all involved, including the Red Cross.

> The teaching of law in prisoner of war camps in Germany was, for an academic teacher, an illuminating experience. It was both chastening and very gratifying. It was chastening because, at the beginning at least, the teaching had to be done without books; and the teacher (who in peace time might have been tempted to regard himself as tolerably well grounded in his own subjects) was compelled to appreciate how small was his actual grasp of the law he professed himself to know. . . . The experience was gratifying because it appeared that such teaching was effective. . . . No person who taught in prison could fail to be impressed by the zeal and devotion of his students.[6]

Meanwhile, within the United Kingdom, the experience of the universities in the war years varied greatly from one place to another. In some cases there was a need to report a loss of life on the part of both students and staff on active service. For

---

[4] (1947–51) 1(NS) *JSPTL* 23, 48–9.
[5] Ibid, 49.
[6] Ibid, 49–50.

example, Hull lost five students after they had gone into the services and London University lost staff.[7] In places, bomb damage was significant, not least at UCL. Elsewhere, it was said, for example, that 'Work at Liverpool continued throughout the war, though at times the conditions were difficult.'[8] In the words of William Geddes:

> For forty years a working arrangement obtained in Liverpool between the University and the profession, whereby law lectures were delivered 'down town' in the legal quarter of the city, under the joint auspices of the Faculty of Law and the Liverpool Board of Legal Studies. The Law Library, the Students' Library, the Lecture Rooms and the Board Room were all situated in Cook Street. During the first week of May, 1941, Liverpool was subjected to a fierce and nightly visitation of the enemy, and one morning we arrived to find the whole block of buildings reduced to a mass of smoking rubble. . . . The Law Library—focal point of the profession for so many years—was no more.[9]

In response, there were numerous initiatives in the city with premises being shared for a while with chartered accountants and the creation of the core of a new library in Dale Street. Temporary arrangements in Abercromby Square gave way in 1945–46 to a finer building in the same place. 'Its distance from the professional quarter of the city, which may be regarded by articled clerks as rather a disadvantage, is counterbalanced by its proximity to the central life of the University itself.'[10]

In Sheffield the Law Department 'escaped serious damage during the heavy raid of December, 1940, but numerous incendiaries fell on the roof, and the preservation of the building was due to the swift and efficient work of student fire-watchers'.[11] In Hull the city

> became one of the most blitzed areas of the country. The College was not evacuated. Students carried on under heavy strain due, not only to loss of rest through frequent and prolonged raids, but also to the insecurity of the Department and their own position. All students did duty in the Home Guard on local gun emplacements, or as wardens or fire-watchers. On some occasions, lectures continued during alerts in the air-raid shelter or its approaches. No lectures were lost on account of raids.

To a considerable extent teaching at Hull was organised and sustained by one man, Mr Taylor.[12]

Elsewhere there were movements of entire departments. For example, Aberystwyth, Bristol and Cambridge received people from London at various times and built up a system of reciprocity in respect of lectures. The law library

---

[7] Ibid, 47 and 27, respectively.
[8] Ibid, 33.
[9] Ibid, 34 (William Geddes).
[10] Ibid.
[11] Ibid, 38 (Denis Browne).
[12] Ibid, 46–7 (Raphael Powell).

of King's College London was taken to Bristol and was largely destroyed when Bristol was heavily bombed in 1940.[13]

More generally there were difficulties in sustaining student numbers. At Oxford before the war there were about 400 reading law; this was halved in the first year of conflict and continued to decline thereafter.[14] At Cambridge the numbers reading for the Law Tripos went down from about 500 to about 50. 'Special courses and examinations were undertaken for the benefit of cadets who were training for the services, but were allowed to give part of their time to academic study.'[15] In some cases the decline in student numbers helped to offset the loss of staff to fighting. Shortly after the start of the war the number of staff available for teaching at the University of Birmingham was cut to less than half, but the reduction in student numbers and changes in course structures made it possible to cope.[16] In Manchester the serious depletion in staff numbers was in part dealt with by assistance from local practitioners, and in part it was offset by the reduction of student numbers from 141 in 1939 to 44 by the end of 1944. Beyond these changes the decline in staffing in Manchester could be managed because at a meeting of staff in September 1939 it was decided that as far as possible the work of those who were absent would be shared out amongst those who remained without extra pay.[17] Surprisingly, one law school reported that the war had not been very eventful for its work. 'There is, in fact, nothing outstanding to report from Leeds, in relation to the war-time experience of the Law School.'[18]

Teaching at the Law Society's School of Law in London was limited. After the autumn term of 1939 it 'would not accept responsibility for students in the London building'.[19] Towards the end of the war it took an initiative under the direction of RE Megarry in the provision of refresher courses for solicitors returning from service, and this idea was taken up around the country with local Law Societies and a number of universities.

In contrast, the Council of Legal Education in London managed to sustain courses for prospective barristers, and its lectures were 'thrown open to members of the British, Dominion and Allied Forces, though not belonging to an Inn; to the Poles and later to the Americans this privilege was most welcome'.[20] The Council went beyond this with a programme for holding examinations overseas, at first in India and then at 14 other places.

> In addition, special examinations were held from time to time for members of the three Forces at numerous service bases and depots from the Faroes to the Pacific, and

---

[13] For Aberystwyth see ibid, 39–40 (DJ Ll Davies), for Bristol see 31–2 (Malcolm M Lewis), for Cambridge see 25–6 (HA Hollond), for King's see 27 (D Hughes Parry).

[14] Ibid (FH Lawson).

[15] Ibid, 26 (HA Hollond).

[16] Ibid, 30–31 (CE Smalley-Baker).

[17] Ibid, 35–8 (RA Eastwood).

[18] Ibid, 33 (JDI Hughes).

[19] Ibid, 43 ('HFJ').

[20] Ibid, 40 (W Cleveland-Stevens).

even in HM Ships. Shortly before HMS Jamaica delivered the final torpedo attack on the German Battle Cruiser Scharnhorst, an Examination was held on board for one of her officers: at the time of the action one of the Council's clerical staff was serving on her.[21]

One wonders, did the candidate pass the examination? Clearly something unusual was happening at the Council of Legal Education. It claimed to be the only substantial educational establishment in London which was neither closed nor evacuated.

> The popularity of the Lectures was a pleasant surprise to the Council. Until after Dunkirk it had been a matter for speculation whether there would continue to be students for the Inns, but towards the end of 1940, with havoc wrought by the bombs, there was the gravest anxiety whether there would be any Inns left for the students. In quick succession the Temples and Gray's Inn ceased to be available; Lincoln's Inn, though somewhat battered, alone remained, and there all the Council's Lectures and Examinations were held for the rest of the war. A further cause for anxiety was the safety of students during air-raids, but with the passing of day attacks this ceased and the emergency measures for their protection were never put to the test. During the Michaelmas and Hilary Examinations, 1940–41, there were many alerts and at times gunfire uncomfortably near, but the students carried on stoically and refused to go to the shelters.[22]

Post-war Respectability and Social Conservatism

Normal work for the SPTL was resumed with a meeting at the LSE on 23 March 1946. There was mention of 'the post -war problems of law teachers' but this was not, it seems, followed up by any significant action.[23] Instead, there was a return to administrative work. For example, an application for membership was received from Mr NC Speed, LLB, BCom, of the Middle Temple, Barrister-at-Law and Head of the Department of Commerce and General Education at Wakefield Technical College. After some delay the General Committee considered this at a meeting on 7 January 1947 and it was resolved that his appointment would 'not fall within the terms of Rule 5'. The interest of this application is the unquestionable nature of Mr Speed's qualifications and no hint of any sort to suggest some scandalous or doubtful background which might have made Rule 4 relevant. If the Committee were following Rules 4 and 5 in combination, the more obvious grounds for rejection were that Wakefield Technical College was not an appropriate body or Mr Speed was not active as a law teacher. It seems likely that the applicant did some teaching of legal topics. If he was engaged in teaching (and there is no recorded evidence on the point) it might be reasonable to suspect

---

[21] Ibid, 41–2 (W Cleveland-Stevens).
[22] Ibid, 41 (W Cleveland-Stevens).
[23] General Committee Minutes, 23 March 1946 and 12 July 1946, A.SPTL 1/5.

prejudice against an *institution* which was seen as lacking in prestige. It looks as if the SPTL's General Committee was as unenthusiastic about certain institutions as it was about the admission of women. In any event Mr Speed remained unelected.[24]

The likelihood of opposition towards such teachers is strengthened by a comparison of the early version of Rule 5 with the one in operation in the 1940s. As we saw in chapter 2, the side note to the early Rule refers to 'Definition of public teachers'. The substance of the early Rule states:

[T]he expression 'public teachers of law in England or Wales' shall include all gentlemen engaged in teaching law in England or Wales in virtue of appointment or official recognition by any university, *college*, incorporated society, council, board of studies, or other body, not being a body established or existing for the purpose of making pecuniary profit divisible among its members. The General Committee may require evidence of such qualifications if it think fit; and on any question that may arise as to the interpretation and application of this rule the decision of the Committee shall, unless and until reversed by a general meeting of the Society, be conclusive. Provided that a member ceasing for one year to be engaged in the teaching of law shall, ipso facto, cease to be an ordinary member of the Society.[25] (emphasis added)

This contrasted with the rule now in force which defined the expression 'public teachers of law' as being

all gentlemen regularly and continuously engaged in teaching law in Great Britain or Northern Ireland by virtue of appointment or official recognition by any university, *university college*, the Council of Legal Education, the Law Society of Northern Ireland, the Inn of Court of Northern Ireland, or other body approved by the General Committee, not being a body established or existing for the purpose of making pecuniary profit divisible among its members.[26] (emphasis added)

It is reasonable to conclude that the application from Wakefield Technical College never had any prospect of success. Such a place was a college but not a university college and it appears that it was not likely to be approved by the General Committee by way of an exception. The rules of the Society were now less 'open' than they had been in the early decades and this was having an impact.

In December of the same year the Committee considered whether it would admit an organisation of 'European Law Teachers' to Associate membership by invitation. The committee concluded (for reasons which are not recorded) that this would be inappropriate and in doing this it also rejected an Hungarian application for membership.[27] In February 1949 the General Committee received a letter from the British Council revealing that

Professor Roger Pinto had visited England at the request of the University of Lille and the Institut de Droit Compare in the University of Paris for the purpose of establishing

---

[24] General Committee Minutes, 9 January 1947, A.SPTL 1/5.
[25] Rules of the Society for 1910. For the location of these rules, see ch 2, n 7.
[26] For discussion of this rule, see General Committee Minutes, 10 May 1950, A.SPTL 1/5.
[27] General Committee Minutes, 18 December 1947, A.SPTL 1/5.

an association of British and French teachers of law and political science and post-graduate research students, with the object of facilitating the study of political and legal institutions and current legal developments in both countries.

In response the Committee did 'not feel it could take any action at present'.[28] In contrast to these negative responses, the *Journal* provides proof of constructive continental initiatives by individual British law teachers at this time, and the SPTL did respond to exchanges on a number of occasions, sending members to Anglo-French meetings in Paris and London.[29] There was particular interest in a meeting of comparative lawyers in Paris which was attended by some in 1948.[30]

There was also interest in prestigious transatlantic links with the granting of Honorary Membership to Mr Justice Frankfurter and Professor Williston. There was cheerful news from Australia. In early 1947 the Society was told by Professor Paton in Australia that 'We have just founded an Australian Universities Law Schools Association—the inspiration for which came from the SPTL. We had a very successful meeting in Sydney in June.'[31] The Society's committees were at ease with the English-speaking world.

In the post-war years there was an interest in the staffing levels in 'provincial law schools'. After initial discussion in March 1948 the General Committee voted by a majority not to proceed with an investigation into this topic, but the Committee had second thoughts and in July RE Megarry said the issue would go to the Annual General Meeting. The latter recommended the creation of a Standing Committee on Staffing in Law Schools. The committee was established and its importance was signalled by its membership, which included the President, Vice-President and Professor Crane who had recently been elected to the General Committee as a representative from the new University of Nottingham.[32] General references suggest that this became the focus of further, largely unrecorded discussion.

For reasons that are not clear this initiative came to nothing. It may have been aired as an issue to persuade one particular university (not identified by name) to raise the pay of part-time law teachers. Whatever the explanation, the significance of this not being taken further was very considerable. With hindsight the Society could have attempted to require a minimum staff/student ratio in all Law Schools. Because of the expense involved, this would, surely, have made it difficult for some of the provincial centres to survive and would have thereby reduced the opportunity for numerous people to study law. But in other respects the imposition of a ratio would have had notable benefits. In the course of the second half of the century staff/student ratios in some law schools came to exceed 1:30 and this very seriously reduced the capacity to give individual attention to students,

---

[28] General Committee Minutes, 24 March 1949, A.SPTL 1/5; (1947–51) 1 *JSPTL* 287.

[29] For instance (1947–51) 1(NS) *JSPTL* 121 and 285.

[30] General Committee Minutes, 16 July 1949, A.SPTL 1/5.

[31] General Committee Minutes, 9 January 1947, A.SPTL 1/5.

[32] General Committee Minutes, 18 December 1947, 10 July 1948, A.SPTL 1/5; (1947–51) 1(NS) *JSPTL* 286.

many of whom were commencing their studies at the age of 18 or 19. The contrast with subjects in 'health' is vivid with areas such as medicine, nursing, midwifery and physiotherapy being protected by ratios which rarely exceed 1:15. Of course these areas have been sheltered by the demands of powerful professional bodies containing practitioners as well as teachers, but the SPTL does not seem to have made an effort to look for support in this context from either the Bar or the Law Society. Whatever one may think about the merits of this inaction, it was to prove to be of the first importance for the future. In comparative terms, legal education could be done on the cheap.

In contrast to this inaction in regard to the level of resources for Law Schools, some in the Society were positive about the creation of the Institute for Advanced Legal Studies in 1947. It was acknowledged that this would replace an informal system which had grown up under the guidance of Professor Wortley of Manchester for exchanging information about research projects amongst members of the society. 'The Institute of Advanced Legal Studies had now taken over from Professor Wortley the collation and exchange of information regarding research in law.'[33] In this respect, one of the major hopes of reformers in the 1930s was being realised and some in the SPTL could claim credit for having done all they could to ensure that it came into existence. But it was scant consolation during a generally inactive and in some respects introverted period for the Society.

The Admission of Women

The admission of women to the Society was a major exception to this lack of interest in change. As we have seen, the meeting of 1939 in Edinburgh had not produced a conclusive result. It was therefore significant that the Honorary Secretary, Professor DJ Ll Davies of Aberystwyth, writing on 21 February 1949, pointed out that 'In the past some members strongly opposed any suggestion that women should be admitted to the Society, but that opposition now appears to have died down.'[34] He also would have had in mind what happened at the meeting of the General Committee two months before on 16 December 1948. It was held at the new Institute for Advanced Legal Studies and the discussion was recorded as follows:

> Women Members:—The Hon Sec reported that an application for ordinary membership had been received from Miss SMB Tolson, Assistant Lecturer in Laws at Kings College London. The provisions of Rules 4 and 5 and the instructions of the Annual Meeting in 1939 on the admission of women were considered. The Committee resolved, Mr Landon dissenting, that duly qualified women teachers should be eligible

---

[33] (1947–51) 1(NS) *JSPTL* 286.
[34] Letter from DJ Ll Davies to RA Eastwood, 21 February 1949, A.SPTL 2/42.

for membership and the Hon Sec was requested to submit to the next meeting a draft amendment in the Rules to give effect to the extension. The President undertook to explain the position to Miss Tolson, and the committee resolved that an invitation to attend the 1949 Annual Meeting at Nottingham be issued to Miss Tolson, if necessary as a guest.[35]

On 24 March 1949 the Committee further resolved

> that the only necessary amendment in the Rules to admit duly qualified women to membership would be the substitution of the word 'persons' for the word 'gentlemen' in Rule 5 . . . and it was resolved to recommend the General Meeting to amend the Rule accordingly.

The Committee was clearly concerned about the practical implementation of the change. It 'also resolved that on various grounds it was undesirable for the Committee to invite women to the General Meeting next July, but that at the next meeting of the Committee applications for membership by women would be considered'.[36] On 16 July the Committee met at Nottingham and it was agreed 'with regard to the few women now known to be teaching law' that action would be taken to notify them of their eligibility to apply and be admitted to the Society.[37]

The Nottingham dinner of 1949 was therefore the last occasion on which women could not attend such a function as a member. It took place at a time when rationing still applied, but the menu reflected an effort to make the occasion convivial and rivalled the food at the LSE in 1946 and, for that matter, at Birmingham in 1947 and the London Senate House in 1948.[38] The surviving records of the Society have a way of telling us more about food than the debates over membership, particularly the membership of women.

Educational Conservatism

The post-war years saw a firm assertion of a distinctive way of looking at the study of law on the part of many of the most influential members of the Society. In 1946 Judge Rayleigh Batt gave the Presidential Address and spoke at formidable length; it must have a good claim to being the longest Presidential address on record. (It appears to be over 9,000 words in length.) He had a high regard for many practitioners working with the common law. He was uncontroversial in requiring that undergraduates should 'have a firm grasp of the principles of the Common law'. He had a favourable view of legal history but thought it should be 'subsidiary to the law'. 'I am inclined to think that many law teachers are too

---

[35] General Committee Meetings, 16 December 1948, A.SPTL 1/5.
[36] General Committee Meetings, 24 March 1949, A.SPTL 1/5.
[37] General Committee Meetings, 16 July 1949, A.SPTL 1/5 and see (1947–51) 1(NS) *JSPTL* 283.
[38] A.SPTL 4/7.

preoccupied . . . with legal history when they are expounding the modern law.' He had little time for Roman law and even less for jurisprudence. He could not tolerate 'the smart, rather cheeky young man whose wit and readiness in speech and writing mask his essential incompetence and incapacity to concentrate or apply himself to study'. 'What every law student should know is that his future clients are not buying his brains so much as his technical knowledge and scrupulous unremitting and assiduous care in the conduct of their affairs.' Nor was there much (if any) merit in the more speculative forms of intellectual enquiry. What mattered was preparation for legal practice and an associated respect for professional demands. It would be hard for the listener to conclude that it was worth attempting something novel in legal education.[39]

The restricted view of the scope of legal education put forward by Raleigh Batt was repeated on other occasions at this time and has been mentioned by Abel-Smith and Stevens in their book, *Lawyers and the Courts*, published in 1970. They point out that when WTS Stallybrass was President of the Society in 1947–48 he commended the fact that the Oxford Law School 'has been wise in excluding from its course those branches of the Law which depend on Statute and not on precedent'.[40] Nor should there be speculation about what the law ought to be. The latter:

> gets us near to the field of sociology. My own profound conviction at the present day is that the first essential of University teaching is that it should be objective and objectivity is difficult when you come to Sociology. I feel that that is one of the great dangers of the increasing development of social studies in the University.[41]

Abel-Smith and Stevens observe that in this context objectivity had different aspects. For example, Stallybrass also argued that:

> It is quite true that lawyers, I think it was Maine said it, are bound to be conservative; that is inevitable, because you cannot be a good lawyer unless you have a respect for property, life and order. Unless you have respect for these things you cannot possibly be entrusted to uphold our most precious British possession of freedom. . . . But a conservative bias does not prevent an objective approach to law or history.[42]

Similar things were said in the years which followed the Stallybrass presidency. Not long after he had done what he could to block the admission of women to the

---

[39] (1947–51) 1(NS) *JSPTL* 4, 7, 8, 11.

[40] B Abel-Smith and R Stevens, *Lawyers and the Courts: A Sociological Study of the English Legal System, 1750–1965* (London, Heinemann, 1970) 365–6; WTS Stallybrass, 'Law in the Universities' (1947–51) 1(NS) *JSPTL* 157, 163. Note that in 1947 CE Smalley-Baker had delivered an address in Birmingham under the title: 'The Teaching of Law as One of the Social Sciences' (1947–51) 1(NS) *JSPTL* 69. It chiefly commended forms of legal history and comparative law and seems to have had little impact. But it contains interesting observations as where the author points out that the University Grants Committee of that time had no lawyer on it: see 71.

[41] (1947–51) 1(NS) *JSPTL* 157, 164.

[42] Ibid. Stallybrass was killed in an accident soon after giving the address and his views are touched on in an obituary at 170.

Society, Mr Landon (Trinity College, Oxford) was elected President for 1951–52. His address to the Annual Meeting of 1952 informed the audience that 'no school boy has a vocation to become a law teacher' and that the speaker had fallen into teaching law in part because his great-uncle, Lord Halsbury, had recommended the Bar and this had not led anywhere after 'an unnecessary attempt to display legal learning before a County Court Registrar' and other forensic misadventures. By implication, teaching law required something of an apology. In turning to legal change, he thought that while 'law teachers should certainly take an active interest in law reform he hoped that their teaching would never degenerate into expounding sociology to potential lawyers'.[43] Most of the audience apparently agreed with these views, which, interestingly, also included support for law teachers gaining experience in foreign jurisdictions, albeit only those that were English-speaking.

Taken as a whole, the tone of the talk was too much for Professor JL Montrose from Belfast.

> He could not agree with the view implied in the latter part of the President's remarks, that the task of the law teacher was confined to descriptive exposition of legal rules; some judgment about these rules had to be expressed. He agreed that adverse criticism confined to the use of derogatory epithets was inadequate: it was necessary to go beyond emotional language in juristic criticism. But approval as well as disapproval went beyond exposition, and just as it was inadequate to express disapproval of rules and decisions by derogatory epithets, so it was inadequate for the expression of approval by laudatory epithets.[44]

In this minority view it was at least possible for academic lawyers politely and with restraint to criticise judicial decisions. But there is no record of anyone coming to his support. The full explanation for the intensity with which Stallybrass and others were putting forward their views at this time lies beyond the scope of the present study. But it may be that it involved, in part, an increasing sense of isolation within the universities for law teachers as other disciplines strengthened in self-confidence in the post-war years. In part, too, it may have linked in with a resurgent interest in a conservative view of the common law within the legal professions as they faced the radical reforms of the post-war Labour government. As to the beliefs of the individuals involved, there are useful comments in FH Lawson's *The Oxford Law School 1850–1965*. Of Landon, he writes that 'He had taken a first in Greats and spent some years at the Bar. In the meantime he had shed his earlier membership of the Fabian Society and become a firm, one might even say reactionary, Conservative.' He could be an excellent lecturer, a stimulating tutor and 'very fair-minded examiner'. Lawson adds: 'It will not now be unkind to allude to a rather quaint snobbishness which he would himself have regarded as a proper respect for rank and family.' He wrote little:

---

[43] (1952–54) 2(NS) *JSPTL* 32.
[44] Ibid, 33.

'But he was believed to be capable of writing much more than he did.' In a foot-note Lawson adds 'As President of the Society of Public Teachers of Law he rather characteristically refused to write down his Presidential Address but left it to be reported by others from memory fortified by notes.'[45] In respect of another President during these years, GRY Radcliffe, Lawson remarked that 'His Toryism was more extreme and went back to an earlier age than Landon's.'[46]

These ideas were being put forward in a context that offered little resource for law teaching in many parts of the country. For example, a survey of library provi-sion retrospectively revealed sharp contrasts. At the depleted end some English universities were spending very little. In two universities over the period 1951–55 the average annual expenditure on law books was respectively £282 and £125. Seven returns on the total number of law books in libraries (excluding law reports, legislation and legal periodicals) ranged from 11,331 to 1,285. In a sad way it was pointed out that Harvard had nearly three-quarters of a million law books.[47]

In effect, by the early years of the 1950s members of the Society were faced with a choice. There could have been further Presidents who repeated the post-war hostility to, say, the study of statutes and the attempt to use sociology for the contextual analysis of law. In England and Wales at least there could have been an almost exclusive focus on the detailed exposition of certain parts of the common law. Or there could have been a contentious departure with the development of interests in new ideas about legal studies. Montrose apart, there was little overt sign of interest in new ideas. The most striking demand for reform during these years came from outside the Society in Professor Gower's article of 1950 in the *Modern Law Review* which was an expanded version of his inaugural lecture at the LSE.[48] He vigorously questioned what he took to be complacency on the part of the professional bodies and the universities. In response (to quote the later words of Gower when he was President of the Society in 1977)

> the Law Lords summoned to their presence the General Editor of the Modern Law Review and solemnly reproved him for publishing something that had ventured to criticise judges for the patronising attitude that they had been wont to adopt when addressing a group of academic lawyers such as this.[49]

We will see below that this experience may have made an impression on the Review's General Editor of the day, Lord Chorley.

---

[45] FH Lawson, *The Oxford Law School 1850–1965* (Oxford, Clarendon Press, 1968) 130–31 n 2 and see (1952–54) 2(NS) *JSPTL* 32–3.

[46] Lawson, above n 45, 131 n 6. On Stallybrass, ibid, 129–30.

[47] JL Montrose, 'University Law Libraries' (1957–58) 4(NS) *JSPTL* 1, 7.

[48] LCB Gower (1950) 13 *Modern Law Review* 137.

[49] (1976–79) 14(NS) *JSPTL* 155.

Towards an 'Active Role in the Play'

By the summer of 1954 there were indications that new initiatives might materialise. There was a novel intellectual restlessness amongst some members. The senior editor of the *Journal*, HF Jolowicz, supported the idea of publishing more than just one volume a year. A single volume was sufficient to report the activities of the Society, the Presidential Address and a few other papers. But now he wanted a second number each year which would normally print only articles of educational interest, together with reviews and possibly some correspondence.[50] Butterworths were helpful and the Society had more funds having raised its subscription.[51] It was agreed that the journal could be published twice a year.[52]

In the General Committee's view the annual meeting of July 1955 was particularly valuable. It had a lively, assertive quality.

> The Annual Meeting was probably the most successful in the Society's history both from the point of view of members attending and the extensive programme. The Committee remain most grateful to the University of Edinburgh and to the legal profession there for their generous hospitality and for their willing assistance with the arrangements. The Committee welcomed with great pleasure a large and distinguished group of members (and their wives [*sic*]) from Commonwealth countries.[53]

Lord Chorley gave a Presidential Address which mixed praise with critical and impatient reflections on the Society.

> We have . . . developed the happy tradition of electing to our Presidential Chair most of those who have been so successfully occupied during our generation with building up the law schools which are so prominent a feature in the organisation of our modern universities.

The Society had done something to thwart the exploitation of its members.

> During his early years at the Bar when briefs are few, the young barrister is peculiarly open to exploitation. That this should occur in connexion with the educational work of a great local authority like the London County Council is deplorable enough, but when it is also found that a law school in a university is being built up on the services of part-time teachers who are being exploited in this way, it is difficult to restrain one's language to the sober verbiage of the lawyer, and not to pass over to the rhetoric of the politician. . . . In connexion with the LCC salary scales in evening institutes we have assisted the Bar Council and the Law Society in their not very successful efforts to

---

[50] (1952–54) 2(NS) *JSPTL* 189.

[51] We are grateful to Prof Geoffrey Samuels for information about these events, including a copy of a letter from H Kay Jones, Publishing Manager for Butterworth and Co to Prof Gower, 17 March 1954. Prof Montrose also provided useful support in a note of May 1954. Clearly, some of the unorthodox members of the Society were now being taken more seriously.

[52] (1952–54) 2(NS) *JSPTL* 228.

[53] (1955–56) 3(NS) *JSPTL* 236.

secure redress. The other case is still under discussion and we are hopeful of a satis-factory outcome.[54]

Looking at the work of the Society over almost half a century he could point to a significant increase in membership. He thought there had been 82 members in 1909, 105 by 1920, 176 by 1939 and, now, in 1955 there were about 230. Reflect-ing on these figures, he argued that 'the Solicitors Act of 1922, under which more finance became available for salaried appointments, was possibly the dominant cause'.[55] As to status, he doubted 'whether the work of Maine, Maitland, Dicey, etc, did much to heighten the prestige of the teaching branch of the profession'. Whereas 'My experience now is that practising lawyers have a high regard for the academic branch as a whole.' Perhaps in the hope of even better things to come he remarked that 'I have the impression that the Deans of the great American law schools have the prestige of High Court judges in England'.[56]

However, these arguments did not reveal that the Society had been notably successful.

> You will have observed that in this short sketch of a highly significant development within the legal profession the SPTL has not appeared. This does not mean that our Society has not taken part in the process, but it would be wishful thinking to attribute more than a subsidiary significance to this. Indeed, it has never cast itself for an active role in the play. In this it would be interesting to contrast our work with that under-taken by the Association of American Law Schools, which I gather has great influence in the USA.[57]

In short, the Society was bigger and law teaching was more respected (at least within the professions) but the Society had not had a major role in bringing about this change. By inference Jenks's individual success in working for the statutory reform of 1922 had been the catalyst for change because it provided legislative and financial foundations for teaching in provincial law schools. In blunt terms it was Chorley's view that the impact of the Society had been marginal on these important issues faced by law teachers.

The expression of such a forceful view in combination with an interest in an additional annual volume of the *Journal* had an impact. There was an increased interest in what we would now call seminar papers at SPTL functions.

> On Friday, September 21, 1956 papers on the work of the Franks Committee on Administrative Tribunals and Enquiries were given. The first and main paper was by Mr JAG Griffith (London School of Economics). In the discussion which followed, Dr Mary Bell Cairns (University College of N Staffordshire) described her experience of teaching law to arts students.[58]

---

[54] The Rt Hon Lord Chorley, Presidential Address, Edinburgh, 13 July, 1955, 'The Progress of Academic Law in the United Kingdom' (1955–56) 3(NS) *JSPTL* 65, 67.

[55] (1955–56) 3(NS) *JSPTL* 68.

[56] Ibid, 68, 70.

[57] Ibid, 70.

[58] Ibid, 197.

Mary Bell Cairns may have been the first woman to establish a new programme of legal studies in England. Her college was shortly to become Keele University. In 1959 she was to be the first woman to join the General Committee of the Society of Public Teachers of Law.[59]

For 1956–57 JL Montrose was President, and given his preparedness to challenge others this in itself was significant. In his address in September 1957 he spoke of 'Law, Science and the Humanities'. 'I think that the best preparation for the legal profession is a truly academic education in a faculty of law followed by a truly professional training.' He set out to explore the significance of what made for a good education. Ignoring what had been said by certain Presidents, he argued that 'It is a tribute to the advocacy of my predecessors who have dealt with this subject that it is now a commonplace to say that a university faculty of law has to provide a liberal education.' Within this, 'research is an integral part of the task of a university'. Further 'teaching and research are in close-knit relationship'.

> It is this insight that at a university the undergraduate assumes responsible adult status—acquires freedom to think for himself, rejecting subordination to mere authority, liberating himself from prejudice but accepting bondage to truth—that provides perhaps the most important characteristic of liberal education. It is the critical approach to his subject, making full use of his creative imagination, which leads the student of law, as of every subject, to philosophy and sociology.

A little later he added 'Criticism in law cannot ignore the social sciences.' Further 'the subject matter of law is humanity: . . . in faculties of law we join hands with the other humanities which inquire into the nature of man and of his response to the universe'. 'Ehrlich's statement that the centre of gravity of legal development lies in society itself can, I think, be modified by saying that the growing point for rational law lies in the social sciences.'[60] His argument was unrelenting.

> It needs but little analysis of our legal rules to see how implicated they are with propositions in psychology, in economics, in sociology—in the social sciences generally. . . . It surely is one of the great tasks of the legal researcher to keep himself in touch with developments in the social sciences, to see how they necessitate corresponding changes in our laws, and to make himself proposals for legal reform. . . . I conceive of judge and jurist as partners in the task of statesmanship called for in adapting laws to the march of science and society.[61]

In response Lord Chorley (LSE) agreed that the relation of the social sciences and humanities to law should be discussed. It was 'high time' for this to happen. More precisely,

> He agreed that lawyers should be prepared to go beyond what had hitherto been the orthodox legal methods into kinds of methodology more particularly associated with

[59] (1959–60) 5(NS) *JSPTL* 226.

[60] JL Montrose, The Presidential Address, Belfast, 18 September 1957, (1957–58) 4(NS) *JSPTL* 61, 62, 63, 65.

[61] (1957–58) 4(NS) *JSPTL* 69, 71, 72.

the social sciences, but he thought it was a formidable task. His own experience at the London School of Economics and as editor of the *Modern Law Review* was that attempts to bridge the gap between law and social sciences usually petered out after a little time.[62]

Dr Glanville Williams agreed with the thrust of the talk but thought that in such a vast potential for work each faculty should be selective and concentrate upon certain areas. 'He himself would say that our greatest deficiency now was in the field of penology and criminology.'[63] Professor Lawson agreed with Lord Chorley in that there was 'extreme difficulty in getting law studied along with other disciplines'. One way forward was to 'prune the legal curriculum of unnecessary information in order to find room for what the President had at heart'.[64]

Montrose continued to advance his radical ideas whenever he could. In respect of libraries, he argued that

> Those who do not wish for any diminution in the influence of the study of the humanities may derive comfort from the considerable increases which have taken place in the faculties of law since the first world war, and more dramatically since the second world war. It is true that colleagues in faculties of arts may express doubts whether the development has been entirely in the field of liberal studies, and among law teachers divisions may be found which suggest a dichotomy indicated by the 'vituperative epithets' each side may apply to the other of 'metaphysician' and 'technician'. But the overall picture is one of resistance to influences in the direction of limited vocational studies and a strengthening of the attitude that legal study provides a liberal education for the undergraduate, a mental and moral training, and a life of university scholarship for the teacher and researcher.[65]

In general terms he spoke of 'the true function of university faculties of law—one of co-ordination with, but not subordination to, professional training'.[66]

Montrose in Belfast was assisted by new initiatives elsewhere. Scottish ideas about legal education were of national interest at this time, not least because of the active work of students. David Walker gave a report of the activity of the Scottish Union of Students in putting on a two-day conference in Edinburgh on the theme of reform in legal education and training. It was addressed by a number of speakers including Professor Monteath and Sir Earnest Wedderburn. A sub-committee was elected to draw up a report and an 'Association of Law Students and Apprentices' was formed to sustain debate on the issues. Detailed discussion about particular topics and courses were put in a wide-ranging context about the purposes of legal education. There was a felt need to justify the place of law as a university subject. In the words of the Report when it appeared, it is 'an aspect of the development of the human mind and of social organisation, a study not of facts merely but of principles, in sum a humane study and a liberal

---

[62] Ibid, 73.
[63] Ibid.
[64] Ibid.
[65] JL Montrose, 'University Law Libraries' (1957–58) 4(NS) *JSPTL* 1.
[66] Ibid.

education in itself'. It spoke of the 'intrinsic value of the academic study of law for the ultimate good of the profession . . . It is vital for the preservation of Scots law from the dead hand of precedent unenlightened by principle that research should be encouraged'.[67] This is remarkable in being a very rare intrusion of student ideas into SPTL debates during the first half century of the Society's existence. For David Walker it was welcome in its principles if not in all its detail. For him, the value of the Report lies in the 'recognition within the student body that law is properly a liberal study, that the academic study of the law must be extended and improved, and that a degree which covers only professional subjects is not good enough'.[68] Soon he was pleased with the reformation of a system in which there had been undue professional influence: in an article of 1959 he thought it was possible to say that: 'Glasgow University is shaking itself free from professional domination and narrow vocationalism.'[69]

But there were also less optimistic voices, and these could include those of foreign visitors. The Dean of the Harvard Law School, Erwin N Griswold, spoke clearly and forcefully about 'English and American Legal Education' to a joint meeting of the SPTL and the Section of Legal Education of the American Bar Association. After pointing out that there was much in common in the two systems of legal education, he explored contrasts such as the difference in the age of students, the dissimilarity in approach to professional topics, and the distinct qualities of the respective legal systems. In regard to the latter the federal arrangements in the United States made its law 'vastly more complicated'. Comparison was also made difficult by the contrasts in the way the professions were organised. A further and challenging difference of a more intellectual nature was apparent. The Dean remarked that one of the previous speakers had said that the objective in his school was 'to teach law and not how to think'. In response he stated

> Now we would think this impossible. In the United States, the average law teacher regards it as far more important that his students be taught how to think than that they should be taught any specific rules or system of law. This is one of the things that makes law teaching interesting and stimulating and worth while.[70]

After the middle of the decade there was no general agreement amongst Society members on how legal education should be approached within the United Kingdom. Instead there was increasingly lively debate and an openness to new ideas. The sense of there being new possibilities gathered momentum and by 1960 there were debates that would never have surfaced in the immediate post-war years. Presidents such as Professor Lawson (1959–60) made a virtue of discussion. In July 1960 the Society met in Southampton and there was nothing dull about the

---

[67] Quoted in DM Walker, 'Student Thoughts on the Present Discontents' (1957–58) 4(NS) *JSPTL* 41.

[68] (1957–58) 4(NS) *JSPTL* 43.

[69] (1959–60) 5(NS) *JSPTL* 19. This article gives references to the contemporary debates in Scotland about the reform of legal education.

[70] (1957–58) 4(NS) *JSPTL* 131, 134 and 135.

proceedings. For example, there was discussion about the topics which would be raised at the Conference of American, Canadian and British Law Teachers in New York in September 1960. There was lively disagreement over the extent to which teaching should reflect professional demands. Professor LCB Gower (LSE) argued that 'There was no true distinction between academic and vocational subjects.' Further 'there were only two ways of teaching—teaching well or teaching badly'.[71] There were references to international experience and a paper on 'The Public Responsibilities of the Academic Law Teacher'.[72] Further contributions from RB Stevens (Yale), Dean Read (Dalhousie), Colwyn Williams (Belfast) and FE Dowrick (Trinity College Dublin) would have been very unsettling just a few years before. Many of the proposals looked to the study of the context of law, and some were simply directed at the idea of syllabus review and reform for its own sake. Thomas from Cambridge pointed out that the University was considering courses 'which would allow those going into business and other professions to do some law and those going into legal practice to do some other, wider papers'.[73] More generally, there was regret amongst some that little was done by way of teaching professional ethics. In a further session on 'Responsibilities' Professor PG Stein (Aberdeen) explored 'The desirability of the academic law teachers actively participating in public affairs'.[74] Professor Seaborne Davies pointed out that some provincial universities had a document for use when promotions were being considered (circulated initially at the instance of scientists) which listed publications. Perhaps, he suggested, public work should be taken into account. Another paper looked to 'the Obligations of the Academic Teachers of Law Towards Legal Reform'.[75] Further papers were on subjects such as 'Torts' and 'Administrative Law'. One study considered 'The Academic Lawyer's "House of Intellect"', based on a paper by Professor Montrose. It is also noticeable that there were international participants from, for example, Tulane, and from Australian universities.

Within a few years the Society had experienced an intellectual regeneration that could be compared with the early years of its existence between 1909 and 1914. But, as before, there was no guarantee that this would be permanent.

[71] (1959–60) 5(NS) *JSPTL* 207.
[72] Ibid, 209.
[73] Ibid, 210.
[74] Ibid.
[75] Ibid, 211.

6

The First Fifty Years: A Summary

There is a curious anecdote about Edward Jenks, the man who more than anyone else created the SPTL. In chapter 3 we saw that when he was teaching at Oxford he gave a *viva* to FE Smith, an undergraduate who in later years became Lord Chancellor and Lord Birkenhead. In the course of this *viva*, land law was discussed and the candidate was asked, perhaps in somewhat aggressive tones, 'What is the rule in Shelly's case?' Smith replied that he did not know the rule but—whatever it might be—he would abolish it if he ever became Lord Chancellor. As a *viva* the encounter did not go well and 'FE', as he was often known, failed to obtain the 'First' to which he felt he was entitled. In later years 'FE' did become Lord Chancellor and he did abolish the rule in Shelly's case and, unusually for a Lord Chancellor, he was never elected an Honorary Member of the SPTL. In fact the archives of the Society reveal successful opposition in the 1920s whenever the Lord Chancellor's name was put forward. Contemporaries believed that 'FE' and Jenks disliked each other intensely. Some even thought that the Lord Chancellor ensured that Jenks was never appointed a King's Counsel.[1]

The anecdote reveals a great deal about the context in which the Society had to work during its first half century. In many ways, the 'world' in which it operated was dominated by assumptions nurtured in Oxford, Cambridge and within the legal professions in London. Throughout the early years this triangle was the focus of the Society's activities; after all, it was only in the second half of the 1920s that annual meetings came at times to be held outside this area. In such a setting reputation was everything and relationships with others, whether good or bad, could be intense. It was of critical importance to the Society that there were not too many feuds with powerful lawyers such as FE Smith. It was equally important as a counterbalance that it obtained the positive support of people such as, say, Goudy, Geldart or Dicey in the academic community, and of influential practitioners in the professions such as Viscount Haldane. A new society with, inevitably, a dispersed membership and small numbers needed this type of recognition. Certainly, it was a notable achievement for Jenks to bring these 'major' names together in the Society. Reputation, or 'standing', was a prerequisite

---

[1] PH Pettit, 'The Society of Public Teachers of Law—The First Fifty Years' (1983) 3 *Legal Studies*, 231. Prof Pettit refers to the comments of Prof Goodhart at (1963) 7 (NS) *JSPTL* 231.

if early statements by Presidents were to be taken seriously. Professor Goudy's ambition was unlimited as he urged members to

> remember that the future reform of the laws, and consequent amelioration of the social and political conditions of this country, may largely depend upon the knowledge we impart to, and the ideas we instil into, the minds of our pupils.[2]

In its early years the Society was making large claims on its own behalf and it needed reputations which would make these claims look convincing.

The strength of the reputations and the ambitious declarations of intent concealed important structural weaknesses that became clear by the end of the 1920s. The Society had annual subscriptions from its members but it lacked large capital donations from individuals, or the professions or the universities or anywhere else. In financial terms, at best the Society could 'balance its books'. In respect of resources it could hardly compete with professional organisations in, say, the United States. It was in no position to give sustained financial support to legal education or research or even generally to its own members. When individuals were distracted by the First World War, and attendance at annual meetings fell, it took effort and determination to ensure that the organisation survived. The restoration of morale in the 1920s was a notable achievement but, again, it was dependent on individual initiative rather structural strength. On top of this a small membership made it difficult to use economies of scale. To take just two examples of concern to members, the Society tried and failed to fund teaching in legal history; and it tried with unconvincing results to ensure that law lecturers putting on courses at outside bodies such as the LCC had reasonably satisfactory pay. Saying this does not reflect adversely on the individuals who did the Society's work. Quite the reverse: it was the individual effort of successive Secretaries, Treasurers and others that kept the organisation going during these years. Annual meetings did take place, one year after another. The General Committee continued to convene in response to the effort of successive Secretaries and others operating from the Law Society or one of a small number of universities.

In this context the creation of a *Journal* in 1924 was a triumph for a few persistent reformers. The capacity to write on educational issues in the new *Journal* did much to enliven the Society, and by the mid-1930s there were important debates reflected in articles and the published records of Annual General Meetings. The extent to which the teaching of law was a matter for the universities or the professions, or a combination of both, was, as ever, of interest, but in the inter-war years it came to have a particular focus. The degree to which the teaching in provincial centres should be integrated with the local professions under arrangements where the latter provided lectures, library facilities and the like, or, alternatively, should be left exclusively to the universities, was explored with some feeling. In practice, comparatively small numbers of students and the financial weakness of many contemporary universities often made professional

---

[2] Minutes of General Meetings, First Annual General Meeting, 1 July 1909, A.SPTL 1/1. The address was also printed and a copy may be found in A.SPTL 3/3: see 4.

support essential. In 1935 Jenks pointed out that the society had 138 people engaged in teaching. Nationally there were, he thought, about 1,879 students on academic courses and 1,825 on professional programmes. In respect of the academic students the distribution was very uneven: 1,010 were divided between Oxford and Cambridge and 307 were in London. Manchester, for example, had 90 students (with an additional 49 on professional courses) and Southampton had 8 (with an additional 54 on professional studies).[3] In most contexts a significant professional role was inevitable and university teachers were grateful for it, but at the same time it was significant that some were challenging the idea of strong professional links. What was more, these public arguments were reflected in private debates between members about the best 'way forward'. As we saw in chapter 4, Professor Eastwood of Manchester supported a role for the professions and suggested that Professor Hughes of Leeds was acting as a 'stalking-horse' for Oxford and Cambridge in putting forward a different view. 'Hughes' Presidency' he wrote 'has given dissatisfaction to a number.' He went on to say that this was

> not because people do not like Hughes. We all do. But more than any other among the provincial teachers he represents the Oxford point of view, and not the point of view held by many of us that legal education in a city should be the result of the cooperative efforts of the local legal profession and the teachers.[4]

These debates, public and private, were part of the intellectual setting for initiatives during the 1930s. The latter included the work of the Lord Chancellor's Committee on Legal Education, and attempts at systematic law reform and even an effort to created a national centre for advanced legal study. None of these projects were successful at this time, but they reflected interest in debate and pointed to possible future achievements. Conversely, in certain contexts the opening up of discussion on legal education had the potential to cause intense dissent. It is obvious (despite the later 'weeding' of the records) that the arguments of 1939 about the admission of women to the Society produced considerable feeling and that for the moment these competing views were unresolved.

In the Second World War the Society largely ceased to function other than as a loosely organised membership with shared objectives on many issues. It did not meet and it did not organise initiatives. But its earlier work, and the knowledge that the Society would be revived after the conflict, surely assisted the numerous efforts of many law teachers, not least in the major programme of legal studies for the armed services. Thanks to the existence of the Society the teachers of law had at least come to know teachers in other universities. It was presumably for this reason that after the war the Society became the focal point of accounts of what had happened to the various law schools during the war years.

The Society's activities for the period 1945–55 reveal a time dominated by a powerful form of academic conservatism. Presidents spoke openly of the need to focus on common law cases to the exclusion of other forms of study. There were

[3] (1935) 51 *Law Quarterly Review* 169–74.
[4] Letter, 10 July 1932, A.SPTL 2/28.

doubts about the use of statutes in legal education. There was outright condemnation of sociology and anything hinting of the contextual explanation of law. Most striking of all, there were open declarations that the study of law reform did not come with the work of the law teacher—an interesting intellectual position given the capacity of the common law itself to be an instrument of reform. Instead there was praise for the legal practitioner, and in particular for the barrister or judge, with, its seems, the implicit assumption that barristers and judges of the day shared this very restrained view of legal education. We do not know why this view came through with such force at this time, but it may have been linked to resentment towards the radical social reforms of the post-war Labour Government, with the common law being seen as a desirable source of alternative and unchanging values. It may also have reflected a wish to seek professional approval during years when law degrees were being eclipsed in universities by an interest in new subjects. It is not anachronistic to say that this was a phase of introverted thought about legal education on the part of the Society which would have astonished the intellectually adventurous creators of the organisation in 1909.

These conservative ideas produced a reaction from the middle of the 1950s, particularly in the outspoken words of Professor Montrose from his base at Queen's University, Belfast. As we have seen in the preceding chapter, he continued to argue that law had to be explained and criticised as a part of a wide movement of thought in both the humanities and the sciences. It had to be understood with reference to subjects such as sociology and psychology, and, where appropriate, the law should be reformed. He was not alone in seeking change. Professor Walker writing on developments in Scotland pointed in the same direction with an interesting emphasis on the need to consult student views. Within a short space of time diversity of view and debate had come to be valued. In effect members were increasingly in agreement that they would never agree on precisely what it was that made for the ideal law teacher and ideal law course. Rather, the point was to sustain and develop a debate. Women were now (at last!) members of the Society and some, such as Mary Bell Cairns from Keele, had executive roles (but note that there were limits to the pace of change in this respect: the Society's records for these years frequently refer to 'members and their wives').

Certainly, for some the role of the Society remained open to question. Lord Chorley in his Presidential Address of 1955 pointed to a steady increase over the years in membership. He thought it had now risen to about 230. For him it was significant that its Presidents came from the ranks of those who had been 'building up' the law schools. The status of law teaching within the legal profession had been considerably enhanced. But he could be brutally frank in his criticisms of the SPTL. In his view these improvements could not be attributed to the Society. The legislation of 1922 which established foundations for the financing of legal studies in provincial universities (through linking their role to the education of solicitors) was not the product of a Society initiative. (It was achieved by Jenks operating outside the Society.) Nor, in the view of Lord Chorley, could the Society claim a lot of credit for the increased standing of law teachers. To repeat what was mentioned in the previous chapter, he argued that the Society had not 'cast itself for an active role in the play'.[5]

Blunt comments such as these were to some extent historically misjudged in their failure to recognise the extent of the acute difficulties faced by the members of the Society during its first 50 years. Survival had been in itself an achievement. It could be said that Lord Chorley's observations of mid-century simply cele-brated the fact that changing conditions now made it possible to conceive of a much more active and successful role for the Society. However, at its heart there was much truth in his raw analysis. With rare exceptions, the Society had not developed a dynamic role in legal education or in its relations with the legal professions; at best it had sometimes sustained debate. With encouragement for diversity of views and the context of increasing membership and a shared sense of enhanced status there was now the potential for the Society to take on 'an active role'. The experience of the Society during the next 50 years had the poten-tial to be more adventurous than that of the first half century.

---

[5] The Rt Hon Lord Chorley, Presidential Address, Edinburgh, 13 July 1955, 'The Progress of Academic Law in the United Kingdom' (1955–56) 3(NS) *JSPTL* 55.

7

The Swinging Sixties

> I am reminding myself that the most important parts of the Conference are the
> three business meetings, not the wining and dining and outings, though the
> latter take most time to organise.
>
> (Letter from Professor FE Dowrick (conference organiser)
> to Professor JND Anderson (President), April 1969)

The SPTL and the Expansion of Higher Education

As the new decade began, the SPTL, like the rest of academia, was caught up in
the changes effected by government policy on higher education. By 1960, the
University Grants Committee (UGC), the Committee of Vice-Chancellors and
Principals (CVCP) and the government wanted to engage in some long-term
planning of the higher-education system. If higher education was to fulfil its
potential in terms of social policy, the UGC argued that there was a need for
some broad assessment of the amount and kind of higher education which was
to be developed.[1] Pressure for change also came from a range of reformers, who
argued that the talent of young people in Britain was being wasted by an
outdated education system.[2] It appears that the relevant government ministers
wanted to see a small committee of experienced persons, with an independent
chairman, rather than having a Royal Commission, so the committee could work
more speedily and be more flexible.[3]

The chosen instrument for advising on long-term development was a
committee set up in February 1961 under the chairmanship of Lord Robbins, a
leading academic economist, well respected at the Treasury, where he had worked
during and after the war, and a convinced liberal in university matters.[4] The
Committee had the following terms of reference:

---

[1] WAC Stewart, *Higher Education in Postwar Britain* (London, Macmillan, 1989) 96–7.
[2] D Sandbrook, *Never Had It So Good: A History of Britain from Suez to the Beatles* (London, Abacus, 2005) 427.
[3] Stewart, above n 1.
[4] Ibid.

> To review the pattern of full time higher education in Great Britain and in the light of national needs and resources to advise Her Majesty's Government on what principles its long term development should be based, (and) whether there should be any changes in that pattern, whether any new types of institution are desirable and whether any modifications should be made in the present arrangement for planning and co-ordinating the development of the various types of institutions.[5]

It started its work by setting out four aims of higher education. The expression of these aims immediately reflects the tensions between the intellectual and the vocational approaches to education which, then as now, underlie the university sector, and which can be seen in law schools as much (if not more so) than in the rest of academia.

The aims of higher education were, the Committee said, 'to provide instruction in skills suitable to play a part in the general division of labour', while also aiming 'to produce not mere specialists but rather cultivated men and women'.[6] In addition, universities should seek to 'advance learning', both in terms of teaching and research, and finally, they should be concerned with 'the transmission of a common culture and common standards of citizenship', meaning by this, not the forcing of all individuality into a common mould, but to provide 'that background of culture and social habit upon which a healthy society depends'.[7] Overall, the Committee reaffirmed the value of a liberal education, while simultaneously emphasising the importance of skills and practicality.[8]

The Committee quickly established what became known as 'the Robbins principle'—that all young people qualified by ability and attainment to pursue a full-time course in higher education should have the opportunity to do so if they wished.[9] The consequent increase in the number of students would require much bigger institutions of higher education, and many more of them.[10] In the event, the UGC did not sanction quite the number of new institutions which Robbins recommended, on the grounds that some of the increased numbers could be more cheaply accommodated by the expansion of existing universities. (In his book on the period, WAC Stewart, himself a former vice-chancellor, comments that it is probable that most vice-chancellors of existing universities were opposed to the Robbins scheme, seeing it as a threat to the growth of existing universities.[11]) However, the Report was an extremely important driver behind the expansion of higher education in the twentieth century, and its effects were seen almost immediately: the 1960s witnessed a period of great expansion in the higher-education sector. Thirteen additional universities came into being in this

---

[5] *Higher Education* (the Robbins Report) (1963) Cmnd 2153, HMSO, London, para 1.
[6] Ibid, paras 25 and 26.
[7] Ibid, paras 27 and 28.
[8] R Stevens, *University to Uni: The Politics of Higher Education in England since 1944* (London, Politico Publishing, 2004) 23.
[9] Ibid, para 31.
[10] Ibid, ch VI.
[11] Stewart, above n 1, 100.

period,[12] with another ten 'technological universities' being created from former colleges of advanced technology.[13]

The need for expansion of higher education being considered by the Robbins Committee was also reflected in the life of the SPTL. During the 1960s, there are several references in the Minutes of the General Committee to the need to increase the amount of legal education available. In 1961 it was decided to produce a memorandum on this topic, the Committee having been reminded that provincial law faculties, who offered approximately 550 places to undergraduates annually, received nearly ten times that number of applications.[14] For some members, initial progress with the memorandum was too slow. At the meeting of the General Committee in November 1962, Professor JC Smith, on behalf of the constituency of the University of Nottingham, indicated that the constituency was dissatisfied that no steps had been taken by the General Committee on the question of the need for increased facilities for law teaching in England and Wales as had been raised on previous occasions.[15] This complaint appears to have had some effect; the matter was being considered by the Legal Education Sub-Committee which, led by its Chair, Professor JL Montrose (Queen's University, Belfast), sprang into action and recommended that the Society should undertake a comprehensive survey of the state of legal education in the UK, with a view not only to influencing the UGC's next quinquennial review, but also to 'correct widespread misapprehensions about legal education [which] were present among colleagues in other faculties within universities, and apparently among the Vice Chancellors and governing bodies of the new universities, as well as among the public generally'.[16] It was agreed that arrangements should be put in place for a survey of legal education to be undertaken, and that meanwhile a memorandum should be submitted to the Robbins Committee.[17]

The SPTL Submission to the Robbins Committee

The memorandum sent by the Society to the Robbins Committee was comprehensive in the issues it addressed. Its introduction sets the tone:

[12] Five were previously university colleges: Southampton (1952), Hull (1954), Exeter (1955), Leicester (1957) and Keele (1962). Newcastle became a separate university from Durham in 1963 and in June 1964 Strathclyde became the first university to be founded in Scotland since Edinburgh in the sixteenth century. Lampeter and Sussex were established in 1961, and six new universities were established with no previous 'apprentice' period as university colleges: York and East Anglia (1963), Essex and Lancaster (1964), Kent and Warwick (1965). After Robbins recommended another Scottish university, Stirling was created in 1967 and the New University of Ulster opened in 1967; Stewart, above n 1, 108.

[13] Aston, Bath, Bradford, Brunel, City of London, Heriot-Watt, Loughborough, Surrey (1966); Salford, UWIST (1967); Stewart, above n 1, 108.

[14] General Committee Minutes, 15 December 1961, A.SPTL 1/5.

[15] General Committee Special Meeting Minutes, 2 November 1962, A.SPTL 1/5.

[16] General Committee Minutes, 14 December 1962, A.SPTL 1/5.

[17] General Committee Minutes, 25 January 1963, A.SPTL 1/5.

> The main theme of this memorandum is that law is an important branch of university education, admirably fulfilling many current needs both for undergraduate studies, providing an excellent mental training and broad human perspectives, and also for scholarly research, providing valuable critiques of many problems of social organization. Law has a long history as a university subject, it constitutes an area of scholarship as renowned as any other, it has kept abreast of progress in scientific and philosophical thought. Its study constitutes, on the one hand, a liberal education for students serving as a bridge between the humanities and the sciences, and, on the other, it constitutes a preparation for the important profession of the law and for many other professions and careers. It cannot be taught or studied in this traditional and progressive manner outside adequately staffed and equipped Faculties of Law. It is in the interests of both universities and the community that adequate resources be available for the development of legal studies within universities.[18]

The memorandum itself reiterates the view of law as an academic discipline, pointing out that for many years law was largely conceived of as a training for the legal profession, but with post-war changes such as the development of international organisations, the end of colonialism and the establishment of the welfare state, legal curricula had been subjected to profound changes, with much greater prominence given to governmental, international and comparative law studies, and a greater recognition of 'legal sociology'.[19] There was also an acknowledgement that there were diverse views among law teachers about the nature and purpose of legal education, broadly emerging from two different attitudes to legal study:

> One sees the purposes of university education adequately fulfilled by limiting legal study to the understanding of rules and legal institutions. The other calls for the study of the relations between legal and other institutions, for appreciation of the relations between law and social sciences and philosophy.[20]

Despite this, the memorandum tries to draw a picture of a united constituency of law teachers 'The attitude of all law teachers may be summarized by saying that the major function of a Faculty of Law is to provide students with a liberal education through the medium of law.'[21]

The memorandum is firm in putting the case that more resources need to be allocated to the discipline of law. It argues that since students and employers no longer regarded law as exclusively a preparation for a career in the legal profession, there had been an increased demand for places, a demand which university law schools could not satisfy, because they were allocated quotas on a historical basis and this inhibited expansion. Law teachers were also being asked to provide law teaching for other disciplines, increasing the burden on staff.[22]

---

[18] *Memorandum Submitted to the Robbins Committee on Higher Education* (1962–1963) 7(NS) JSPTL 107.

[19] Ibid, 110.

[20] Ibid, 111.

[21] Ibid, 112.

[22] Ibid, 112–3.

The memorandum also makes the point that, while all disciplines are facing difficulties in recruiting staff, there is a particular problem in law.

> The inducements for a man with a good honours degree to take up a career of useful service, as well as high monetary reward, outside universities, are considerable. The legal profession has always proved a great attraction for men of high intelligence.[23]

Not only was adequate remuneration important, but the conditions of service also needed to be improved: 'Too often, a law teacher is asked to carry too many law subjects, resulting in a heavy burden of teaching and insufficient time for research.'[24] Equally, there was a need for more Chairs in law; the situation in the United Kingdom compared unfavourably with that in the United States, where many more appointments of comparable status were available.[25] Further resource issues laid out in the memorandum include the need for more postgraduate opportunities in law, and the need not only to improve law libraries but also to improve the means of copying materials for teaching purposes.[26]

Finally, the memorandum turns to the particular responsibilities of law faculties in relation to the Commonwealth, pointing out that as the home of the common law, there are special obligations on law faculties in the United Kingdom not only to provide training for students and future law teachers, but also to assist with the establishment and development of Commonwealth law schools, by a policy of secondment.[27]

This memorandum has a significant place in the history of the Society; not only does it provide a window into a range of issues relating to legal education in the early 1960s, but it also provides material for submissions by the SPTL to other bodies, such as the Heyworth Committee on the Future of Social Studies.[28] It also provided the catalyst for the establishment of a series of empirical surveys of legal education, which were to provide future members of the Society with invaluable empirical evidence about the state of the legal academy.

National Incomes Commission

The effects of the expansion of higher education which took place as a result of the Robbins Report were felt by members of the SPTL as much as anywhere else in the academy. At the meeting of the General Committee held in March 1965,

---

[23] Ibid, 114.

[24] Ibid, 114.

[25] Ibid, 115. Throughout the 1960s the number of senior posts in universities was limited by Government quota; see AH Halsey and MA Trow, *The British Academics* (London, Faber & Faber, 1971) 179.

[26] *Memorandum Submitted to the Robbins Committee on Higher Education* (1962–1963) 7(NS) *JSPTL* 115–9.

[27] Ibid, 119.

[28] See below.

Professor PS James (Leeds) informed the Committee that he was finding considerable difficulty in filling junior academic posts with suitably qualified persons. In the discussion which followed, it appeared that there were about 30 such posts unfilled in law schools in the UK and the problem was in no way confined to any particular area of the country. It was felt that the difficulty arose from the fact that universities were engaged in a process of rapid expansion at a time when many other attractive openings in the legal profession and in industry were available to good graduates.[29]

Another reason for the difficulties in appointing staff may have been the poor levels of pay on offer in universities. In his speech at the Society's Annual Dinner in 1962, Professor GW Keeton argued that inadequate pay was a particular problem for law schools, because of the counter-attractions of the profession, of commercial enterprises and, in particular, the higher salaries offered to law teachers in commercial and technical colleges.[30] Nationally, the Association of University Teachers (AUT) was arguing that university salaries were about 25 per cent below comparable jobs, such as the civil service.[31] In 1963 the Society submitted a substantial memorandum to the National Incomes Commission (NIC). This body had been set up in July 1962 as part of the government's strategy to control wages and thereby inflation.[32] Issues for consideration could be referred by the parties immediately concerned or the government, and the Commission was empowered to take evidence from interested parties.[33] Following advice from the UGC that there was an urgent need for an increase in university salaries in the interests of the expansion programme following the Robbins Report, the government decided to refer the remuneration of university staff to the Incomes Commission, and it was in this context that the SPTL submitted its memorandum.[34]

In its evidence to the NIC, the profession of law teacher was characterised as that of a scholar:

> The law teacher in the universities of the United Kingdom considers himself, like his colleagues in other Faculties, as primarily a scholar engaged in the various tasks which belong to membership of a university. He teaches the generations of law students that important section of the culture of man embraced by systems of law, patterns of socially controlled behaviour, and ideas of justice, recognising, however, that legal institutions and ideas are part of the broader complex of human institutions and ideas. Consequently, law as taught at a university is closely allied to the social sciences.[35]

---

[29] SPTL General Committee Minutes, 19 March 1965, A.SPTL 1/5.

[30] 'Extract from the President's Speech at the Annual Dinner of the Society' (1962–63) 7(NS) *JSPTL* 54–5, 54.

[31] Halsey and Trow, above n 25, 174.

[32] See White Paper (1962) *Incomes Policy: The Next Steps*, Cmnd 1626, HMSO, London; JL Fallick and RF Elliott (eds), *Incomes Policies, inflation and Relative Pay* (London, Allen & Unwin, 1981) 266.

[33] *National Incomes Commission* (1962) Cmnd 1844, 3.

[34] Ibid, vii and viii.

[35] Memorandum for National Incomes Commission, 24 June 1963, A.SPTL 1/5 1.

The memorandum goes on to make a case for increased remuneration for law teachers, based on a growing demand from established universities, and the expectation that newly created universities will also wish to open law departments in due course. It is noted that larger local authorities are forming law colleges (such as the Holborn College of Law) and that these institutions are able to offer salaries capable of attracting teachers away from universities. In addition, there is a demand for law teachers to staff law schools in the Commonwealth, where posts of sufficient status and salary also attract British law teachers (a point confirmed by the reference in General Committee minutes for March 1960, which refer to the advertisement of a post teaching English law in Cairo, which, it was pointed out, would carry a high salary, while taxation in Egypt was low).[36]

Quite apart from the availability of well-paid lecturing jobs outside British universities, law graduates were not only attracted to join the legal profession, but were also sought by the civil service, industry and commerce; in all of those professions they could earn a better salary than as a university lecturer. As a result of all these pressures, the memorandum argues that law schools experienced great difficulties in recruiting staff:

> There are of course some dedicated scholars who prefer an academic career with its disadvantages to other careers, but it is not possible to recruit adequate numbers of teachers from such men. There are men with admirable intellectual and other qualities to whom at present the rewards of law teaching do not make sufficient appeal.[37]

The memorandum paints a picture of law schools that had been for years unable to appoint to the most junior 'assistant lecturer' posts, while at the lecturer level, appointments were rarely made at the bottom of the scale, and even then the richer institutions tended to entice them away by paying higher salaries.[38] Generally, academic salaries remained low, particularly when compared with the legal profession. One institution reported 'the loss of a lecturer aged 26 to a firm of solicitors who promised him a salary rising within three years to that payable to the professor'.[39]

The memorandum records that 'Hitherto, the Society has concerned itself with the scholarly aspects of legal education' and the tone of the submission is somewhat apologetic; there appears to have been some reluctance to take action at all, but the President 'eventually' decided that 'such representations should be made'. The memorandum notes that 'examination time' conditions have hampered the work of the relevant committee, there is no hard data, since the intended survey of university law teachers is not yet complete and as a consequence 'the statements in this memorandum are largely impressions, which though subjective are, it is hoped, responsibly stated and reasonably accurate within the limitations of the generalisations so produced'.[40] Hardly a statement

---

[36] General Committee Minutes, 25 March 1960, A.SPTL 1/5.
[37] Memorandum for National Incomes Commission, 24 June 1963, A.SPTL 1/5 4.
[38] Ibid, 5.
[39] Ibid, 6.
[40] Ibid, 7.

designed to ensure that the arguments contained in the memo had maximum impact. Nevertheless, the Society did make a submission, and also selected five professors to appear before the Commission.[41] It was reported in December of that year that oral evidence given on behalf of the Society had been well received by the Commission.[42]

The result of the reference to the National Incomes Commission was positive for legal academics as it was for all university teachers, in that the Commission recommended an increase in academic salaries across the board:

> We have found that existing salaries are not adequate to enable the Universities and the Colleges to recruit and retain sufficient staff of the calibre necessary to maintain their high academic standards, and the main object of our recommendations is to put them in a position from which they will be able to compete on terms with other claimants for the limited number of persons of high academic ability.[43]

However, as Halsey wryly notes 'The recommendations of the Commission did nothing to allay AUT discontent' and salary levels in academia continued to be a source of dissatisfaction throughout the 1960s.[44] New salary scales were proposed in 1964 as a result of the NIC's report, but these were then reviewed by its successor, the National Board for Prices and Incomes, which did not report until December 1968, and the matter still had not been settled by the end of the decade.[45]

Survey of Legal Education

It was in the context of a need to expand legal education that the idea of under-taking a comprehensive survey of legal education had been raised with the SPTL General Committee.[46] In presenting the case for such a survey, the Chair of the Legal Education Sub-Committee, Professor Montrose, argued that this would be an appropriate development of the Society's activities:

> The Society had before the War expressed its views on the desirability of the establish-ment of a Law Reform Committee, and after the War it had helped in the re-establish-ment of that Committee. The Society had taken corporate action in proposing the for-mation of a Criminal Law Reform Committee, and it appears to me that the members of the Society generally would approve of further corporate activity by the Society. However, if the Society were to speak with any authority on behalf of its members, it

---

[41] General Committee Minutes, 22 July 1963, A.SPTL 1/5.
[42] General Committee Minutes, 13 December 1963, A.SPTL 1/5.
[43] *National Incomes Commission* (1962) Cmnd 1844, para 213.
[44] Halsey and Trow, above n 25, 188–9.
[45] Ibid, 177.
[46] General Committee Minutes, 25 January 1963, A.SPTL 1/5.

was necessary there should first be ascertained what in fact were the conditions of legal education, what were the policies at present implemented and what policies were contemplated as desirable for the future[47].

Members of the Sub-Committee unanimously agreed with their Chairman, although they indicated that it should be made clear that there was no question of formulating any policies; the autonomy of law faculties was regarded as key.

The Sub-Committee hoped to be able to find funding for a secretariat to carry out the survey, but resolved that even if this were impossible, the survey should go ahead. This plan of action was subsequently agreed by the General Committee.[48] In July 1963 Mr JF Wilson (Southampton) agreed to oversee the survey on the basis of an honorarium and some replacement teaching costs.[49] Professor JND Anderson, Director of the Institute of Advanced Legal Studies, was successful in obtaining a grant from the Nuffield Foundation to enable the project to be undertaken. A questionnaire was designed, with the help of an advisory committee, chaired by Professor AL Goodhart.[50] The survey enjoyed a high response rate (100 per cent of law schools and 78 per cent of law teachers, plus large numbers of practitioners, and colleges of further education), suggesting that it enjoyed a high degree of support from the legal community.[51]

There were at the time of the survey 23 universities in the UK running full degree courses at undergraduate and postgraduate level: 17 in England, 4 in Scotland and 1 each in Wales and Northern Ireland.[52] Numbers of law students had doubled since before the Second World War, with expansion largely in the provincial universities.[53] Postgraduate students were concentrated in Oxford, Cambridge and London, and the majority of them came from outside the UK.[54] Facilities for research outside the 'golden triangle' of Oxbridge and London were poor, with consequent effects both on staff research and postgraduate teaching.[55]

Law degrees were generally composed of 14 courses; of these, 10 were compulsory (though at Leeds there were 13 compulsory courses). The subjects which were identified as forming the compulsory core at the majority of law schools were: contract, constitutional law, criminal law, jurisprudence, land law, equity or trusts, torts and legal system. Roman law remained compulsory in only 10 law schools. There was considerable disagreement about legal system, with a significant number of law teachers regarding a separate legal system course as being

---

[47] Report of Legal Education Sub-Committee of the SPTL 1962, A.SPTL 1/5.

[48] General Committee Minutes, 14 December 1962, A.SPTL 1/5.

[49] General Committee Minutes, 22 July 1963, A.SPTL 1/5.

[50] JF Wilson, 'A Survey of Legal Education in the United Kingdom' (1966–67) 9(NS) *JSPTL* 1–144, 5.

[51] Ibid, 6–7; responses were received from 450 barristers, 1,250 solicitors and 275 colleges of further education.

[52] Ibid, 8; contrast the position in 2008, when 99 law schools offered qualifying law degrees: 81 in England, 6 in Wales, 10 in Scotland and 2 in Northern Ireland; see www.sra.org.uk/students/academic-stage.page and www.lawscot.org.uk .

[53] Ibid, 13.

[54] Ibid, 22.

[55] Ibid, 23–4.

of little value.[56] The most common optional subjects were evidence, conflicts, administrative law, industrial law and family law.[57] Generally students were given two lectures a week and a fortnightly tutorial in each subject, though some law schools only had enough staff to deliver monthly tutorials. Group sizes ranged from four to eight, though increasing student numbers were causing group sizes to increase.[58]

In terms of staffing, the report noted that the overall staff–student ratio was poor, especially in the older provincial universities, where there was difficulty in finding staff. One in four law teachers was employed on a part-time basis, with an even greater proportion of part-timers both at Cambridge and in the older provincial universities: 'the tendency is to recruit local solicitors to lecture on the more practical subjects, such as conveyancing, evidence, procedure and administrative law'.[59] The survey found that law teachers preferred the appointment of full-time academics, though a substantial number recognised the value of part-time lecturers 'for lecturing on practical subjects and for bringing a flavour of the law in action into the teaching of more theoretical subjects'.[60] Sixty-seven per cent of law teachers thought that university law teachers were seriously underpaid, with 58 per cent believing poor pay was a deterrent to suitably qualified candidates entering academic life.[61]

Looking at the qualifications of law teachers, the survey found that two-thirds of law teachers held a degree from either Oxford or Cambridge, with the rest almost equally divided between London and provincial universities.[62] (This statistic gives an insight into the significant influence of Oxbridge on the development of legal education at this time.) Seventy-eight per cent of law teachers held a professional qualification, while only 26 per cent had a PhD or equivalent.[63] There was little mobility among law teachers, with two-thirds having only had experience of teaching at one law school (over 40 per cent were teaching at the university at which they obtained their first degree).[64] However, in contrast to this apparent provincialism, more than 50 per cent of law teachers had international experience: 25 per cent had studied abroad, 21 per cent had taught in the United States, and 10 per cent had taught in Commonwealth universities.[65]

Research was under pressure, and a shortage of suitable candidates for academic posts, combined with the recent expansion in student numbers, led to a heavier teaching load and a wider coverage of subjects for the average law teacher.[66] Many law teachers complained that their research was confined to

---

[56] Ibid, 44.
[57] Ibid, 44.
[58] Ibid, 48.
[59] Ibid, 28.
[60] Ibid, 28.
[61] Ibid, 35.
[62] Ibid, 29.
[63] Ibid, 29–30.
[64] Ibid, 30.
[65] Ibid, 31.
[66] Ibid, 33.

vacations and sabbatical leave (though at the majority of universities there was no formal entitlement to sabbatical leave). They also criticised the facilities for research; only 26 per cent of law teachers at older provincial universities and 13 per cent at newer provincial universities thought that the research facilities were adequate.[67] Eight of the provincial universities had law libraries that fell below the SPTL's recommended minimum standard.[68]

Teaching facilities were also far from ideal in many cases. The report comments that:

> As law is not a subject which requires special provision to be made in the way of laboratories, it has not fared so successfully in regard to accommodation as have many other disciplines. The majority of university law schools are located in converted houses or other university buildings, and rarely are lecture rooms specifically appropriated for their use.[69]

Although there were some exceptions to this general observation, with Aberystwyth, Birmingham, Liverpool and Manchester acquiring new buildings, 62 per cent of law teachers considered their accommodation inadequate for teaching purposes.

This survey of legal education was a very important achievement for the Society. It was the first of a series of such surveys, which have documented the changing nature of legal education for well over 40 years, and which have provided information that has been used extensively, both to press for improvements in resources and facilities, and to assist researchers in the field.[70] It is thus important to acknowledge the role of the then Chair of the SPTL's Legal Education Committee, Professor JL Montrose. As the co-ordinator of the survey, Mr Wilson, observed, this enterprise might never have been undertaken had it not been for the work and initiative of Professor Montrose, since it was he who realised the paucity of information available, and had the foresight to realise the value of gathering such data.[71] The Society was also fortunate in finding John Wilson to co-ordinate the first survey.

Legal Academic Life through the Eyes of Presidents

The subject-matter of Presidential Addresses in the 1960s included some substantive legal topics, such as 'The House of Lords and Criminal Law' or 'Judiciary

---

[67] Ibid, 34.

[68] Ibid, 38.

[69] Ibid, 36.

[70] During the period 1966–93 three surveys and two interim supplements were published; in 1996 Harris and Jones published a similar survey; for details see F Cownie (2004) *Legal Academics: Culture And Identities* (Oxford, Hart Publishing) 42–3. These have been followed by a survey by Harris and Beinart published in 2006: P Harris and S Beinart 'A Survey of Law Schools in the United Kingdom 2004' (2005) 39(3) *The Law Teacher* 299–366.

[71] Wilson, above n 50, 5.

and Constitutional Struggle 1660–88', but at least half of the Addresses focused on some aspect of legal education, from 'The Academic Lawyer as Jurist' to 'Examinations for Law Degrees'.[72] From the Addresses which focused on legal education, it is possible to gain some insights into the world of the academic lawyer of those times.

In 1960, Professor FE Lawson (Oxford), in urging members of the Society to play a more active part in the making of law, not merely the teaching of it, argues that such activity would help to raise the profile of academic lawyers:

> We certainly need something of the kind, for Law is, by and large, not thought well of in our universities. At Oxford, at any rate, the Faculty as a whole, and the Professors and Readers in particular, are much less numerous in proportion to the number of undergraduates reading Law than is the case with many other populous subjects. In other words, Law is run on the cheap. I imagine its treatment in other universities is not very different. Moreover, I doubt whether even now it is considered entirely respectable. But for the undeniable quality of the great pioneer generation: Pollock, Maitland, Dicey, Holland and Anson, it might never have acquired any prestige, and even those illustrious persons had very little opinion of those who came into contact with the undergraduates. Hazel used to tell with relish the story of how he and his colleagues among the College tutors forced themselves upon the notice of the Professors. It has continued to be an uphill fight.
>
> Academic law has had to compete with practice, whereas History can only be academic. Law teachers are not paid competitive wages, like teachers of medicine. Law teaching still appears to the outside world like the teaching of a trade, or at best the transmission of a body of received doctrine, and that other faculties no longer regard as the prime task of a university.[73]

Lawson was also self-critical about the standard of scholarship achieved by academic lawyers in the UK 'We academic lawyers know that our teaching of law is by no means entirely vocational . . . we know that, on the whole, we try to teach Law in a liberal, non-vocational way.'[74] But, he goes on, on considering the matter, he was surprised to find how few among contemporary legal academics in the UK were writers of significant books fit to be set beside the great books of French and German law.

> Moreover, there has been a tendency to till over and over again the field occupied by the traditional subjects of examination. . . . We should at any rate not be satisfied until we have covered scientifically all the contents of such comprehensive books as Planiol in France or Enneccerus in Germany.[75]

---

[72] See D Seaborne Davies, 'The House of Lords and the Criminal Law' (1961) 6(NS) *JSPTL* 104; GW Keaton, 'The Judiciary and Constitutional Struggle 1660-88' (1962) 7(NS) *JSPTL* 56; FH Lawson, 'The Academic Lawyer as Jurist' (1960) 5(NS) *JSPTL* 182; JA Coutts 'Examination for Law Degrees' (1967) 9(NS) *JSPTL* 399.

[73] Lawson, above n 72, 184.

[74] Ibid, 185.

[75] Ibid, 185.

He ends on an upbeat note, but nevertheless urges his contemporaries to achieve higher standards:

> When I remember that I am only in the third generation of high-class law teaching at Oxford—and for that matter, in England—for I learnt my law from Holdsworth, who learnt it from Dicey, Pollock, Holland and Anson, I do not think we have done too badly. But it is now time for us to spread our wings.[76]

It is salutary to realise that just over 50 years since the SPTL was founded, its President reminds its Members that academic law in the UK was still finding its feet in the academy.

Robert Megarry, the President in 1966, was, as he made clear in his address, primarily a practising lawyer, who enjoyed some part-time teaching.[77] He chose to examine the differences between law as taught and law as practised, high-lighting, for example, the different approaches to law and fact:

> In the law school, the facts are always certain; any uncertainty is in the law. A problem question . . . sets out the facts explicitly; a candidate merely has to wrestle with the law. . . . In daily practice, the position is usually the reverse.[78]

It is interesting that Megarry made a plea for students to be provided with copies of statutes in examinations, suggesting that this may not have been common practice in the mid-1960s. He was also in favour of long problem questions covering disparate areas of law.[79] The second half of his address focuses on law teaching, arguing that it is important that lectures are of the highest quality:

> A good lecture is satisfying, enlivening, absorbing. With a little imagination, there can be curiosity, suspension and humour. . . . The bad lecture is sheer murder. Indeed, among law lecturers, two types of genius may be discerned. There are those who can breathe life into the dullest and most technical of subjects . . . [but] the other type can make the most enthralling subject dull and repellent.[80]

He goes on to criticise the assumption that 'anyone can lecture', and is also concerned about the lack of support for lecturers, in terms of teaching technique, both at the beginning of their career and later on:

> So many things may be wrong. A lecturer may be a voice-dropper, a word-swallower, a coin-jangler. . . . Complex thoughts may be expressed in sentences so labyrinthine that barely one in ten will understand the words and only one in thirty comprehend the thought. Or platitudinous reiterations of the obvious may turn the thoughts of the audience to murder or suicide. . . . The material may be presented as from a pogo-stick, hopping all over the place, or hobby horses may be pursued at inordinate lengths, leaving untouched vast intervening tracts of important law.[81]

---

[76] Ibid, 185.
[77] R Megarry 'Law as Taught and Law as Practised' (1966-67) 9(NS) *JSPTL* 176–89, 176.
[78] Ibid, 176.
[79] Ibid, 185.
[80] Ibid, 187.
[81] Ibid, 188.

Surprisingly, in view of his critique, Megarrry did not argue for a teacher training course for law lecturers, but after urging members of the Society to cultivate 'an awareness of the problems and a determination to resolve those that are soluble', he suggested that peer observation of teaching and student feedback might help improve matters, thus foreshadowing much that was to become commonplace in universities by the end of the twentieth century.[82]

In many ways Robert Megarry might be regarded as a controversial choice as President of the SPTL. As Neil Duxbury points out in *Jurists and Judges*, when Megarry delivered the Hamlyn lectures in 1962, he was somewhat less than complimentary about academic lawyers, characterising them as 'far too ponderous, leisurely, genteel, impractical and unworldly to be able to carry out the work of a judge. Faced with such work, the legal academic would probably prove unreliable or crack under pressure.'[83] Duxbury may not be alone in wondering how it was that someone who adopted such a critical attitude towards legal academics could be elected President of the SPTL only three years later. Perhaps, as Duxbury suggests, it provides some insight into the collective psyche of legal academics during that period, and their general lack of self-confidence.

The following year, Professor JA Coutts (Bristol) used his Presidential Address to consider the question of law examinations, during the course of which he commented:

> First, I suggest that we need to pay heed to what Lord Rosebery said in 1906, as Chancellor of the University of London, namely that examiners are in as much need of training as teachers. . . . Casual, though extensive, conversation with members of this Society leads me to believe that we think little of Institutes of Education and less of the professors therein. Off-hand, I can think of only one member of this Society who holds a Diploma in Education. I would none the less suggest that there should be established a Professor of Legal Education, surrounded by a suitable entourage of research assistants, and attached perhaps to the Institute of Advanced Legal Studies, if it would have him.[84]

It is noticeable that successive Presidents express quite fundamental criticisms of the quality of legal education on offer in the 1960s. Perhaps this reflects not only a time when standards were in need of improvement, but also a milieu in which teaching arguably had a higher profile than it was to have in later decades, so that it was 'on the radar' of Presidents in a particularly acute way.

---

[82] Ibid, 188 and 189.

[83] N Duxbury, *Jurists and Judges* (Oxford, Hart Publishing, 2001) 75.

[84] Coutts, above n 72, 411. The first Professor of Legal Education attached to the Institute of Advanced Legal Studies was not appointed until 1995, when Prof Avrom Sherr became the first holder of the Woolf Chair of Legal Education. See http://ials.sas.ac.uk/about/staff/staff.asp?ID=37, accessed 16 March 2009

The SPTL and Admission to University

Statistics gathered for the Robbins Committee in 1963 showed that there were considerable differences between the patterns of admission to Oxbridge, as compared with other universities. For example, in 1960 only 30 per cent of males admitted to Oxbridge had attended maintained schools, while the proportion for other universities was 7 per cent.[85] Significant differences between Oxbridge and provincial universities relating to regional origin and gender were also uncovered, with few places at Oxbridge being won by northerners or women.[86] In relation to gender differences, one researcher commented: 'One possible explanation for this fact is that girls from professional families are more likely to attend a local direct grant day school whereas the sons more usually go to independent boarding schools.'[87]

The segmented pattern of higher education had implications for recruitment to the professions, industry and commerce. Recruitment to Branch A of the Foreign Office (one of the most prestigious parts of the Civil Service) was 94.2 per cent from Oxbridge.[88] Lowe argues that despite a growing awareness of the injustices of the situation, access to university was not one of the major debates of the early 1960s.[89] Nevertheless, some change was facilitated by the acceptance in 1962 of the report of the Anderson Committee, which compelled local education authorities to fund all full-time students in higher education taking courses requiring two or more A levels.[90]

The disproportionate influence of the 'golden triangle' of Oxford, Cambridge and London was reflected in the law student population. Presenting a survey of law school statistics to the SPTL General Committee in December 1961, Professor Parker (Exeter) reported that law undergraduates were distributed as follows: Oxford and Cambridge 1,220; London 575; provincial (England and Wales) 1,304. He also reported that provincial universities had approximately 50 postgraduates, of whom about half were at the University of Manchester.[91] Provincial university law departments were also major providers of vocational training, with 355 articled clerks taking their 'statutory year courses' in provincial law departments.[92]

One of the significant events affecting admission to universities in the 1960s was the creation of UCCA (the Universities' Central Council on Admissions). Until 1960, each candidate made separate applications to each university until he/she was accepted or eventually settled for rejection. Universities had no

[85] *Higher Education* (the Robbins Report) (1963) Cmnd 2153, HMSO, London, para 218, Table 32.
[86] R Lowe, *Education in the Post-War Years: A Social History* (London, Routledge, 1988), 156.
[87] G Boehm, 'Which Girls' Schools Lead to Oxford and Cambridge?' (1963) 13 *Where* 4–6.
[88] Lowe, above n 86, 157.
[89] Ibid, 158.
[90] Ibid, 171.
[91] General Committee Minutes, 15 December 1961, A.SPTL 1/5.
[92] Ibid.

guarantee that those offered places would in fact turn up, which made planning very difficult. Equally, students rejected by one institution had no certain way of locating other institutions with vacancies. The SPTL convened a Committee on the Procedure for Admissions which proposed, in its Second Report, that a clearing house be established to put rejected candidates in touch with universities who had vacancies. Professor Marshall (Sheffield) undertook to organise this.[93] The scheme began on a small scale (in 1960 22 candidates used the scheme, 7 of whom found places);[94] but in the following year Professor Marshall reported that there was a large surplus of candidates; over 100 were without places, and he appealed for help from members in placing them.[95]

The situation was greatly improved when the universities agreed to a proposal emanating from the CVCP that a central, largely standardised system of university admissions should be established, and UCCA was born. A pilot programme ran in 1962 and 1963, following which all the universities in England, Scotland and Wales (except for Oxford, Cambridge and parts of the University of London) began to operate a common scheme in 1964.[96] It would appear that the UCCA system resolved the problems which the SPTL had been trying to address, since the minutes of the General Committee contain no further references to the SPTL's own scheme.

SPTL Conferences

The SPTL conferences in the 1960s continued to be the central activity of the Society. It is difficult to gain an accurate picture of the number of *legal academics* attending the conferences, since numbers given in the reports published in the JSPTL each year are for 'members and their wives'. This number rose from 'over 100' in 1960 to 'some 300' in 1969. However, we are fortunate in having more detailed information about the 1969 Durham conference, which reveals that there were nearly 300 delegates (214 academics (including guests) plus 62 wives/husbands).[97] Comparing these numbers with those in the Wilson survey for the 1965–66 academic year when there were 335 full-time and 113 part-time law teachers, and assuming that the majority of academics attending would have been the full-timers, it would appear that the conference attracted well over half the law teachers in the UK.

Wives continued to attend the annual conferences in relatively large numbers during the 1960s. Sometimes, organisers remembered to mention husbands as

---

[93] General Committee Minutes, 25 March 1960, A.SPTL 1/5.
[94] General Committee Minutes, 16 December 1960, A.SPTL 1/5.
[95] General Committee Minutes, 22 September 1961, A.SPTL 1/5.
[96] Stewart, above n 1, 89
[97] Letter from the then President, Prof FE Dowrick (Durham) to Prof JND Anderson (IALS), dated 19 September 1969, A.SPTL12.

well. The Preliminary Notice for the 1966 conference states that 'All members attending the Meeting are cordially invited to bring their wives or husbands with them to all functions.' In 1968, at Cambridge, the programme included a 'Reception for Wives' given by the wife of the President and a guided visit to the Fitzwilliam Museum 'for wives and others who have indicated a wish to take part'.[98] Despite the fact that women could now be admitted to membership of the SPTL, they did not feature much in the life of the Society, except as wives.

Conferences lasted three days, starting after lunch on day one, and finishing at lunchtime on day three. Generally, there were no more than two substantive sessions during the whole conference, and no parallel sessions except for the Young Members' meeting, which took place at the same time as the General Committee meeting. Topics addressed in the substantive sessions ranged from 'The Uses of Computers for Lawyers' (1965) to 'Statutory Interpretation' and 'Procedure and Evidence following the Criminal Justice Act' (1967) to 'The Work of the Parliamentary Commissioner' (1968) and 'Comparative Law—Expanding Horizons' (1969).[99]

The social programme was prominent. The schedule for the Manchester conference in 1965 is typical: day one contained no business meetings at all—a tour of the Rylands Library was followed by tea, after which time was specifically allocated to allow delegates to change for dinner, before visiting the new Law Faculty building and the Arts library, followed by attendance at an honorary degree ceremony at which degrees were bestowed upon Lord Radcliffe and the distinguished constitutional lawyer, Sir Ivor Jennings. A sherry party was hosted by the University, followed by the Annual Dinner. The following morning, delegates could listen to the Presidential Address on 'Legal Research', followed by a discussion led by Professors FH Lawson (Oxford) and H Street (Manchester). After coffee, there was an address by Colin Tapper (Magdalen College, Oxford) on 'The Uses of Computers for Lawyers' followed by discussion. Lunch was sponsored by Sweet & Maxwell, and the afternoon was spent visiting the radio telescope at Jodrell Bank. In the evening, a buffet supper and reception was sponsored by Butterworths. On the final morning, the General Committee met, and at the same time a meeting was called by AA Bradley (Trinity Hall, Cambridge) 'for members of under five years' standing, to discuss matters of concern to members in the early stages of law teaching'. A demonstration of 'teaching machines and programmed learning, with specific reference to the teaching of law' was followed by coffee and the AGM, before members departed.[100]

The 1966 conference, held in London, and organised by the CLE, was held in

---

[98] SPTL Annual Conference 1968 Second Circular, A.SPTL 26/1.

[99] SPTL Annual Conference 1965 'Provisional Programme; SPTL Annual Conference 1967 'Second Circular; SPTL Annual Conference 1968 'Second Circular'; SPTL Annual Conference 1969 'First Circular', A. SPTL 26/1 and 16/1.

[100] Provisional Programme, SPTL Conference 1965 A.SPTL 26/1; for more information on teaching machines and programmed learning, see FG Healey, J Freeman and JR Hartley 'Programmed, Instruction, Teaching Machines and their Possible Uses in Teaching Law' (1964–65) 8(NS) *JSPTL* 275–83, 281.

July, rather than in September. The date was chosen 'because the courts will still be sitting, and it is hoped that it will be possible for members to meet more judges and practitioners during the meeting than would otherwise be possible'.[101] This conference offered a considerably less ambitious social programme ('Afternoon free; the courts will be sitting') but sessions remained plenary, and the leisurely pace of events is reflected in the fact that the only event on day one was the Presidential Address, and the entire conference contained only one substantive session (a discussion on the Wilson Survey of Legal Education).[102] It is not recorded whether some members sloped off to watch the World Cup Quarter Final on 23 July, although football certainly affected the domestic arrangements of the conference, since hotels in London were full. Delegates were requested to stay with friends if possible, and the organisers made arrangements for private hospitality for those who were unable to find accommodation themselves.[103]

A noticeable feature of the conferences in the 1960s was the continuing presence of judges as speakers. It appears to have been customary to invite at least one judge to speak at the Annual Dinner; thus we find Lord Radcliffe in 1965, the Lord Chancellor and Lord Pearce in 1966, Mr Justice Widgery in 1967, Lord Morris of Borth-y-Gest in 1968 and Lord Kilbrandon in 1969.[104] On other occasions, judges were part of the substantive programme—in 1968, Mr Justice Scarman (as he then was) addressed the conference on 'Law Reform—The Experience of the Law Commission' and in 1969 Lord Wilberforce spoke on 'Educating the Judges'.[105]

Annual conferences continued to be held at different geographical locations, and it appears there was a conscious decision on the part of the Society's officers to try and visit as many different universities as possible. It was still common for the conference to be held at a different university to that of the President, although it appears that by the end of the 1960s, practice was changing, and more conferences were being held at the President's university. Correspondence relating to the Durham Conference shows that when the conference was not held at the President's own institution much liaison took place between organiser and President:

> It would help if you could give me an idea of the seating-plan for High Table, either by letter or on the phone on Monday morning, as the seating plan for all the rest does to some extent depend on the former. . . . If you would like to make suggestions about who sits with whom (and whom to keep apart) at the Dinner . . . we will have time to incorporate these suggestions.[106]

[101] SPTL Annual Meeting 1966, 'Notice', A.SPTL 26/1.
[102] SPTL Annual Meeting 1966 'Programme', A.SPTL 26/1.
[103] http://www.planetworldcup.com/CUPS/1966/wc66index.html; SPTL Annual Meeting 1966 'Notice', A.SPTL 26/1
[104] SPTL Annual Conference 'Programmes'—1965–69, A.SPTL.26/1 and A.SPTL 16/1.
[105] SPTL Annual Conference 'Programmes'—1968 and 1969, A.SPTL.26/1.
[106] Ibid

Holding the conference at a different institution to that of the President did have its advantages; as the Honorary Secretary wrote in 1967 in response to a query from Professor JND Anderson, Director of the Institute of Advanced Legal Studies, who had written suggesting that he might hold the conference out of London:

> Naturally in the normal case Presidents prefer to entertain the society on home ground eg Bristol, Manchester and Birmingham in recent years, but there is little problem since in the normal course of events visits to any particular law faculty would be few and far between. On the other hand, visits to London, Oxford and Cambridge would be more frequent and they are all places where there are difficulties in organising hospitality— as was evidenced last year on the accommodation side. Personally I think there are many advantages in breaking new ground. Members prefer a change of scenery (as you say, this would be the third visit to London in six years), new law schools welcome a conference as giving a boost to their acticities and otherwise we should never visit certain law schools if it depended upon the luck of one of their members being elected President.[107]

Wherever it was held, the conference continued to be the highlight of the Society's year.

The Annual Dinner

The Annual Dinner appears to have been an occasion of some formality. Delegates received specific instructions about the dress code in their conference instructions, and were generally expected to wear dinner jackets, although in London in 1966 'in view of the difficulty that some members might have in arranging to return to their accommodation to change for the Annual Dinner', it was decided that 'dress for the Dinner shall be dinner jackets if convenient but otherwise ordinary suits'.[108] A similar 'dinner jacket, if convenient' dress code applied at Manchester in 1965.[109]

The menu for the 1969 conference at Durham shows a four-course meal (Florida soup, salmon mayonnaise, roast duckling and meringue and apricot) accompanied by sherry (Amontillado/Harvey's Club), white wine with the fish, red with the meat and port, brandy or liqueur (Drambuie or Cointreau) with the coffee. Toasts were given to the Queen, the guests, and the Society, with appropriate responses, and it appears that the whole event was relatively lavish. The conference organiser (Professor Dowrick, Durham) was able to report that

> As we are not so hard pressed for money for the dinner as we once expected to be, I have arranged with the Bursar that the waitresses should press all guests to a second or

---

[107] Letter from J Wilson (Southampton) to Prof JA Anderson (IALS), dated 9 May 1967 SLS Archive; uncatalogued.
[108] SPTL Annual Conference 1966, A.SPTL.26/1.
[109] SPTL Annual Conference 1965 'Provisional Programme', A.SPTL.26/1.

third glass of claret. Cigars will cost us a bit: we thought that those who smoke cigarettes would prefer their own brands. [110]

Despite the hospitality, since the dinner (costing less than £2 a head) attracted sponsorship from Sweet & Maxwell and the University of Durham, the organiser was also able to report that it was not necessary to have an increased conference fee.[111]

The Young Members' Group

The idea that more opportunities should be provided for new law teachers to meet as a group came at the Annual General Meeting of the Society held in September 1964, put forward by Mr AW Bradley (Cambridge). When this idea was considered by the General Committee the following December, it was agreed that, as an experiment, 'a session should be set aside for "junior members" at the meeting in Manchester in 1965', and the President would ask Mr Bradley to prepare a paper for discussion at the session.[112] Accordingly, the programme for the Annual Conference in Manchester announced:

> Meeting called at the suggestion of AW Bradley Esq, MA, LLB, of Trinity Hall, Cambridge, for members of under five years' standing, to discuss matters of concern to members in the early stages of law teaching.[113]

At the following meeting of the General Committee, Mr Bradley reported that a Young Members' Group Committee had been elected at the Manchester meeting, and at its first meeting had decided that membership of the group should be open to members with not more than seven years' experience of law teaching. Its purpose would be 'to provide opportunities for the discussion of matters of common interest to the younger members of the SPTL', and a general meeting of the group would be held annually during the SPTL conference.[114]

The first meeting of the Young Members' Group took place in September 1966, and was a conference on 'The Concept of a Law Degree'. The report of the conference in the *Journal* notes that it was decided 'to proceed from the general to the particular by way of an overall emphasis on the relationship of law and the social sciences'. This approach was intended to promote discussion, particularly the last issue, upon which it was felt opinions were very sharply divided.[115] The

---

[110] Letter from Prof FE Dowrick (conference organiser) to Prof JND Anderson (President) 15 April 1969, A.SPTL.12.

[111] Ibid.

[112] General Committee Minutes 11 December 1964, A.SPTL 1/5.

[113] SPTL Annual Conference 1965 Manchester, letter dated August 1965 from BA Wortley (President) to members, A.SPTL 26/1.

[114] General Committee Minutes December 1965, A.SPTL 1/5.

[115] A Taylor, 'The 1966 Meeting of the Young Members' Group: Introduction' (1966–67) 9(NS) *JSPTL* 328–34, 328.

establishment of the Young Members' Group clearly caused some ripples inside the Society. The report of this first conference notes, with some amusement, that:

> Right up to the eve of the conference, anxieties were still being expressed by persons whose experience ought to have immunized them from the temptation to wild sur-mise. Was the Young Members' Group a band of latter-day Young Turks? Was the conference a political platform? Were we an anti-SPTL and anti-Bar conspiracy? . . . By the close of the conference, the misconception had changed . . . we were 80 or so aca-demics, talking shop; the discussion in the end revolved around four inter-related issues, law and education, the student, the professions and the social sciences.[116]

In the event, the Young Members' Group was to become an important constit-uent of the Society. Its Chair sat on the General Committee, and reports of its meetings continued to appear in the *Journal* throughout the decade. A pattern emerged of the meetings being held immediately after the main conference, and in this way Young Members discussed law examinations at Bristol in 1967, aspects of law degree reform (in particular the new course at Warwick and the four-year degree at Belfast) at Cambridge in 1968, where the first woman (Miss DH Pink, Keele) was elected to the Committee of the Young Members' Group and 'New Developments in Legal Methods' at Durham in 1969.[117] The latter meeting included a paper given by Mr Colin Tapper about computers and the law. He commented that formidable technical problems needed to be overcome, 'but he was confident that with suitable developments in things such as memory banks and optical reading devices, computers would be made useful tools of legal research and practice'.[118]

Socio-Legal and Interdisciplinary Studies

Although socio-legal studies was emerging as an important aspect of the legal academy, it was not yet accepted as completely mainstream.[119] In 1961, for instance, in the context of a report on law libraries, it was noted 'with pleasure' that in many cases the law library was situated in, or in close proximity to, the law department:

> The library being to the lawyer what the bench is to the engineer and the laboratory to the scientist, it is clearly essential that the law library be situated in the closest proxim-ity to the place where tutorial and seminar work is taking place, since the solution of a single problem may well require reference simultaneously to law reports and statutes, treatises and periodical literature.[120]

---

[116] Ibid, 328–9.
[117] See reports of Young Members' Group Meetings: (1966–67) 9(NS) *JSPTL* 396, (1968–69) 10(NS) *JSPTL* 86 and 244.
[118] The 1969 Meeting of the Young Members' Group of the Society (1968–69) 10(NS) *JSPTL* 244.
[119] WL Twining, 'Some Jobs for Jurisprudence' (1974) 1 *BJLS* 149–74.
[120] General Committee Minutes 24 March 1961, A.SPTL 1/5.

There was no thought here of the possibility of legal scholars needing to consult materials in disciplines other than law. However, by 1964, in the context of submitting a memo to the University Grants Commission on libraries, several members of the General Committee 'expressed disquiet at the recommendation that wherever possible the law library should be housed as a separate entity in the law building'.[121] While the discussion does not specifically mention socio-legal studies, the implication is clear that at least some members of the Committee did not wish to pursue such an isolationist policy with regard to the library.

In 1963 the Society submitted a memorandum to the Heyworth Committee on the Future of Social Studies. The purpose of the memo was 'to present and support the view that legal studies within universities falls within the field of social studies research'.[122] The submission consisted of the memo already submitted to the Robbins Committee on Higher Education, together with some additional material. It was pointed out at the General Committee Meeting in December 1963 that the memo submitted to the Robbins Committee had presented law as a social science; in particular stating that:

> The full range of legal studies can only be appreciated when it is realised that the study of law is not confined to the study of rules of law. . . . The jurist is concerned not only with rules of law, but also with the social facts which create law, and which law seeks to control—with human nature itself.[123]

The Legal Education Sub-Committee, led by Professor Montrose, went on to point out that:

> Although sociological jurisprudence is pre-eminently a social science, so too are other branches of jurisprudence and so too is the entire field of law. Legal institutions are organs of social control, and their exposition and consideration constitute social studies, which fall not only within the ambit of faculties of Law, but in many instances are the subject-matter of topics in the list circulated by the secretaries of the Committee on Social Studies. . . . The methods used by the social sciences are employed by legal studies other than penology or criminology. The scope of such empirical studies extends to all fields of law, as the writings of US legal scholars abundantly demonstrate. In the UK, however, it is true that sociological research in law is not as well developed. But it is growing apace as sociological theories of law become more generally adopted.[124]

Interestingly, the eventual memo submitted to the Heyworth Committee adopted a completely different tone, and did not at first make the case for law as a social science, but concentrated on arguing for increased funding for legal studies, including increased numbers of postgraduates and of research institutes similar to the Institute of Criminology at Cambridge, one of the principal functions of

---

[121] General Committee Minutes 11 December 1964, A.SPTL 1/5.
[122] General Committee Minutes 19 September 1963, A.SPTL 1/5.
[123] Memorandum Submitted to the Robbins Committee on Higher Education (1962–1963) ?? (NS) *JSPTL* 115.
[124] General Committee Minutes 13 December 1963, A.SPTL 1/5.

which would be to propose law reform. The introduction was followed by a series of sections making the case for the need for (socio)legal research in various fields, each written by an expert in the area. In some of these sections, there were strong arguments for the need for the development of socio-legal work, though in others the point was made less clearly, or not at all. There were 12 sections, all but one written by academics working in the universities of London or Oxford and Cambridge, the exception being that on general comparative law, written by Professor Wortley of Manchester.[125] The difference between the two versions of the memorandum for the Heyworth Committee would seem to reflect the divergent views held by members of the Society at this time.

The outcome of the Heyworth Committee was not good for law. As a result of the Committee's report, the Social Science Research Council was established. In a circular sent to Vice-Chancellors in 1966 outlining its plans for the award of research grants, it was made clear that law was not to be considered as a discipline qualifying for a specific quota of grants. We shall never know to what extent this decision was influenced by the changes made to the Society's evidence—neither does history record the reaction of Professor Montrose or his sub-committee members.

Even those who were enthusiastic about socio-legal studies had concerns about the capacity of legal academics to develop this new approach. In correspondence in November 1966 with the then Chair of the Young Members' Group, Professor Twining referred to a 'widespread feeling' that

> one of the principal obstacles to the development of a legal literature that is based on a contextual approach to law is the fact that very few members of the law teaching profession have been equipped to undertake the kind of research on which such literature should be based.[126]

He urged the Young Members' Group to address this problem, and received a sympathetic response from his correspondent, David Perrott (Exeter) 'I thoroughly agree about the need for the preparation of law teachers in methodology. . . . Presumably there would have to be some sort of preliminary discussion on what *kind* of preparation this would, or could, be.'[127] Professor Twining responded by expressing concern that

> I feel that there is a danger that too many conferences will be devoted to discussing programmes and not enough time and resources will be devoted to the concrete application of general ideas . . . there would have to be some planning, but I don't see any fundamental difficulties about this. [128]

The diversity of views, even among those who were keen on socio-legal studies, is clearly reflected in some of the papers given at the first Young Members' Group

---

[125] Memorandum Submitted to the Committee on Social Studies (1964–65) 8(NS) *JSPTL* 131–52.
[126] Letter from WLTwining to David Perrott (Exeter), dated 18 November 1966, A.SPTL18/2.
[127] Letter from David Perrott to WL Twining, dated 1 December 1966, A.SPTL 18/2.
[128] Letter from WL Twining to David Perrott (Exeter), dated 17 December 1966, A.SPTL18/2.

conference. KW Wedderburn (LSE) argued that law teachers should bring in 'the socially important factors which the law often leaves out'.[129] However, he saw little room for this approach in the undergraduate curriculum:

> I am convinced that the first few years of an undergraduate course are bound to be taken up with legal technique, and that the most we can do is gradually to infiltrate the social context and a functional approach into our teaching at that point. [130]

Taking a completely different approach, PJ Fitzgerald, talking about the new university at Canterbury (ie Kent University), explained that in Part 1 of their degree students would take courses in economics, economic history, politics and sociology, with one option chosen from law, accounting and statistics. In Part 2, law students could concentrate entirely on law, or take law with one other subject. As far as the approach to teaching law was concerned, it was intended that in teaching Part 2 of the law degree, the Kent law school would try to 'get students to go further and look beyond the actual law itself to its actual functioning in society'.[131]

Some members of the SPTL were also involved in interdisciplinary work. In his Presidential Address in 1969, Professor JND Anderson, Director of the Institute of Advanced Legal Studies, discussed 'the law in its wider setting', and in particular what he termed the 'experiment' carried out throughout the 1960s at the Institute, whereby a number of interdisciplinary discussion groups had been formed, beginning in 1960 with lawyers and economists, followed by lawyers and sociologists (though this group also included psychologists, psychiatrists and others), lawyers and theologians, and lawyers and criminologists.[132] These groups, though very informal, had not been without influence:

> It is significant, I think, that the Lord Chancellor's Committee on the Enforcement of Judgements, under the chairmanship of Mr Justice Payne, was composed almost entirely of some of those who had participated in a discussion on the thesis that 'The methods of enforcing judgements in civil cases create social upheavals disproportionate to the private benefits they produce'; while half the members of the group appointed by the Archbishop of Canterbury to advise him on the reform of the law of divorce—the group which eventually produced the report entitled 'Putting Asunder' were drawn from the group of Lawyers and Theologians which had already, on more than one occasion, discussed that subject. And I am told that other practical results from these discussions may be anticipated before long, chiefly in the field of family law.[133]

While modern readers may cavil at the 'old-boy network' implications of these meetings, which, the President informed members, had resisted any suggestion that their proceedings should be reported 'so as to ensure that all participants,

---

[129] KW Wedderburn, 'Law as a Social Science' (1996–67) 9(NS) *JSPTL* 335–43, 338.
[130] Ibid, 339.
[131] PJ Fitzgerald, 'The Canterbury Plan' (1966–67) 9(NS) *JSPTL* 344–9, 349.
[132] JND Anderson, 'Presidential Address' (1968–69) 10(NS) *JSPTL* 245–53, 251–2.
[133] Ibid, 253.

some of whom hold official positions, may feel at liberty to speak freely', it is nevertheless an indication of the developments that were beginning to take place in socio-legal studies at this time.[134]

Membership Issues

The most controversial issue that the Society faced in the 1960s was the question of precisely who should be eligible to become a member of the Society, and, in particular, whether to admit teachers of law who taught in institutions of higher education other than universities. A substantial number of applications was received from such persons, and by the mid-1960s the officers of the Society were finding it difficult to 'hold the line'. In 1962, the Society resolved to allow members of the College of Law to be eligible to be members of the Society.[135] But the really controversial issue was whether to admit law teachers who worked in polytechnics:

> [T]he name of the Society gives no clear indication of the criteria of eligibility for membership. This has led in recent years to a substantial number of applications being received from law teachers at other institutions where they are engaged in 'the public teaching of law'. The resultant correspondence, often involving detailed explanation of the Society's Rules, has thrown a considerable burden on the officers which at times has been accompanied by a considerable degree of embarrassment.[136]

The matter was referred to a sub-committee, which came to the conclusion that the preferable solution to the problem was to change the name of the Society to the Society of University Teachers of Law. It was felt that membership based on some form of minimum standards would be very difficult to implement, while an extension of membership to all persons engaged in law teaching would fundamentally change the nature of the Society.[137] At the 1966 AGM, therefore, a resolution was put forward proposing that the name of the Society be changed to the Society of University Teachers of Law.[138] This resolution proved to be very controversial; JAG Griffiths and KW Wedderburn wrote urging opposition to the resolution:

> We understand that [the name change] is consequential on the policy of excluding from membership of the Society those teachers of law who are teachers of law in institutions of higher education which do not have university status. In our view, this policy is wholly regrettable and must help to create divisions within the profession of law teaching.

---

[134] Ibid, 253.
[135] General Committee Minutes Special Meeting, 2 November 1962, A.SPTL 1/5.
[136] Letter from JF Wilson (probable date 1966), A.SPTL 18/1 2.
[137] Minutes of General Committee, 18 March 1966, A.SPTL 1/5.
[138] AGM 1966 Agenda, A.SPTL 26/1.

> We write to ask for your support for this view and we hope you will express your opinion by voting against the resolution proposing a change of the Society's name.[139]

At the AGM, opinions were so obviously divided that it was decided to refer the matter back to an expanded sub-committee for further consideration. The first action of the new sub-committee was to circulate a letter to all members of the Society, setting out the background to the debate, together with all the possible options, and asking them to complete a questionnaire detailing their views on the proposed changes.[140] A wide range of possibilities was canvassed, including a change to institutional, rather than individual membership, and the radical step of extending membership to all persons engaged in the public teaching of law, whether at universities, professional law schools, colleges of commerce or technical colleges. The latter option, it had been argued at the AGM, 'meant that the Society would be able to speak with authority on all branches of legal education'.[141] However, there was concern that a radical extension of membership would change the fundamental nature of the Society, especially as the number of law teachers working in colleges of further education was more than three times greater than the number working in universities—in time, university teachers might become a minority within the Society, and there was the risk of a university 'break away' to form a separate society. In addition, the Association of Law Teachers (ALT) had just been created, with membership drawn primarily from colleges of further education. Any radical extension of membership by the SPTL would bring it into direct conflict with the ALT. The consultation paper also included the suggestion that it might be possible to form some 'federal structure' in conjunction with the ALT 'which would incorporate both societies, though allowing each to run its own activities on a sectional basis'.[142]

When the responses were received (with a 60 per cent response rate), there was overwhelming support for the preservation of the existing membership rules, and for a change in the name of the Society, with strong support for some kind of close collaboration with the ALT by the creation of a permanent liaison committee. As a result, the sub-committee reiterated its view that it would be undesirable to change the rules relating to membership of the Society, and recommended that steps should be taken to form a permanent liaison committee to work with the ALT However, it did not recommend that the proposed name-change should be implemented.[143] This brought to an end, at least for a while, the debate over membership.

---

[139] Letter from Griffiths and Wedderburn, dated 13 July 1966, A.SPTL 18/1.

[140] Report of the Sub-Committee on Membership AGM 1967, A.SPTL 26/1.

[141] Minutes of 52nd Annual Meeting 1966, A.SPTL 18/1.

[142] Letter from J.F. Wilson (undated—probable date 1966), A.SPTL 18/1 5.

[143] The Sub-Committee did recommend that a postal ballot of all the membership should confirm any proposed change to the basic constitution of the Society, but did not recommend that such a ballot should be instigated at that time. AGM 1967 Agenda & Report of the Sub-committee on Membership, A.SPTL 26/1.

It is clear that this was not one of the happiest periods in the Society's history. Many of those law teachers who were deemed ineligible to join the Society would have liked to have become members. In the foreword to the history of the first 25 years of the ALT, Jack Jacob wrote:

> Before the creation of the Association of Law Teachers in 1965, law teachers outside the universities could not gain admission to the Society of Public Teachers of Law, which, with anomalous exceptions, limited membership to law teachers within the universities. Law teachers outside the universities felt excluded, without a 'home', with no organisation to which they could belong, and which could represent them in matters relating to legal education . . . establishing a body in parallel with the SPTL, a kind of younger sibling, was clearly sensible, realistic and practical. It has enabled its members to find their identity, integrity and interdependence in their profession as law teachers, but, in truth, the creation of the Association of Law Teachers was an act of faith, which history has fully vindicated.[144]

The decision to exclude many law teachers from membership of the SPTL meant that it has not, since that time, been possible for any one learned society to speak for all law teachers, thus arguably weakening the political strength of the Society. There is little doubt that the decision caused much anger, as reflected in the oblique but pointed comments made in the first issue of the ALT's *Journal* by Stanley Marsh, one of the leading lights in the establishment of the ALT. The purpose of the ALT, and of its *Journal*, he wrote, was to 'help achieve effective teaching of law at all levels, and to provide for maximum communication between teachers of law wherever and whatever they teach'. The result of this philosophy, he went on,

> must be, on the part of the Association, a total rejection of the narrow basis upon which some societies conduct their affairs, a total rejection of the artificial barriers that are raised, barriers based upon levels of subject matter taught or upon academic qualifications as such. At some stage in their careers most teachers probably welcome assistance; such assistance should not be denied merely because of the nature of the work being undertaken by the individual.[145]

Over time, the relationships between the two associations settled down: the joint liaison committee with the ALT (which was mentioned in the SPTL's consultation paper on membership) was successfully established, and had its first meeting in January 1969, at which the representatives discussed, among other things, the evidence to be submitted respectively by the two societies to the Ormrod Committee on Legal Education.[146]

---

[144] J Jacob, 'Foreword' in S Marsh, *A History of the Association of Law Teachers: 1965–1990* (London, Sweet & Maxwell, 1990).

[145] 'Comment' (1967) 1(1) *Journal of the Association of Law Teachers* 1.

[146] 'Report of the General Committee for 1968–1969' 10(NS) *JSPTL* 289–91, 290.

International Relations

It is striking that during the 1960s the Society made continuous efforts to establish and maintain contacts with law teachers in other parts of the world. Some of these efforts were more successful than others; it was reported to the General Committee in March 1960 that a Professor Gledhill had arrived at Allahabad at the stated time to attend a meeting of the Indian Law Teachers Association, but no meeting had taken place. (The SPTL nevertheless paid the £20 which had been authorised for his travel expenses to New Delhi.[147]) The significance of international relations is also reflected in the fact that the SPTL had a liaison officer for the British Council.[148]

The minutes of the General Committee also frequently record requests for English teachers of law to spend one or two years in an overseas university. In 1960 such a request was made for someone to teach in Cairo as part of a comparative law programme. Members were informed that 'the post would carry a high salary and taxation in Egypt was low'.[149] When the Denning Report on the Legal Education of African Students was published in that year, it recommended that each British university law department should be enabled to create an extra post so that at any time one member of staff could be serving in Africa for at least six months.[150] The General Committee responded by resolving that in the light of this suggestion, and of the calls upon university lecturers in the UK, the UGC should be forthwith informed that an increase in the staff of law faculties was essential if they were to play the important role envisaged by Denning.[151]

The following year it was agreed to indicate to the Canadian Association of Law Teachers that it would be valuable experience for UK law teachers to teach for a time in a Canadian university.[152] By 1964, the Canadian Association of Law Teachers had decided to create a committee to investigate the possibility of organising a regular system of exchange between Commonwealth and Canadian law teachers. The General Committee welcomed the idea, and suggested that it could act as a clearing house for information regarding British law teachers who were interested in participating in such a scheme.[153]

Legal education in Africa was considered again in 1963 by an informal committee convened at the suggestion of Mr WL Twining, who suggested that there should be an informal meeting of law teachers in Africa and law teachers in Britain to discuss means of mutual assistance and co-operation.[154] That meeting duly took place, and in 1966 a second informal meeting was held in London

---

[147] General Committee Minutes, 25 March 1960, A.SPTL 1/5.
[148] General Committee Minutes, 24 March 1961, A.SPTL 1/5.
[149] General Committee Minutes, 25 March 1960, A.SPTL 1/5.
[150] *Report of the Committee on Legal Education for Students from Africa* (1961) Cmnd 1255 para 55.
[151] General Committee Minutes, 24 March 1961, A.SPTL 1/5.
[152] Ibid.
[153] 'Editor's Pages' (1965–65) 8(NS) *JSPTL* 31.
[154] General Committee Minutes, 22 March 1963, A.SPTL 1/5.

under the auspices of the British section of the International African Law Association. The meeting focused principally on the recruitment of staff, interchange of staff and students, linking arrangements between British and African faculties, and joint schemes of research and publication.[155]

However, with relatively few resources, there were limits to the Society's overseas commitments. The General Committee regretfully turned down a request from Mr Hannigan of the Royal College in Nairobi asking the SPTL to sponsor or co-ordinate a conference in East Africa, though there was lengthy discussion, and members expressed considerable sympathy towards the request. It was suggested that members who were seconded to African universities or visited them as external examiners might be able to help.[156]

During 1964, there was a great deal of discussion at the General Committee about the arrangements for a joint meeting of the SPTL with the Australian Universities Law Schools Association, an idea which was enthusiastically supported by both societies.[157] Professor Montrose was very active in securing financial support from bodies such as the British Council and the Leverhulme Trust.[158] He led a delegation from the SPTL to the conference, which was held at the University of Sydney, and timed to coincide with the Third Commonwealth and Empire Law Conference. A suitably inscribed gavel and block were presented to the Australian Association, and the trip appears to have been very successful, not only for those who attended, but also in establishing further links with law teachers outside the UK.[159] The Honorary Secretary reported to the following General Committee meeting that while attending the conference he had made enquiries about the possibility of setting up formal machinery for the exchange of law teachers between the UK and Australia, but this seemed impossible, due to the financial difficulties involved. Nevertheless, it was suggested that the Secretary should act as a link to channel information about vacancies in either country.[160]

In 1968 the Society was approached by the organisers of the Philip Jessup mooting competition, which was sponsored by the American Society of International Law, and generally attracted competitors from American law schools. The organisers were keen to draw in teams from UK and Canadian law schools, and Professor Parker, a member of the General Committee, agreed to organise the UK competition.[161] Five teams emerged to form a Southern Division (two from Cambridge and one each from Oxford, UCL and Kings College London), while the Northern Division consisted of four teams (Aberdeen, Durham, Manchester and Sheffield).[162]

[155] 'Second Informal conference of Teachers from British and African Law Faculties', Editor's Page (1966–67) 9(NS) JSPTL 154.
[156] General Committee Minutes, 13 March 1964, A.SPTL 1/1–2 .
[157] General Committee Minutes, 29 May 1964, A.SPTL 1/1–2 .
[158] General Committee Minutes, 11 December 1964, A.SPTL 1/5.
[159] 'Joint Conference of the Society and the Australian Universities Law Schools Association' (1964–65) 8(NS) *JSPTL* 248.
[160] General Committee Minutes, 19 March 1965, A.SPTL 1/5.
[161] General Committee Minutes, 21 March 1969, A.SPTL 1/6.
[162] General Committee Minutes, 10 December 1969, A.SPTL 1/6.

Overall, the Society devoted considerable attention during the 1960s to matters international; it is doubtless the case that more could have been done, but compared with some other periods of the Society's history, it was at this time relatively open to the rest of the world.

Law Libraries

The Society took another step forward when in March 1961 the Library Sub-Committee reported that the Society's 1958 Statement of Library Holdings was now accepted as representing the desirable minimum holdings for law libraries.[163] The statement was to be one of the lasting achievements of the Society, updated from time to time as new developments in information science necessitated adjustments in the holdings. In the wake of the Robbins Report, the Society was also alert to the resource implications of those law schools establishing new law libraries. In 1969 Professor Dowrick (Durham) presented a paper to the General Committee written by himself and Professor Fitzgerald (Kent) which showed that there were considerable variations in the amount of capital and income made available by the UGC to new law schools for establishing a law library. It was agreed that the report of the Minimum Holdings Sub-Committee should include recommendations as to the financing and staffing of law libraries, although a direct approach to the UGC was felt to be inappropriate.[164]

Relations with the Legal Profession

It would appear that the relations between legal academics and practising lawyers continued to be uneasy throughout the 1960s. In his Presidential address in 1960, Professor FH Lawson (Oxford) urged members of the SPTL to consider whether academic lawyers were playing their part in the making, not merely the teaching, of law. A comparatist, he suggested that members of the Society

> should shed such modesty as they may have, and assume as a matter of course something like the responsibility for developing the law that has been exercised by the great jurists of France and Germany, and even in our sister common-law country, America.[165]

One of the reasons he was keen that legal academics should become involved in pressing for new legislation was that

---

[163] General Committee Minutes, 24 March 1961, A.SPTL 1/5.
[164] General Committee Minutes, 19 December 1969, A.SPTL 1/6.
[165] Lawson, above n 72, 183.

Now, generally speaking, lawyers' law has no well-organised pressure group; for the Bar, as a body, is apathetic, and the Solicitors, though they have occasionally stimulated reform, have acted spasmodically, under the spur of some outrage to the feeling for justice. The academic lawyer alone can look comprehensively at even a portion of the law, let alone the law as a whole. Hence it is his responsibility to act with his fellows as a pressure group for reform.[166]

In general, relations with the legal profession during this period proved to be somewhat cool. At the beginning of the decade, the 'new scheme' for training solicitors proved controversial, and the General Committee recommended that a meeting be set up between representatives of the Law Society and a representative from each university in England and Wales to discuss the proposals.[167] Later in 1960, the Law Society approached the universities of Bristol and Manchester with a view to providing courses for Part 1 of the Law Society's examination from October 1962.[168] The universities gave a cautious welcome to the approach, emphasising that their agreement would depend not only on their involvement in the delivery and assessment of the course, but also on an appropriate financial package to cover the costs of additional staff. In response to an enquiry from the Law Society, the General Committee also indicated that 'there was in principle no objection to a student being under articles while studying for a degree, provided that it was realised that during term-time this would require full-time attendance at the University'.[169]

A special meeting of the General Committee was held in 1964 to discuss the decision by the Council of Legal Education to abolish the December Bar examinations. After discussion, it was acknowledged that this decision fell solely within the jurisdiction of the Council, and that it was done to improve the academic standing of the exam, with which the Society did not disagree, but considerable disquiet was expressed about the lack of consultation with law schools, whose students were affected by the decision.[170]

Further evidence of the uneasy relations between the Society and the legal professions emerged when new regulations for Part 1 of the Bar examinations were introduced in 1966. Although they were generally welcomed by members of the General Committee, some members questioned the value of a compulsory paper in substantive legal history, and concern was expressed about the precise requirements for this paper, and the new papers in constitutional and administrative law, as well as the exact grounds upon which claims by students for exemptions would be considered.[171] By the following year, members were reporting a range of difficulties, and a meeting was set up with representatives of the Council of Legal Education.[172] However, no general scheme for granting

---

[166] Ibid.
[167] General Committee Minutes, 25 March 1960, A.SPTL 1/5.
[168] General Committee Minutes, 16 December 1960, A.SPTL 1/5.
[169] Ibid.
[170] General Committee Minutes, 29 May 1964, A.SPTL 1/1–2.
[171] General Committee Minutes, 18 March 1966.
[172] General Committee Minutes, 22 September 1967, A.SPTL 1/5.

exemptions emerged, and as the decade drew to a close, members reported that the Council of Legal Education had in a number of ways adopted 'unexpected attitudes' with regard to exemptions:

> In particular, law schools had been asked for particulars of courses, and second class performance had been required from students taking mixed degrees where law students had been asked for a third class performance in precisely the same paper. Both matters appeared to be infringements of the principles which had been agreed with the Bar the previous year.[173]

Although some progress was made in the relationship between the Society and the professions when the Law Society invited the SPTL to nominate a person to sit on its Legal Education Committee, overall, relations between the legal professions and the Society during the 1960s seem to have been lukewarm at best.[174]

The Ormrod Committee

Relations with the legal profession were brought to the fore again towards the end of the decade when, on 20 December 1967, the Lord Chancellor announced in the House of Lords that a Committee was to be established under the chairmanship of Lord Ormerod with the following terms of reference:

> 1. To advance legal education in England and Wales by furthering co-operation between the different bodies now actively engaged in legal education.
> 2. To consider and make recommendations upon training for a legal professional qualification in the two branches of the legal profession, with particular reference to:
>   (a) the contribution which can be made by the universities and colleges of further education
> and
>   (b) the provision of training by the Law Society and the Council of legal Education, the co-ordinating of such training and of qualifying examinations relating thereto.

The SPTL was well represented on the Committee: Mr Ll Armitage (Cambridge), Professor Crane (Queen Mary) and Professor JF Wilson (Southampton) were all members. The Society submitted substantial evidence to the Committee, and was able to use the information gathered in the survey of legal education, benefiting from the foresight of Professor Montrose and others who had instigated the survey.[175] Having noted the upward trends in student numbers, the memorandum argued that facilities for legal education need to be increased—not by adding to the number of institutions offering Law, but by enabling established institutions to cope with greater numbers of students.[176]

---

[173] General Committee Minutes, 19 December 1969, A.SPTL 1/6.
[174] Ibid.
[175] Lord Chancellor's Committee on Legal Education: Memorandum from the Society of Public Teachers of Law (1968–69) 10(NS) *JSPTL* 157–68, 157.
[176] Ibid, 158.

The memorandum gives a further insight into relations between legal academics and the legal profession. It was critical of the professional exams, with their emphasis on rote learning, and of the arrangements for granting exemptions; it noted that:

> many university law teachers are of the opinion that the recent changes in the structure of professional requirements have not been sufficiently thoroughgoing, nor are they satisfied that the objectives of the professional examination have been sufficiently defined . . . [leading] to unnecessary duplication between university and professional teaching and to the omission of certain vital aspects of professional training.[177]

The point was made that law teachers wished to place emphasis on legal techniques and the depth of intellectual training, rather than on the 'coverage of a prescribed number of branches of the law as found in current textbooks'.[178] Anticipating closer links between Britain and Europe (regardless of whether the UK would join the EEC) knowledge of other legal systems is seen as desirable, and the memorandum also argued that:

> certain aspects of the social sciences, such as economics and sociology may increasingly be regarded as an acceptable part of a [law degree]. Developments of this kind will be brought about as much by greater attention being given by the university law teacher to the economic and social aspects of his subject as by the inclusion within the degree curriculum of new courses taught by specialists from other disciplines.[179]

Law departments, it was stressed, did not exist solely to offer basic legal education to the future practitioner, but were also responsible for furthering scholarship and research in law 'both of the traditional kind and also in newer forms employing methods which are increasingly likely to be inter-disciplinary'.[180]

It would appear that the SPTL had concerns that the Ormrod Committee might bow to pressure from the legal profession, and make recommendations which would curtail the freedom of university law schools to organise their own affairs:

> Law faculties recognise their responsibilities to the legal profession and to the public which the profession serves, but their immediate academic responsibility is to their own universities. It would neither be consistent with this responsibility, nor in the best interest of the future development of legal education, if the reform of the legal profession led to external restrictions on the freedom of each faculty to choose its students, to construct its own degree courses, and to regulate its own teaching and examination methods...This diversity must not be endangered in the interests of establishing uniform entry requirements for the legal profession.[181]

In order to facilitate negotiations between the legal profession and the universities in this controversial area, the memorandum suggested that a joint standing

---

[177] Ibid, 158.
[178] Ibid, 159.
[179] Ibid, 159.
[180] Ibid, 160.
[181] Ibid, 161.

committee 'fully representative both of the universities and the two branches of the profession' should be established, pointing out that if this arrangement were to receive the full support of law schools, it would have to have parity of representation between the universities and the legal profession.[182]

The memorandum ended with a plea for more research into legal education since 'Without this, it is likely that Law will not benefit from the increasing amount of research now being done into university and professional education.'[183]

Law Reform

In 1965, the newly established Law Commission invited the Society to set up a process so that its members, as well as the Bar and the Law Society, would be in a position to comment on the Commission's proposals.[184] The Society responded by establishing a Law Reform Co-ordinating Committee in January 1966, which set up specialist sub-committees, made up of both senior and unpromoted members of the Society, and drawing members from a range of universities.[185] The first six sub-committees were tort, contract, criminal law, family law, public law and transfer of land.[186] A report by the Society's Treasurer, Professor Crane (Queen Mary) notes that in the first seven months of the existence of this system, the Law Commission sent 13 memoranda for consideration:

> Our Sub-Committees and Convenors have, I believe, acted quickly and efficiently. Nevertheless, we are part-time law reformers, with activities geared to University terms and requirements, dealing with a full-time Commission, charged by statute with the duty of formulating proposals for reform and a timetable geared to its internal workings and legislative possibilities. (Thus our May/June preoccupation with examinations was inevitably irrelevant to the Commission's timetable on Restrictive Covenants). [187]

Despite the pressures of other work, members of the Society continued to be active in law reform matters throughout the 1960s. The Society was represented on the Working Party on Restrictive Covenants in 1967, and several members were appointed to an Advisory Committee to assist the Commission in its project to codify the law of contract.[188] In addition to routine work on law reform, the Law Commission was the subject of a plenary address at the Annual Conference in 1968, and two seminars were held jointly with the Law Commission (one in

---

[182] Ibid, 164.

[183] Ibid, 168.

[184] The Law Commission was established by the Law Commissions Act 1965; see Scarman J, 'Law Reform—The Experience of the Law Commission' (1968–69) 10(NS) *JSPTL* 91–100.

[185] General Committee Minutes, 18 March 1966, A.SPTL 1/5.

[186] 'Report of the General Committee for 1965–1966' (1965–66) 9(NS) *JSPTL* 259–62, 261.

[187] General Committee Minutes, 23 July 1966 (Law Reform Report by Prof Crane), A.SPTL 1/5.

[188] 'Report of the General Committee for 1966–1967' (1965–66) 9(NS) *JSPTL* 452–5, 454.

September 1968 at Nottingham to discuss codification of the criminal law and one the following year at Birmingham on classification).[189] At the request of the Law Commission, the Family Law Sub-committee produced in 1969 a study of 'The Illegitimate Child in English Law', which was the first time the Society had been approached in this way.[190]

The SPTL in the 1960s

The 1960s saw the SPTL caught up in the expansion of higher education brought about largely as a result of the Robbins Report, with new law departments opening, and increasing numbers of law students and law teachers. During this decade, the Society argued for better remuneration for law teachers, being specifically mentioned by Halsey and Trow, in their study of British academics, as one of the bodies which submitted evidence to the National Incomes Commission, along with the Royal Veterinary College, the British Medical Association and the Royal Society.[191] This was also the decade which saw the first of the large-scale surveys of law schools and law teachers, conducted by John Wilson under the auspices of the SPTL. This initiative was to become one of the most significant and enduring contributions to legal education research and policy-making that the Society has ever achieved.

On the other hand, we learn from Presidential Addresses that there was much to be critical about in the state of legal scholarship and education. It is also clear that the Society's conferences were largely social affairs, with little academic input, and it was during the 1960s that members of the Society were deeply divided over the question of whether to admit polytechnic law teachers to membership of the Society. The failure to do so may be seen as one of the bleakest moments in the Society's history.

Yet this was the decade which saw the birth of the Young Members' Group—a group which was to become highly significant in changing the Society from its rather gentle 1960s existence to a somewhat more dynamic body.

---

[189] 'Annual Meeting of the Society 1968' (1968–1969) 10(NS) *JSPTL* 85; Report of the General Committee for 1968–1969 (1968–69) 10(NS) *JSPTL* 288–91, 290.
[190] 'Report of the General Committee for 1968–1969' (1968–69) 10(NS) *JSPTL* 288–91, 290.
[191] Halsey and Trow, above n 25, 184.

8

The 1970s: Reform Begins

[T]he SPTL as at present organised has shown itself incompetent to fulfil the very considerable responsibilities that have been put upon it and that it has light-heartedly accepted. For lack of any alternative it is the universities' law schools' pressure group, but it still behaves like some kind of universities' law schools' club.

(Memorandum from Professor GP Wilson for discussion at Special Meeting of SPTL, November 1973)

Reforming the Society

The Young Members' Group began the decade with a bang, by taking up the challenge of the outgoing President in 1970, Professor Cross (Oxford), to consider the future activities of the Society. A memorandum was drafted by the Young Members' Group Committee and submitted to the General Committee at the AGM in 1971. It noted the marked expansion in the number of law teachers and law students as a result of the Robbins Report, and the rapid increase in membership of the Society, from 256 members in the first edition of the Directory (published in 1952) to 1,201 in the 19th edition (published in 1970).[1] Equally, the content of the curriculum, teaching methods and degree structures were changing, with 'wide acceptance of the idea of "law as a liberal study" and some movement away from purely vocational subjects', as well as an increasing number of joint degrees.[2]

Against this background of change and expansion, however, the memorandum suggested that there was some feeling that the Society was 'inflexible,

---

[1] The 1,201 members in 1970's Directory included 604 Ordinary Members, 426 Overseas Members and 171 Honorary, Emeritus and Associate Members; 'The Future of the Society of Public Teachers of Law', Memorandum from Young Members Group presented at Annual Conference 1971, A.SPTL 26.1, paras 1.i and 1.ii The relatively large proportion of overseas members is perhaps an indication of the comparative dearth of similar associations in other jurisdictions.

[2] 'The Future of the Society of Public Teachers of Law', Memorandum from Young Members Group presented at Annual Conference 1971, A.SPTL 26.1 para 1.iii.

rigid and incapable of coping with the developments that have occurred'.[3] The formation of the Young Members' Group in 1966, it argued,

> was indicative of a feeling of frustration or disappointment among some members with the direction pursued by the main Society. The formation of the Association of Law Teachers in 1965 highlighted the limited and restrictive role this Society seems to wish to play. And Professor Cross's public invitation to members to consider the future activities and essential functions of the Society recognised the need for reappraisal that individuals had long been admitting to privately.[4]

The memorandum listed ten of the main failings of the Society. Foremost among these was the restrictive and elitist attitude of the Society in terms of membership, excluding, in effect, all teachers of law except those in universities: 'at present, the exclusion of such teachers who are engaged in full time law teaching appears to be nothing short of ridiculous'.[5] Apathy and lack of interest in the Society was reflected in poor attendance at SPTL functions and meetings.

> A popular conception of the annual meeting as a social gathering where members may sip free champagne is one sad example of this. The complaint is not against the social gathering as such, nor, of course, the free champagne—but that this appears, with justification, to be the main function of the meeting.[6]

Members felt uninvolved—there was little decision-making to be involved in, and the structure of the Society, with its large General Committee, representing institutions rather than individuals, was 'antiquated and inappropriate'.[7] As a representative body of law teachers the Society was ineffective, and, perhaps most damning of all, it was seen as failing to cater for the professional interests of its members in any significant way. 'No initiative is taken to stimulate or inform members working in specialist fields.'[8]

This catalogue of criticisms was seen as reflecting a general malaise within the Society, which the memorandum then sought to address by suggesting some guiding principles which should be reflected in the way the Society was organised and developed. These included consideration of the extent to which the Society should engage in 'trade union' activities to protect and further its members' interests, and thinking about its responsibilities towards those areas of activity in which its members were involved, such as legal publishing, by, for example, sponsoring a new book series or stimulating co-operation between members in the preparation of new books of readings or casebooks.[9] The Society was urged to think more broadly about its responsibilities towards legal education, in terms of

---

[3] Ibid, para 1.v.
[4] Ibid, para 1.vi.
[5] Ibid, para 2(i)a.
[6] Ibid, para 2 (i)b.
[7] Ibid, para 2 (i)c–f.
[8] Ibid, para 2 (i)g–h.
[9] Ibid, para 3A and B.

having policies on the establishment of new law faculties or departments and colleges of further education teaching law, as well as on co-operation with, and criticism of, the other branches of the legal profession.[10] The Society was also urged to think about its responsibilities to the law itself, not only in terms of involvement in law reform, but also by setting up specialist groups to keep up to date with and engender new developments in the law.[11] 'Finally', the memorandum concluded: 'if there is a theme running through the previous considerations, it is that a Society representing law teachers in Great Britain should be an active body, not merely a polite social grouping.'[12]

The memorandum then turned to specific reforms that it urged the SPTL to implement. Foremost among these was that membership of the Society should be open to all those engaged in teaching law for a degree course—whether a university degree or a degree of the Council of National Academic Awards.[13] The Society was also urged to set up its own specialist bodies to deal with matters such as library holdings, the Ormrod Report, law student concerns, law publishing and liaison with the legal profession. Specialist groups in substantive areas of law should hold workshops and publish newsletters. 'Underlying all this is the conception of the Society being an active rather than a passive body.'[14] The Annual Conference should not be a mainly social gathering, but should involve a series of business meetings looking at the problems of law teaching generally, as well as other matters within the competence of the Society, and it should also be a time for holding meetings of the specialist groups.[15]

The memorandum also suggested that the Society's *Journal* should be wider in outlook, and should be supplemented by newsletters and bulletins which would facilitate the circulation of news and information between members whose work on specialist topics would benefit from sharing of views and ideas, as well as containing news about ongoing and planned research projects.

> It seems to us that a further clear value of such a newsletter, appearing several times a year, would be the opportunity for creating just that sense of 'identity' and 'purpose' in the body of the Society which seems to be lacking at present. The editorial correspondence published in the newsletter, and the short notes and comments which members could submit, would enable continuing discussions to take place throughout the year on matters of general interest and importance.[16]

Finally, the memorandum urged the Society to reform its 'cumbrous and ineffective' structure, in particular the General Committee, which was seen as too large to be a workable decision-making unit. Equally, consideration should be given to

[10] Ibid, para 3C.
[11] Ibid, para 3C.
[12] Ibid para 3E.
[13] Ibid para 4a.
[14] Ibid, para 4b.
[15] Ibid, para 4c.
[16] Ibid, para 4d.

establishing a full-time secretariat, to relieve pressure on the (voluntary) Honorary Secretary.[17]

At the AGM in 1971, on the basis of a motion submitted by the Young Members' Group, the Society agreed to set up a Working Party to consider the proposals in the memorandum and to make recommendations for a new constitution for the Society.[18] The Working Party was duly established under the chairmanship of Professor PS James (Leeds), then President of the Society.[19]

Reforms as a Result of the Young Members' Group Memorandum

The President in 1973, Professor RH Graveson (London), appears to have been all too aware of communication difficulties within the Society, and he used his Presidential Address to urge members to try and overcome these:

> [But] in this endeavour, it is for our senior members to take the initiative. It was one of our former Presidents, Professor Archie Campbell, who remarked to me that for the first half of his career he knew only the young members, and for the second half only the old ones . . . if we bring this problem into the open, we shall at least have a chance of dealing with it, as I hope we shall all try to do.[20]

Spurred on by the publication of a *Newsletter* by the Young Members' Group, and the points made in the memorandum, the General Committee decided to publish a general *Newsletter* for the Society, to 'deal with all matters of more topical interest which are of concern to the Society'.[21] Writing in the Foreword to the first issue in March 1973, Professor Graveson noted that difficulties in communication were a natural by-product of increasing size and dispersion, as well as diversity of interests and specialisation, and the need for effective communication of topical matters within the Society was self-evident.

The Young Members' memorandum was also effective in getting the Society to reform its somewhat cumbersome administrative structure, whereby the only decision-making body was the General Committee, which consisted of all the Officers of the Society, plus a representative from each constituency. Amendments to the Society's Rules were agreed which established an Executive Committee to manage the Society's affairs between meetings of the General Committee, which was renamed the Council of the Society. The Executive Committee was to consist of the Officers and three other members of Council, two of whom were to be of less than ten years' standing as members of the Society. These constitutional

---

[17] Ibid, para 4e.
[18] Ibid, 'Conclusion'.
[19] 'Annual Report of the Society 1971–72' (1972–73) 12(NS) *JSPTL* 277.
[20] RH Graveson, 'Presidential Address' (1974–75) 13(NS) *JSPTL* 7.
[21] *SPTL Newsletter* No 1 March 1973, A.SPTL 17.

changes were passed by 'overwhelming majorities' at the AGM in 1973, and the first meeting of Council was held on 13 December 1973.[22]

It is clear from the *Newsletter* that in the years after the publication of the Young Members' Group memorandum, the Society made an effort to become more active and to involve members in its activities. The *Newsletter* continued to appear regularly, and contained a large number of notices about conferences, symposia and colloquia of potential interest to SPTL members, including the International Congress of Comparative Law held in Tehran, and a colloquium on Welsh medieval law focusing on 'the law of women'.[23]

The increased amount of activity generated by the reforms which the Society implemented during the early 1970s necessitated an rise in the price of members' subscriptions in 1975. In particular, Butterworths 'had felt obliged to reconsider the terms of the agreement reached with the Society in 1955 regarding the sharing of the cost of publishing the Directory and the *Journal* (which in 1955 began to appear twice yearly)'.[24] Under the new agreement, Butterworths would still make a substantial contribution, but the Society would be required 'to bear a fair share of the considerable publishing costs involved'.[25] Since there had been no change in membership rates since 1957, an increase was long overdue. However, it was clearly controversial. Announcing the proposed subscription increase to Council, the Honorary Treasurer gave detailed reasons for its implementation and also indicated that it was being kept to a minimum; at the same time as the subscription increase was proposed, Council was being advised by the Executive Committee of various economies which were being contemplated, including the possibility of the Directory being published biennially, with amendment lists in the intervening years, and the reversion of the *Journal* to one issue a year.[26]

It was the financial issues of the mid-1970s that also provided the catalyst for reform of the content of the Society's *Journal*. Since its establishment in 1924 the *Journal* had been a mixture of an academic journal and a newsletter. However, in 1975 it was decided to revert to publishing only one edition a year, as had been the case when the *Journal* was first published. The Editor was no longer to regard himself as under an obligation to publish reports of the proceedings of the annual meetings, and, most significantly, the *Journal* was no longer to focus exclusively on legal education, but would include articles 'of more general legal interest'.[27] The Senior Editor of the *Journal*, Professor JA Jolowicz, encouraged members to send in contributions; his appeal is somewhat apologetic, perhaps reflecting the lack of status which the Journal enjoyed at that time:

[22] *SPTL Newsletter* No 1 March 1973, A.SPTL 17; *SPTL Newsletter* No 3 November 1973 A.SPTL 17, 5; *SPTL Newsletter* No 4 March 1974, A.SPTL 17, 4. SPTL AGM 1973 Leeds; Agenda, private papers of WL Twining.
[23] *SPTL Newsletter* No 4 March 1974, A.SPTL 17, 6.
[24] *SPTL Newsletter* No 6 May 1975, A.SPTL 17, 1.
[25] Ibid.
[26] *SPTL Newsletter* No 5 December 1974, A.SPTL 17, 2; *SPTL Newsletter* No 6 May 1975, A.SPTL 17, 1.
[27] *SPTL Newsletter* No 6 May 1975, A.SPTL 17, 4.

I appreciate that members will feel that their articles are likely to reach a wider audience if published in one of the other periodicals, but I very much hope that, in future, members will be willing to submit articles of general legal interest to the Society's Journal.[28]

Reverting to the publication of only one issue of the *Journal* per year also necessitated a change in policy as regards book reviews. While these would continue to feature, it was decided that the Editor should not feel obliged to publish reviews of new editions of established textbooks, or of practitioners' books, and that review essays surveying current thinking on legal education in a particular area were of particular interest, as would reviews indicating the utility of a book to the teaching of a subject.[29] This policy is consonant with the other efforts which were being made at this time to improve the standing of the *Journal* by developing it into a general academic publication.

Reforming the Society was not an easy undertaking; members had to be persuaded that the increased costs involved would be worthwhile, and it would appear that not all members appreciated the need for the SPTL to speak with a more confident voice, illustrated by the memorandum on 'Preparation of Legislation' which was submitted to the Renton Committee.[30] Members were informed of the terms of reference of the Committee and invited to send in evidence, which was in line with the efforts to reform the Society.[31] However, the response itself is hedged about with qualifications:

> [The memorandum] does not purport to represent the views of all, or even a substantial number of SPTL members, rather it represents a number of points which a comparatively small but fairly representative committee of members felt were worthy of consideration by Sir David Renton and his colleagues. Some of the points were unanimously endorsed by the committee, some by majority, some only by minority but accepted by majority as suitable to be put forward.[32]

By the time the Renton Committee had digested all the qualifications, one wonders how persuasive was the actual evidence submitted. The tentative tone gives weight to the Young Members' view that the Society lacked strong leadership.

Some Presidents of the Society also expressed reservations which indicate that they were not at ease with the new reforms. In December 1974 the then President, Professor Parker (Exeter), appears to be so concerned by the difficulties of representing the collective view of the Society that he urges complete inaction:

> I am only too well aware that criticism has often been levelled at the Society in that it has been too slow or even completely silent when it should have expressed quickly and

---

[28] *SPTL Newsletter* No 6 May 1975, A.SPTL 17, 4.
[29] *SPTL Newsletter* No 7 January 1976, A.SPTL 17, 2–3. A large number of book reviews were also published in the Society's *Newsletter*.
[30] 'Preparation of Legislation: Memorandum' (1974–75) 13(NS) *JSPTL* 96.
[31] *SPTL Newsletter* No 3 November 1973, A.SPTL 17, 7.
[32] 'Preparation of Legislation: Memorandum' (1974–75) 13(NS) *JSPTL* 96.

with force the views of University Law Schools on matters which fall within its ambit. But I always wonder if such critics would really welcome the Society, through its Officers, speaking out on important matters, ostensibly in the name of the Society, when the views expressed are quite likely to be diametrically opposed to the views held by many of its members. . . . Indeed, perhaps the only principle to which we in this Society should subscribe is the principle of complete freedom of opinion as to the aims and purposes of legal education. But this makes it extremely difficult, even impossible, for the Society to present a collective view to the outside world.[33]

Such sentiments hardly represent a rallying-cry for radicalism, but they do serve as a reminder that not all members of the Society were equally critical of its somewhat conservative nature, and that considerable obstacles stood in the way of those who were.

Activities of the Young Members' Group

The Young Members' Group continued to play a leading role in reforming the Society. Thus in 1973 its Chairman, Ian Fletcher, wrote to the SPTL Honorary Secretary, James Read, to press for progress in introducing elected members of the new Executive Committee:

I suppose that the idea of electing, by convention, the Chairman and immediate past Chairman of YMG may be one of the proposals to be canvassed: I feel it would be invidious of me to communicate this suggestion directly to the President, although as a matter of fact this was the arrangement which the YMG specifically envisaged at its 1972 Annual General Meeting, so it would certainly be welcomed by the Group if it came about![34]

This received a sympathetic response from the Honorary Secretary, who shared his own disappointment that the process of electing constituency representatives annually seemed to have fallen by the wayside; 'It is a little sad that some members are hardly aware of the elections.'[35]

The academic part of the Young Members' Group annual meetings continued to address a variety of topics, including 'small claims' at Leeds in 1972, 'police methods and their propriety' and 'environmental pressure groups for the enactment of legislation' at Sheffield in 1973, and 'legal teaching techniques' at Cardiff in 1974, followed by devolution in 1976.[36] There was a particularly lively

---

[33] *SPTL Newsletter* No 5 December 1974, A.SPTL 17, 1.

[34] Letter from Ian Fletcher, Chair, Young Members' Group, to James Read, Hon Sec SPTL 10.9.1973, A.SPTL 26.

[35] Letter from James Read, Hon Sec, to Ian Fletcher, Chair, Young Members' Group, 20.9.1973, A.SPTL 26.

[36] *SPTL Young Members' Group Newsletter* November 1972, 1, A.SPTL 26; SPTL Young Members' Group Conference Programme, Sheffield, 1-2 September 1973(note that the date is wrongly typed as 1972 on the original document), A.SPTL 26; SPTL Young Members' Group Booking Form 1974 Cardiff, private papers of WL Twining; *SPTL Newsletter* No 9 February 1977, A.SPTL 17, 22.

programme at Manchester in 1978 when speakers included a Home Office pathologist and Baroness Lockwood, Chair of the Equal Opportunities Commission.[37] Baroness Lockwood's talk was subsequently reported in *The New Law Journal*.[38]

The Young Members' Group talks on 'legal teaching techniques' in 1974 were delivered by Professor William Twining (Warwick) and Professor JC Smith (Nottingham).[39] Accepting the invitation, Professor Twining comments:

> The topic you suggest is a bit broad, and your description of the occasion makes it sound as if you are inviting a series of oldies to try to teach their grandchildren how to suck eggs—however, since it will be my fortieth birthday the following day, this will no doubt be appropriate in my case.[40]

Notes of the talk given by Professor Twining indicate that he asked his audience whether they had read any of a list of nine books about pedagogy, including Donald Bligh's *What's the Use of Lectures?* (1971), Benjamin Bloom's *Taxonomy of Educational Objectives* (1956) and Tansy and Unwin's *Simulation and Gaming in Education* (1969). He also wanted to know if they had read any of a list of six titles about *legal* education, including articles by Laswell and McDougal on 'Legal Education for Public Policy', and by Coutts on 'Examinations for Law Degrees'.[41] He followed this up by giving participants a questionnaire, demanding yes/no answers to a series of further questions, including:

Have you ever:
a)   Formulated in writing the objectives of a course you are teaching?
b)   Set a multiple choice examination?
c)   Used algorithms in teaching?
d)   Seen a video recording of yourself teaching?
e)   Seen notes written by students in your lectures?
f)   Invited students to assess your course after it is over?
g)   Sat one of your own examination papers under exam conditions?
h)   Taken a course on teaching methods?
i)   Participated in a seminar/course on legal education?
If the above questions were a test of educational professionalism for law teachers, do you consider that on your performance you deserved to be awarded:
   a) a distinction b) a credit c) a bare pass d) a fail?
Is this a fair test for members of the SPTL, YMG? If not, why not?
What general points about law teaching and teaching in general has the questionnaire been designed to get across?
What pedagogical devices and techniques have been used in this questionnaire?[42]

---

[37] *SPTL Newsletter* No 13 March 1979, A.SPTL 17, 26.

[38] See [1978] *NLJ* 966.

[39] SPTL Young Members' Group Conference Flier 1974; private papers of WLTwining.

[40] Letter dated 29 November 1973 from Prof William Twining to Jim Schofield, Secretary, Young Members' Group, private papers of WL Twining.

[41] Notes by WL Twining for his talk to the Young Members' Group, Cardiff, 1974, private papers of WL Twining.

[42] Notes for a talk by Prof William Twining at SPTL Young Members' Group Conference 1974, private papers of WL Twining.

Perhaps the Young Members' Group got more than they bargained for! The report of the meeting describes Professor Twining's presentation as 'totally disconcerting'.[43] Nevertheless, the experience cannot have been that bruising, since the Group invited Professor Twining to address them again in 1979 at Leicester, on the topic of 'Four Year Degrees in Law'.[44]

The Ormrod Report on Legal Education and Relations with the Professions

The Ormrod Committee on Legal Education reported in March 1971, and the progress of its implementation was followed closely by the Society.[45] At the Annual Conference in Edinburgh later that year, speakers recognised the key recommendation of the Report as being that a law degree should be the normal condition of entry to the legal profession, not merely allowing law graduates to gain exemptions from parts of the professional examination, but being recognised without more as permitting law graduates to complete the academic stage of training.[46] The effect of this proposal would be to exclude the legal profession entirely from having any significant influence over the academic stage of legal education. However, the shift in the balance of power from the professions to academia which this recommendation represented was to prove far from uncontroversial.

The report of the discussion groups held at the Annual Conference in 1971 reveals that it was generally agreed that the Ormrod proposals gave law schools some freedom to develop their interests within a basic framework, but underlying concerns about relations with the legal profession were also voiced 'it was felt that it was necessary for professional bodies to accept the qualifications granted by universities without detailed specification'.[47] Equally, it was noted that many law students did not wish to enter the legal profession, and that their needs and requests should also be catered for. On the other hand, it was reported that:

> Great advantages were seen in a system whereby practitioners were involved in law teaching, as happens in the medical profession . . . one result of involving practitioners in teaching would be an increase in interchange of ideas between academic and practitioner as well as possible increase in status, reputation and remuneration.[48]

This latter comment is perhaps most revealing in its indication of a considerable

---

[43] *SPTL Newsletter* No 5 December 1974, A.SPTL 17, 10.
[44] Letter dated 5 January 1979 from RCA White (Leicester) Chair, Young Members' Group, to Prof WL Twining, private papers of WL Twining.
[45] Report of the Committee on Legal Education (1971) Cmnd 4595.
[46] Ibid, para 103; 'The Ormrod Report' (1972–73) 12(NS) *JSPTL* 39–55.
[47] 'The Ormrod Report', above n 46, 49.
[48] Ibid.

lack of self-confidence among some legal academics, who clearly saw members of the legal profession as superior in status and reputation. Nevertheless, the report of the discussions also reveals that a significant proportion of contributors were clear that, so far as the academic stage was concerned, law teachers were the experts, and should resist undue interference in academic matters by the professions.

Commentators at the time recognised that the relationship between the legal academy and the legal professions was key. Harry Arthurs, offering a reaction to the Ormrod Report from a Canadian perspective, noted that:

> Of all the issues raised by the Report, none is more thoroughly explored, and yet less clearly resolved, than that of the profession's influence over the education of its prospective members.[49]

Arthurs's concerns were echoed by Robert Stevens, comparing the situation in the UK with that of the USA. Commenting that 'A powerful elite profession is not likely to hand over powers of admission to a group of academics over whom it has no control—at least, not without a fight', Stevens noted that the Report itself stressed the need for mutual trust and respect.[50] His scepticism about whether the legal professions would in reality leave legal education entirely to academics was pithily expressed: 'As a good trade unionist, my natural instinct is to enthuse over such sentiments. For the success of the proposals, however, I can only say that I hope the statements are realistic.'[51] Arthurs and Stevens were both offering an outsiders' perspective on the report. But insiders also had concerns: Geoffrey Wilson, writing in the *Modern Law Review,* also concluded his analysis of the report by focusing on future relations between the profession and academia, noting that 'it has yet to be seen' what progress has been made in furthering co-operation between 'the different bodies now actively engaged in legal education'.[52] Phil Thomas and Geoff Mungham expressed similar concerns in their analysis of the Report, questioning the precise nature of the co-operation envisaged between the professional bodies and the law schools, and commenting:

> While we do not suggest that the relationship between the schools and the profession is likely to plummet to the level of internecine warfare, we are aware that the influence of the professional bodies on law school curricula would tend to be exercised in a conservative direction.[53]

In the event, the aftermath of Ormrod proved to be one of the biggest disappointments the Society had faced. After the Report had been delivered, the members of the Ormrod Committee, apparently feeling that they had achieved enough, suggested that its recommendations should be implemented by another

---

[49] H Arthurs, 'The Ormrod Report: A Canadian Reaction' (1971) 34 *MLR* 642.
[50] R Stevens, 'American Legal Education: reflections in the light of Ormrod' (1972) 35 *MLR* 248.
[51] Ibid, 248–9.
[52] GP Wilson, 'Reflections on the Ormrod Committee' (1971) 34 *MLR* 641.
[53] PA Thomas and G Mungham, 'English Legal Education—A Commentary on Ormrod' (1972) 7 *Valparaiso University Law Review* 119.

committee.[54] The Lord Chancellor's Advisory Committee on Legal Education was established to do this. However, although the Chairman of the Committee, Lord Cross, was appointed by the Lord Chancellor, the Committee itself was established by resolution of the four Inns of Court and the Law Society.[55] The then Lord Chancellor, Lord Hailsham, decided to devote no further resources to it, and when Lord Cross appeared at the Society's Annual Conference in Cardiff in 1974, he admitted that the Advisory Committee 'was not really the sort of Committee which had been envisaged by the Ormrod Committee . . . it had no independent financial support and was dependent on the legal profession for its secretarial services and expenses'.[56] The Advisory Committee was thus very much a creature of the professions. Nevertheless, Lord Cross maintained that the recommendations of Ormrod regarding the academic stage of legal education had been implemented.[57]

However, when the Advisory Committee published its first report, on the academic stage of legal education, the Committee could not reach agreement, with practitioner members of the Committee stressing the necessity of having 'core' subjects, and the academic members arguing forcefully against an insistence on the 'core'. [58] Marcel Berlins, writing in *The Times Higher Education Supplement* in 1973, commented that 'The two branches of the profession are reluctant to relinquish any control over educational standards.'[59] He also noted that an announcement about the academic stage had recently been made by the Law Society. 'What is significant about the announcement', he continued, 'is that it was made unilaterally, outside the context of the advisory committee, and with the knowledge that it did not have the support of the academic representatives on the committee.'[60] Describing the situation as a 'crisis' in legal education, he concluded that the Advisory Committee

> has been a disappointment to almost all who sit on it and to everyone who hoped that Ormrod would provide the impetus not only for a reorganisation and reassessment of the structure of legal education, but also for a change in attitude towards the training of lawyers which would be more relevant to the needs of today's society.[61]

The SPTL certainly appears to have singularly failed to capitalise on the momentum for reform engendered by the Ormrod Report. Although Ormrod had recommended that there should be five core subjects, the professional bodies argued for the recognition of the law of trusts as a sixth core subject, as well as for the expansion of constitutional law to include administrative law, and the

---

[54] See LCB Gower, 'Looking Back' (1976–79) 14(NS) *JSPTL* 158.

[55] Thomas and Mungham, above n 53, 129.

[56] M Berlins, 'Law Teachers Keep Strangely Quiet About Crisis in Legal Education' (1973) *The Times Higher Education Supplement* 7 September, 2; 'Whatever Happened to Ormrod?' (1957) 13(NS) *JSPTL* 199.

[57] 'Whatever Happened to Ormrod?' (1957) 13(NS) *JSPTL* 199.

[58] Ibid, 204.

[59] Berlins, above n 56.

[60] Ibid.

[61] Ibid.

Cross Committee accepted both of these proposals.[62] The implications of legal academia's failure to secure the implementation of Ormrod's fundamental recommendation that the law degree should be recognised, without more, as enabling students to fulfil the academic stage of legal training continue to haunt successive generations of law teachers.[63]

It took a couple of years for the Society to realise that the Cross Committee was generally inclined to do as the professions suggested. At that point, the Society decided to review the work of the Advisory Committee, and held a special meeting to discuss the issue.[64] In a memorandum discussed at that meeting, Professor Geoffrey Wilson (Warwick) was highly critical of the way in which the Society had failed to follow up on Ormrod, and he drew attention to:

> the apparent lack of initiative by the Society with regard to legal education, particularly its lack of effort to discuss questions of general policy in order to guide the representatives on the Advisory Committee or even to provide a method whereby those representatives could test opinion within the Society about the possible effects or desirability of proposals made in the Advisory Committee.[65]

The seriousness of his criticisms was reinforced by his further observation that:

> Much of this is now water under the bridge, but it is not so uncharacteristic of the way in which the SPTL operates as not to raise serious questions about its general handling of situations like this where representatives are appointed , or even committees or that matter, and nothing more is heard [from the Society].[66]

As if this were not enough, Professor Wilson's assessment of the Society's handling of Ormrod in particular was damning:

> The fact is that the professions have taken all they can from it but the Society has not. The profession has successfully offloaded the Part 1 teaching but without giving the universities any greater freedom, in fact giving them less. Far from being the beginning of a new partnership of equals in the total process of legal education the universities have been successfully kept in their place.[67]

His assessment of the general effectiveness of the Society at this time was equally forthright:

> More generally the SPTL as at present organised has shown itself incompetent to fulfil the very considerable responsibilities that have been put upon it and that it has light-heartedly accepted. For lack of any alternative it is the universities' law schools'

---

[62] Memorandum from CLE, November 1978, 'The Teaching of Administrative Law', private document of WL Twining.

[63] For a discussion of the continuing tensions between the legal academy and the professions, see A Bradney *Conversations, Choices and Chances: The Liberal Law School in the Twenty-First Century* (Oxford, Hart Publishing, 2003) 164–70.

[64] *SPTL Newsletter* No 3 November 1973, A.SPTL 17, 1.

[65] Memoranda from Prof GP Wilson and Prof JF Wilson for discussion at Special Meeting of SPTL, November 1973, A.SPTL 26, 2.

[66] Ibid, 2.

[67] Ibid.

pressure group, but it still behaves like some kind of universities' law schools' club. . . . The honorific nature of the Presidency is such that for the most part Presidents are only too thankful, and rightly so, to get through the year with as little disturbance of their normal lives as possible, and the same goes for members of Council.[68]

Professor John Wilson (Southampton), who had been a member of the Ormrod Committee, also submitted a note for consideration by the Society:

> As the one surviving member of Ormrod who still has an indirect connection with its successor, I must say I am appalled by the way things have developed over the last eighteen months and I fear all the ground we gained on Ormrod has been lost. . . . I tend to agree with Geoffrey Wilson that the Society should seriously consider taking a more positive line in future negotiations with the professional representatives . . . the attitude of the professional side is becoming increasingly inflexible. . . . From my brief experience of the Cross Committee, I found the Committee . . . ready to leave all the running to the professional bodies.[69]

In an effort to counter the disappointment about the Advisory Committee, and enable the Society to 'operate more effectively on behalf of university law schools', the Society decided to recommend that a Legal Education Sub-Committee of the Society should be established, consisting of law school heads or their representatives, 'which could meet with the Society's representatives on the Advisory Committee, the Law Society Legal Education and Training Committee etc'.[70] Soon afterwards, at the first meeting of Council in December 1973, it was decided 'to investigate the support which would be forthcoming for the formation of a Standing Committee of Heads of University Law Schools'.[71] By September the Heads of University Law Schools Committee had held its first meeting; the then SPTL President, Professor Parker (Exeter) was elected as the first Chairman. [72]

It was also agreed to publish in the *Newsletter* not only a report of the special meeting, but also the Second Report of the Advisory Committee on Legal Education, together with the Note of Dissent written by Mr JA Jolowicz and supported by other members of the Committee, including two other SPTL representatives. All members of the Society were invited to express their opinions on the Report, which focused on 'mixed degrees and non-law graduates'.

The main concern expressed in the Note of Dissent was about the Report's recommendation that non-law graduates would only have to pass the six 'core' subjects for their degree to qualify them for entry to the legal profession.[73]

> For the academic stage of legal education the present Report is crucial for, unlike the First [Report] it determines the minimum academic study of legal subjects which should be required of graduate entrants to the legal profession. For all practical pur-

[68] Ibid.
[69] Ibid, 3.
[70] *SPTL Newsletter* No 3 November 1973, A.SPTL 17, 1.
[71] *SPTL Newsletter* No 4 March 1974, A.SPTL 17, 4.
[72] *SPTL Newsletter* No 5 December 1974, A.SPTL 17, 3. This body was soon to evolve into the separate Committee of Heads of University Law Schools.
[73] *SPTL Newsletter* No 3 November 1973. A.SPTL 17, 3.

poses, the present Report fixes as this minimum the study of six core subjects over one year. It is my belief that in an era of rapid social and legal change and at a time when the profession must endeavour to meet demands for a great variety of legal services . . . it is essential that the profession should demand more of the academic stage of a legal education than that. [74]

A number of law schools expressed their support for the Note of Dissent[75], but the reforms objected to were in fact implemented by the professional bodies, giving another indication of the relative lack of power of the legal academy over legal education at this time.[76]

The aftermath of Ormrod, and particularly the activities of the Advisory Committee, was undoubtedly a great disappointment to many members of the Society, as reflected in Professor Gower's Presidential Address delivered in 1977. Gower, himself a member of the Ormrod Committee, was candid in his assessment of the situation, deeply regretting the extent to which the professional bodies resiled from the idea of giving independence to law teachers over the academic stage of legal training.[77]

Part of the blame for this rests with the Ormrod Committee itself. We had been set up not only to make recommendations about the reform of the existing arrangements, but also as a Standing Advisory Committee to promote co-operation between the academic and professional sides. Foolishly, as I think all the members now agree, having spent three years preparing our initial report, we felt we had had enough, and that the Standing Advisory Committee should be a new body which we hoped would be more representative, particularly of younger members of the profession. So we recommended our demise. This, as we should have foreseen, was a fatal error. Instead of the Advisory Committee proving to be a forum in which the professional bodies and the universities and the polytechnics can work out any difficulties in implementing the Ormrod recommendations, it has become one in which the professional bodies can seek legitimation for watering down those recommendations—notwithstanding they were based largely on their own submissions. The first step was to add a further core subject to the five unanimously suggested after lengthy discussion by Ormrod. This was just silly, rather than calamitous. The latest step, which was more serious, was an apparent attempt to dictate to the universities and polytechnics how they should assess their students—something which the members of Ormrod never contemplated for one moment and to which they would have taken the greatest exception.[78]

That relations with the professions during this decade were, to say the least, uneasy, is amply reflected in the tussle over the teaching of administrative law. The profession felt that little time was devoted to administrative law, and once the Advisory Committee accepted that it should be added to the 'core', the Council of Legal Education issued a discussion paper, noting that the professions

[74] *SPTL Newsletter* No 3 November 1973, A.SPTL 17, 3.
[75] *SPTL Newsletter* No 4 March 1974, A.SPTL 17, 5.
[76] See 'Whatever Happened to Ormrod? Memorandum by Lord Cross' (1974–75) 13(NS) *JSPTL* 204.
[77] Gower, above n 54.
[78] Ibid.

expected the time to be devoted to administrative law should be not less than two-fifths of the course, but that universities and polytechnics were finding it difficult to maintain such a proportion, and making suggestions about how the desired aim could be achieved, as well as noting that this was a matter which the Council of Legal Education would like to be further discussed by the professions and academics.[79] The extent to which at least some members of the Society felt that this was an unacceptable interference in academic freedom is reflected in a statement issued by six eminent public lawyers which was sent to the Law Society's Legal Education Committee in February 1979.

> We are all concerned in teaching a subject which, variously entitled, embraces the matter to be found in, for example, de Smith's *Constitutional and Administrative Law.* We make academic decisions of many kinds based on our perceptions of the best way to teach undergraduates this complex subject. Some of us have been doing so for thirty years. The resolution of the academic problems in this field has been, and continues to be, one of our principal concerns.
>
> We respectfully suggest to the authors of the paper from the Council of Legal Education that the decision how to achieve the proper balance between constitutional and administrative law is an academic decision which should be left to those in the Universities and Polytechnics whose expertise is likely to be the best available.
>
> Prof JF Garner (Nottingham), Prof JAG Griffith (LSE), Prof J Jowell (UCL), Prof N Lewis (Sheffield), Prof JPW McAuslan (Warwick), Prof H Street (Manchester).[80]

This was just another salvo in the continuing battle between the professions and members of the Society. It is also a painful reminder of the difficulties which could have been avoided, had the Society succeeded in securing the implementation of the Ormrod Report.

Vocational Training

One of the most controversial recommendations made by the Ormrod Committee, as far as the legal professions were concerned, was that the vocational stage of professional training should no longer be delivered by the Council of Legal Education and the College of Law but that it should be transferred to some polytechnic and/or university law schools. Solicitors in particular wished to maintain the status quo, and complex discussions took place between the professions, the Lord Chancellor's Department, the University Grants Commission and the Department of Education. Universities had not been consulted, until the Committee of Vice-Chancellors and Principals stepped in on behalf of law schools. The University Grants Commission was concerned that any reforms should not merely result in the transfer of the costs of professional legal training to the public purse, and had said that if universities were involved in vocational

---

[79] Ibid .
[80] Statement attached to letter from Prof JAG Griffiths to Mr C Snowling (Secretary to the Advisory Committee on Legal Education) dated 14 February 1979, A.SPTL 26.

training, they would demand control over course content and admissions, which had not gone down well with the professions.[81] The Society set up a committee 'to consider what contribution universities can make in the provision of "vocational year" training for solicitors', but in fact the status quo was maintained, and the professions continued to be responsible for vocational training.[82]

Law Commission

Members of the Society enjoyed rather a different relationship with those members of the legal profession with whom contact was made because of their role as Law Commissioners. The annual meetings with the Law Commission continued throughout the decade, with the Chair of the Commission emphasising the value placed by members of the Commission on the assistance they received from members of the Society.[83] By 1974 the Society had seven specialist law reform committees (conflict of laws having been added since the other six were established in 1966). Although each committee was limited to a maximum of eight members to facilitate the preparation of reports, the Society tried to ensure, as far as practicable, a balance of participation between members of different ages and from different law schools, and other members of the Society were also encouraged to send in individual comments on Law Commission consultation.[84] In this area of its activities it would appear that those responsible (in this case Professor Crane (Queen Mary) the Society's Law Commission Liaison Officer, and the convenors of the relevant committees) took steps to ensure that participation was spread as widely as possible among members.

Relations with the Law Commission appear to have proceeded smoothly throughout the decade, and by 1979 some tentative discussions were taking place about the possibility of legal academics spending periods of research leave at the Commission. The Chairman of the Law Commission at that time, Lord Justice Kerr, made it clear that both he and the Commission welcomed such developments, even though lack of resources meant that the relationships between the Commission and legal academics could not be as extensive as in Canada and Australia. But, he wrote, 'meanwhile, we are very anxious to do what we can'.[85] Unsurprisingly, the SPTL's relations with the Law Commission were very much more straightforward than those with the professional bodies.

---

[81] 'The Ormrod Report' (1972–73) 12(NS) *JSPTL* 48.
[82] *SPTL Newsletter* No 4 March 1974, 5.
[83] *SPTL Newsletter* No 2 June 1973, A.SPTL 17.
[84] *SPTL Newsletter* No 5 December 1974, 4.
[85] Letter dated 3 September 1979 from Kerr LJ to Prof William Twining, President SPTL, private papers of WL Twining.

Royal Commission on Legal Services

At the end of the decade, the Society had another opportunity to define its relationship to the legal professions when it made a submission to the Royal Commission on Legal Services (which was set up in 1976 under the chairmanship of Lord Benson). The SPTL reiterated its support for the Ormrod Committee's recommendation that a law degree should be an integral part of the qualification for the legal profession, emphasising that the function of the law degree is not merely 'to give the student a comprehensive coverage of all the law he may later require in practice' but rather to provide a student with the knowledge and skills needed 'to ascertain the law as and when he wants it'.[86]

> The study of law at a University, like the study of the other arts subjects, is a humane one, and aims at providing insights into the law in historical, social, economic, philosophical and political contexts.[87]

The memorandum adopted a direct approach to the vexed question of the role of the professional bodies in academic legal education, stating that 'the content of University curricula should not be dictated by the professional bodies' and noting that 'we would regard any attempt by the professional bodies to inhibit the discretion of Universities to frame their courses according to desirable academic criteria as detrimental both to University and professional training'.[88] It would appear that the lesson of Ormrod had struck home. The memorandum was unequivocal in putting forward the Society's views. It was also used by the Society as an opportunity to repair the early damage wreaked by the Cross Committee, making the point that it hoped the Advisory Committee on Legal Education would be improved. 'Meetings of the Committee have become sporadic, and far too many pronouncements by the professional bodies are made *ex cathedra*, without reference to the Committee.'[89] This may be thought by many to be bolting the stable door after the horse has bolted, but at least by the end of the decade the Society had gained sufficiently in self-confidence to be more assertive about protecting the position of the legal academy.

Socio-Legal Studies

The first conference of the SPTL's Socio-Legal Group took place in Manchester in December 1972. About 25 people attended, and papers were delivered by WG Carson (Bedford College) on 'Instrumental and Symbolic Aspects of Early

---

[86] SPTL Submission to Royal Commission on Legal Services, A.SPTL 26/12, paras 7 and 8.
[87] Ibid, para 8.
[88] Ibid, paras 9 and 10.
[89] Ibid, para 14.

Factory Legislation 1802–47', Dr Pauline Morris (Legal Advice Research Unit, Nuffield Foundation) on 'Research into the Provision of Legal Services', Paul Wiles (Sheffield University) on 'Some Criminological Lessons for Socio-legal Studies' and Professor ID Willock 'Getting On with Social Scientists'. Further meetings were planned and the organiser, Colin M Campbell (Edinburgh University), was careful to state that 'Although the Society's members provide the primary focus for the Group, in view of the nature of the topics covered interested members of social science departments and polytechnics will also be welcome.'[90] Members of the Socio-Legal Group were also, it appears, determined not to reflect the narrow membership of the main Society.

The Socio-Legal Group grew rapidly—150 members joined in its first year— and had an ambitious programme, with weekend meetings three times a year in Manchester.[91] Significantly, its activities tended to be reported within the Young Members' section of the *Newsletter*, where it described itself as 'one of the most thriving [groups] within the SPTL' and was enthusiastic in encouraging members to attend its meetings 'All young members are encouraged to attend at least once, if only to become aware of what is happening to some of their colleagues!'[92] The Young Members' Group was clearly interested in socio-legal work. Quite apart from the socio-legal nature of many of the contributions at its annual meetings, in 1976 it advertised in the *SPTL Newsletter*, soliciting information from any members of the Society who had experience of the practice of the Social Science Research Council in making awards for legal research, and in 1977 they invited Professor Geoffrey Wilson (Warwick), Chair of the SSRC Committee on Social Sciences and Law, to talk about the role of the committee.[93]

Another indication of the interest in socio-legal studies in the 1970s is given by the comments of Professor William Twining, when he is providing some background information about the Society's Working Party on Law Publishing. Explaining that the move by some legal academics to challenge the prevailing doctrinal orthodoxy is a controversial matter in which he has been actively involved, he goes on:

> I do not see [the Working-Party] as part of a polemical campaign to broaden the study of law, but more as an attempt to contribute to the solution or palliation of a practical problem of great importance to all academic lawyers.[94]

The reference to the controversial nature of the doctrinal/socio-legal debate reflects the nature of the wider discussion about the relationship of law and soci-

---

[90] *SPTL Newsletter* No 1 March 1973, A.SPTL 17.

[91] *SPTL Newsletter* No 3 November 1973, A.SPTL 17, 10.

[92] *SPTL Newsletter* No 4 March 1974, A.SPTL 17, 8.

[93] *SPTL Newsletter* No 7 January 1976, A.SPTL 17, 12; *SPTL Newsletter* No 11 December 1977, A.SPTL 17, 23.

[94] Letter dated 8 April 1974 from Prof William Twining to Dr Peter Mann, private papers of WL Twining.

ology which was taking place at this time, as the contributions to the first volume of the newly established *British Journal of Law and Society* clearly illustrate.[95]

Meanwhile, SPTL members wishing to embark on some socio-legal research may have been encouraged by a letter from the Director of the Legal Action Group (LAG), Susan Marsden, expressing the view that 'there is a fund of skill and knowledge among LAG's academic members which we are not yet drawing fully upon for the LAG Bulletin'.[96] She went on to indicate that LAG was particularly interested in receiving short reports of research findings, concluding by offering a long list of possible topics for investigation, which amount to a socio-legal research agenda. Some of the suggestions include: what's happened to the enforcement of County Court judgments, the power of barristers' clerks, McKenziemen, what actually goes on in your local courts—quality of representation, what happens at pre-trial reviews, what's the system for parcelling out work among solicitors at the magistrates' court, what trends are showing up in the judicial statistics? Authors were also solicited to write articles on particular areas of 'hard' law, such as the law relating to seamen, houseboat residents and caravan dwellers, illegitimacy, environmental nuisances, the Defective Premises Act 1972 and numerous other topics.[97] The number of suggestions listed in this contribution indicates a perception that socio-legal research at this time was somewhat limited in scope, but that it had huge potential.

A significant proportion of the *Newsletter* was devoted to socio-legal matters in 1977, when the Officers reported on their meeting with some members of the Committee for Social Sciences and Law of the Social Science Research Council (SSRC).[98] This Committee had been established as a result of the SSRC's decision, taken in 1970, to allocate substantial resources to socio-legal studies. That decision had led to the establishment of the Centre for Socio-Legal Studies at Oxford, and also to the establishment of a new SSRC subject-committee (the Committee on Social Sciences and Law) to support research and training in the socio-legal field.[99] Professor Geoffrey Wilson, Chair of that Committee, contributed a substantial article to the *Newsletter*, explaining the role of the Committee, which was not only to consider research grant applications, but to 'develop plans for stimulating interest and fostering research study in the socio-legal field'. In the course of his discussion, Professor Wilson notes considerable growth in socio-legal activity since '[t]he pessimistic comment of the Heyworth Committee in 1960 that "in the United Kingdom the study of law has been mainly concerned with the professional training of barristers and solicitors"'. This outdated view had been replaced by the 'more optimistic demand by the Ormrod Committee on Legal Education that lawyers should be exposed to the methods and insights

---

[95] The first volume of the *BJLS* (1974) contained articles on 'Getting on with Sociologists' (ID Willock), 'Legal Thought & Juristic Values' (CM Campbell), 'Social Action and Methodology for the Sociology of Law' (C Grace and P Wilkinson) and 'Some Jobs for Jurisprudence' (WL Twining).

[96] *SPTL Newsletter* No 7 January 1976, A.SPTL 17, 5.

[97] Ibid, 6–8.

[98] *SPTL Newsletter* No 9 February 1977, A.SPTL 17, 1.

[99] *SPTL Newsletter* No 13 March 1979, A.SPTL17, 12.

of the social sciences even in the course of their professional training'.[100] Although there had been numerous developments in the undergraduate law curriculum 'designed to emphasize the social function and context of law, and the relevance of the literature, perspectives and methods of other social sciences', socio-legal work still did not lie within the mainstream of law school activities, and law lacked a strong tradition of graduate teaching and research.[101] Nevertheless, the picture was optimistic. The Committee had recognised a postgraduate course at Sheffield, and there were signs of interest from other institutions. Professor Wilson concluded by noting that '[a]lthough the United Kingdom has not started later than many other countries, the real test will be the speed and success with which it develops now that it has started.'[102]

As a result of the meeting with the SSRC, it was decided to seek information about the nature of research in university law departments and to discover whether financial difficulties were interfering with that research. A survey was carried out by Professor Aubrey Diamond, Director of the Institute of Advanced Legal Studies, and the final Report was published in the *Newsletter* in 1979. A response rate of about 39 per cent was achieved, and the Report contained a range of information about the state of legal research.[103] However, Professor Diamond includes many caveats about his methodology, observing, for instance, that in relation to the question on research, 'I must admit that the form was designed so that a nil return would be difficult', and in relation to a question on the types of research materials used, 'Even here, however, I admit to some arbitrariness in classification, since I included the Public Record Office in this category', while the category of those using 'unwritten materials' included 'a few who made use in their research of their personal experience as magistrates or as members of committees or commissions'.[104] While acknowledging these difficulties, it is nevertheless interesting to note the information about the nature of legal research, where the Report concludes that 'pure' doctrinal research 'seems to be rare today, because the authoritative sources are likely to be supplemented by textbooks and articles in legal periodicals'.[105] As far as empirical research was concerned, it was 'usually carried out by, or under the direction of, social scientists, or lawyers and social scientists working in collaboration. A few lawyers are however acquiring experience in this type of research.'[106] Overall, Professor Diamond concluded that 'a very considerable amount of research into law and the legal system is going on, but I am left in no doubt that lack of funds is hindering research'.[107] While junior staff faced difficulties in relation to out-of-

---

[100] *SPTL Newsletter* No 9 February 1977, A.SPTL 17, 2.
[101] Ibid.
[102] *SPTL Newsletter* No 9 February 1977, A.SPTL 17, 4.
[103] *SPTL Newsletter* No 13 March 1979, A.SPTL 17, 1–16.
[104] Ibid, 2, 3, 4.
[105] Ibid, 7.
[106] Ibid.
[107] Ibid, 13.

pocket expenses, such as rail fares, more senior staff faced difficulties in finding resources to pay for research assistants, and at all levels 'inadequate secretarial help hinders and slows down research work'.[108] Recommending that more information be gathered about matters such as photocopying charges, travel grants and so on, Professor Diamond concluded that the best institutional answer to this problem would be for the SSRC to take responsibility not just for socio-legal research, but for pure legal research as well.[109]

Socio-legal studies also featured prominently in the *Newsletter* in 1978, when a substantial 'Postscript' to Professor Gower's Presidential address was published.[110] The article focuses on Professor Gower's remark that:

> We have not succeeded in persuading the Social Science Research Council that legal research even into topics of paramount social importance (such as family law) is worthy of their support unless the lawyers work in conjunction with social scientists—and 'mere' lawyers, apparently, are not deserving of that description.

The author argues that the assumption by some lawyers may be that all that is needed to engage in empirical research is 'a crash course in research methods, a bit of cash . . . and off they go'. This would, however, be 'hopelessly naive', failing to take account not only of the assumptions inculcated by location in a particular discipline, but also of the complexity of social science methodology.[111]

> In fact the lawyer will discover that sociology differs fundamentally from his own discipline in that whereas law involves a particular methodology about which all lawyers are more or less agreed, sociology does not. . . . Having opened this Pandora's box he/she will discover a gaggle including Weberians, Marxists, structuralists, ethnomethodologists, phenomenologists ready to jump out, each vehemently asserting a claim to the unique validity of their widely differing viewpoints.[112]

The other question which is addressed is Professor Gower's question about whether law courses provide an understanding of the relationship of law to the social and economic environment. Here, the article argues for courses which offer a much greater theoretical insight into the nature and working of law in society, regarding the need for more theoretically aware lawyers to be 'pressing'.[113]

The amount of SPTL activity relating to socio-legal studies during the 1970s suggests that there was considerable interest in this new approach.

---

[108] *SPTL Newsletter* No 13 March 1979 A.SPTL 17, 13.
[109] Ibid, 14–5.
[110] *SPTL Newsletter* No 12 September 1978, A.SPTL 17, 9–13.
[111] Ibid, 9.
[112] Ibid, 10.
[113] Ibid, 13.

Insights Into Legal Education

Expansion after Robbins

The Society's new *Newsletter* provided the opportunity for sharing of news about law schools around the country. From this we learn that the Robbins Committee recommendations for expansion of higher education continued to reverberate, with the University Grants Committee stating in its guidance to universities for the 1972–77 quinquennium that there should be an increase by one-third in the provision of places in law schools in England and Wales. Most of the expansion was to take place within existing law schools, with the exception of Reading, where the existing Department of Law relating to land was to be developed into a new law school.[114] The SPTL tried to gather information from constituencies about the position around the country. Although only a few responses were received, the *Newsletter* reported in 1973 that:

> the major expansion of legal education recommended by the Ormrod Report has begun to take place. Appointments to Chairs (seven) have been, or are to be, made at Hull, Keele, Kent, Reading, Sheffield, UWIST and Warwick. Lectureship appointments (at least 18) are envisaged for Aberystwyth (1), Birmingham (several), Bristol (2), Durham (2), Hull (1), Leeds (2), Nottingham (1), Reading (4) Sheffield (2) and Warwick (3).[115]

Further *Newsletter* items in the same year reveal that Cambridge envisaged appointing six new lectureships during the quinquennium to meet the increase in numbers of undergraduates reading law, while Exeter was increasing its student numbers from 200 to 300 by 1976. At Liverpool, the law school was hoping to decrease its reliance on part-time teaching provided by legal practitioners and make a significant increase in the numbers of full-time staff, as well as broadening the range of subjects taught 'and a development in research interests on a scale not hitherto possible'. Newcastle was bucking the trend by wishing to 'retain the intimacy of a small law school'; student numbers there would merely increase from 50 to 60. Nottingham, meanwhile, had big plans for expanding its student numbers from an intake of 58 to an intake of 110 by the end of the quinquennium, accompanied by an increase in staff. In common with most other universities, money had been allocated for additional library provision to cater for expansion and the purchase of EEC materials; Nottingham was taking over the current main university library building as the Law Library. New law school buildings were either completed or nearly so at Liverpool, Nottingham and Aberystwyth, reflecting the expansionist nature of law schools at this time.[116]

---

[114] *SPTL Newsletter* No 1 March 1973, A.SPTL 17.
[115] *SPTL Newsletter* No 2 June 1973, A.SPTL 17.
[116] Ibid.

Expansion of provision also encouraged some law schools to offer different types of law degree. In 1974, Brunel announced its first undergraduate law degree, which was a four-year course, incorporating three periods of placements in occupations connected with law, and in the first two years involved the study of other social science subjects as well as law.[117] The School of Oriental and African Studies began offering undergraduate degrees in law for the first time in 1975, drawing on its particular expertise to inform the curriculum by including material on the legal systems of Asia and Africa, as well as religious laws and the customary laws of African peoples. Several joint degrees were also offered, including anthropology and law, and law and a south-east Asian/African language. These developments give an indication of some small increase in the diversity of legal education offered during this decade.

However, the effects of the expansion brought about by the Robbins Committee caused concern in some quarters. In 1977, one of the sessions at the Annual Conference considered the question 'Are There Too Many Law Schools and Law Places?', with the ensuing discussion reported in the Society's *Journal* by GA Seabrooke, who noted 'considerable concern', with the CNAA expressing concerns about the over-production of law graduates and shortage of suitably qualified staff, while the UGC gave a qualified 'no' to the question.[118] Underlying these concerns may have been an increasing awareness of the decreasing resources available to higher education alongside the growth that was taking place. The Fifth Report of the Lord Chancellor's Advisory Committee on Legal Education, published in the same year, noted that:

> Government cuts in University expenditure, originally estimated at 4–6% in real terms, were later announced by the Secretary of State as being only of the order of 1% for 1977–78 and about 2% in 1978–79. It has since become clear that these latter figures bear little relation to reality and that in the ensuing session Universities face a cut in real terms of at least 4% or thereabouts, possibly significantly more, with no clear indication how far salaries and other costs will have to escalate above Government forecasts before the amount of grant is adjusted. Similar problems have been experienced by the polytechnics. Not only is there a widespread freeze on additional appointments but many posts falling vacant are not being allowed to be filled because of anxiety about future finance. Law schools are obviously not immune from the effects of staffing cuts of this kind.[119]

European Community Law

During this decade, members of the SPTL were concerned in a number of ways with the effects on legal education of the UK's newly acquired membership of the

---

[117] *SPTL Newsletter* No 3 November 1973 A.SPTL 17, 6.

[118] GA Seabrooke, 'Are There Too Many Law Schools and Law Places?' (1978) 14(NS) *JSPTL* 161.

[119] Lord Chancellor's Advisory Committee on Legal Education, 'Fifth Report: The Undergraduate Teaching of European Community Law in University and Polytechnic Law Schools', *SPTL Newsletter* No 12 September 1978, A.SPTL 17, 5–6.

Common Market, an event duly acknowledged by the then President, Professor PS James (Leeds) when he delivered his Presidential Address in 1972. His opening remarks included the observation that:

> I speak today at a milestone of our history, whether political or legal; for we are about to cross the European threshold . . . anxious though we be to cherish the traditions which our long isolation has evolved, and thereby, we pray, to make our contributions to the common good, let us remind ourselves that though winds are sometimes wayward, the *trade* winds of western culture blow neither North to South nor South to North nor West to East but follow the sun from East to West.[120]

The Society acted quickly to establish a Committee on European Law (including law of the European Communities) with the broad function of advising the Society on all matters connected with the study and teaching of European law.[121] The Society's Journal carried a report of a symposium on 'Legal Education and the Common Market' held at Leeds University in September 1972, when delegates were addressed by Professor Tunc (University of Paris 1), His Excellency Judge Donner (formerly Professor of Law at the Free University of Amsterdam) and Professor Grisoli, Director of the Centre of European Community Studies, University of Pavia. In the ensuing discussion, it was agreed that teaching the economic and political aspects of the Community was very important; law teachers who tried to expound only the legal aspects would be 'distorting reality'.[122] One of the plenary speakers at the 1973 Annual Conference was Lord Mackenzie Stuart, a judge at the Court of Justice, whose address on' The Court of Justice of the European Communities and the Control of Executive Discretion' was reprinted in the *Journal*.[123]

Members of the Society engaged in various activities designed to increase their knowledge of the European Community. In 1974 the Young Members' Group had a discussion on 'Teaching Common Market Law' led by Dr Gillian White (Manchester) and Dr Kurt Lipstein (Cambridge), in which attention was drawn to the lack of textbooks, and discussion took place as to whether there should be a special course on EEC law or whether European aspects should be integrated into existing courses.[124] The following year the *Newsletter* carried extensive coverage of the establishment of the United Kingdom Association for European Law; Professor J Bridge (Exeter) was the SPTL representative on the Association's Advisory Council and Professor JDB Mitchell (Edinburgh) and Professor FG Jacobs (LSE) were its Secretaries. The Association's President was Lord Wilberforce, and it was a constituent member of FIDE, the Fédération International pour le Droit Européen.[125] In the same year members of Birmingham

---

[120] PS James 'Presidential Address: The Lawyer and The Times' (1972–73) 12(NS) *JSPTL* 217.

[121] 'Annual Report of the Society for 1971–72' (1972–73) 12(NS) *JSPTL* 277.

[122] FEDowrick, 'Legal Education and the Common Market; Report of a Symposium' (1972–73) 12(NS) *JSPTL* 248.

[123] Lord Mackenzie Stuart (1974–75) 13(NS) *JSPTL* 16.

[124] *SPTL Newsletter* No 4 March 1974, A.SPTL 17, 4; *SPTL Newsletter* No 5 December 1974, A.SPTL 17, 10.

[125] *SPTL Newsletter* No 6 May 1975, A.SPTL 17, 5.

and Aberystwyth law schools joined forces to take advantage of reduced-price group travel from London to Luxembourg, and had a highly successful trip, meeting some of the judges and advocates general, as well as officials from the Commission and the Parliament, and from the European Investment Bank.[126]

By the end of the decade, the Lord Chancellor's Advisory Committee on Legal Education discovered that 'in a very short time and with severely limited resources, the law schools have established European Community Law as an integral part of the undergraduate syllabus through a range of courses which is rapidly expanding'.[127] At least 20 university and 8 polytechnic law schools offered full courses devoted to areas of substantive community law; all law schools dealt with the institutional structure of the Community and some basic concepts.[128] Community law was also included in some substantive courses such as labour law and company law. The Committee also noted some of the difficulties experienced by those teaching Community law, including inadequate resources, and the lack of sufficient staff expertise, so that if one such teacher left, there was difficulty in replacing them.[129] Other difficulties included reduced library budgets, and a lack of resources to send staff and students to Europe to study the workings of the Community institutions, and to facilitate staff exchanges.[130] In its Fifth Report the Committee made a number of recommendations about the teaching of Community Law, including a strong preference for the provision of separate Community law courses. It concludes by noting the need for additional resources for law schools, 'if they are to be able to play their part effectively in developing the study of European law'.[131]

Human Rights Law

Although a great deal of progress was made in towards the effective teaching of European Community law, the same was not true of human rights law. In 1973 the British Institute of Human Rights announced that it was organising a conference on 'Education for Human Rights and Responsibilities', aimed at a range of interested parties, including law teachers. Under the auspices of UNESCO, the Institute had already conducted a survey of human rights teaching in universities, which had revealed that 'rarely in the UK was a detailed examination of the European Convention on Human Rights undertaken, although courses, usually in Constitutional Law or Public International law, did include consideration of various aspects of the subject'.[132]

---

[126] *SPTL Newsletter* No 7 January 1976, A.SPTL 17, 9.
[127] Lord Chancellor's Advisory Committee on Legal Education, 'Fifth Report: The Undergraduate Teaching of European Community Law in University and Polytechnic Law Schools', *SPTL Newsletter* No 12 September 1978, A.SPTL 17, 1.
[128] Ibid, 2.
[129] Ibid, 5.
[130] Ibid, 6.
[131] Ibid, 7.
[132] *SPTL Newsletter* No 2 June 1973, A.SPTL 17.

Library Resources

The Society had first produced a Statement of Minimum Holdings for Law Libraries in 1958. In 1969 the General Committee had set up a sub-committee chaired by Professor JC Smith to revise the Statement. When it reported in September 1970, apart from bringing the Statement up-to-date, the sub-committee added an introduction, which sought to explain the 'special needs' of law libraries, in the hope that this would be of assistance to law schools in procuring library resources. An attempt was also made to estimate the costs involved in implementing the Statement.[133] In 1975, the Society published a similar Statement on 'the Law of the European Communities and of their Member Countries'. The introduction to this Statement notes that there are some basic works in language other than English which are needed for the study of the law of the Communities in adequate depth. It also notes that minimum holdings for the law of each Member State is included in the Statement, but emphasises that it was not the intention that every library should collect the law of every Member State. Rather, libraries were encouraged to specialise, and to enter into co-operative agreements with other nearby libraries to facilitate comprehensive holdings in convenient geographical areas.[134] The Statement of Minimum Holdings was to prove one of the enduring contributions which the Society made to legal education.

Pedagogy

During the 1970s, members of the Society were concerned in a number of different ways with the actual practice of teaching. In 1971 a sub-committee was established under the chairmanship of Professor Glanville Williams to consider 'the use of audio-visual aids in law teaching' which produced a 'progress report' the following year, announcing that it had decided to take steps towards the establishment of an SPTL collection of audio-visual aids on legal topics, from which law teachers could borrow materials.[135] The Society also wrote to the Government, asking it to give full consideration to the establishment of legal information retrieval systems, and to consult with all interested parties on such matters. [136]

In his Presidential Address in 1976 Professor FR Crane (Queen Mary) considered the use of various methods of assessment in legal education. While he mentions a range of methods, including open-book, multiple-choice examina-

---

[133] JC Smith 'Statement of Minimum Library Holdings for Law Libraries in England and Wales' (1970–71) 11(NS) *JSPTL* 90.

[134] SPTL Committee on Libraries, 'Statement of Minimum Holdings of the Law of the European Communities and of their Member Countries' (1974–75) 13(NS) *JSPTL* 113.

[135] 'The Use of Audio-Visual Material in Law Teaching' (1970-71) 11(NS) *JSPTL* 161.

[136] 'Report of the General Committee for 1970–71' (1972–73) 12(NS) *JSPTL* 57–8.

tions and coursework, he remarks that in his experience, other disciplines seemed to use a wider range of assessment methods than law faculties. His extended description of what he terms 'the limited open-book examination' (permitting students to take in to the examination room statutes, casebooks and their own notes, including lecture handouts) and his reference to the experimental nature of this innovation in his own department, suggests that this was not common practice in other law schools at the time.[137]

Law Teachers

Towards the end of the decade, two successive Presidential Addresses offer some reflections on law teachers themselves. Professor Harry Street (Manchester), President in 1978, took as his subject 'The University Law Teacher'.[138] Noting that 'There is no job satisfaction unless you enjoy teaching' he went on to consider the research and publication required of the modern law teacher.[139]

> My overall view of English law teachers' periodical writing is that the standard is indefensibly low. . . . The choice of topics is often unimaginative. Article after article on the same area, normally only because there are conflicting decisions which others have also written about. Too much detailed examination of isolated decisions or tedious reanalysing of groups of decisions.[140]

He went on to say in his view that the most exciting development in legal research was the increasing number of opportunities for lawyers to collaborate with other social scientists, with the SSRC and the Nuffield Foundation offering both training and funding, so that there were plenty of opportunities for those wishing to do socio-legal research.[141] Much of Street's enthusiasm for such research was pragmatic, as he saw it as a way of influencing policymakers. He was also keen to highlight the contribution which academic lawyers had made to the development of welfare law, an area with little practitioner input, where legal academics had written high-quality work and made a real impact.[142] Although he acknowledged that law teachers were not particularly well paid, Street offered a number of ways in which legal academics could increase their earnings—by publishing (where there were particularly lucrative opportunities in the core subjects), chairing tribunals and journalism, to name but a few.[143] He also believed that they had opportunities to be active in 'public life', both inside and outside the university. 'Never have so many law teachers served on Royal

---

[137] FR Crane, 'Presidential Address: Reflections on Land Law and Its Teaching'(1976–79) 14(NS) *JSPTL* 71
[138] H Street, 'The University Law Teacher' (1979) 14(NS) *JSPTL* 243.
[139] Ibid, 246–7.
[140] Ibid, 247.
[141] Ibid, 247–8.
[142] Ibid, 248.
[143] Ibid, 250

Commissions and departmental committees as in recent years.'[144] Overall, he is reasonably optimistic, characterising university law teaching (tongue firmly in cheek) as 'not such a bad choice of career'.[145]

The following year, Professor William Twining delivered his Presidential Address: 'Goodbye to Lewis Eliot: The Academic Lawyer as Scholar', providing a slightly different perspective on the academic lawyer in the 1970s. He began by acknowledging the tendency of academic lawyers to be defensive when asked about research in law, a reaction which he related to the fact that 'the notion that academic lawyers might have serious scholarly aspirations, comparable to those of historians or biochemists, for example, has not yet gained universal acceptance'.[146] He went on to note that, in England and Wales at least, academic law had been structured, financed and conducted on the basis of 'a set of remarkably low expectations about sustained research and scholarship'.[147] In his Address, Professor Twining sought to argue that such attitudes were no longer appropriate, and that the SPTL had a potential role to play 'in fostering a different set of expectations and ideas about legal scholarship'.[148]

The stereotype of an academic lawyer as a marginal man of low visibility in academia (to which the Lewis Eliot alluded to in the title of the address was a notable exception) could now be regarded as outdated, but some vestiges of that inheritance remained. Professor Twining noted the small minority of law teachers with research degrees, the marginal position of law in relation to funding bodies, and the continuing existence of law schools in which academics were prevented/discouraged from applying for research leave.[149] Compared to most disciplines law was perceived by others in academia as not having a highly developed tradition of committed and sustained scholarship.[150] However, Professor Twining went on to argue that the position of academic law as it entered the 1980s was significantly different. Developments such as the increasing numbers of full-time law teachers, the marginal involvement of law schools in vocational training and the growth of socio-legal studies had all contributed to the convergence of the law school with the rest of academia. This had the result, among others, that academic lawyers were expected to carry out research in the same way as scholars in other disciplines, and this expectation was reinforced by promotion procedures.[151]

Turning to the nature of legal research, Professor Twining acknowledged the strengths of the traditional expository tradition, but also expressed some reservations about the nature of this type of legal research. His reservations were:

[144] Ibid, 249.
[145] Ibid, 252.
[146] WL Twining, 'Goodbye to Lewis Eliot: The Academic Lawyer as Scholar' (1980) 15(NS) *JSPTL* 2.
[147] Ibid.
[148] Ibid.
[149] Ibid, 4.
[150] Ibid, 5.
[151] Ibid, 6.

first, that an acceptable conception of legal scholarship must encompass much more than exposition and analysis of existing doctrine; secondly, that the expositor needs to examine, articulate and refine his epistemological and methodological assumptions. Concentrating on expository work does not provide immunity from theorising. Thirdly, that no expository work, which claims to be based on *understanding* can disregard the historical background, the perceptions and definitions of the problems and the other matters which provide the context of legal doctrine. This even the legal scholar who conceives of his primary task as exposition has to be a contextualist, if he is to be in a position to claim that he is advancing understanding as well as knowledge.[152]

As far as the 'non-expository' approach was concerned, Professor Twining saw the challenge as being whether research of this nature could be done in ways which satisfy scholarly values and standards at least as well as good expository work. He was also sceptical whether law schools would be places in which really intellectually ambitious programmes (such as 'a macro-theoretical sociology of law') or radical changes of perspective (such as the development of an empirical science of law) would be possible.[153] These were the challenges that law teachers would face in the future.

International News

During the 1970s the Society appears to have attempted to maintain at least some overseas links. A five-person delegation represented the Society at the Commonwealth Law Conference in New Delhi in 1971; members included not only the President, but also the Chair of the Young Members' Group.[154] The following year the Society was also represented at one of the founding meetings of the Commonwealth Legal Education Association.[155] The *Newsletter* made regular attempts to keep members informed about developments in legal education in other jurisdictions. In 1973, there was a report on the annual meeting of the Australasian Universities Law Schools Association, noting the names of convenors of specialist groups so as to encourage interested SPTL members to contact them, as well as an article about legal education at the University of South Africa, a fully accredited university delivering its teaching almost exclusively by correspondence, where the Law Faculty, with 3,400 students, offered a range of legal education, including law degrees and diplomas.[156] In 1974 members were informed about a workshop on 'vocational courses, practical training facilities and requirements, clinical education etc' organised by the newly

---

[152] Ibid, 16.
[153] Ibid, 17.
[154] 'Report of the General Committee for 1970–71' (1972–73) 12(NS) *JSPTL* 57.
[155] 'Annual Report of the Society for 1971–72' (1972–73) 12(NS) *JSPTL* 277.
[156] *SPTL Newsletter* No 3 November 1973, A.SPTL 17, 7.

established Commonwealth Legal Education Association (of which the SPTL was a member).[157] During the same year, the Law and Economics section of the American Association of Law Schools (AALS) placed a small article in the *Newsletter*, wishing to establish contact with UK scholars sharing similar interests. Professor Maurice Kay (Keele) offered to act as a link with the AALS group, and wished to hear from anyone interested to join the American group or to form a similar one in the UK.[158] 1977 saw a report of a conference on legal education in Australia, organised by the Law Council of Australia, which examined the education of lawyers from admission to law school to continuing education for the practitioner. Much discussion focused on the relationship between what is taught at the undergraduate level, and its relationship to how the law actually works in practice. The author of the article, Professor Brian Harvey (Birmingham), noted that

> in Australia there is much closer control of undergraduate law courses by representatives of the profession than we are used to in the UK and this factor is clearly unpalatable to some. . . . [However] the close relationship of practitioner and teachers does have some benefits. Academics are less prone to retreat into ivory towers and leading practitioners are educated much more thoroughly than normally occurs in the UK in the broad objectives of university education and the detailed problems of devising and developing the law syllabus.[159]

During this decade the *Newsletter* also continued to carry information about opportunities for British academic lawyers to spend time abroad. In 1974 the University of Singapore was keen to attract visiting scholars to teach subjects such as torts, land law and trusts, as well as company law, revenue law and banking law. Visitors were encouraged to consider co-teaching with Singapore staff, and it was hoped they would also be willing to participate in seminars on teaching techniques and research as well.[160] In 1977 there was a letter from an American judge, who also taught in several law schools in the United States, and who wished to teach for a period (somewhat optimistically, in the summer) in the UK.[161]

After the first two years of the decade the Society did not send its representatives abroad on a regular basis. It is not entirely clear why this is the case—perhaps lack of inclination on the part of individual Presidents, or a reflection of straitened financial times (the 1970s was, after all, the decade of the three-day week).[162]

---

[157] *SPTL Newsletter* No 5 December 1974, A.SPTL.17, 5.
[158] *SPTL Newsletter* No 4 March 1974, A.SPTL 17, 7.
[159] *SPTL Newsletter* No 9 February 1977, A.SPTL 17, 12–4.
[160] *SPTL Newsletter* No 5 December 1974, A.SPTL17, 8.
[161] *SPTL Newsletter* No 11 December 1977 A.SPTL 17, 3.
[162] For analysis of the economic situation of Britain in the 1970s, see R Coopey and N Woodward (eds), *Britain in the 1970s; The Troubled Economy* (London, UCL Press, 1996) esp ch 1.

Annual Conferences

Conferences in the early 1970s continued to take much the same form as in the previous decade. The usual pattern was to arrive on a Thursday afternoon, listen to the Presidential address, then have a reception and dinner. On the Friday, there would be two talks in the morning, while the afternoon was devoted to outings, followed by the Annual General Meeting and the Annual Dinner. On Saturday morning there was another talk before the conference ended. The talks were often delivered by non-academics (thus we find Lord Reid in 1971, Mark Carlisle QC MP, the Minister of State at the Home Office in 1972, Advocate General Warner and the Director General of Fair Trading in 1975).[163]

However, the agitation by the Young Members' Group may have had some effect, since it is noticeable that during this decade the proportion of contributions from academics increases, not only in plenary sessions, where it becomes increasingly common to have panels of speakers where at least one member of the panel is an academic, but also in the inclusion of 'group discussions' or 'working groups' where members of the Society actively participated both in delivering papers and in the ensuing discussion. [164] Participation by members of the Society in the academic aspect of the Annual Conference was also facilitated by the growing number of specialist groups within, or closely connected with, the Society. A good example is the announcement in the *Newsletter* in 1973 by Professor AW Bradley (Edinburgh) and Professor JF Garner (Nottingham) that '[f]ollowing the recommendation oft repeated at the Annual Meetings that specialist groups should be convened within the Society' they proposed to establish an Administrative Law Group. [165] It met for the first time at Nottingham in 1973: speakers included JPWB McAuslan on 'Planning Law and Administrative Law—Some Teaching Problems' and DGT Williams on 'Research into Tribunals and the Council on Tribunals'.[166] When the Administrative Law Group extended an invitation to any members of the Association of Law Teachers who might like to attend, it was expressly distancing itself from the restrictive policy of the main Society, reflecting the wide variety of opinion found within the Society on this issue.[167] It appears far from coincidental that AW Bradley had been a leading figure in the establishment of the Young Members' Group in the mid-1960s.[168] Other specialist groups on Welfare Law, Criminal Law and Revenue Law were also founded during this decade.[169]

---

[163] Annual Conference 1971 First Circular, A.SPTL 16/2; Annual Conference 1972 Programme, A.SPTL 10/3; Annual Conference 1975 Programme, A.SPTL 16/2.

[164] See eg SPTL Annual Conference Southampton 1977 Second Circular, A.SPTL 16/2; SPTL Annual Conference Cardiff 1974 Programme, A.SPTL 16/2.

[165] *SPTL Newsletter* No 1 March 1973, A.SPTL 17.

[166] Ibid.

[167] *SPTL Newsletter* No 2 June 1973, A.SPTL 17.

[168] General Committee Minutes, 11 December 1964, A.SPTL 1/5.

[169] *SPTL Newsletter* No 13 March 1979, A.SPTL 17, 24; *SPTL Newsletter* No 8 May 1976, A.SPTL 17, 2; *SPTL Newsletter* No 10 July 1977, A.SPTL 17, 5.

However, the level of participation in the Annual Conference open to ordinary members of the Society was very much dependent on the attitude of the President, who was responsible for organising the conference. At the beginning of the decade, the 1970 conference at Oxford, under the Presidency of Professor Cross, included a session described in the programme as 'The Role of the Academic Lawyer—a discussion with a panel of judges and practitioners including Lord Diplock, Lord Justice Edmund Davies, Lord Justice Cross and Mr Desmond Ackner QC' where discussion was clearly expected from the academics, but they were confined to the role of audience.[170] However, the following year, at the Edinburgh conference, the programme included discussion groups on the Ormrod Report on legal education in England and Wales, followed by 'working sessions' at the Sheffield conference in 1973 and 'discussion groups' on contract, criminal law, family law, labour law and land law at Cardiff in 1974.[171] Some officers of the Society, at least, were making conscious efforts to increase the academic side of the programme, as is clear from the correspondence in 1973 between the then Honorary Secretary, James Read, and Professor Glanville Williams about his plans for the following year's conference:

> In principle, I certainly favour more, and more intensive, working sessions based also on preparatory papers. I think we did this year step up the working sessions—or the opportunity therefore—somewhat, and should do so again next year. Your proposal takes account of a lesson learnt this year—that on a warm afternoon after a good lunch members are disinclined to attend working sessions![172]

Such developments came to a grinding halt at the Exeter conference in 1975, however. Writing to Peter Glazebrook (Cambridge), convenor of the newly formed specialist group on Criminal Law, the President, Professor CF Parker (Exeter) made his position very clear:

> I can say that I do not intend to have Discussion Groups on a variety of topics as at Cardiff. This is not to say, by any means, that they were not successful there, but they do not fit into my plans for our Conference here at Exeter.[173]

Nevertheless, participation was on the agenda again in 1977 at Southampton. Despite the fact that the panel discussing the Report of the Royal Commission on Legal Services included only one academic, the intention was clearly to allow maximum opportunity for audience participation, since the topic occupied two sessions, taking up the whole of the Friday morning.[174]

---

[170] 'The Annual Meeting of the Society 1970' (1970) 11(NS) *JSPTL* 65.

[171] SPTL Annual Conference 1971 First Circular, A.SPTL 16/2; letter dated 12 September 1973 from James Read to Glanville Williams, A.SPTL 16/2; SPTL Annual Conference Cardiff 1974 Programme, A.SPTL 16/2.

[172] Letter dated 12 September 1973 from James Read to Glanville Williams, A.SPTL 16/2.

[173] Letter dated 4 November 1974 from Prof CF Parker (SPTL President) to PR Glazebrook, A.SPTL 16/2

[174] SPTL Annual Conference Southampton 1977 Second Circular, A.SPTL 16/2

It appears likely that, as far as the Annual Conference was concerned, the memorandum received from the Young Members' Group had had some effect in stimulating the Officers of the Society to think about increasing both the academic content of the conference and the active involvement of members in the conference programme. It was with some satisfaction, perhaps, that the report of the 1974 meeting of the Young Members' Group commented that with the proliferation of discussion groups at the main conference that year, 'the Young Members' Group could no longer claim to provide the sole source of intellectual stimulation'.[175] From 1976 onwards the Young Members' meeting ran concurrently with the main SPTL conference, which also helped to increase the academic content of the conference, although necessitating some hard choices for members about which sessions they attended.[176]

Annual Dinners

The Annual Dinners continued to be relatively grand affairs throughout the 1970s. Generally they consisted of four courses, with two different wines and port or brandy with the coffee. The dinner in 1971 in Edinburgh, under the Presidency of Professor TB Smith, reflected its local heritage, with a starter of pheasant paté and oatcake or game soup, followed by saddle of hill lamb, soufflé Royal Stewart, coffee and petits fours; it was accompanied by Chabret, Claret 'Walter Scott' and port. This dinner also featured musical entertainment—in the form of a programme of pipe music played by a Pipe Major from the Army School of Piping.[177] At Cardiff in 1974 under the Presidency of Professor Glanville Williams the menu consisted of melon en parapluie, consommé julienne, cold Teifi salmon mayonnaise, Welsh saddle of lamb, cassata, a selection of cheeses, coffee and mints, accompanied by Liebfraumilch, Tabarin and port. Guests were entertained by a Welsh choir, originally founded to compete in the international 'Let the People Sing' competition, which had numerous television appearances to its credit and was conducted by a lecturer in music education at University College Cardiff.[178] Interestingly, it was only when the dinner was held outside England that music was a feature; all other conferences in the 1970s were held at English universities, none of them featured music and at only one (Exeter, in 1975) was there any reference to local produce (Exe salmon and Devon beef).[179]

[175] *SPTL Newsletter* No 5 December 1974, A.SPTL 17, 10

[176] *SPTL Newsletter* No 13 March 1979, A.SPTL 17, 26. Prof Peter Birks, Hon Sec 1989–96 and President 2002–03 pointed out in conversation with one of the authors that the concurrent programme of Young Members' events with those of the main conference also decreased networking opportunities for young members.

[177] Menu for Annual Dinner 1971, A.SPTL 16/1. Prof TB Smith, President of the Society in 1970–71, was only the second Scot to hold the office of President (the first Scottish President was Prof Goudy, the first President of the Society); see (1971) 12(NS) *JSPTL* 3.

[178] Menu for Annual Dinner 1974, A.SPTL 16/1.

[179] Menu for Annual Dinner 1975, A.SPTL 16/1.

Formal toasts remained a feature of the Annual Dinners throughout the decade. The first toast was always 'The Queen', generally followed by 'The Society' and 'The Guests'; on occasion, additional toasts were added, such as the Chancellor of the relevant university or 'The Host Colleges'.[180] Usually, the President proposed a toast to the Society, and the Vice President to the guests; in each case there would be a response, usually by a distinguished judge, so we find the Lord Chancellor (Lord Hailsham) in 1970, Lord Kilbrandon in 1971, the Lord Chief Justice in 1973, followed successively by Lord Diplock, Lord Edmund Davies, Lord Denning and Lord Justice Scarman.[181] Towards the end of the decade, respondents included Lord Goodman and the Chancellor of the Duchy of Lancaster, while at the 1979 dinner, under the presidency of Professor William Twining, the speakers were Dean Erwin Griswold, former US Solicitor-General, and the left-wing barrister, Geoffrey Robertson.[182]

Other Visitors

It is noticeable that at the beginning of the decade at least, participant lists reveal that attendance at the Annual Conference included a significant number of academics from abroad, mainly from Commonwealth countries, but also from other parts of the world. In 1971 at Edinburgh, 239 academics attended, of whom 17 were from abroad, including 5 from Australia, 3 from Canada, 2 from the United States and 1 each from South Africa, Malta, Nigeria and New Zealand.[183] In 1972 at Leeds, 221 academics attended, of whom 30 came from abroad, 6 each from Canada and the United States, 3 each from South Africa and New Zealand, 2 each from Germany, Australia and Japan and 1 each from Belgium, Malta, Cameroon, Uganda, France and Italy.[184] It is not possible to say whether this level of participation by overseas academics continued throughout the decade, but in Exeter in 1975, only 6 out of 174 academics attending were from abroad (3 from Canada and 1 each from the United States, Kenya and New Zealand).[185] Wives continued to attend the Annual Conference in relatively large numbers, and some husbands (very few) also attended. For each of the years where participant lists exist (1971, 1972 and 1975) 22 per cent of the total attendees at the Annual Conference were spouses.[186]

---

[180] Menu for Annual Dinner 1971; Menu for Annual Dinner 1974, A.SPTL 16/1.
[181] See menus for Annual Dinners 1970–77, A.SPTL 16/1.
[182] Menu for Annual Dinners 1978 and 1979 A.SPTL 16/1.
[183] SPTL Annual Conference Edinburgh 1971 List of Participants, A.SPTL 16/2.
[184] Annual Conference Leeds 1972 List of Participants, A.SPTL 10/3.
[185] SPTL Annual Conference Exeter 1975 Registration List, A.SPTL 16/2.
[186] SPTL Annual Conference Edinburgh 1971 List of Participants, A.SPTL 16/2; Annual Conference Leeds 1972 List of Participants, A.SPTL 10/3: SPTL Annual Conference Exeter 1975 Registration List, A.SPTL 16/2.

Improving the Conference

Looking at the available evidence about the Society's conferences in the 1970s, it is hard not to agree with the Young Members' Group that they were largely social events. At the beginning of the decade, at least, it is clear that the academic part of the conference generally took up a mere four and a half hours (three sessions) of a 48-hour conference.[187] The first paragraph of the report of the 1971 conference published in the Society's *Journal* gives an indication of the leisurely pace of the Annual Conference:

> The conference opened on the afternoon of Thursday September 16th, with a reception and tea, which was followed by the Presidential address. After dinner at Pollock Halls, members and their wives were entertained at a reception given by Messrs Butterworth & Co (Publishers) Ltd in the attractive setting of the Upper Library Hall, Old College, University of Edinburgh.[188]

The report of the annual meeting of the Young Members' Group, in contrast, began with a session on 'Understanding Judges' in which a sociologist (Gavin Drewry), a legal academic (Professor Fleming James, Harvard) and a practising lawyer (Mr Brian Gill) discussed the feasibility of different research approaches, as well as substantive issues. This was followed by a session on teaching European law, while the following day was taken up with a series of sessions on 'The Role of the Young Law Teacher', which included consideration of the Ormrod Report on Legal Education, the Young Members' Group memorandum on the future of the Society, and consideration of lawyers and social science research methods.[189]

The criticisms voiced by the Young Members do seem to have had some effect, in that some 'working' or 'specialist' groups occasionally featured in the conference programme, but at least in the early part of the decade, the Society continued to devote a whole half-day to pleasurable outings, on which many members were accompanied by their spouses (predominantly wives). However, some change was apparent, at least in some years, and even the Annual Dinner may have 'loosened up' a little, if the invitation to the 1976 Dinner at Nottingham was anything to go by—dress, it solemnly announced, was 'optional'.[190]

Law Publishing

The 1970s witnessed a considerable amount of concern among members of the Society about legal publishing, against a background of rising costs in the printing and publishing industries, resulting in fewer books being published.

---

[187] SPTL Annual Conference Oxford 1970 First Circular, A.SPTL 16/2.
[188] 'The Annual Meeting of the Society 1971' (1971) 12(NS) *JSPTL* 1.
[189] 'The 1971 Meeting of the Young Members' Group of the Society' (1971) 12(NS) *JSPTL* 2.
[190] SPTL Annual Conference 1976 Nottingham, Programme, SLS Archive, uncatalogued.

This situation meant that 'established scholars had difficulty in publishing their works and for young men the prospect was even bleaker'.[191] At the Sheffield Annual Conference in 1973 a session on law publishing, with a panel of publishers as speakers, was attended by more than 100 members of the Society. Topics ranged from the editing and production of law books to marketing and book-selling. The publishers were adamant that it was simply not commercially viable to publish most monographs which were offered to them, but argued that they were not without regard for the advancement of learning, and did sometimes take risks.[192]

One of the participants in the Sheffield seminar was Professor William Twining who took up the invitation issued by the President at the seminar that any member who wished should follow up the matter so that it could be discussed by the General Committee. In November 1973 Professor Twining wrote to the President to propose 'an SPTL-sponsored Working-Party on law publishing and legal scholarship'.[193] The core of the problem, as he saw it

> is simply stated: nearly all law publishing in this country is run on commercial lines, but much scholarly legal writing (including writing and anthologising for education purposes) is commercially unprofitable. Market forces have a particularly inhibiting or distorting influence on specialized monographs, on educational works in new or neglected fields and on legal publishing generally in the smaller jurisdictions. . . . The world of publishing is changing rapidly, and a number of factors, such as rising costs, are likely to have serious implications for legal scholarship and legal education during the next ten to fifteen years.[194]

It took some persistence on Professor Twining's part to ensure that this idea was considered by the Executive Committee; its agenda was too full in December 1973, and there were also concerns that funding was being requested, with the Honorary Secretary writing that: 'the Hon Treasurer, Neville Brown, clucked a little at the financial aspect—the cupboard is not bare, but we are hard hit, like everyone, by inflation. Could even your relatively modest £200 be pared down without undue loss?'[195] Professor Twining reduced his financial request to £150, and at the end of February 1974 the proposal was approved by the Executive Committee, which asked Professor Twining to chair the Working-Party.[196]

[191] FE Dowrick, 'Law Book Publishing' (1974–75) 13(NS) *JSPTL* 27.
[192] Ibid.
[193] Letter dated 23 November 1973 from Prof WL Twining to Prof JS Read, Hon Sec SPTL, private papers of WL Twining.
[194] Ibid.
[195] Letter dated 8 January 1974 from Prof JS Read, Hon Sec SPTL, to Prof WL Twining, private papers of WL Twining.
[196] Letter dated 18 January 1974 from Prof WWL Twining to Prof JS Read, Hon Sec SPTL, private papers of WL Twining. Members of the Working Party were: Prof WL Twining (Warwick) Convenor; Dr Peter Mann, Department of Sociology (Sheffield), who had undertaken a survey on 'Books and Students' for the National Book League, and had spoken at the SPTL Annual Conference at Sheffield (see Letter dated 23 November 1973 from Prof WL Twining to Prof JS Read, Hon Sec SPTL, private papers of WL Twining); Prof John Rear (Brunel), Secretary and Treasurer; Prof Kenneth Simmonds (Queen Mary); Mr Don Daintree (librarian, Trent Polytechnic, representing BIALL); and David

Financial assistance was limited to £50, however, (it was hoped that additional finance could be raised elsewhere).[197]

Explaining the context of the Working Party to one of its members, Professor Twining wrote that:

[T]he main stimuli to the project are twofold: the first is that there appears to be a vaguely defined sense of dissatisfaction among some law teachers (I suspect especially some younger ones with career worries) about the present situation and future prospects for finding publishing outlets—queues for learned journals, a squeeze on monographs and fringe subjects etc. There is also a contrapuntal and equally vague feeling that 'too much is being published'. The nature, scale, realism, intensity etc of these concerns needs to be investigated. . . . Second, there is currently a fairly widespread reaction taking place against the dominance of legal education and research by what might be called 'the expository orthodoxy' as exemplified by the dominant role of the standard legal textbook in legal education. This is a controversial matter, and I have been in the thick of the controversy . . . I think that I should reveal my biases in this respect, but I would hope as convenor of the Working-Party to give ample breathing-space to upholders of this orthodoxy and to other points of view.[198]

The Working-Party proved to be extremely energetic. It consulted widely, not only seeking the views of SPTL members in general, but also interviewing a wide range of people concerned with legal academic publishing and research, including Professor Herbert Hart, to whom Professor Twining wrote 'Your connection with OUP (or more precisely, your experience of their approach and their problems) suggests that you might be able to advise and help us in a number of ways.'[199] The Assistant Director of the Scottish Arts Council provided information about subsidies obtained by the Universities Committee on Scottish Literature.[200] Meetings were held with the major law publishers, and information gathered from university presses.

The Working-Party published its first Interim Report in time for the 1974 Annual Conference, and circulated copies to every law school. One of its main purposes was to encourage feedback to inform its future work. By that stage, discussion papers were being developed on the problems of smaller jurisdictions, law publishing in the USA and Australia, and on the copyright problems of photocopying as they affect law schools. With the assistance of the British and Irish Association of Law Librarians (BIALL), a questionnaire had been sent to law

Trimble (Queens University Belfast; until Spring 1975 only). 'Interim Report of the SPTL Working Party on Law Publishing and Legal Scholarship', August 1975, private papers of WL Twining.

[197] Letter dated 27 February 1974 from Prof JS Read, Hon Sec SPTL, to Prof W Twining, private papers of WL Twining.

[198] WLT 7, letter dated 8 April 1974 from Prof W Twining to Dr P Mann, private papers of WL Twining.

[199] WLT 6, letter dated 3 March 1974 from Prof W Twining to Prof H Hart, private papers of WL Twining.

[200] Letter dated 12 April 1974 from Trevor Hoyle, Assistant Director, Scottish Arts Council to Prof W Twining, private papers of WL Twining.

librarians about the likely impact of economic pressures on law libraries.[201] A second Interim Report was published in the following year.[202]

The second Interim Report emphasises the economic crisis facing academic publishing generally, with rising production and printing costs at a time when libraries, students and academics had less money to spend on book purchases. Although there was some evidence that publishers would have more conservative publication policies, the Working Party was of the view, on the basis of the evidence it had uncovered so far, that there were not a substantial number of good monographs 'lying in bottom drawers because they have failed to find a publisher'. On the contrary, 'more than one publisher associated with a university press has commented to us on the surprisingly small number of law manuscripts which have been submitted to him'. [203] Similarly, there was little evidence of huge queues for publication in scholarly law journals; this may have been the case in relation to some of the most prestigious journals, 'such as the Law Quarterly Review, Modern Law Review and Cambridge Law Journal', but elsewhere there was often space available.[204] The Working Party took the view that while some retrenchment in publishing was likely,

> there is also evidence to suggest that not all academic lawyers have a realistic picture of the world of law publishing . . . and it may be the case that some individuals have been unduly pessimistic, unduly submissive and unduly unimaginative in the face of certain kinds of direct or indirect economic pressures.[205]

The second Interim Report concludes with a few 'home truths' for law teachers:

> It is evident from listening to law teachers . . . that there is a widespread feeling that commercial publishers are the villains of the piece, and that if they would only be less grasping and more efficient there would be no difficulty in students getting books cheaper, in law teachers having them free, in having all publishing proposals accepted and PhD theses published, and in finding room in prestigious journals for every article submitted irrespective of length. Even in less exaggerated form, this opinion is naive . . . where certain types of publications are considered desirable by academic law-yers, but are commercially unattractive to publishers, then we must recognise that the problem is *our* problem rather than theirs. It is also plain that law teachers can to a cer-tain extent help themselves in the current situation by marketing their manuscripts more effectively. . . . A proposal rejected by one publisher is not a proposal rejected by all.[206]

Despite all its activity, the Working Party had been very short of resources; it had received small grants from the SPTL, Butterworths and Sweet & Maxwell, but

---

[201] 'Interim Report of the SPTL Working Party on Law Publishing and Legal Scholarship', above n 196, para 2.

[202] A.SPTL 10/7.

[203] 'Interim Report of the SPTL Working Party on Law Publishing and Legal Scholarship', above n 196, para 12.

[204] Above n 202, para 13.

[205] Ibid, para 15.

[206] Ibid, para 53.

nothing substantial. However, it was able to embark on a much more substantial enquiry when a grant was secured from the Nuffield Foundation, facilitating the employment of Mrs Jenny Uglow as a researcher.[207]

In its second phase, the Working Party was even more active. Such a mass of material was collected that a series of substantial Working Papers was published: 'Marketing Your Manuscript to Commercial Publishers', 'Law Journals', 'Institutional Production of Educational and Research Materials', 'Subsidisation of Scholarly Work'and 'New Methods and Techniques'.[208] With the support of the Commonwealth Legal Education Association a research project was undertaken on the special problems of smaller jurisdictions and a paper on this subject was subsequently submitted to a project run by the International Legal Centre.[209]

Overall, the conclusions in the Final Report do not differ greatly from those of the second Interim Report. The evidence confirmed that market forces were having an inhibiting effect on monographs, educational works in new or emerging fields, and on law publishing generally in the smaller jurisdictions. The rising costs of books also presented problems of access for students, both in terms of libraries and personal ownership. Periodicals were unlikely to expand in size, so would not be able to accommodate the increasing number of articles being produced by legal academics. Commercial pressures were causing publishers to go for short print runs, so that books went out of print, and second editions were not commissioned until after a considerable demand had built up. The Working Party found a clear conflict between the requirements of commercial publishers and those of scholarship. Publishers were concerned with their perception of the market, while academics were concerned with intellectual or teaching matters.[210]

When the Working Party began its work, rising costs appeared to present a serious problem. Production costs rose more than 30 per cent per year between 1971 and 1975; in the same period book prices overall rose almost 70 per cent. However, by the time the Final Report was published in 1977, publishers did not feel in crisis; they had got used to the conditions of the market, and taken steps to reduce the accompanying risks. Lists were pruned, and books allowed a much shorter period to achieve profitability, while publishers also experimented with various ways of reducing production costs. These latter experiments were not always successful, sometimes resulting in an unacceptable reduction in production quality. Royalties were also reduced; some publishers offered none at all. However, law journals seemed to be less hard hit, and two new journals, the *European Law Review* and the *British Journal of Law and Society*, were established during this period. A growth in the number of small publishers taking an interest

---

[207] SPTL Working Party on Law Publishing, 'Final Report on Law Publishing and Legal Scholarship' (1977) s 1, para ii; A.SPTL 10.7.

[208] These titles comprise, in order, Working Papers 1–5, A.SPTL 10/7

[209] SPTL Working Party on Law Publishing, above n 207, s 1, para v; A.SPTL 10.7.

[210] Ibid, s 2, paras 6 and 7; A.SPTL 10.7.

in law also mitigated the situation to some extent.[211] The picture was also brighter for socio-legal work; in the time between the Working Party first looking at the outlets for such work in 1973, and the publication of the Final Report in 1977, there was a growth in outlets, with an increasing number of publishers perceiving a demand for such work.[212] Nevertheless, the Working Party concluded that certain categories of material faced particular problems. These included works dealing with the law of smaller jurisdictions, monographs, educational books dealing with new fields, 'think-books' (books which seek to change established ideas or ways of thinking so that textbooks and courses are changed thereafter) and ambitious scholarly projects such as the Bentham project.[213]

In seeking to address the problems it had uncovered, the Working Party made a number of recommendations. Chief among these were that there should be an SPTL Publishing Committee to keep the situation under review, establish an SPTL publication fund, primarily to support the publication of teaching materials and to act as editorial committee for a proposed SPTL book series. In addition, the Society was urged to promote the establishment of a new general law journal, to encourage research into the information needs of law students and to support efforts to initiate a general enquiry into the problems of academic publishing and their implications for scholarship.[214]

By the end of the decade, The Working Party had achieved at least some of its aims. The Society established a Standing Committee on Law Publishing, which recommended that negotiations should take place with a view to establishing an SPTL Law Series. In line with efforts to promote increased openness within the Society, it invited expressions of interest in the job of General Editor (particularly senior members of the Society, but any interested members of whatever standing were invited to get in touch with Professor William Twining, the Chair of the Committee.[215] In 1979 Professor PS Atiyah (Oxford) was formally appointed as Editor of the SPTL Law Series.[216]

In contrast to many aspects of the Society during this time, the Working Party was very energetic and productive, making concrete proposals for change which were broadly accepted by the Society.[217] It is a tribute to the members of the Working Party, and in particular its Chair, Professor Twining, and its researcher, Mrs Jenny Uglow, that this was the case.

[211] Ibid, s 2, paras 11–6; A.SPTL 10.7.
[212] Ibid, s 2, para 17; A.SPTL 10.7.
[213] Ibid, s 2, para 21; A.SPTL 10.7.
[214] Ibid, s 2, para 75; A.SPTL 10.7.
[215] *SPTL Newsletter* No 13 March 1979, A.SPTL 17, 23.
[216] SPTL Council 13 September 1979 Minute C13/79, A.SPTL 10/5.
[217] SPTL Council 16 December 1977, Minute C35/77, Report of the Society's Working Party on Law Publishing, 'General approval was given to the contents of the report', A.SPTL 10/5.

Conclusion

During the 1970s, the SPTL underwent significant structural changes due to the energy of the Young Members' Group in pressing for reform of the Society. The establishment of an Executive Committee offered the opportunity to undertake more activity, at a greater speed, than had been possible when the only decision-making body was Council. Equally, the establishment of the *Newsletter* indicates that the Society wished to improve communications among its members. However, reform was not consistent. It is clear that some members of the Society (and some Presidents) did not share the view that reform was either desirable or urgent. Consequently, it was a case of two steps forward, one step back. The after-math of the Ormrod Report was a major disappointment. It is all too clear that at the crucial time, the Society lacked the political leadership which would have enabled it to capitalise on the Report, which was generally very favourable towards the legal academy.

Although women had been eligible to become members of the Society since 1950, the number of female legal academics listed in the Society's Directory of Members grew slowly. The Directory for 1970 lists 604 Ordinary members of whom 54 were women (9 per cent).[218] By 1979 the Directory lists 896 ordinary members, of whom 146 were women (17 per cent), although in 1979 the number of women is inflated by the 21 female teachers at the College of Law (if the College of Law members are omitted, the percentage of women members in 1979 drops to 14 per cent).[219] Unsurprisingly, those attending the Annual Conference were also largely male. Attendance lists exist for three Annual Conferences in this decade: 1971, 1972, and 1975.[220] They show that female legal academics (as opposed to wives of male members) make up 9, 14 and 11 per cent, respectively, of the academics attending in those years. None of the Officers of the Society were women during this decade, although women did play a part in the Committee of the Young Members' Group.[221]

As the decade ended, the question of eligibility for membership of the Society remained controversial. In 1971 a proposal had been made to extend eligibility to law teachers in polytechnics, but this was defeated. During his presidency in 1978–79, Professor William Twining decided to raise the issue again. Comment-ing on this decision, the Vice-President, Professor JC Smith wrote:

---

[218] SPTL Directory of Members 1970, A.SPTL 7. Note that there was no standard template for information in the Directory, so different law schools used different conventions to designate gender. Generally, it is easy to identify women, though on a few occasions, where initials only are used, it is impossible to verify the gender of the person concerned.

[219] SPTL Directory of Members 1970, A.SPTL 7.

[220] SPTL Annual Conference Edinburgh 1971 List of Participants, A.SPTL 16/2; Annual Conference Leeds 1972 List of Participants, A.SPTL 10/3; SPTL Annual Conference Exeter 1975, Registration List, A.SPTL 16/2.

[221] See eg SPTL Young Members' Group Newsletter November 1972 reporting that the YMG Committee for 1972–73 included Jennifer Temkin, A.SPTL 26.

The point that is likely to be most controversial is that concerning the ALT. You may very well be right in saying that there is a 'growing' body of opinion in the society that law teachers in Polytechnics should be eligible to be full members of the society, but I wonder if there is any evidence that this is so? There is certainly another view that it would be best to let sleeping dogs lie and that to reopen the issue would be divisive. It may be that this is mainly the attitude of senior members of the society whose opinions I naturally hear more often than those of younger members with the exception of those in my own department.

I think that you put the practical difficulties very fairly, if I may say so . . . There is a fear on the part of some of our colleagues, which may be completely unfounded, of being 'swamped'. I think that they would need to be reassured.[222]

In December 1978, on the proposal of Professor Twining, Council voted to establish a Working Party to explore the possibility of extending membership to law teachers in institutions teaching law at degree or professional level. The Working Party reported in the summer of 1979 and a motion, embodying its recommendations, was submitted to the AGM in 1979, but was withdrawn on the advice of Council because, it was suggested, members had not had time to consider the report.[223] The decade therefore ended with the matter of membership unresolved.

---

[222] Letter dated 27 September 1978 from Prof JC Smith to Prof WL Twining, private papers of WL Twining.

[223] SPTL AGM 13 September 1979, Minute 8, A.SPTL 26/1.

9

The 1980s: A Difficult Decade

If the new world of budget centres, management priorities, and bureaucratic obedience to university administrators and Government takes priority over the creation of that sense of academic community within which academics are encouraged and enriched, the maintaining spirit of our university system will be lost.

(Professor John Andrews, Presidential Address, 1989)

The Society's *Journal*

The decade began with a very noticeable change for the Society. In 1980 the final issue of the *Journal of the Society of Public Teachers of Law* (*JSPTL*) was published. The relaunched journal was to be known as *Legal Studies*. It had become increasingly apparent that a journal focusing on legal education, which at the same time carried out the intention of the original founders of the publication that it should be 'for the permanent recordation of the Society's various activities', was no longer appropriate.[1] The Editor from 1962 until the final issue of the *JSPTL* was Professor A Jolowicz (Cambridge), whose father had been the *Journal*'s first editor from 1924 until his death in 1954. Professor Jolowicz had for some time been trying to move the *Journal* towards being a more general legal journal, but his initial suggestion was made in 1974, at a time when the Society was very concerned about its finances, and instead of developing the *Journal*, the decision was made to decrease the number of issues from two to one a year.[2] In the midst of all the financial discussions, Professor Jolowicz's paper suggesting changes to the *Journal* was not put before members, although an editorial advisory committee was established, and a new editorial policy decided upon, which freed the editor of the *Journal* from an obligation to publish reports of the proceedings of the annual meetings, and stated that although a 'certain priority' would be given

---

[1] WS Holdsworth 'The Society of Public Teachers of Law' (1924) 1 *JSPTL* 36.
[2] 'Meet the Editors: Statement by the Senior Editor of the Society's Journal for the Third Session of the Society's Annual Meeting 1978', private papers of WL Twining.

to articles concerned with legal education, an attempt would be made to publish more articles of general interest.[3]

As Professor Jolowicz acknowledged in a paper he wrote about the *Journal* for the 1978 Annual Conference, that change of policy was not very effective in moving the *Journal* in a more general and scholarly direction: it was still the practice to publish the Presidential Address and some material from the Annual Conference, and space for articles of a general nature was very limited.[4] In the same year, the *Journal's* Editorial Committee produced a report on the future of the *Journal*, stating that:

> It is the committee's opinion that it would be to the advantage of the Society and of legal publishing in the U.K. if the Society's Journal could now adopt much more of the role of a general scholarly publication, and, at the same time, seek to reach a wider readership than at present.[5]

The Committee did not underestimate the size of the task which lay ahead in establishing a new image for the *Journal*. Its report went on:

> The principal difficulty will be to get started . . . it has to be recognised that at present established academic legal writers do not regard the Journal as an appropriate outlet for the results of their research.[6]

Professor Jolowicz made it clear that he wished to retire as Editor, feeling it appropriate that the new *Journal* should start with a new editor. The vacancy was duly publicised, and four expressions of interest were received, from which Professor John Andrews (Aberystwyth) emerged as the first editor of the new journal.[7] Butterworths, the publishers of the *Journal*, were supportive of the new venture, and suggested that their support might be increased so as to enable the publication of two, or even more, issues a year.[8]

A number of titles were canvassed for the new journal. Noting that there were possible objections to each of 'United Kingdom', 'British' and 'British and Irish', Professor Twining (Warwick), the Chair of the Society's Working Party on Law Publishing, suggested:

> How about 'The Jurist'? (Other titles which have occurred to me are 'Legal Studies'; 'The (British and Irish) Journal of Academic Law'; 'The Legal Scholar'; 'Law'. I am not sure I would wish to be blamed for any of them.[9]

---

[3] Ibid.

[4] Ibid; see also '*JSPTL*—Adieu' (1980) 15(NS) *JSPTL* 78–9.

[5] 'Report of Editorial Committee Concerning Future of the *JSPTL*', November 1978, private papers of WL Twining.

[6] Ibid.

[7] Letter dated 5 March 1979 from Prof WL Twining (Chair, SPTL Working Party on Law Publishing) to Prof JA Jolowicz (Editor, *JSPTL*), private papers of WL Twining; *SPTL Newsletter* No 14 March 1980, A.SPTL 17, 1.

[8] Letter dated 11 August 1978 from Prof WL Twining (Chair, SPTL Working Party on Law Publishing) to Prof JA Jolowicz (Editor, *JSPTL*), private papers of WL Twining.

[9] Letter dated 15 June 1979 from Prof WL Twining (Vice-President) to Prof JA Jolowicz, private papers of WL Twining.

Finally, the formal announcement appeared in the Society's *Newsletter* in March 1980. Henceforth, with the generous support of Butterworths, the *Journal* would appear three times a year, under its new title of *Legal Studies*, aiming to be a scholarly journal of broad general appeal.[10] In the following *Newsletter*, the new Editor made the editorial policy clear:

> As a matter of editorial policy, *Legal Studies* will publish articles on a wide range of subjects, limited only by the criteria of scholarly merit and legal interest. We shall not publish the traditional case notes or statute notes, but we do hope to include a number of shorter articles whose main consideration might be a decided case or cases or a recent statute. However we would expect contributions of this sort to be of scholarly and permanent interest and they may range over all areas of legal investigation, historical, philosophical, statistical, sociological or indeed any area of scholarship within the compass of the journal.[11]

In the event, the new incarnation of the *Journal* was to be very successful in a remarkably short period. Five years later, the Editor was able to report in the *Newsletter* that at the end of its fourth year as *Legal Studies* the journal was enjoying an increasing number of subscriptions, with a high level of academic readership not just in the UK but internationally.[12]

Financial Stringency

As Kogan and Hanney's study of higher education policy reminds us, the election of Margaret Thatcher in 1979 heralded a period of financial stringency for universities:

> The Secretary of State for Education, Sir Keith Joseph, was concerned more than any other spending minister to reduce levels of public expenditure, driven as he was by a monetarist ideology . . . in addition, questions were being voiced by ministers . . . over whether much of the HE output was economically valueless . . . and whether therefore HE should be both reduced in scale and somehow drastically reformed .[13]

In 1981 a Public Expenditure White Paper announced cuts in resources which would mean universities losing between 11 and 15 per cent in real terms between 1980/81 and 1983/84.[14] This was followed by other policy announcements including a Green Paper in 1985 and a White Paper in 1987 which emphasised

---

[10] *SPTL Newsletter* No 14 March 1980, A.SPTL 17, 1.
[11] *SPTL Newsletter* No 15 February 1981, A.SPTL 17, 1.
[12] *SPTL Newsletter* Summer 1985, A.SPTL 17, 3.
[13] See M Kogan and S Hanney *Reforming Higher Education* (London, Jessica Kingsley Publishers, 2000) 89.
[14] Ibid, 118.

the need for universities to be more efficient, and confirmed that funding of research would be increasingly selective.[15]

The continuing financial cutbacks caused concern among members of the SPTL, as elsewhere in higher education. In his Presidential Address at the Annual Conference in 1982 Professor Grodecki (Leicester) made clear that he saw them as a real threat, commenting: 'There is every reason to fear that universities and conditions of work in them will never be the same again.'[16] He noted a recent survey carried out by the Committee of Heads of University Law Schools, which reported decreasing student numbers, academic posts being frozen and early retirement programmes being implemented almost everywhere.[17]

Faced with such a serious financial situation the Society wrote in 1984 to the University Grants Committee (UGC) to protest that 'It is already the case that public provision for legal studies in the UK is less than for other social studies and less than in the EEC or North America'.[18] The Society also lent its support to the detailed response produced by the Committee of Heads of University Law Schools (CHULS) on the implications for law as a discipline of the 'Swinnerton-Dyer letter,' from the then Chairman of the UGC, detailing the cutbacks.[19] The CHULS response was reproduced in full in the *Newsletter*.[20] It made the point that Law as a discipline had changed from one primarily focused on teaching an undergraduate curriculum mainly involving exposition of legal doctrine with a view to preparing students for private practice to one in which there was increasing diversity both in teaching and research, and in particular an increase in socio-legal research and in interdisciplinary approaches to law, such as law and economics, law and medicine, and sociology of law, as well as in international and comparative law.[21] It went on to indicate that any expansion of the 'core' subjects in the undergraduate degree would be a matter of 'grave concern', and argued for a return to the Ormrod principle of recognition of degrees as a whole 'in place of the tendency to emphasize detailed coverage of particular topics on a subject-by-subject basis'.[22] The suggestion that two-year degrees might be introduced was rejected by all heads of law schools, with the exception of Professor Casson (Buckingham), whose comments were appended to the response. Apart from this one dissenting voice, the legal academic community was united in its resistance to the threat posed by continuing Government cutbacks.

> We do not accept that further reductions in the resources available to the University
> sector, following closely on the recent severe cuts, would be in the public interest, nor

[15] DES (1985) *The Development of Higher Education into the 1990s* Cmnd 9524 HMSO, London; DES (1987) *Higher Education: Meeting the Challenge* Cm 114 HMSO, London.

[16] *SPTL Newsletter* Winter 1982–83, A.SPTL 17, 5.

[17] Ibid, 6.

[18] *SPTL Newsletter* Summer 1984, A.SPTL 17, 10.

[19] Circular Letter from the Chairman of the UGC No 16/83, 'the Swinnerton-Dyer letter'.

[20] *SPTL Newsletter* Summer 1984, A.SPTL 17, 11–25.

[21] Ibid, 13.

[22] Ibid, 16 and 23–4.

that the UGC should passively accept assumptions about such reductions as a basis for planning.[23]

It is noticeable, however, that although the SPTL expressly supported the CHULS response, its own response was couched in much more general terms; the Council minute notes 'as a considerable number of Council members had not seen the [CHULS] document, it would not be possible to endorse its contents specifically'. The President was asked to indicate 'that the Society was concerned at the level of support for law teaching and research in universities and hoped that serious consideration would be given to the representations in that regard made by the CHULS'. [24] This somewhat understated response suggests that the Society was not capable at this time of providing strong leadership in important matters of legal education policy.

However, by the end of the decade, the Executive Committee was much more active, agreeing that the President should write to the Chair of the UGC to complain about the financial cutbacks in higher education, noting that:

> the teaching of law as a university subject has not benefitted [*sic*] from the historical averaging method of calculating its funding. This method reflects the position which once operated when the subject was taught by more junior staff at the lower end of the salary scale and when staff student ratios were higher than under current conditions. Incremental drift and higher costs, for example for the purchase and installation of new technology, have made the current level of funding inadequate.[25]

In his letter the President expressed the Society's concern at the low unit of resource in law and argued that this should be raised to a level equal to that of other social sciences. He also raised the question of the forthcoming Research Assessment Exercise (RAE) and the importance of recognising the 'diverse nature of research in law' and the Society's firm view that a member of the Society should sit on the panel assessing law.[26] This showed more willingness on the part of those leading the Society to participate actively in debates on matters of educational policy than had previously been the case.

The Society itself was not immune from the effects of the financial cutbacks experienced by law schools. By the end of the decade it acknowledged that although in the past it had been able to draw upon the assistance of various departmental secretarial facilities to provide administrative assistance for the running of the Society, this would no longer be the case, as law schools no longer had the necessary surplus capacity, and Council agreed that the Executive Committee should consider setting aside a sum of £1,000 towards secretarial assistance.[27]

---

[23] Ibid, 16.
[24] SPTL Council Minutes 16 March 1984 Minute C54/84, A.SPTL 10/5.
[25] SPTL Executive Committee Minutes 14 June 1989 Minute E18/89, A.SPTL 20/5.
[26] Letter dated January 1989 from Prof J Andrews to Chair, UGC, A.SPTL 20/5.
[27] SPTL Council Minutes 21 September 1989 Minute C19.5, A.SPTL 20/5.

Collective Voice

For some time, the Society had been struggling with the question of its collective voice, and this became particularly obvious during the 1980s. In 1983 Council agreed that the President should have authority to write to the press and make public the views of the Society on relevant matters such as legal education. However, the reluctance of Council to go too far down this route is reflected in the qualification that 'the President should only write in this way where the view of Council was known and was undivided'.[28] This ensured that the President could only make pronouncements on completely uncontroversial matters; the Society was compelled to be silent on anything at all controversial where arguably it should have been making its presence felt.

The Society's minutes record a large number of responses to consultation papers being organised by various members on behalf of the Society. These were often drafted by ad hoc groups of subject specialists, and many of them appear to have been managed without controversy. In these cases the Society appeared to be developing more confidence in the ability of such individuals to gather views and draft responses without constantly having to refer back to Council.[29] However, responses were extremely variable in the confidence with which they represented the Society's views. Two responses in 1984 (on 'Discovery of Documents and Disclosure' and 'Legal Aid') were both authoritative in tone; divisions of opinion among members were recorded, but only in passing.[30] However, an ad hoc group convened to respond to a consultation paper from the Home Office on 'Trespass on Residential Premises' in 1983 began by stating:

> Unfortunately, our views are divided at the outset. One of us (Professor Prichard) is persuaded of the necessity of a general offence of trespassing with intent to annoy, frighten etc any person on the premises. . . . The others of us, however, are not convinced that a case has been made out for a general criminal offence.[31]

While these statements are in the best tradition of academic debate, it might be thought that this was a style unsuited to responding to consultation, where a more robust approach might better reflect the Society's authority and legal expertise to the 'outside world'.

In 1989 the Government issued three Green Papers relating to the reform of the legal profession. They represented a serious move on the part of the Government to introduce free-market principles to the supply of legal services.[32] There were howls of protest, not only from the legal profession, but also from the

---

[28] SPTL Council Minutes 18 March 1983, Minute C7/83, A.SPTL 10/5.
[29] See eg SPTL Council Minutes 16 March 1984, Minute C62/84 and Minute C63/84, A.SPTL 10/5.
[30] *SPTL Newsletter* Sumer 1984, A.SPTL 17, 4–10.
[31] *SPTL Newsletter* Winter 1983–84, A.SPTL 17, 3–4.
[32] See F Cownie, 'The Reform of the Legal Profession or the End of Civilisation as We Know It', ch 12 in F Patfield and R White (eds), *The Changing Law* (Leicester, Leicester University Press, 1990) 216–7.

judiciary, anxious to protect their independence.[33] Lord Lane, the Lord Chief Justice, described the Green Paper as 'one of the most sinister documents ever to emanate from Government', while Lord Hailsham accused the Government of 'thinking with its bottom and sitting on its head'.[34] While many of the issues raised did not directly concern legal academics, the Society submitted a response which focused on issues pertaining directly to legal education.[35] In relation to the Lord Chancellor's Advisory Committee, it welcomed the continued existence of a Committee, but argued for an enlarged body so that it could have two sub-committees—one to supervise legal education and one to regulate professional conduct. A strong case was made for increased academic representation on the Committee, whatever form it took.[36] Commenting on the academic stage of legal education, the response noted that in different sections of the Green Paper at least three subjects (evidence, financial regulation and European Community law) were mentioned as candidates for addition to the existing core. It made clear that considerable resistance could be expected from the legal academy to any proposal for an increase in core subjects, especially given the fact that a substantial proportion of law graduates would not enter the legal profession. Equally, there was likely to be little support for any proposal to teach trusts and land law together, at least insofar as it involved a halving of the time devoted to teaching each subject.[37] The response ended by making some general points, including the need for an expansion of student numbers so as to provide the legal practitioners of the future, and the Society's view that if solicitors were given advocacy rights, a career at the Bar would not be of much attraction to future law graduates. Finally, there was a strong submission about the underfunding of university law schools, and the difficulties of appointing good staff, especially in the commercial and financial fields:

> Bearing in mind that we are talking of competition for first class graduates it is virtually impossible to see how the system will continue to cope with a situation in which articled clerks beginning in London firms are paid more than lecturers with years of service and a Professor in a law school receives a salary which a reasonably successful solicitor hopes to overtake before the age of thirty. The poor response to recent advertisements for posts and the departure of young (and not so young) academics from the universities and polytechnics into legal practice, or other equally lucrative careers, bears witness to this.[38]

Although one reading of this submission might be that the Society took the opportunity to try and strengthen the Society's position in relation to the legal profession, the response came in for some sustained criticism from Professor

[33] Ibid, 217.
[34] Ibid, 222.
[35] *SPTL Newsletter* Summer 1989, A.SPTL 17, 12; Green Paper, *The Work and Organisation of the Legal Profession* Cm 570.
[36] *SPTL Newsletter* Summer 1989, A.SPTL 17, 12.
[37] Ibid, 14–5.
[38] Ibid, 16.

Patrick McAuslan, writing in the *Journal of Law and Society*.[39] In the context of expressing his concern about the failure of legal academics to take a proactive role in current debates about the future of legal education, he characterised as 'frankly pathetic' the SPTL's response to the Green Papers, remarking that it was 'likely to confirm the view of the Government that legal academics need not be taken seriously in their future plans for the profession'.[40] In fairness, Professor McAuslan did not just single out the SPTL for criticism; he was equally scathing about individual legal academics, law schools and law journals who, in his view, were similarly failing to engage in a debate about the future of legal education. However, as far as the SPTL is concerned, his comments serve to underline the difficulties the Society was experiencing in providing an authoritative collective voice on matters which were directly relevant to its members.

Relations with the Professions

Relations between the Society and the legal profession continued to be tetchy. In 1981 the Society expressed disquiet about a number of matters relating to the Law Society's professional examinations, including the lengthy delay in publishing the results of the Part II Examination, and the inability of the Law Society to publish results in such a way that the results of the various teaching institutions could be compared, which hindered law teachers advising students.[41] The Law Society did not agree to do this, and Council reluctantly decided to drop the matter.[42] However, after further lobbying by the SPTL, the Law Society eventually agreed to circulate to polytechnics running vocational courses more information about applicants for places at the College of Law.[43]

During this time, the SPTL did have representation on the Education and Training Committee of the Law Society, where over the years, a series of representatives attempted to maintain a dialogue, representing the Society's views to the profession, and reporting back to the Society on the Law Society's views and proposals.[44] The Society was also represented, for at least some of the 1980s, on the Board of Studies of the Council of Legal Education.[45] However, representation on the professional bodies was not particularly effective in preventing friction between members of the SPTL and the professions. In 1981 the Bar announced without warning that it was going to introduce new minimum entry requirements, together with new rules governing priority for places on the

---

[39] P McAuslan, 'The Coming Crisis in Legal Education' (1989) 16(3) *Journal of Law & Society* 310.
[40] Ibid, 312.
[41] SPTL Executive Committee Minutes 8 January 1981, Minute E 11/81, A.SPTL 10/5.
[42] SPTL Council Minutes 16 September 1982, Minute C 18/82 (i), A.SPTL 10/5.
[43] SPTL Council Minutes 19 September 1984, Minute 6, A.SPTL 10/5.
[44] See eg SPTL Council Minutes 20 March 1987, Minute C5.3, A.SPTL 20/3.
[45] SPTL Council Minutes 9 December 1988, Minute C52.1, A.SPTL 20/5.

Council of Legal Education (CLE) practical courses. The Society sent a letter of protest to the CLE, about the lack of consultation with the Society, with law schools and with the Advisory Committee on Legal Education prior to the introduction of the new arrangements.[46] The apparently high-handed way in which the Bar had acted caused long-standing resentment among SPTL members, which is reflected in a long article published in the *Newsletter* in 1983 by Peter Wallington (Lancaster). The main issues were the new requirement that the minimum entry qualification for the Bar from 1983 onwards would be a 2(2), as well as the imposition of a quota on entry to the Inns of Court School of Law of 1,000 students per year, with preference given to those professing an intention to practise at the English Bar. The background to these changes from the Bar's point of view was the increasing difficulty in finding pupillages and especially tenancies, and overcrowding on the vocational course exacerbated by students wishing to obtain a qualification to be used in their home countries. It was the manner of the announcement of these changes which was controversial, since the Bar had failed to consult the Lord Chancellor's Advisory Committee on Legal Education until after the formal announcement had been made. This had provoked a lot of complaints from academics, which had led to assurances that normally there would be consultation over such changes.[47]

Wallington was sympathetic to the annoyance caused, but urged legal academics not to withdraw completely from dialogue with the professions. While there was undoubtedly lingering resentment about the treatment meted out to the Ormrod Report, especially by the Law Society, he argued for increased participation in any consultation processes that were undertaken. However, he also noted that the Bar did not really understand universities' concerns about possible impacts on student numbers, nor did it take seriously their concerns about academic independence. The assumption made by the professions was that law degrees were simply the academic stage of a professional qualification 'rather like the pre-clinical medical degrees', and this attitude was increasingly reflected in the approach of the professions to matters such as granting exemptions.[48] As Wallington commented, these matters were bound to be resented:

> [N]ot only on the traditional ground of academic independence, but also because of the apparent failure to grasp that, both in intent and in reality, Law degrees are offered increasingly as a form of education as well as a step towards a professional qualification.[49]

This episode did nothing to improve relations between members of the SPTL and the professions.

To make matters worse, the Society also discovered that two additional core subjects (company law and evidence) had been introduced, without consultation,

---

[46] SPTL Council Minutes 18 December 1981, Minute C35/81, A.SPTL 10/5.
[47] *SPTL Newsletter* Summer 1982, A.SPTL 17, 5.
[48] Ibid, 7.
[49] Ibid.

by the Northern Irish legal professions.[50] The Society reacted by attempting once more to increase the effectiveness of its members when negotiating with the legal professions, by appointing 'liaison officers' for the Law Society and the CLE.

> The role of the Liaison Officers with the professions is to act as repositories of infor-
> mation concerning individual constituencies' relations with the professional bodies so
> that they can pass on this accumulated wisdom to any University which finds itself in
> disharmony with one of the professions in relation to matters such as exemptions.
> Universities which have had recent dealings with either professional body should
> please inform the appropriate Liaison Officer of the result of the discussion so that that
> experience can be added to the file of wisdom.[51]

Meanwhile, the question of admission to the Bar remained a matter of concern. The Society attempted to get the Bar to agree that the 2(2) requirement should not apply to those who did not wish to practice at the English Bar. It was also concerned that the requirement had merely been introduced to assist the Inns of Court School of Law in keeping to its entry quota. Both of these points were rejected by the Bar. The letter conveying these decisions is reprinted in full in the *Newsletter*, and its inclusion is another indication of the seriousness with which the Society viewed the new admission rules.[52] The matter was still troubling the Society in 1989, when the Executive Committee noted 'that the lower second class requirement for admission to the Bar operated with unnecessary severity on intending overseas practitioners' and asked the President to reopen the matter with the Bar.[53]

When the Society submitted a response to the Committee on the Future of the Legal Profession (the Marre Committee) in 1986 the opportunity was taken to make the point that 'there have in the past been some unhappy failures of consul-tation between the profession on the one hand and universities and polytechnics on the other'.[54] The response also emphasised the independence of the legal academy by reiterating the Ormrod Committee recommendation that

> the academic stage of legal education should . . . be left to the academic institutions
> and the control exercised by the profession therefore limited to approval or disapproval
> of a degree course as a whole.[55]

It goes on to point out that any change proposed by the profession which relates to the nature or quality of a law degree 'is of immediate concern to all institu-tions offering degrees in law' and suggests that consultation with those institu-tions prior to the introduction of any change 'should be a matter of course and possibly of rule'.[56] Another matter raised in the response to the Marre Committee

---

[50] SPTL Council Minutes 19 March 1982, Minute C10/82, A.SPTL 10/5.

[51] *SPTL Newsletter* Summer 1982, A.SPTL 17, 1.

[52] *SPTL Newsletter* Summer 1985, A.SPTL 17, 4–5.

[53] SPTL Executive Committee Minutes 14 June 1989, Minute E13.2, A.SPTL 20/5.

[54] The Committee on the Future of the Legal Profession: response on behalf of the SPTL, A.SPTL 20/2.

[55] Ibid.

[56] Ibid.

was the inclusion of a legal academic on the governing bodies of the professions. The SPTL had for some time been trying to persuade the Bar Council to include an academic lawyer on the Senate of the Inns of Court and Bar, but to no avail.[57] In its response to Marre, the SPTL once again made a case for such representation:

> [G]iven the recognition of an 'academic stage' as an essential element of qualification, the voice of those responsible for that stage should be heard at the highest level in each profession.[58]

When the President was invited to lunch to meet members of the Marre Committee, he was able to reinforce the SPTL's view that any proposed increase in the number of core (compulsory) subjects 'would not be welcomed by the academic branch of the profession'.[59] However, the Marre Committee appeared unimpressed by the SPTL's representations. In its final Report, its views on the academic stage of legal education were uncompromising:

> We appreciate that a law degree cannot be regarded as a vocational course at university level . . . however, we consider that the universities have an obligation to recognise that most law students will enter the legal profession, and that the profession have a right to expect that such graduates should be properly equipped to enter the vocational stage of training.[60]

Although the Marre Committee recommended that the number of core subjects should not be increased, it did recommend that 'consideration should be given to teaching trusts and land law as a composite subject', a matter which encroached directly on the territory of legal academics.[61]

Towards the end of the 1980s, relations with the professions appeared to be slightly less contentious. Discussions about the College of Law's decision to change its admissions procedure from a continuous process of 'first come first served' to a process which would involve a window for submission of applications and a selection procedure giving priority to those applicants who had demonstrated their commitment to the solicitors' profession (eg by having applied for enrolment as a student member of the Law Society) proceeded without controversy.[62] The College of Law announced in 1988 that it was to open an additional branch at York, which it was hoped would ensure the demand for places would be met by supply, and Council merely noted that this was the case, together with the desirability of notifying members through the *Newsletter* of the new arrangements.[63] Equally, at an informal meeting organised by the Bar Council in January

---

[57] See SPTL Council Minutes 18 March 1983, Minute C10/83, A.SPTL 10/5 and SPTL Council Minutes 13 December 1985, Minute C131.2, A.SPTL 20/1.

[58] The Committee on the Future of the Legal Profession: response on behalf of the SPTL, A.SPTL 20/2.

[59] SPTL Council Minutes 17 September 1987, Minute C18.3, A.SPTL 20/3.

[60] 'A Time For Change: Report of the Committee on the Future of the Legal Profession', General Council of the Bar & Council of the Law Society, London, para 13.2.

[61] Ibid, paras 13.18 and 13.24.

[62] SPTL Council Minutes 11 December 1987, Minute C42.1/87, A.SPTL 20/4.

[63] SPTL Council Minutes 11 March 1988, Minute C8.88, A.SPTL 20/4.

1989 where representatives of the Bar explained their proposals to improve arrangements for obtaining tenancies, they also undertook, wherever possible, to support the universities' case for improved resources.[64] There was also a suggestion that legal academics might be involved in providing continuing education for members of the Bar, and the Society agreed to support such initiatives as a matter of general principle.[65] Even the Advisory Committee seemed to be a little more positive, with the Chairman expressing the view in 1987 that:

> [I]t was desirable that members of the academic branch of the legal profession should enjoy a greater role in the formulation of policy concerning the future of legal education.[66]

Despite the generally uneasy relations between practitioners and academics throughout the 1980s, it was clear that not all practitioners were mindless of the contribution of legal academics to the development of the law. In the Foreword to *Legal Studies* in 1983, written to mark the 75th anniversary of the Society, Lord Hailsham wrote:

> We cannot do without *Legal Studies* or the Society of Public Teachers of Law if we are to do our work properly as judges, advisers or legislators, and if we sometimes resent your criticisms of our work as being unfounded, we are all the better for having been subjected to them. May our dialogue long continue.[67]

The experience of the Society during the 1980s was that even maintaining a dialogue was not easy. Overall, it had not succeeded in asserting the interests of the legal academy in the face of decisive action by the professions.

Relations With Other Outside Bodies

Regular meetings with the Law Commission continued to take place. The importance placed by the Commission upon its relations with the SPTL is reflected in the length of the meetings; the general pattern was for the Commissioners to meet the Officers of the Society in the morning and the Convenors of Special Interest Groups in the afternoon.[68] The *Newsletter* regularly published details of the Commission's work, keeping members up to date with the latest reports and consultation papers. At the beginning of the decade the Chairman of the Commission, Mr Justice Kerr, welcomed the fact that some legal academics had expressed an interest in working on a Law Commission project, either at the Commission during a period of sabbatical leave, or in other ways.[69] He wrote:

---

[64] SPTL Executive Committee Minutes 17 February 1989, Minute E5/89, A.SPTL 20/5.
[65] SPTL Executive Committee Minutes 14 June 1989, Minute E13/89, A.SPTL 20/5.
[66] SPTL Council Minutes 11 December 1987 Minute, C37.1, A.SPTL 20/4.
[67] Lord Hailsham, 'Foreword' (1983) 3(3) *Legal Studies* 228.
[68] See eg SPTL Council Minutes 19 March 1982, Minute C14/82, A.SPTL 10/5.
[69] *SPTL Newsletter* No 14 March 1980, A.SPTL 17, 2.

> The Commission is most appreciative of this suggestion, particularly because I had to make it clear at our meeting that we could not offer any financial reward as things stand at present and in the foreseeable future. However, any such assistance with our work would of course be greatly appreciated and mentioned in our Annual Reports.[70]

He invited members who were interested in working with the Commission in the areas of private international law, contract and commercial law, or family law to get in touch. This invitation evoked little response, but it was agreed at the next meeting with the Commission that this might be because the announcement had been too generalised and had placed too much emphasis on sabbatical leave; it is an indication of its wish to co-operate with legal academics that the Commission undertook to repeat the invitation in a different form which might attract early-career academics.[71]

During the following year the Law Commission held a series of open days to enable law teachers to gain an insight into the way in which the Commission operated, and to met Commissioners and staff.[72] The Law Commission's efforts to involve academic lawyers in its work continued in 1982 when the then Chairman of the Commission, the Honourable Mr Justice Ralph Gibson, wrote an open letter to the SPTL. Acknowledging the assistance which the Law Commission had already received from various SPTL members, he indicated a range of topics on which research would be particularly valuable to the Commission in its law reform work, especially on topics in which the Commission had a long-term interest, but where detailed work had not yet been carried out.[73]

At the annual meeting with the Law Commission in 1982 a suggestion was made that there should be some joint co-operation in connection with the reform of civil procedure. Professor Jolowicz (Cambridge) subsequently met with the Chairman of the Law Commission and it was proposed that a small one-day meeting of academics, judges and practitioners should be held to discuss the establishment of some form of review body. An expert paper written by Sir Jack Jacob would form the basis of discussion, and a report produced after the meeting would be used to try and arouse Government interest in setting up some sort of permanent review body. Having established an outline plan, Professor Jolowicz wrote to ask for the official sanction of the Society:

> I also think that it is most desirable that the SPTL should take the opportunity of getting in at the beginning in this way [but] . . . I am very far from clear what my authority is . . . I hope you will agree that this ought to be an SPTL enterprise, even though, at the beginning, it will involve only very few members.[74]

---

[70] Ibid.

[71] Minutes of a Meeting between the Law Commission and Representatives of the SPTL held at Conquest House, Thursday 21 May 1981, Minute 4, A.SPTL 10/5.

[72] Ibid.

[73] *SPTL Newsletter* Summer 1982, A.SPTL 17, 12.

[74] Letter from Prof JA Jolowicz (Cambridge) to the SPTL President (Prof PH Pettit, Bristol), dated 15 December 1982, A.SPTL 10/8.

He was pleased to get the President's agreement, and by March 1983 the plan had been agreed by the Executive Committee and Council, although there are no records of its outcome.[75]

The cordial relations with the Law Commission continued throughout the decade. The Commission repeatedly made clear that it was open to a range of possibilities allowing it to take full advantage of the work done by academic lawyers in the field of law reform, including secondment of academics, contract work, legal research, sabbatical leave being spent at the Commission, and the appointment of research assistants.[76]

Advisory Committee on Legal Education

The Society continued to be represented on the Advisory Committee on Legal Education, but the Committee proved to be largely ineffective in providing a forum for influencing the legal professions in matters relating to legal education and training.[77] During the saga of the Bar entry qualifications, the SPTL Council decided to request a meeting of the Advisory Committee (which had been by-passed by the Bar) to try and ensure that in the future adequate consultation would take place, noting that 'The Advisory Committee has not met for a year, although it did discuss the Bar's decision at its last meeting, which was after the Bar had come to its decision without consultation.'[78] The Society asked for a meeting to discuss the lack of finance for legal research, raised in Professor Grodecki's Presidential Address the previous September, and the question of admission to the Inns of Court School of Law.[79] When this meeting finally took place in March 1983 the Advisory Committee had not met for more than two years. The matter of lack of support for legal research received a sympathetic hearing, and the Chair of the Advisory Committee agreed to write to the Chairmen of the UGC and the Social Science Research Council (SSRC) to try to get funding policies changed.[80] Two further meetings were then held in relatively quick succession to discuss the restriction on entry to the Inns of Court School of Law, where the SPTL representatives tried to ensure that any selection procedures were as fair as possible.[81]

By 1986 the position was unsatisfactory again; Council minutes record that the President was to write to the Lord Chancellor 'expressing the Society's regret that it had yet to receive any information concerning the appointment of a new

[75] See letters from Prof JA Jolowicz (Cambridge) to Prof PH Pettit (Bristol), dated 5 January 1983 and 24 March 1983, A.SPTL 10/8.
[76] See eg *SPTL Newsletter* Summer 1985, A.SPTL 17, 21.
[77] SPTL Council Minutes 19 March 1982, Minute C11/82, A.SPTL 10/5.
[78] SPTL Council Minutes 16 September 1982, Minute C23/82, A.SPTL 10/5.
[79] SPTL Council Minutes 18 March 1983, Minute C8/83, A.SPTL 10/5.
[80] SPTL Council Minutes 22 September 1983, Appendix 1, President's Report to Council, A.SPTL 10/5.
[81] SPTL Council Minutes 22 September 1983, Appendix 1, President's Report to Council, A.SPTL 10/5.

Chairman of the Advisory Committee'.[82] Nevertheless, all was not lost. When it did next meet, the Committee considered a concern expressed by the Dean of the Council of Legal Education that students lacked sufficient knowledge of EEC law, but was not prepared to suggest that EEC law should become an additional compulsory subject.[83]

The story of the Advisory Committee during this decade is largely one of frustration and inactivity. It was small comfort that the professions appeared to have very little interest in legal education at this time.

Ministry of Justice

In 1988 representatives of the Society met with Sir Derek Oulton, the Permanent Secretary of the newly created Ministry of Justice. Both sides expressed their desire for co-operation, with the Society outlining the role of the special-interest groups, whose members might provide expert advice and the possibilities of empirical research. On learning that in appropriate circumstances the Law Commission paid academics' travelling expenses, though not fees, the Ministry agreed to investigate the practices of other departments with regard to the payment of fees for commissioned pieces of research. It was agreed that future meetings should be convened, and meanwhile the Ministry would also consider the balance between the desire of academics to publish the results of their work and the need to maintain confidentiality in relation to the development of Government policy.[84]

Representatives of the Society also met with Ministry of Justice officials the following year, when they discussed the Society's concerns about the very small representation of academics on the proposed new committee to advise the Lord Chancellor on matters of legal education and conduct, and also the dominant representation of lay members on a single committee concerned both with matters of conduct and with legal education. The minutes record that 'The Society gained the impression, however, that both the linkage of education and conduct and the dominant representation of lay members was a key part of the Government's strategy.'[85] The Society's Executive Committee was nevertheless hopeful that academics might be better represented on any sub-committee dealing specifically with legal education'.[86] In the light of the Society's previous experience with the Advisory Committee on Legal Education, this view could be thought somewhat naïve.

[82] SPTL Council Minutes 12 December 1986, Minute C176.2, A.SPTL 20/3.
[83] SPTL Council Minutes 20 March 1987, Minute C5.1(ii)., A.SPTL 20/3.
[84] Minutes of a Meeting with the SPTL 24 February 1988, A. SPTL 28; see also SPTL Executive Committee Minutes 13 June 1988, Minute E13/88, A.SPTL 20/4 and SPTL Council Minutes 11 March 1988, Minute C3.1, A.SPTL 20/4.
[85] SPTL Executive Committee Minutes 17 February 1989, Minute E7/89, A.SPTL 20/5.
[86] SPTL Executive Committee Minutes 14 June 1989, Minute E13.3, A.SPTL 20/5.

Research Matters

In the 1980s the Society's *Newsletters* carry a considerable proportion of items about research-related matters, providing some evidence that it was not only the *Journal* which was becoming more scholarly, but that there was a general move within the Society to be more active in relation to legal research. In 1980, in addition to an item about opportunities for working on research projects in partnership with the Law Commission, there was also an item soliciting contributions for *Current Legal Problems*.[87] The following issue carried the editorial policy of the Society's new-style *Journal*, emphasising its scholarly nature, as well as a note about the establishment of a new specialist group on property law (encompassing all aspects of land law, including planning, and landlord and tenant) and notices of three conferences, including an international congress on civil procedure and a one-day conference organised by the Society's own Consumer Law Group.[88] In 1983 the SSRC decided to develop a programme of research into the ways in which contemporary family structures and relationships developed. As a preliminary step, a multidisciplinary register of existing research on the family was being compiled, and members were invited to contact the project consultant if they wished their work to be included.[89] Other research-focused items included annual announcements of a Colloquium on Comparative Law, which preceded the Annual Conference. In 1986 this focused on the application of international conventions in domestic law; other topics included computers and the law (Leicester 1982), liabilities of Government agencies in tort (Bristol 1983), product liability (Edinburgh 1984), Government torts and compensation (Birmingham 1985), and legal regulation of reproductive medicine (Cambridge 1987).[90] In 1987 the *Newsletter* for the first time carried publicity about the Critical Legal Conference. This innovation may have been because the conference theme was 'Critique in Legal Education', a topic which was likely to interest SPTL members, but its inclusion suggests greater openness to different approaches to legal scholarship than might have been the case in previous decades.[91]

The SPTL Book Series

Another way in which the Society contributed to its members' research activities was by the establishment of the SPTL book series. Its purpose was 'to make a modest contribution towards meeting the difficulties sometimes facing authors

---

[87] *SPTL Newsletter* No 14 March 1980, A.SPTL 17, 2.
[88] *SPTL Newsletter* No 15 February 1981, A.SPTL 17, 5–6.
[89] *SPTL Newsletter* Summer 1983, A.SPTL, 14–15.
[90] *SPTL Newsletter* Summer 1982, 2; *SPTL Newsletter* Summer 1983, 2; *SPTL Newsletter* Winter 1983–84, 1; *SPTL Newsletter* Winter 1984–85, 3; *SPTL Newsletter* Summer 1987, 1, A.SPTL 17.
[91] *SPTL Newsletter* Summer 1987, A.SPTL 17, 3.

who may be unable to find a normal commercial outlet for their work, and at the same time to mark in a special way works of high scholarly merit'.[92] Professor AS Atiyah (Oxford) was the General Editor of the series, and authors were encouraged to get in touch with him:

> Books will be considered for inclusion even if they are not yet complete, provided that an adequate synopsis and at least one or two draft chapters are available for scrutiny. However, no firm contract or commitment to publish will normally be given except for a completed ms.[93]

Although the series aimed to encourage authors, and its existence clearly benefited members of the Society wishing to write scholarly monographs, it was not an easy option; authors had to take the risk of writing a book for which there was no guarantee of publication.

However, the book series was to be very short-lived. It had been clear from the outset that the series was likely only to be marginally profitable, and in 1985, after the publication of only two titles (*Foundations of the Modern Bar* by Raymond Cocks and *Public Legal Services, a Comparative Study of Policy, Politics and Practice* by Jeremy Cooper) the series was discontinued.[94]

> It was intended that the Series should offer an opportunity for the publication of works of legal scholarship which would otherwise be too specialised to find a publisher. With the development of new methods of book production, it has become clear that the need for the Series is not as great as was originally envisaged, and it has therefore been discontinued.[95]

Although the book series did not last for long, it did provide concrete evidence that the Society was attempting to take seriously the publishing concerns of its members, and actively to do something to assist.

Other Research Initiatives

In 1987 the Society decided to establish an Academic Purposes Fund to make small grants in support of legal research. Members could apply for assistance in relation to any research or scholarly activities, including attendance at or the organisation of conferences.[96] The then President, Professor Jolowicz, had been instrumental in securing agreement to this innovation, and when only two applications (both for conference funding) were made in the first year of its existence, he urged members to put in more applications:

[92] *SPTL Newsletter* No 15 February 1981, A.SPTL 17, 6.
[93] Ibid, 7.
[94] See letter from Hugh Jones (Director, Sweet & Maxwell) to Prof PH Pettit (President, SPTL, Bristol) dated 4 March 1983 and SPTL Council Minutes 12 September 1985, Minute C117.3, A.SPTL 20/1.
[95] *SPTL Newsletter* Winter 1985–86, A.SPTL 17, 4.
[96] SPTL Council Minutes 20 March 1987, Minute 06/87, A.SPTL 20/3.

> I hope and believe that this paucity of applications was due to the novelty of the scheme and, perhaps, to lack of knowledge of its existence among members of the Society. I find it difficult to believe that there are no ordinary members who would not welcome even relatively modest financial help with their research. I ask you, therefore, to read the Rules and note the possibilities offered.[97]

In the same year, the Society decided to include details of members' research interests in the Directory of Members; one of its uses, it was hoped, would be to enable funding bodies to identify those working in relevant fields.[98]

The Society and the Research Assessment Exercise

Among the many policy initiatives introduced by the Conservative governments of the 1980s was a new approach to the determination of universities' financial allocations, which would involve the selective allocation of research funding.[99] The first RAE took place in 1985, when the UGC asked universities to provide details of their research plans, and to provide profiles of individual subject areas ('cost centres') which were to include the titles of not more than five recent books or articles published by individual academics.[100] On the basis of the assessment of the material submitted the UGC divided the cost centres into four bands and published the results. As Henkel notes, this exercise 'provoked widespread criticism on the grounds of lack of transparency and failure to meet the UGC's own criteria for effective performance indicators'.[101]

There is no record in the Society's archives of any discussion having taken place within the Society about the introduction of the first RAE, but in 1988 the *Newsletter* included a copy of the SPTL response to a consultation paper on the 1989 RAE, which was the second RAE carried out in the UK.[102] The response welcomed the inclusion of learned societies in the process, and proposed the President as a member of the appropriate assessment committee. It went on to argue for disclosure of the identities of the experts appointed to carry out the assessment, and for a separate law panel (rather than law submissions being judged by non-lawyers), and also argued strongly against the use of funded research income as an indicator of quality, and against the proposal that departments should be required only to submit a selection of publications, commenting that 'each university should be invited to submit as comprehensive a list of publications as it thinks appropriate'. Finally, it made some suggestions, including that

---

[97] *SPTL Newsletter* Winter 1987–88, A.SPTL 17, 2–3; *SPTL Newsletter* Winter 1988–89, A.SPTL 17, 3.

[98] *SPTL Newsletter* Winter 1987–88, A.SPTL 17, 7.

[99] DES (1987) *Higher Education: Meeting the Challenge* Cm114.

[100] M Cave et al, *The Use of Performance Indicators in Higher Education: The Challenge of the Quality Movement* (London, Jessica Kingsley Publishers, 1997) 79.

[101] M Henkel, *Academic Identities and Policy Change in Higher Education* (London, Jessica Kingsley Publishers, 2000) 114.

[102] On the Research Assessment Exercise, see A Jenkins, 'The Research Assessment Exercise: Funding and Teaching Quality' (1995) 3(2) *Quality Assurance in Higher Education* 4–12, 5.

the criteria by which work is to be judged should be published in advance, and that there should be an appeals mechanism.[103]

When Professor HK Bevan delivered his Presidential Address at the Annual Conference at the University of Hull in 1988 he supplied some background to the RAE consultation process, noting that the Society had not originally been included in the list of 143 learned societies which the UGC intended to consult, but that persistence on the part of the Society had been rewarded with the agreement that it could submit a response. Professor Bevan commented that he could bear with a degree of equanimity the fact that the Committee of Heads of Law Schools, the Inns of Court School of Law and the Law Society had all originally been on the list of consultees, but felt 'some irritation' that the SPTL was excluded when 'for example, the Association of University Teachers of Economics' was included.[104] He mentions this saga, he adds,

> in order to leave you with the thought that over the years the Society may have been too introspective and not sufficiently assertive in self-publicity. I doubt whether it can afford to continue that stance in an age of education conditioned by a philosophy of central Government which ... demands efficiency and value for money in return for public expenditure.[105]

Professor Bevan's view that the increasing tendency of central government to interfere in areas of academic life which had hitherto remained largely immune from outside pressures made it particularly important that the Society was proactive in this area was clearly shared by others; the Society remained closely involved with the RAE, ensuring that it nominated members for consideration for appointment to selection panels.[106] However, his remarks also serve to underline a sense that the Society was not always as effective as it might have been in representing the interests of law teachers in the 'outside world'.

Specialist Groups

The Society's specialist groups thrived during the 1980s. New groups were established, and many of the existing ones held regular meetings, sometimes to coincide with the Annual Conference, sometimes at a different time of the year. The new specialist group on property law, established in 1980, found time to have a meeting with the Contract Law Group to explore the possibility of future joint meetings, while in 1986 both the Tort Group and the Consumer Law Group held one-day conferences (on 'Recent Developments in Professional Negligence' and 'The Nationalised Industries, Privatisation and Consumer Representation',

---

[103] *SPTL Newsletter* Winter 1988–89, 6–7. See also letter dated 1 August 1988 from Prof HK Bevan, President, SPTL to UGC, A.SPTL 17. See also SPTL Executive Committee Minutes 13 June 1988, Minute E16/88, A.SPTL 20/4.

[104] Bevan, letter, above n 103, 2.

[105] Ibid.

[106] SPTL Executive Committee Minutes 17 February 1989, Minute E4/89, A.SPTL 20/5.

respectively).[107] Regular items appeared in the *Newsletter* throughout the decade informing members of the activities of the specialist groups, and inviting participation in responding to Law Commission Working Papers and similar consultation exercises.[108]

Some of the specialist groups were particularly active; for instance, the Administrative Law Group held its own annual conference each year, usually in April, while 1981 saw the Law Commission agree to a proposal made by the Criminal Law Group that 'a team of its members should, under the aegis of the Commission, consider and make proposals in relation to a criminal code'.[109] The team was led by Professor JC Smith (Nottingham) and its members were Professor E Griew (Leicester), Mr P Glazebrook (Cambridge) and MI Dennis (UCL). The hope was that a comprehensive statement of the principles which should govern criminal liability would provide Parliament with 'the necessary framework within which codification of the principal criminal offences can be considered'.[110] Such activities clearly demonstrated the potential of the specialist groups to marshal the expertise of SPTL members to make a contribution to wider debates about the role of law in society.

The Society also had a number of Special Committees (eg on criminal law, family law, private international law) which were established within the Rules of the Society; their Convenors and members were appointed by Council to formulate and express the views of the Society on matters within their area.[111] An item in the *Newsletter* reminded members of the technical distinction between the special interest groups and the special committees.

> Members are reminded of the distinction between Special Committees of the SPTL Council and Special Interest Groups. The former are established within the Rules of the Society; their Convenors and members are appointed by Council to formulate and express the views of the Society on matters within their remit. The latter, although often using the occasion of the SPTL conference to arrange meetings, are established informally without any official link with the Society; membership of these groups is independent of appointment by Council, and may include non-members of the Society.[112]

Of the Society's special committees, the Criminal Law Reform Sub-Committee was particularly active, under the convenorship of Mr P Glazebrook. In July 1982, together with the Society's Public Law Reform Sub-Committee, a response was produced to the Law Commission's Working Paper No 82 on public order offences, followed by comments in April 1983 on the Law Commission's Working

---

[107] *SPTL Newsletter* Winter 1985–86, A.SPTL 17, 3; *SPTL Newsletter* No 15 February 1981, A.SPTL 17, 4.

[108] See eg *SPTL Newsletter* Summer 1982, A.SPTL 17, 4.

[109] *SPTL Newsletter* Winter 1981–82, A.SPTL 17, 2; *SPTL Newsletter* No 16 June 1981, A.SPTL 17, 1.

[110] *SPTL Newsletter* No 16 June 1981, A.SPTL 17, 2.

[111] *SPTL Newsletter* Winter 1987–88, A.SPTL 17, 3.

[112] Ibid, 6.

Paper No 84 on criminal libel and in June 1983 to the CIRC's Working Party on Offences Relating to Prostitution. All are substantial documents.[113]

Socio-Legal Studies

The development of socio-legal studies continued to be reflected within the Society. In 1981, the *British Journal of Law and Society* announced a conference on 'Policing in the Eighties', at which speakers would include Stuart Hall, Professor of Sociology at the Open University, the Director of the Institute of Race Relations and two lecturers in social administration, as well as a member of the Royal Commission on Criminal Procedure. SPTL members were invited to propose papers for panel sessions and workshops, and this was clearly a serious attempt by the Editor of the *British Journal of Law and Society*, Philip Thomas (Cardiff), to involve members of the Society in an important interdisciplinary conference.[114]

Socio-legal studies played a leading role in the special edition of *Legal Studies* published in November 1983 to mark the 75th anniversary of the Society. Lord Hailsham contributed a Foreword in which he wrote that he hoped the dialogue between practitioners, legislators, judges and academics would long continue. But he expressed some concern that there might be a hindrance to this dialogue.

> My only abiding concern for its future is my fear that the study and practice of law may become too narrowly based and tend to divorce itself from the general culture of which we are all part, and in which history, language, literature, the physical sciences and philosophy have an equal and distinctive part to play in the framing of our institutions and our system of justice.[115]

The emphasis on a broad approach to the practice and study of law, coming from a member of the senior judiciary, suggests that the influence of socio-legal studies was continuing to grow.

The developments which had taken place in the field of socio-legal studies were amply recorded in the 75th anniversary issue of *Legal Studies* in an article by Donald Harris, Director of the Centre for Socio-Legal Studies at Oxford.[116] He saw the most important development in socio-legal studies as being the influence of sociology on the teaching of law.

---

[113] All these documents can be found in A.SPTL 10/8.
[114] *SPTL Newsletter* No 16 June 1981, A.SPTL 17, 2–3.
[115] Hailsham, above n 67.
[116] DR Harris, 'The Development of Socio-Legal Studies in the United Kingdom' (1983) 3(3) *Legal Studies* 315.

> Even without any formal change in the syllabus of law courses, the content of many courses has been transformed by emphasis on the social effects of law and by reference to theories of the role of law in society.[117]

Supported by the establishment of new series of textbooks, such as the Law in Context series published by Weidenfeld & Nicolson, and new journals such as the *British Journal of Law and Society*, and the *International Journal of the Sociology of Law*, as well as by growing numbers of edited collections of essays and monographs, often reporting the results of empirical studies, Harris saw socio-legal studies as a thriving field.[118] In including his article in the anniversary edition of *Legal Studies* the SPTL's journal was also acknowledging the importance of this relatively new approach to legal education and scholarship.

However, law remained marginal as far as the Research Councils were concerned, and the Society did not make substantial progress in improving the situation. Sometimes this appears to have been due to the existence of widely differing views on the subject held within the Society. An invitation in 1981 to join other learned associations in the social sciences to consider the establishment of an Academy of Social Sciences was politely refused by the then President, Professor Stein (Cambridge):

> Thank you for your letter. . . . As you may know, the SSRC does not consider law as such to be a social science and is only prepared to support research in subjects which relate to law *and* another social science.
>
> In the circumstances, I do not think that my Society would wish to take any initiative in setting up an Academy for British social scientists. However, if such an Academy were set up we would like to have the opportunity of joining if we felt we could contribute usefully to it.[119]

Yet later in the same year Council expressed interest in this very same project and the Society's Honorary Secretary attended the inaugural meeting of the Association of Learned Societies in the Social Sciences in February 1982.[120] Council was not overly enthusiastic about the new organisation, merely agreeing that the Society 'should indicate its continued interest in the Association without making any commitment' but nevertheless it clearly did not wish to be completely outside the new association.[121]

The inconsistency of the Society's views, particularly in relation to socio-legal studies, is further illustrated by the fact that although at times its interest in socio-legal matters appeared lukewarm, on other occasions it responded much more positively to the role of law as a social science. In 1982 the President, Professor Grodecki, urged the Officers to respond quickly to a letter which he had

---

[117] Ibid, 316.

[118] Ibid, passim.

[119] Letter dated 24 April 1981 from Prof P Stein to Prof J Eldridge (President, British Sociological Association), A.SPTL 10/4.

[120] SPTL Council Minutes 18 December 1981, Minute C28/81, A.SPTL 10/5; SPTL Council Minutes 19 March 1982, Minute C7/82.

[121] SPTL Council Minutes 19 March 1982, Minute C7/82.

received from Lord Rothschild, who had been asked to conduct a review of the SSRC. Since one of the terms of reference was to examine 'which areas, if any, at present supported by the Exchequer through other bodies could better be covered by the SSRC', there was an opportunity for the SPTL to try once more to gain some research funding for law. Professor Grodecki wrote to the Society's Honorary Secretary (Professor Brown, (Birmingham):

> The matter is obviously of considerable significance. This is our opportunity to express our dismay at the fact that the SSRC is not supporting legal research adequately. Lord Rothschild's brief paragraph iii clearly gives us an opening.[122]

He reported to Council that he had responded to Lord Rothschild, stressing the importance of socio-legal studies, but stating that 'pure research into law is not funded by any Government body at all', and urging a wider interpretation of the SSRC's terms of reference so as to include a wider area of legal research.[123]

The SSRC did not endear itself to the Society when the next contact it made was merely to consult about a suitable new name for itself.[124] Passing on the letter to the new President, Professor PH Pettit (Bristol), Professor Grodecki wrote:

> My original impulse was to write a rude reply stressing that the new titles for the Council, even more than the present, showed the Council's lack of concern for law and legal research. If you feel like saying something like that you have my fullest support.[125]

Professor Pettit's reply to the Council made the SPTL position clear:

> As you are doubtless aware my Society is very dissatisfied with the present position under which most legal research is not regarded by the SSRC as eligible for its support. We would be more interested in proposals to extend the effective range of research covered by the Council in the discretion of Law, than in proposals which are merely concerned with a change of name. On this latter question the Executive Committee did not have any views it wished me to send to you.

However, despite his exasperation with the SSRC, Professor Pettit further developed the Society's policy of trying to gain more research funding for law, and tried to introduce some consistency into its approach. He advised Council that it would be inconsistent to urge the (newly renamed) Economic and Social Research Council (ESRC) to acknowledge law as a social science, while simultaneously urging the UGC to treat law as a separate discipline from the (other) social sciences. He recommended pursuing the ESRC, since there appeared to be no particular disadvantage in being grouped with other social sciences by the UGC.[126]

In 1984 the ESRC finally announced a new policy in respect of research grants to law: 'The Committee would now regard any legal research with policy

---

[122] Letter from Prof J Grodecki to Prof LN Brown, dated 19 January 82, A.SPTL 10/8.
[123] SPTL Council Minutes 19 March 1982, Minute C6/82, A.SPTL 10/5.
[124] Letter from Mr M Posner, SSRC, to Prof J Grodecki, dated 14 February 1983, A.SPTL 10/8.
[125] Letter from Prof J. Grodecki to Prof PH Pettit, dated 18 February 1983, A.SPTL 10/8.
[126] SPTL Council Minutes 22 September 1983 ESRC & UGC Note by the President, A.SPTL 10/5.

implications as being within the criteria for eligibility.'[127] From the SPTL's point of view, that was a good result. However, it did not mean that academic lawyers immediately became major players on the ESRC stage. A note prepared for Council in 1987 by the Honorary Treasurer, Clive Weston (Birmingham), reports on some research undertaken to find out about SPTL members' experiences in gaining funding for research.[128] Only a small number of members were applying for funding, with socio-legal studies and European law being the two main areas where applications were made. Concerns were expressed about the tendencies of funding bodies to prefer 'socially useful' research, rather than 'pure' or 'theoretical' research, and also about the difficulties of getting funding for cross-disciplinary research. Respondents noted that funding bodies appeared to prefer previously successful applicants 'that is, (like publishers) to back winners rather than hitherto unknown steeds'. Finally, it is noted that feedback from those sitting on funding bodies suggests that the quality of applications from academic lawyers could be improved. Academic lawyers 'might be handicapped by diffidence or amateurishness in making applications for financial assistance'.[129] However, there is no record in the Society's archives of any initiative being taken to address the concerns raised in this report, reflecting once more its rather inconsistent approach to socio-legal issues.

Legal Education/Teaching Matters

Alongside its increasing interest in research, the Society continued to support its members' interests in legal education. Members appear to have been much concerned with the use of information technology for teaching purposes. In 1981, an article by Philip Britton (Warwick) told members about a documentary film made by Warwick University about the Thalidomide case, suggesting that it could be used effectively to arouse students' interest in a variety of legal issues:

> What other modern real-life story could not only expose so cruelly the inadequacies of tort law and civil procedure but also show the need for state regulatory intervention to protect the public against risks from drugs, exemplify a fundamental conflict between protecting legal processes and encouraging high quality investigative journalism and even demonstrate an international court hearing being used as a lever to force a government to reform recent case-law? . . . 'The Sunday Times Case' takes the starting-point that a case-study approach to law teaching can be more effective than traditional expository techniques—especially with unfamiliar institutions and procedures like those of the European Convention—and that film is the ideal medium to fire the imaginations of students coming to examine the issues raised by thalidomide and the Sunday Times litigation for the first time.

[127] SPTL Council Minutes 12 September 1985, Minute C117.1, A.SPTL 20/1.
[128] 'For SPTL Council Sept 17th 1987; a note from the Hon Treasurer', A.SPTL 20/3.
[129] Ibid.

Audio-visual aids for teaching were also discussed in 1984 when the *Newsletter* carried an extensive review of a videotape and teaching materials based on a personal injury action in the High Court, devised by Martin Dockray and produced by the University of London Audio-Visual Centre. Under the heading 'The New Teaching Medium', the reviewer is generally enthusiastic about the use of technology to aid teaching. Some minor reservations are expressed about the quality of the acting, but on the whole, the package is recommended as 'an excellent first attempt at producing an interesting way of introducing law students to civil procedure'.[130] In the same year Mr P Seago (Leeds) appealed in the *Newsletter* for information about the use of such aids by individual law schools, and invited interested members to get in touch with a view to future co-operation.[131] Finally, a new Information Technology Group was proposed by Mr S Saxby (Southampton) 'to encourage discussion about the impact and use of information technology in the curricula and teaching methods of legal studies within universities and polytechnics'.[132] It appears that some members of the Society were actively embracing the new technologies, and that the Society provided law teachers with a means of encouraging co-operation and exchange of ideas on the subject.

Other new approaches to legal education, such as socio-legal studies and clinical legal education also featured in the pages of the *Newsletter*. In 1982, Dr Nigel Fielding (Sociology, Surrey) encouraged members to participate in a survey on the teaching of sociology of law that he was conducting.[133] Two articles contributing to contemporary debates on legal education were published in the *Newsletter* in 1986. The first was written by Dr Gordon Woodman (Birmingham), who was a Visiting Professor at the Faculty of Law in the University of Papua New Guinea, and had first appeared in the newsletter of the Commonwealth Legal Education Association. He put forward a strong plea that law degrees should not be regarded solely as an instrument for preparing students for legal practice, but that law degrees should be conceived of much more broadly, as offering an education which might lead to a wide variety of careers.

> We should have confidence in the value of our type of education, and do our best to see that it is widely spread. Furthermore, we should encourage all students to acquire similar confidence, to consider themselves fitted for a variety of jobs of which legal practice is only one sub-category. We should also look critically at our existing courses. . . . If we could escape from tradition and come to regard legal education as a study of the entire 'enterprise of subjecting human conduct to the governance of rules' (L Fuller *The Morality of Law, passim)* we would make important changes. We could give more attention to laws of social importance, such as those of governmental administrative processes, those of social welfare practice. . . . We would view whole areas of law, such as property, family and contract law, as primarily modes of organis-

---

[130] *SPTL Newsletter* Winter 1983–84, A.SPTL 17, 27.
[131] *SPTL Newsletter* Summer 1984, A.SPTL 17, 4.
[132] *SPTL Newsletter* Winter 1984–85, A.SPTL 17, 5.
[133] *SPTL Newsletter* Summer 1982, A.SPTL 17, 4.

ing social activity, rather than implements for gaining advantages for clients. We would re-design our syllabuses, re-write our textbooks, and make many new discoveries.[134]

The second article, focusing on clinical legal education, first appeared in *The Times Higher Educational Supplement*, and was written by Patricia Woodward and Patrick Dalton. It also starts off by criticising the teaching of law as a set of rules, without paying attention to their operation in practice, and goes on to argue that clinical legal education can offer students a more realistic view of law, as well as offering the pedagogic advantage of being able to marry practice with theory. Acknowledging the difficulties involved in running legal clinics, they advocated a simulated case-study approach:

> The students come to appreciate through experience that those legal rights, principles and doctrine which have been set in concrete in the pages of legal texts and judgments may in fact be available to the citizen in spite of, rather than because of, the operation of the rules and personnel of the legal system, and that the law has real practical rather than merely intellectual consequences.[135]

When the Law Schools Admissions Test (LSAT) was introduced by some law schools in 1987, the Executive Committee agreed that the Society should not adopt a particular position on the value of the test, but the Lord Chancellor's Advisory Committee on Legal Education decided to write to the Department of Education and Science expressing its concern as to the reliability and predictive value of the test.[136] Considering the matter further the following year, the situation was inconclusive: Council noted that Nottingham Law School had devised its own aptitude test, which it felt offered a more reliable prediction of subsequent performance at degree level than did A levels, but that the Law School at Manchester University had operated an aptitude test which had been found to offer no predictive value. The Executive noted that whatever admissions criteria were operated was a matter for individual law schools, but that 'the Society should continue to emphasize that the predictive value of LSAT was not established'.[137] In agreeing with this, Council added that 'The principal objection to LSAT was its use in schools, since there was the possibility that it might discourage potential applicants of some merit from studying law at university if they had performed badly at LSAT.'[138] The Society was, in the end, content to sit on the fence as far as LSAT was concerned.

---

[134] *SPTL Newsletter* Summer 1986, A.SPTL 17, 8.

[135] Ibid, 13.

[136] SPTL Executive Committee Minutes 9 June 1987, Minute E24/87.1, A.SPTL 20/3.

[137] SPTL Executive Committee Minutes 5 February 1987, Minutes E2.1.1–E2.1.6, A.SPTL 20/4.

[138] SPTL Council Minutes 11 March 1988, Minute C37.3.87, A.SPTL 20/4.

Library Matters/Information Technology

Copyright

During the 1980s, the Society was concerned with a number of matters relating to copyright law which affected both research and teaching. In 1980 it made a submission on 'Copyright and Sources of Law', in which it endorsed the recommendation of the Whitford Committee that primary legal materials should be free of any copyright restriction.[139] Copyright was of concern again when the Library Committee drew the attention of Council in 1983 to the likely implications of the establishment of the Copyright Licensing Agency (CLA). The Committee was particularly concerned about the possibility that photocopying charges would rise to a prohibitive level, and that authorisation of single copies for the purposes of research or private study would be threatened.[140]

Copyright was to receive continuing attention during the next few years as universities engaged in a somewhat acrimonious dispute with the CLA, during which the CLA threatened a number of universities with legal action, including the University of Warwick. The Head of the Law Department at Warwick, Dr S Picciotto, briefed the Committee of Heads of University Law Schools about the situation, and when a Working Party was set up under his chairmanship, invited the Convenor of the SPTL Libraries Committee, Mr W Steiner, to be a member. He also sent his discussion paper to Mr Steiner, making the point that law schools are particularly affected by any restrictions relating to the copying of primary materials, as well as by those relating to secondary materials.[141] When the relevant legislation went through Parliament, the SPTL Libraries Committee was active in making various suggestions about possible amendments to the Copyright Bill to the Department of Trade and Industry, although without much success.[142]

Information Technology

The Society's Libraries Committee were responsible for drawing up a revised 'Statement of Minimum Holdings for Law Libraries' which was published in 1986. Along with an explanation of the ways in which the Statement had been updated (eg by including a section on comparative law), the introduction to the Statement notes that:

[139] *SPTL Newsletter* No 14 March 1980, A.SPTL 17, 4.
[140] Letter dated 26 April 1983 from WA Steiner to Prof DB Casson (Surrey), Hon Sec SPTL, A.SPTL 10/8 part 2.
[141] Letter dated 25 March 1985 from Prof S Picciotto to Mr W Steiner, A.SPTL 11/7; Briefing Paper, Agenda Item 9, Committee of Heads of University Law Schools meeting 1 March 1985, A.SPTL 11/7.
[142] SPTL Special Committee on Libraries, Minute 3, 25 November 1988, A.SPTL 11/3.

It is becoming increasingly necessary for academic law teachers to have on-line access to, at least, one legal database, and for law students to become familiar with on-line searching. The Committee recommends, therefore, that each Law School subscribe to at least one database though no specific base is recommended.[143]

The Statement is one of the Society's enduring contributions to legal education on a national level, and its periodic revision allowed it to keep up with developments in information technology so that it remained current and useful.

When members reported in 1983 that Lexis/Butterworths was renegotiating its contracts with law schools for the use of its online database on less favourable terms, the Society suggested that the constituencies involved should get in touch with Professor Diamond (IALS) 'so that SPTL members could present a united front in negotiations'.[144] Although no further mention is made of the issue at that point, the matter was clearly not resolved, because in 1987 the Society set up a committee under the chairmanship of Professor I Fletcher (Aberystwyth) to investigate the costs and use of Lexis in law schools.[145] Information gathered as a result of a questionnaire circulated to all Council members revealed that the majority of law schools had, or were about to acquire, Lexis but the pattern of usage varied considerably, with a relatively small group where usage was high and the application of Lexis in a teaching context was well established.[146] In the majority of law schools few members of staff were trained to use Lexis and little or no attempt was made to give students experience of using it. Consequently, most law schools had a lot of unused hours out of their annual entitlement. Lack of training for staff was seen as a major stumbling block to increased use. Butterworths were insistent that in return for having the system available at less than commercial rates, law schools should undertake to introduce students to Lexis. The Committee had explained to Butterworths the impracticality of doing this using the current system which involved using a dedicated Lexis terminal. It was successful in getting Butterworths to agree that Lexis could be accessed via JANET (the Joint Academic Network—the UK universities' intranet). This was an important step forward, as it made it much easier to introduce groups of students to Lexis, as well as significantly increasing the ease of use for members of staff for research purposes. The other major achievement of the Committee was to get Butterworths to agree to provide training for staff in law schools without them having to travel to London to receive it.[147]

In its handling of the Lexis situation, the Society showed that it was able not only to be effective in representing the interests of its members, but in martialling them to act together on occasion. Further evidence of the increasing willingness

[143] 'Statement of Minimum Holdings for Law Libraries in England and Wales (Revised 1986)' (1986) 6(2) *Legal Studies* 195.

[144] SPTL Council Minutes 22 September 1983, Minute C35/83(iv), A.SPTL 10/5.

[145] SPTL Council Minutes 20 March 1987, Minute C7/87, A.SPTL 20/3.

[146] Letter from Prof I Fletcher dated 28 May 1987, A.SPTL 11/4 and *SPTL Newsletter* Winter 1988–89, A.SPTL 17, 9–10

[147] SPTL Committee on Information Technology Report on Pricing Policy for the Use of Lexis, A.SPTL 20/3; *SPTL Newsletter* Winter 1988–89, A.SPTL 17, 9–10.

of the Society to be proactive in this area is provided by its reaction to the issue of Crown copyright. When the Society was alerted by Butterworths to the fact that the Crown was claiming copyright in primary sources of law, Council immediately urged members to write to their MPs pointing out the need for amendments to the Copyright Bill so as to ensure the future accessibility of primary legal documents in the public interest.[148]

The *Newsletter*

One of the lasting legacies of the agitation by the Young Members' Group in the 1970s was the Society's *Newsletter*. At first it was edited by the Honorary Secretary, but it was soon realised that the work involved meant that a separate editor was needed, and Mrs Mary Hayes (Sheffield) was appointed as Editor in 1981.[149] She wasted no time in encouraging members to submit items for publication, suggesting that the *Newsletter* could carry items varying from information from the Law Society or Bar on matters affecting law students and short articles containing views on matters of legal education, adverts for books for sale and offers to exchange houses during vacations.[150] In 1983, she resigned due to other commitments (in addition to her academic duties at Sheffield University, she was a JP and was expecting her fifth child).[151] Her successor was Nigel Gravells (Nottingham).[152] Under his editorship the *Newsletter* continued to carry a wide range of items, from information about internal matters, such as the Annual Conference, to news from bodies such as the Commonwealth Legal Education Association and the Law Commission, as well as topical items such as letters to the UGC and responses to consultation papers.

One item of news which did not make it into the *Newsletter* (but unusually was reported in *Legal Studies*) was the celebration of the 100th birthday of the Society's first Honorary Assistant Secretary, Mr Arthur Bowers. Arthur Bowers had worked as Secretary to the Director of the Law Society's School of Law, Edward Jenks, who was the moving spirit behind the foundation of the SPTL. As a consequence, he had been intimately involved in the meetings and discussions which led to the formal establishment of the Society. A survivor of the Boer War, Mr Bowers also served in the First World War and was mentioned in despatches after the battle of Passchendaele. A small group from the Society called on him

---

[148] SPTL Council Minutes 11 December 1987, Minute C40/87, A.SPTL 20/3. See also letter dated 2 December 1987 from Prof J Adams (Kent) to Hon Sec SPTL (Prof David Casson, Buckingham) and document from Butterworths entitled 'Crown Copyright and Law Publishing', A.SPTL 20/3.

[149] Letter dated 9 February 1981 from Prof JA Andrews (Aberystwyth) to Prof P Stein (Cambridge), A.SPTL 10/4; SPTL Council Minute 17/81, A.SPTL 10/5.

[150] *SPTL Newsletter* Winter 1981–82, A.SPTL 17, 1.

[151] Letter dated 20 January 1983 from Mrs M Hayes (Sheffield) to Prof PH Pettit (Bristol), A.SPTL 10/4.

on his birthday, and presented him with a leather-bound volume containing the new index to the Society's *Journal* and a copy of the latest Directory of Members, to signify the enormous expansion of the Society during Mr Bowers' lifetime. He reminisced about the early days of the Society, and also about the personalities involved, including Edward Jenks, who had rather a peppery temperament: reference to the Society as 'Jenks's trade union' apparently caused him immense annoyance.[153]

As the decade closed, Council decided that it was not always satisfactory for the Editor of the *Newsletter* to rely upon information received from members about their law schools on a voluntary basis, and that a more formal arrangement might be more effective, with Constituency representatives completing a questionnaire.[154]

Summer 1989 saw the first issue of 'Constituency News' carried in the *Newsletter*. The first request for such news received a modest response, with only seven constituencies responding. Of these, some were only a couple of lines long. However, the contributions from Brunel, Leeds and Manchester, which all submitted a few paragraphs, covering items such as promotions and appointments, and detailing academic developments such as the establishment of a law–Chinese joint honours degree at Leeds, or the research contract secured by Brunel from the Transport and Road Research Laboratory to study cognitive and social aspects of unlawful driver behaviour, showed the potential offered by this aspect of the *Newsletter* to increase communication by and about individual law schools. In the Winter 1989–90 issue of the Newsletter, Constituency News continued to grow. Once again some entries consisted merely of a couple of lines reporting appointments and promotions, but other entries contained news of curriculum developments and international links, giving clear examples of the potential offered by this part of the *Newsletter* for members to exchange news about developments in their law schools which would otherwise go unnoticed.

Young Members' Group

Although the Young Members' Group held a conference on 'Recent Developments in Civil Liberties' in Hull in 1980, during the early 1980s the Group appears to have withered quietly away.[155] When asked in 1984 what had happened to the Young Members' Group, the President replied that 'this group appeared to have lost its impetus having been supplanted by the special interest

[152] SPTL Council Minutes 18 March 1983, Minute C13/83, A.SPTL 10/5.
[153] Draft of note eventually published as 'Celebration—AD Bowers' (1982) 2 *Legal Studies* 327, A.SPTL 10/8.
[154] SPTL Council Minutes 16 March 1989, Minute C3.3, A.SPTL 20/5.
[155] SPTL Executive Committee Minutes 22 February 1980, Minute E2/80(ii), A.SPTL 10/5.

groups of the Society'.[156] The passing of the Young Members' Group was more of a cause for celebration than otherwise. By this stage the position of Young Members within the Society was much more secure than it had been when the Group was established. Many of the criticisms raised by its members had been addressed, largely as a result of the Memorandum submitted to the Society by the Young Members in 1971. The Annual Conference had a much greater intellectual content, with an increasing emphasis on input from members via the specialist groups, communication with members had been improved by the establishment of the *Newsletter*, and young members were represented on the Society's Executive Committee. All of these developments had strengthened the Society, but they had also decreased the need for a separate group for young members.[157]

Membership of the Society/ALT

The question of eligibility for membership of the Society, which had proved controversial since it was first raised in the 1960s, rumbled on into the 1980s. At the 1980 AGM, 'a considerable majority of those present welcomed the proposed extension of membership to teachers in Polytechnics in principle, provided that the proposed members were teachers at degree or professional level'.[158] At its next meeting, Council also accepted a proposal for the relevant changes to the Society's Rules.[159] However, when the matter was put to the vote at the AGM in 1981, the vote was 41 in favour, 23 against, thus failing to achieve the necessary two-thirds majority.[160] This must have been particularly galling for polytechnic law teachers, since as long ago as 1962, the Society had resolved to allow lecturers at the College of Law to be eligible to be members of the Society.[161]

At the officer level at least, relations with the ALT were amicable enough. In 1981, the President of the ALT, Mr Perry-Oliver, received a request from an American law professor at Nebraska University, enquiring about the possibility of finding a part-time teaching position in the UK to enable him to supplement his research leave allowance and spend a year at a UK university.[162] Mr Perry-Oliver passed the request to the then President, Professor Stein (Cambridge) in the hope

[156] SPTL Council Minutes 16 March 1984, Minute C67/84 (5), A.SPTL 10/5.

[157] 'By the early 1980s, the influx of young teachers was such that they no longer represented [a] minority subset of activity but were very much at the heart of Council representation and conference attendance etc. As far as I can remember, it was thought that the separation out of 'young members' no longer made much sense'. Email dated 9 February 2009 from Prof R Lee (Cardiff), one of the last Chairs of the Young Members' Group, to F Cownie, deposited in SLS archive.

[158] SPTL AGM 18 September 1980, Minute 10.iv, A.SPTL 26/1.

[159] SPTL Council Minute C43/80, A.SPTL 10/5.

[160] *SPTL Newsletter* Winter 1981–82, A.SPTL 17, 6.

[161] General Committee Minutes Special Meeting, 2 November 1962, A.SPTL 1/5.

[162] Letter dated 11 January 1981 from Prof S Kalish to Mr Perry-Oliver, A.SPTL 10/4.

that the SPTL could assist, and received a positive response, with a promise that the matter would be advertised in the SPTL *Newsletter*.[163]

More formal attempts to foster good relationships with the ALT were also made through annual meetings between representatives of the two associations. When they met in 1982 it was made clear that ALT members were welcome at meetings of the SPTL's specialist groups, which were not sub-committees of the Society (and therefore participants did not need to be SPTL members). The two organisations also agreed that they would co-operate in trying to make the Advisory Committee on Legal Education more effective.[164] By 1987 the annual meeting between the two societies had been discontinued, but it was revived by the then President, Professor JA Jolowicz, and Council agreed that the two bodies should once more meet on a regular basis.[165] However, as regards membership of the Society itself, the decade ended with this contentious matter unresolved.

International Relations

During his Presidency in 1979/80 Professor JC Smith (Nottingham) attempted to raise the Society's international profile by making contacts with the Canadian Association of Law Teachers (CALT). He received a positive response, suggesting a number of possibilities. CALT could act as a clearing-house for British legal academics wishing to visit Canada and for Canadian law schools who might wish to have a visiting professor, and details of British visitors actually holding visiting appointments could be publicised in order to facilitate short-term visits by them to other law schools. In addition, depending on the availability of funding, CALT was very interested in organising 'a return visit of a group of British law teachers to Canada, along the lines of the Canadian tour to Britain in 1978'.[166] During this decade, this seems to have been the only initiative taken by any President to foster international links on behalf of the Society.

The Editor of the *Newsletter* in the early 1980s, Mrs Mary Hayes, encouraged members to send in details of scholars visiting from overseas, in order that they might be invited to visit other departments, or to attend conferences and seminars.[167] During her Editorship, she also arranged for Peter Handford, of the University of Western Australia, to act as the *Newsletter*'s 'Australian Correspondent'. Commenting in 1982 on the threat of redundancies faced by UK academics when he spent his study leave at the university where he was formerly employed

---

[163] Letter dated 29 January 1981 from Mr Perry-Oliver to Prof PG Stein (Cambridge), A.SPTL 10/4; letter dated 6 February 1981 from Prof PG Stein (Cambridge) to Mr Perry-Oliver, A.SPTL 10/4.
[164] SPTL Council 18 March 1983, Minute C16/83, A.SPTL 10/5.
[165] SPTL Council 17 September 1987, Minute 18.1, A.SPTL 20/3.
[166] Letter dated 10 July 1980 from Prof Percy (President CALT) to Prof JC Smith (Nottingham), A.SPTL 10/4.
[167] *SPTL Newsletter* Winter 1982–83, A.SPTL 17, 31.

(Leicester), he notes that while such threats appear to have receded, there were similar rumblings in Australia, prompting him to think about staff–student ratios and the use of full-time and part-time staff. Staff–student ratios were, in his view, considerably less favourable in Australia. He goes on to report that in contrast to the UK, where an increasing ratio of staff were full-time, law schools in Australia had, until very recently, been staffed predominantly by part-time staff, and the move towards employing more full-time staff was just beginning.[168] The following year he compared qualification to practice in the two jurisdictions, noting that in many Australian states students took a four-year degree, which included some non-law subjects, while two universities required a pre-law year of non-law study. Articling was not universal in Australia; in some states, students took a skills course at an institution run by the profession, followed by a period of 'restricted practice' during which they must be in the employment of an experienced lawyer. In other states, articles still existed, but a skills course and period of restricted practice existed as an alternative. The most noticeable similarity with the UK was the tension that existed between the legal academy and the legal profession over the extent to which the curriculum could be prescribed by the profession.[169]

The *Newsletter* carried a number of other items which reflected an interest in international perspectives on legal education. In 1982 it noted the expansion of the Butterworth Fellowships for Law Teachers, a scheme established in 1961 that offered fellowships tenable at the Institute of Advanced Legal Studies and allowed legal academics from Africa, India and South East Asia to spend time at the Institute.[170] Several *Newsletters* carried summaries of the business of the Commonwealth Legal Education Association. In 1982 this included details of Commonwealth Fellowship and Award Schemes which facilitated exchange visits by various categories of university personnel to and from Commonwealth countries, as well as information about a seminar for law teachers and researchers from Commonwealth countries.[171] The Government's change of policy on overseas student fees, with the introduction of measures intended to ameliorate to some extent the decision to charge overseas students full-cost fees was also noted.[172] In 1983 there were features on the Arthurs Report on legal education in Canada and the Bok Report, *A Flawed System*, on American legal education, as well as remarks made by the incoming Chair of the UGC indicating that 'tenure went too far in British universities and something like the systems in many American universities was better'.[173] EU matters also continued to feature in the *Newsletters*. For example, in 1983 there was an advert for Jean Monnet Fellowships, tenable at the European University Institute in Florence. With a stipend

[168] *SPTL Newsletter* Winter 1982–83, A.SPTL 17, 24–5.
[169] *SPTL Newsletter* Summer 1983, A.SPTL 17, 16–7.
[170] *SPTL Newsletter* Winter 1982–83, A.SPTL 17, 22.
[171] *SPTL Newsletter* Summer 1983, A.SPTL 17, 10 and 12.
[172] Ibid, 13.
[173] *SPTL Newsletter* Winter 1983–84, A.SPTL 17, 8–10.

and a travel allowance, this attractive opportunity was a clear reflection of increasing UK involvement in matters European.[174] Despite its increasing interest in legal research, these international items reflect the Society's continuing interest in legal education.

Conferences

The Annual Conference continued to focus on plenary sessions in the traditional way, but there was a small but detectable shift in the nature of the contributors. It was no longer inevitable that the majority of speakers would be judges; a wider variety of speakers was invited. At Leicester in 1982 a session celebrating 50 years of *Donoghue v Stevenson* was led by a panel of academics, while another panel considering matters of European Community law was led by Judge Pescatore of the European Court of Justice, a former Advocate General (Sir Jean-Pierre Warner) and two academics (Professor Alan Dashwood (Leicester) and Derrick Wyatt (Oxford).The final session was led by Sir Roger Ormrod who, although a judge, was actually invited in his capacity as Chair of the Committee on the Future of Legal Education.[175] At Edinburgh in 1984 the Lord Advocate (Lord Mackay of Clashfern, later Lord Chancellor) gave an address on 'Public Prosecution', but the other sessions were all led by academics.[176] In 1986, in London, under the Presidency of Professor A Diamond, it was noticeable not only that the sessions were generally led by academics, but that a plenary session was devoted to 'How to Obtain Funding for Legal Research', at which the speakers were 'senior representatives of the Economic and Social Research Council, the British Academy, the Leverhulme Trust and the Nuffield Foundation'.[177]

The financial exigencies experienced in the early 1980s prompted Sweet & Maxwell to question whether in devoting all their sponsorship to the Annual Dinner the Society was making the best use of their financial support. In 1982, in the context of discussions about the SPTL book series, Hugh Jones, one of the Directors of Sweet & Maxwell, indicated that it would be helpful to discuss a number of the projects in which his company was jointly engaged with the Society, but he focused on the question of conference sponsorship.

> Our main concern at the moment, however, is the nature of our support for the Annual Dinner. With the greatest respect to the Leicester organisers (who probably had no control over it), none of us here were very impressed by the quality of the food at the last Annual Dinner. Several of us came away feeling that a great deal of money had been spent on an indifferent meal and that some members of the SPTL (perhaps the

---

174 *SPTL Newsletter* Winter 1983–84, A.SPTL 17, 5.
175 *SPTL Newsletter* Summer 1982, A.SPTL 17, 2.
176 *SPTL Newsletter* Summer 1984, A.SPTL 17, 2.
177 *SPTL Newsletter* Summer 1986, A.SPTL 17, 1–2.

majority) might feel that we could have used the money for more profitable purposes within the Society. We might, for example, have sponsored the attendance of several delegates, enabling some people to attend the conference who might not otherwise have been there . . . your members may feel that this kind of financial support is more suitable for the economy-conscious 1980s than continuing to pay the hotel trade high prices to serve us indifferently cooked banquets that we do not actually need. I am not necessarily proposing that we abandon our support for the Annual Dinner. As a high-light of the conference it serves all kinds of useful and pleasant functions—but perhaps we should avoid pouring *all* our financial subvention into food, and spread the support a little more widely. I do not want your Council, or your wider membership, to think that at a time when some law teachers are struggling to keep their departments going at all Sweet and Maxwell are throwing thousands of pounds a year away on banquets and parties and are unwilling to consider anything else.[178]

After a meeting to discuss these issues had taken place, the then President of the Society wrote to Hugh Jones to thank him for a very useful discussion. On the matter of the sponsorship of the Annual Dinner he wrote:

I am afraid you will have thought us a conservative lot in connection with the Annual Dinner but we do feel that it is important to have such an occasion and we also think that from your point of view it is to your best advantage to be associated in the way that you are with the major social occasion of the Conference. We took your point about the danger of having to pay inflated prices to hotels. I think that it would be the general view of the Society that if at all possible the Annual Dinner should be held on university premises, but this is just not possible on every occasion.[179]

Sweet & Maxwell not only agreed to continue sponsoring the Annual Dinner, but also agreed to increase the value of the Sweet & Maxwell Prize. They were, as Council noted, 'very well disposed towards the Society'.[180]

The conference at Warwick in 1979 was the first time that the SPTL had offered a full-scale exhibition opportunity for publishers. Despite their initial doubts, it had been a great success, with many people visiting the stands. Sweet & Maxwell urged the Society to repeat this innovation in future years.[181]

We at Sweet & Maxwell were not initially enthusiastic about this idea, having much enjoyed in previous years the opportunity to mix freely with Members of the Society, without having to attend at a book stand, and we have also enjoyed escaping the additional burdens in terms of manpower, cost, and time involved. . . . I am now writing to say, however, that we regard the exhibition at Warwick as very successful, and would encourage an exhibition of this kind for next year and for succeeding years.[182]

---

[178] Letter from Mr H Jones, Director, Sweet & Maxwell to Prof PH Pettit (SPTL President, Bristol) dated 8 November 1982., A.SPTL 10/8.

[179] Letter from Prof PH Pettit (SPTL President, Bristol) to Mr H Jones (Director, Sweet & Maxwell) dated 14 December 1982, A.SPTL 10/8.

[180] SPTL Council Minutes 18 March 1983, Minute C 12/83, A.SPTL 10/5.

[181] Letter dated 15 October 1979 from Sweet & Maxwell to Prof JC Smith, A.SPTL 10/4.

[182] Ibid.

It was made clear, however, that the success of the Warwick exhibition had been due in no small part to its location, in such a position that everyone attending had to go through the exhibition area to get lunch, and Sweet & Maxwell suggested 'with great respect' that this was the formula they would like to see repeated.[183] This is a recurring theme in correspondence with publishers about subsequent conferences; they continue to draw to the attention of Presidents the necessity of a good location for the book exhibition. The comment from Professional Books in 1982 is typical: 'we are in agreement with Butterworth's and Sweet & Maxwell, in that we are prepared to participate in an exhibition provided it is a central theme of one of the lunches rather than being held in some annex away from the main event'.[184]

Gradually the Society realised that the focus of the conference was changing. In 1981 Council noted that 'Many members now choose to attend specialist groups rather than the main conference. It may be that the time has come to integrate the main conference with the specialist groups completely, having fewer plenary sessions.'[185] The following year the then President, Professor Grodecki, took the decision to integrate the specialist groups more closely with the main body of the conference.

> In recent years the meetings of the specialist groups prior to the main conference have become increasingly popular. Professor Grodecki, this year's President of the Society, has therefore decided to make specialist groups a feature of the conference. To enable those attending the specialist groups more readily to remain for the main conference, and with an eye on costs, the main conference will be marginally shorter this year.[186]

The specialist groups were not completely integrated into the annual conference, as they generally met before the main conference started.[187] However, they were becoming much less marginal, reflected in the fact that by 1984 the meetings of specialist groups were referred to as preceding the conference in the 'now traditional way'.[188]

The Newcastle conference in 1981 appears to have been the last time that the conference was not held at the university where the President worked. This must have made life much easier for subsequent Presidents, who could work with their own colleagues to organise the conference on 'home turf'. Excursions remained a feature of the conference programme, although exceptionally at the London Conference in 1986 the social programme was reduced to evening receptions and dinners, thus allowing more time to be devoted to the academic programme.[189]

---

[183] Ibid.

[184] Letter dated 18 February 1982 from KD Kirk, Chairman & Managing Director, Professional Books, to Prof J Grodecki, A.SPTL 10/4.

[185] SPTL Council Minutes 18 December 1981, Minute C.31/81, A.SPTL 10/5.

[186] *SPTL Newsletter* Summer 1982, A.SPTL 17, 1–2

[187] This was the case at Newcastle in 1981, 'SPTL Conference Announcement, University of Newcastle upon Tyne', A.SPTL 10/8; Bristol in 1983, *SPTL Newsletter* Summer 1983, A.SPTL 17, 1; also in Edinburgh in 1984, *SPTL Newsletter* Winter 1983–84, 1; also in Birmingham 1985, *SPTL Newsletter* Winter 1984–85, A.SPTL 17, 3.

[188] *SPTL Newsletter* Summer 1984, 2.

[189] *SPTL Newsletter* Summer 1986, A.SPTL 17, 1–2.

The Annual Dinner continued to be a formal event, with toasts to the Queen, the guests and the Society; surviving menus indicate that food was traditional: paté, lemon sole, loin of lamb and lemon soufflé at Cambridge in 1980; melon, poached salmon, beef Wellington and soufflé Rothschild when the conference returned to the same venue in 1987.[190] Overall, the Annual Conference did not change radically during this decade, but showed incremental progress towards a more academic occasion.

Self-Reflection: Presidential Addresses

The advent of *Legal Studies* meant that Presidential Addresses would no longer be published in the Society's journal as a matter of course. However, during the1980s, the majority of Presidential Addresses were published. Half of them appeared in *Legal Studies*, while others were published in the *Newsletter*.[191]

The subject-matter of Presidential Addresses continued to vary, with some Presidents focusing on their own area of legal expertise, while others reflected on matters relating more generally to the nature of legal education and law teaching. In 1980, Professor JC Smith (Nottingham) took as his subject 'An Academic Lawyer and Law Reform', noting the growing influence of academic lawyers not only on legislation, through work with the Law Commission, but on the courts as well.[192] He instanced the adoption of Professor Griew's formulation of deception in *Lambie* and the approval by the House of Lords of Geoffrey Samuel's analysis of the Divisional Court in *Morris v Beardsmore*.[193] He noted that this situation was very different from the early 1950s, when judges 'rarely got beyond the admirable casenotes in the Law Quarterly Review and few practitioners got as far as that'.[194] By the early 1980s, Professor Smith reported,

> Almost every issue of the law reports contains references in the arguments of counsel and in the judgments of the courts to academic writings in journals and textbooks. . . . It is no longer necessary to be a professor at Oxford or Cambridge or anywhere else to have some influence on the development of the law. The impact of an article will depend more on its merits than who wrote it.[195]

[190] Menu for SPTL Annual Dinner 1980; Menu for SPTL Annual Dinner 1987 (uncatalogued).

[191] See, apart from the Addresses mentioned in the text, PG Stein, 'Fundamental Legal Institutions' (1982) 2 *Legal Studies* 1; PH Pettit, 'The Society of Public Teachers of Law—The First Seventy-five Years' (1983) 3 *Legal Studies* 231; N MacCormick, 'The Democratic Intellect and the Law' (1985) 5 *Legal Studies* 172; JA Jolowicz, 'Comparative Law and the Reform of Civil Procedure' (1988) 8 *Legal Studies* 1.

[192] JC Smith, 'An Academic Lawyer and Law Reform' (1981) 1 *Legal Studies* 119.

[193] Ibid; see *R v Lambie* [1981] 1 All ER 332 at 337 and *Morris v Beardsmore* [1982] 2 All ER 753.

[194] 1(2) *Legal Studies* 119.

[195] Ibid, 120.

The change in the attitude of the courts was attributed by Professor Smith to the enlightened approach of a number of judges (he instances in particular Lord Edmund-Davies). Their approach was naturally followed by counsel, who had also had the benefit of a modern legal education, which had taught them the value 'of looking well beyond the practitioners' textbooks'.[196] During his Address, Professor Smith also gave further detailed examples of the influence of academic lawyers on the law, drawing on his experience in writing commentaries for the *Criminal Law Review* and as a member of the Criminal Law Revision Committee. In addressing these issues, Professor Smith was not only attempting to reinforce the growing confidence of academic lawyers in his role as President of the SPTL; he was also reflecting a change in legal culture which had gradually taken place since the 1950s. As Duxbury observes in his study of jurists and judges:

> Throughout the second half of the twentieth century, explicit acknowledgment of the potential value of juristic opinion became increasingly less unusual. Indeed, the case reports of that period attest to the fact that judges have become ever more willing to refer to jurists and their writings.[197]

In his Presidential Address at the Annual Conference in 1982 Professor J Grodecki noted the huge advances made in the professionalisation of law teaching during his own career, from the post-war years when he characterises the average provincial university law department as 'small, parochial, appallingly badly housed and with generally quite awful library facilities' through changes which he regarded as amounting to 'a total transformation of the academic legal scene'.[198] These included a huge expansion in the number of law schools, as well as in student numbers, but more significantly, changes in the nature of legal academics, with law schools no longer staffed by part-time teachers whose real interest was in legal practice and who did not really engage with the rest of the university, to a situation where law schools were staffed by full-time academics and as a result law schools had moved into the mainstream of academic life.[199]

The Society, in Professor Grodecki's view, had a major role to play in ameliorating the threats to law schools from financial cutbacks. Acknowledging the disappointments following the failure to implement the recommendations of the Ormrod Committee and the subsequent continuing difficult relations with the legal profession, he emphasised the sense of self-assurance and confidence which he saw in the legal academic community and issued a rallying-cry to the Society to fulfil its duty as 'guardian of the quality of legal education', and 'to resist any encroachments on the part of the professional bodies on what is our proper domain . . . the present is no time for the Society to rest on its laurels—let the early 50s be a salutary reminder to all its members . . . what is at stake'.[200]

---

[196] Ibid, 120.
[197] N Duxbury, *Jurists and Judges: An Essay on Influence* (Oxford, Hart Publishing, 2001) 101.
[198] *SPTL Newsletter* Winter 1982–83, A.SPTL 17, 3.
[199] Ibid, 4.
[200] *SPTL Newsletter* Winter 1982–83, A.SPTL 17, 12.

In 1988, Professor HK Bevan delivered his Presidential Address at the Annual Conference at the University of Hull. His main theme was the changing nature of higher education and the need for the Society to adopt 'a harder and sharper profile'.[201] Professor Bevan observed that relations with the legal profession were not improved by the publication of the Marre Report, which had accepted what it described as 'clear evidence' from the College of Law and Council of Legal Education that some students had insufficient knowledge of the core subjects, lacked the ability to present clear and concise written arguments, and so on.[202] Another source of friction lay in the fact that when the professions introduced changes to their education/training regimes, they appeared to routinely by-pass the Advisory Committee on Legal Education, thus cutting out academic discussion/consultation.[203]

With regard to the research selectivity exercise, Professor Bevan envisaged an increasing concentration of resources in a few institutions, and suggested that the Society would have an important role to play in supporting members doing meritorious research outside those favoured institutions. The Society had already made moves in this direction by including members' research interests in the Directory of Members. But he noted that regrettably nothing had been done to follow up the links made with research councils and other research funders at the London conference in 1986. However, another success in promoting the research interests of members was the establishment of the Society's Academic Purposes Fund, largely due to the efforts of Professor Jolowicz during his presidency.[204]

Professor Bevan concluded his Address by contemplating some much more ambitious projects which could be undertaken by the Society in order to promote members' research interests, including the establishment of a Law Foundation along the lines of that already existing in countries such as Australia and Canada.[205]

Professor John Andrews's Presidential Address, delivered at Aberystwyth in September 1989, focused on the financial and bureaucratic pressures on law schools.[206] In his view the financial situation facing law schools at the end of the 1980s was very serious; law as a discipline received less funding per undergraduate student than virtually any other subject. Only accounting, he noted, had a figure anywhere near as low as law, while even social sciences received considerably more.[207] There were a number of reasons for this phenomenon, but one which Professor Andrews regarded as particularly insidious was that in the 1960s and 1970s, a rapid increase in law students often offset poor recruitment in other

[201] *SPTL Newsletter* Summer 1989, A.SPTL 17, 2.
[202] Bevan, letter, above n 103, 3.
[203] Ibid, 4.
[204] Ibid, 8.
[205] Ibid, 9.
[206] *SPTL Newsletter* Winter 1989–90, A.SPTL 17, 3.
[207] Ibid.

subjects. Thus law schools expanded while other departments stood still or contracted 'but often maintaining historic levels of resourcing'.[208]

> Most law schools were expanding on the assumption that additional staff would follow the additional students, but increasingly during the later 1970s and early 1980s it became difficult for universities to provide the additional staff. So, the staff/student ratio in Law became the most adverse in the country.[209]

While the UGC had announced a small increase in the unit of resource for law in 1986, in practice, since the mid-1980s the spending on law students had fallen in real terms and the situation was now very serious, with many law schools facing severe financial constraints.[210] Many law schools had responded by increasing the number of overseas students they recruited (international students could be charged 'full-cost' fees, though universities varied in the proportion of such fees that were passed to departments). While this brought benefits in terms of the diversity of the student body, as well as financially, Professor Andrews stressed the dangers of relying too heavily on one source of income.[211] In terms of other sources of income, Professor Andrews noted that very few law schools obtained research income of any significance, and he did not see this changing.

> Obtaining research grants is an attractive challenge, proof of the virility of the research efforts of the law school and providing an opportunity to achieve some research programmes which cannot be carried on with ordinary recurrent funding, but no more than a handful of law schools are likely to see their profile changed to a significant degree by research and other income.[212]

Professor Andrews expressed much the same views in relation to endowments and other funding sources, such as continuing education. He was particularly concerned about the suggestion made by the Government that universities should take additional 'home' students on a fees-only basis. The additional income passed on to law schools was likely to be small, resulting in 'a further disastrous decline in the unit of resources [*sic*] for law students'.[213]

For the Society, Professor Andrews suggested, the task was to campaign to increase the unit of resource for law students, in an attempt to redress the low level of funding from which law had historically suffered.[214] In general, while he acknowledged that it would probably become increasingly necessary to support activities which bring in additional income, Professor Andrews stressed that such activities would have to be balanced with more traditional ones in order to maintain, in each law school, a community of scholars.[215]

---

[208] *SPTL Newsletter* Winter 1989–90, A.SPTL 17, 4.
[209] Ibid.
[210] Ibid.
[211] Ibid, 5.
[212] Ibid.
[213] Ibid, 6.
[214] Ibid,
[215] Ibid, 7.

Staffing was another matter of concern. Not only faced with the loss of staff through early retirement and voluntary redundancy schemes brought in as a result of financial pressures in the early 1980s, law schools had lost well over 100 academics to other jobs. 'It is a good thing to have a safety valve for the disenchanted' but law schools were finding it increasingly difficult to recruit 'the ablest of young lawyers in the face of high rewards and increasingly aggressive recruiting from the professions'.[216] Professor Andrews saw this as a pressing problem, and called for it to be addressed as a matter of urgency. His comments provide a telling insight into the extent of the changes experienced by those working in higher education, and the tensions between increasing managerialism and the traditional values of collegiality.

> To my mind, the creation of the right environment to attract and encourage young academics is a particularly important part of the management of the system. If the new world of budget centres, management priorities, and bureaucratic obedience to university administrators and Government takes priority over the creation of that sense of academic community within which academics are encouraged and enriched, the maintaining spirit of our university system will be lost.[217]

The insights gained from these Presidential Addresses reflect the position of academic lawyers as part of an academy undergoing profound changes, at the same time as the discipline of law itself was changing from its previous largely vocational focus to one which was increasingly more academic in nature.

Conclusion

Overall, the 1980s was a period of mixed success for the Society. The reform of the *JSPTL* was a major achievement; during this decade *Legal Studies* developed into a highly respected academic journal, providing a high-quality publishing opportunity for legal academics. In this respect the Society showed signs that it wished to be taken seriously as a learned society. The initiatives which it took to promote its members' research interests, such as the establishment of the Academic Purposes Fund, and publicising members' expertise in the Directory, indicate that it was moving away from a focus almost exclusively on the teaching aspects of legal education towards a more balanced view, which acknowledged the increasing importance of research for many of its members. The existence of the increasing number of specialist groups meant that there was significantly more opportunity for members to engage with a more varied diet of academic content at the Annual Conference than had traditionally been the case. Even the SPTL book series, short-lived though it was, suggests that the Society was more

---

[216] Ibid, 8.
[217] Ibid, 9.

interested in legal research than it had been hitherto. However, the Annual Conference itself continued to focus on plenary sessions, and many aspects of the conference were very traditional. Surviving attendance lists for conferences in the 1980s reveal that a significant number of people attended the specialist groups but did not stay on for the main conference, suggesting that the main conference was not meeting the needs of many members of the Society.[218] In relation to research matters, the Society failed to have a consistently positive approach to empirical socio-legal research, which hampered it in dealing with the ESRC. It also failed to take any initiative to deal with the problem, specifically drawn to the attention of Council, that academic lawyers were often poor at making grant applications. On the other hand, when members reported problems with the use of Lexis, the Society was active in negotiating a more practical arrangement for the benefit of all law schools, and the Libraries Committee was active in responding to changes in copyright law affecting teaching and research, as well as in producing a revised Statement of Minimum Holdings for Law Libraries, whose practical utility should not be underestimated. Overall, however, the initiatives taken to promote research within the Society were incremental, rather than radical.

The Society was successful in ensuring that its new-found focus on research did not mean that teaching was excluded from its activities. The interest in new technology displayed in the *Newsletter* showed that the Society was able to provide not only a forum for discussion on matters of legal education, but also to facilitate interested law teachers in contacting each other to form discussion groups. Yet, as McAuslan points out, it could have done so much more.[219] Given the enormous changes taking place in higher education which, as Professor Andrews pointed out in his Presidential Address, were affecting law schools as much as any other part of the academy, it is disappointing that the Society did not take a lead in ensuring that academic lawyers engaged fully with the changing environment in which they worked.[220] This was a decade that saw unprecedented numbers of policy initiatives, many of them very unpopular with academics, and the Society did not always appear to lead from the front.[221] It may not have been entirely accidental that the SPTL did not feature among the original 143 learned societies originally consulted about the RAE.

The Society's reaction to the first round of financial cutbacks lacked energy (although by the end of the decade it was much more forceful in making representations to the UGC). For much of the decade, the SPTL seems to have been almost entirely disregarded by the legal professions when they wished to make changes to aspects of legal education affecting the academy, and the Society

---

[218] Participants lists for SPTL Annual Conference 1982, 1985, 1987, 1989, uncatalogued.

[219] P McAuslan, 'The Coming Crisis in Legal Education' (1989) 16(3) *Journal of Law & Society* 310.

[220] J Andrews, 'Presidential Address 1989', *SPTL Newsletter* Winter 1989–90, A.SPTL 17, 3.

[221] For a detailed account of the policy initiatives and their effect on higher education, see R Stevens, *From University to Uni: The Politics of Higher Education in England since 1944* (London, Politicos Publishing, 2004) ch 4.

seemed to be incapable of doing anything effective in response. It found it very difficult to develop a clear collective voice, even on matters central to its interests and those of its members. It also failed to resolve the issue of membership in relation to polytechnic law teachers, and this was another decade in which women did not feature greatly in the Society's life. No women were elected as Officers of the Society, although there was clearly some awareness of the male domination of legal academia, as reflected in the announcement in the Newsletter in 1982 when the organisers of the Socio-Legal Group conference expressed their intention to expand the size of the conference, and urged members to submit papers 'In particular, we would like more papers from women, to counteract the male domination by speakers who have so far responded.'[222]

Professor McAuslan was not the only member of the Society at this time who made his criticisms known. The Winter 1982 *Newsletter* carried a long letter from Tom Hervey, a member of Council, complaining that Council failed to have serious substantive discussions but merely received reports from the Executive, which he characterised as a wholly self-appointing body. 'The most graphic way of describing the structure and content of Council meetings to members who have not had the opportunity to attend', he wrote, 'would be to say that they are very similar to Annual General Meetings, but cosier.' He argued that both the Executive Committee and Council were in need of reform, but was not sanguine about the possibility of this happening, commenting that 'The Society has been ticking over happily if purposelessly for many years now and doubtless could continue to do so indefinitely.' Admitting that his views may not be shared by others, he nevertheless felt bound to express them.[223] The President, Professor Neville Brown (Birmingham), cautioned the Officers not to overreact to Mr Hervey's letter, but agreed that the Society's agenda could be made a little more explicit.[224] The matter was discussed at length by the Society's Council, and it appears that Mr Hervey was not entirely alone in his views, since Council agreed that as much information as possible would be included on the agenda, and the President would prepare a report for each Council meeting, updating members on developments taking place subsequent to the latest available minutes, and Executive Committee minutes would also be circulated.[225]

As this incident shows, in some ways, the Society's problem appears to have been more of style than substance. Although the Society was in fact engaging (at least to some extent) in some of the relevant debates, it was not particularly effective in involving all its members in the initiatives it took. By the end of the decade it appears that the Officers of the Society were not only aware of this problem but were attempting to do something about it. In 1988, under the Presidency of Prof John Andrews (Aberystwyth), the Executive Committee noted that

---

[222] *SPTL Newsletter* Winter 1982–83, A.SPTL 17, 44.
[223] Ibid, 27–31.
[224] Letter from Prof N Brown (Birmingham) to Prof PH Pettit (Bristol) 17 December 1982, A.SPTL 10/8.
[225] SPTL Council Minutes 18 March 1983, Minute C.17/83., A.SPTL 10/5.

legal education faces a period of accelerating evolution and that this would be likely to have consequences for members of the Society individually in the manner in which the teaching of law as a university subject would develop, and for the Society in the role it should seek to fulfil as these and other changes take place. . . . It may be an appropriate time in the Society's history for it to consider the manner in which it should execute its role in the future.[226]

Council members were asked to consult their constituencies about new initiatives which the Society might undertake.[227] In particular, the Executive raised the question of new technology, the possibility of taking greater initiatives in representing the interests of law teachers, such as challenging the UGC on the inadequacy of the unit of resource for law and the possibility of extending the Society's role in responding to consultation papers.[228] As the Society entered the 1990s, therefore, it was undertaking a reappraisal of its role in an attempt to overcome some of the weaknesses that had become apparent during the 1980s.

---

[226] SPTL Executive Committee Minutes 11 November 1988, Minute E33/88, A.SPTL 20/4.
[227] SPTL Council Minutes 9 December 1988, Minute C40/88, A.SPTL 20/5.
[228] SPTL Executive Committee Minutes 11 November 1988, Minute E33/88, A.SPTL 20/4.

10

The 1990s: A Decade of Change

Until quite recently, the SPTL was rather an amateurish, friendly, ineffectual organisation which had almost as much a social as a professional and lobbying purpose.

(CA Weston, Response to President for Special Meeting of Executive Committee, 4 July 1998)

Archival note: Our approach throughout this book has been to try to allow those involved in the Society's history to speak for themselves through the documents we have unearthed. However, we should like to draw the attention of readers to the fact that from 1990 onwards, the Society's archives are not yet open to the general public. We were granted access to records from that date onwards by the Society on the understanding that we would use our discretion in what we made public. In relation to the 1990s, we have only omitted material not otherwise publicly available which, were it to have been included, would have constituted a breach of privacy relating to living individuals.

Readers should also note that all documents in the archives relating to the 1990s are uncatalogued, so have no reference numbers attached.

Changing Higher Education

The reform of higher education by successive Conservative governments in the 1990s continued apace, affecting the Society and its members in many ways, and providing the context within which the Society was working as it moved towards the end of the twentieth century. One of the most far-reaching of these was the abolition of the 'binary divide' in the Further and Higher Education Act 1992, when polytechnics became universities; commentators coined the phrase 'new universities' to refer to former polytechnics, as opposed to 'pre-1992 universities' or 'old universities'.[1] The same statute created new funding councils: the Higher

---

[1] For further information on the abolition of the binary divide, see M Kogan and S Hanney, *Reforming Higher Education* (London, Jessica Kingsley Publishers, 2000) ch 5.

Education Funding Council for England (HEFCE), and its equivalent in Scotland (SHEFCE) and Wales (HEFCW); these Councils would have responsibility in future for conducting the Research Assessment Exercises, and thus be of considerable significance to the Society and its members, as well as to institutions of higher education. The newly appointed Chief Executive of the Funding Councils in Wales for Further and Higher Education was Professor John Andrews, who had been the Society's President in 1988–89.[2]

The 1992 Act also required the Funding Councils to establish quality assurance processes; a system of institutional quality audit was introduced, as well as a quality assurance system for teaching, starting with the introduction by HEFCE of Teaching Quality Assessments (TQAs) in 1991. By 1997 the Quality Assurance Agency (QAA) had been established, to oversee both audit and teaching quality.[3] The extent of the change in academic culture brought about by these developments is summed up by Hanney and Kogan:

> Government's placing of evaluation within publicly prescribed frames led to a reformulation of the nature of academic quality, aided by a veritable industry of definers and prescribers. . . . The creation of quality audit, teaching quality assessment and research assessment, and the associated machinery in the funding councils and the . . . Quality Assurance Agency, were part of the fundamental shift in the relationships between the state and higher education. For the most part, academics were opposed to the changes (while conceding the principle of accountability . . .), whilst those responsible for the system may have taken a different view.[4]

During the 1990s the Society itself was to experience a period of considerable development and change, largely brought about by the determination of a number of its Officers to ensure that the Society was a more proactive and lively organisation, providing a real lead in matters affecting law teachers and legal education. These changes within the Society therefore took place against a background of continuing change in the higher education sector as a whole.

Change within the Society: The Early 1990s

In 1989 Professor Peter Birks (Oxford) had been elected as Honorary Secretary of the Society. It was clear from the beginning of his term of office that he was determined that the Society should be more lively and energetic than it had been previously, and he was instrumental in initiating many of the activities which the Society began to undertake in this period, including the establishment of a series of seminars, the reorganisation of the specialist sections and using his

---

[2] 'Top Appointment Goes to Professor John Andrews', *SPTL Reporter* No 5 Winter 1992, 12.

[3] D Laughton, 'Why Was the QAA Approach to Teaching Quality Assessment Rejected by Academics in UK HE?' (2003) 28(3) *Assessment and Evaluation in Higher Education* 311.

[4] Kogan and Hanney, above n 1, 107–8.

considerable energy to ensure that the Society played a more effective role in relation to the increasing number of outside bodies with which it communicated.[5]
His practical approach was reflected in the guidelines for new Council members
he devised on taking office, outlining their duties, encouraging them to 'Try to
make sure that everyone joins' and exhorting them to read the *Newsletter* regularly so that they could draw colleagues' attention to matters of interest.[6] Peter
Birks also brought to his post a deep interest in legal education, which can be
seen in the columns he wrote for each edition of *The Reporter* during his tenure
as Honorary Secretary. His contributions took the form of an informed commentary written by a knowledgeable insider, sometimes performing the role of
an editorial for *The Reporter*, and reflecting all the major legal education issues of
the day. The energy Peter Birks brought to the Society is reflected in a letter he
sent as his tenure as Honorary Secretary was coming to an end. Writing to Conor
Gearty, who had agreed to stand for election as Honorary Assistant Secretary, he
said:

> I am really delighted to know that you will be (democratic processes allowing) assistant
> sec of the SPTL . . . there being so much still to fight for, and to fight, I personally am
> very glad indeed to be succeeded by people who will not let up or let the Society go
> back to sleep.[7]

Peter Birks was not alone in wishing to reform the Society. The President in
1991–92, Professor Roy Goode (Oxford), published a wide-ranging 'Strategy
Document' in *The Reporter*, suggesting a number of areas where the Society could
make further improvements. These included increasing membership, not just to
aid the Society's finances, but to enable the Society to better promote academic
interchange and scholarly debate; improving the Annual Conference; involving
the membership and constituency representatives more effectively; increasing the
Society's influence among key players in the legal field, as well as with research
funders and policy-makers; playing a more active role in collating and dissemin-
ating information about legal education, and promoting a more international
outlook, both in terms of curriculum and legal research. He also noted a number
of particular issues which he thought the Society should be addressing, including
the funding of law schools and issues relating to equality of opportunity. He
ended by examining the standing of the academic lawyer in the UK:

> It is a regrettable fact that academic lawyers in the UK do not enjoy the standing of
> their counterparts overseas. Though scholarly writings do influence legal development,
> both in the common law and in legislation, academic literature of relevance to a partic-
> ular dispute is all too often overlooked . . . and the citation in judgments of academic
> writings drawn upon in the course of argument is ungenerous compared with the
> approach taken by courts elsewhere . . . Moreover, the contribution voluntarily made
> by academic lawyers to law reform generally, in commissioned research, in service on

---

[5] These and other initiatives undertaken by Professor Birks are discussed in more detail below.
[6] P Birks, 'SPTL Council Representatives' (1989).
[7] Letter dated 21 June 1995 from Prof P Birks to C Gearty.

and submissions to governmental and other committees and in responses to consultation papers, is inadequately acknowledged.[8]

Professor Goode therefore thought that the Society had a role to play in raising not only its own profile, but the profile and standing of the community of academic lawyers. Ultimately, perhaps, the Society could seek the grant of a Royal Charter—but its membership and its activities as a learned society would need to be expanded substantially before that could be contemplated. As will be seen from what follows, some of Professor Goode's suggestions were to influence the Society's development for the rest of the decade.

When Professor David Hayton succeeded Professor Birks as the Society's Honorary Secretary in 1996 he continued the policy of developing the Society's activities. It was unsurprising that persons holding the office of Honorary Secretary played a crucial role in the Society's development. As Professor Hayton wrote, shortly before taking up office, the Honorary Secretary acted as 'de facto Chief Executive Officer'.[9] This role has always been key within the Society, as constitutionally the President only holds office for one year, but the Honorary Secretary can be (and generally is) re-elected each year.[10] Professor Hayton's contribution to the changes taking place in the Society may not have been as radical as those of Professor Birks, but they were equally important in ensuring that the impetus built up by Professor Birks was maintained. One of Professor Hayton's achievements was to secure the appointment of a paid administrator for the Society. The idea of having paid administrative assistance had first been raised by Professor Birks in 1995 during his tenure as Honorary Secretary, but it took some time to come to fruition.[11] In 1997 Peter Niven was appointed as the Society's first part-time paid administrator, working two days a week.[12] The archives contain several boxes of documents which testify to the amount of work that Peter Niven undertook as the Society's administrator, underlining the need for this appointment, and Professor Hayton's contribution to the Society's development in bringing it about.

Changing Membership

Change was in the air from the first year of the decade. At its Annual General Meeting in 1990 the Society finally passed a resolution that provided for the admission to membership teachers of law at degree level from institutions other than universities, the Inns of Court School of Law or the College of Law. This

---

[8] R Goode, 'Strategy Document' *SPTL Reporter* No 4 Spring 1992, 16.
[9] Letter dated 5 June 1995 from Prof D Hayton to C Gearty.
[10] See eg 'The Rules of the Society of Legal Scholars', *SLS Directory of Members 2008–9*.
[11] SPTL Executive Committee Minutes of a Special Meeting of the Executive Committee 22 April 1995, Minute 3.
[12] SPTL Executive Committee Minutes 5 May 1997, Minute E29/97; see also SPTL Executive Committee Minutes 5 February 1998, Minute E63/98.

meant that law teachers in polytechnics were finally permitted to join the Society. In the postal ballot which was needed to confirm this, the vote was overwhelmingly in favour: 303 for and 35 against.[13] Commenting on this development, Professor Birks wrote in the Honorary Secretary's column in *The Reporter*:

> By eliminating the exclusion of colleagues in law schools outside the universities the Society has rid itself of a handicap. It is good that the change has been made by an overwhelming majority. Some members of the SPTL are already members of the Association of Law Teachers. The SPTL will now welcome members from the polytechnics and other colleges which teach law at degree level or above. But there will be no going back on the assurance given to the ALT when the changes were initiated, that there would be no active recruitment drive.[14]

This development brought a formal end to one of the most controversial episodes in the Society's history. The Society could now move forward on an inclusive basis. Nevertheless, for many of the individuals formerly excluded, it would be many years before the wounds healed sufficiently to make membership of the Society an appealing prospect.

The Reporter

Another change that took place right at the beginning of the decade was that the *Newsletter*, now edited by William Swadling (Southampton) was published for the first time as the *SPTL Reporter*, in A4 format, with a much more professional appearance.[15] The new editor explained:

> The change of policy which accompanied the change of name of the Society's journal to *Legal Studies* in 1981 placed more emphasis on the general law review article and less on the topic of Legal Education. *The Law Teacher*, the journal of the Association of Law Teachers does, of course, devote much space to this issue, but it was felt that there was still a place for discussion of the subject within the SPTL and the *SPTL Reporter* hopes to provide that forum.[16]

As a start, the first issue of *The Reporter* contained a review article on the teaching of medical law and three items concerned with the future of professional legal education—the Society's response to the Law Society's document 'Training Tomorrow's Solicitors', an item on the new Legal Practice Course to be introduced from 1993, and a report on the new Bar Finals Course. Another innovation was that as well as including news of all law schools in the 'Constituency News' section, it was hoped to feature one particular law school in each issue of *The Reporter*. The subsequent issues of *The Reporter* show that the Editor fulfilled his

---

[13] 'The Postal Vote', *SPTL Reporter* No 2 Winter 1991, 1.
[14] 'Honorary Secretary's Report' *SPTL Reporter* No 2 Winter 1991, 1.
[15] *SPTL Reporter* No 1, Summer 1990.
[16] Ibid, 1.

intention of providing a forum for discussion and debate about legal education. Topics ranged from reports of meetings with the Lord Chancellor's Advisory Committee on Legal Education and discussions with the professional bodies about the Joint Announcement, to articles on law school funding, legal education in Scotland, and the teaching of joint or 'mixed' degrees.

In 1997, after editing 15 issues of *The Reporter,* William Swaddling resigned as editor. He had succeeded in establishing the renamed *Newsletter* as one of the Society's key publications, and a key instrument in informing members about, and involving them in, current debates affecting legal education. The Society wished to ensure that this aspect of its activities maintained its momentum. The Honorary Secretary wrote to Anthony Bradney (Leicester), to enquire whether he would be interested in taking on this task:

> Would you be interested in taking over the helm from your Leicester base? It should help you and Leicester to become better known, while your experience and specialist knowledge in legal education field should help to further legal education and SPTL interests therein.[17]

The new editor took over from issue 16.[18] His first editorial, entitled 'The Future of Law Schools', gave a foretaste of a change of style:

> In 1998 one would suspect an optimistic academic is likely either to be using Prozac or the more traditional remedy of the excessive consumption of alcohol. Little is there to lighten the gloom. A government which takes seven months to respond to Dearing and finally issues something that has the intellectual depth of a shopping list written on the back of a used envelope probably does not have a very firm grasp on educational policy.[19]

However, the commitment to promoting serious debate about matters affecting legal education continued; in the rest of his first editorial, Bradney urged readers to get involved in debates about the current changes in higher education:

> Now, more than ever, it is important for people to think, talk and write not just about the subjects which they teach and research but also about the discipline of legal education itself and about its place in the university and in society. . . . Today, to ignore discussion of educational theory, practice and policy, in the belief that it will have no impact on one's professional life, is to adopt the same strategy as an ostrich with approximately the same likelihood of finding oneself for sale, pre-packaged, on higher education's equivalent of Sainsbury's exotic meat counter.[20]

Subsequent editorials addressed the shortcomings of the QAA and academic pay.[21] The final editorial of the decade noted the appointment of the RAE panel

---

[17] Letter dated 29 October 1997 from Prof D Hayton to A Bradney.
[18] Anthony Bradney decided that he would sign his editorials 'Tony Bradney' to distinguish his journalistic writing from his academic writing.
[19] T Bradney, 'The Future of Law Schools', *SPTL Reporter* No 16 Spring 1998, 1.
[20] Ibid, 3.
[21] *SPTL Reporter* No 17 Winter 1998; *SPTL Reporter* No 18 Spring 1999.

members for the 2001 exercise. Under the headline 'Sacrifices in an Aztec Temple', Bradney wrote:

> So now we know the names of the 11 colleagues who will be the assessors for the RAE. For the next few months these colleagues will need to buy neither food nor alcohol. Their scholarship, their learning, even their dress sense, rather improbably in some cases, will be lauded as the very model of what a modern academic should be. Of course once they have announced the results of their deliberations these self-same colleagues will find that they can only attend conferences under an assumed name and on condition that they wear a brown paper bag over their heads. Much then will be made of their scandalous addiction to illicit substances, their obvious inability to understand even the most basic concepts in the research literature and their well-known predilection for unusual sexual practices. Like the Aztecs of old, first we pamper our prisoners and then we slit their throats and eat their hearts.[22]

Levity apart, Bradney made some serious points about the RAE, arguing that it had helped to raise standards of research in law, to the extent that 'A discipline whose research did not have enough life in it to even qualify as being dead has become a vibrant and challenging arena.'[23] However, he also emphasised that the RAE was not in itself the reason to do research, and that scholars should keep it in perspective, remembering that 'An RAE panel makes a provisional judgement on something about which the academic community will take decades to make a final assessment.'[24] This mixture of humour and serious debate built on the work done by William Swaddling in establishing *The Reporter* as much more than its predecessor, the *Newsletter*. *The Reporter* established itself during this decade as one of the Society's central publications. Constituency News grew from just over a page in the first edition (1990) to nine pages in the Winter 1999 issue, as law schools realised how useful it was in publicising their activities, as well as giving news of appointments and departures.[25] *The Reporter* itself was substantial publication; in the early years of the decade particularly it often ran to more than 40 pages. It was central to the Society's ability to involve its members because, as Peter Birks noted in his guidelines for new Council members, it was 'the Society's only effective way of communicating with the membership as a whole'.[26] This was particularly true because, for most of this decade, email was yet to arrive as the preferred medium of communication. The potential of *The Reporter* was exploited to the full, as it was used not only to convey news about constituencies and about the Society itself, but also to try and engage members in all aspects of the current debates in legal education. During this decade, nearly every issue of *The Reporter* carried items about matters of academic or vocational legal education, or about matters affecting the sector generally, such as the RAE or the QAA. Both of its Editors contributed to this achievement.

[22] T Bradney, 'Sacrifices in an Aztec Temple' *SPTL Reporter* No 19 Winter 1999, 1.
[23] Ibid, 3.
[24] Ibid.
[25] *SPTL Reporter* No 1, Summer 1990; *SPTL Reporter* No 19, Winter 1999.
[26] Birks, above n 6.

Legal Studies

Meanwhile, The Society's journal, *Legal Studies*, continued to go from strength to strength, although it too experienced a change when Professor John Andrews left academic life and was replaced as Editor by Professor John Bell, Professor of Public and Comparative Law in the University of Leeds.[27] Writing an editorial to mark the end of his tenure as Editor, Professor Andrews drew attention to his aim of publishing 'contributions distinguished by their scholarship, and, so far as reasonably possible, by their having a more general rather than a more specialist interest'.[28] Noting the wide variety of legal scholarship published in the journal, he pointed out that *Legal Studies* did not publish case or statute notes, or short book reviews, preferring instead to publish selective reviews of scholarly significance in their own right. 'It is gratifying', he wrote, 'to note that several academic law journals have moved towards a similar book review strategy, leaving the short descriptive reviews to appear in the more specialist or practitioner-oriented journals.'[29] The new Editor, Professor Bell, decided to continue a similar editorial policy, reiterating that '*Legal Studies* does not restrict its choice of material save by the criteria of scholarly merit and legal interest', merely adding that

> Since 1981 the nature of legal education has become a matter of heightened interest both among academics and more generally. It is also a matter of great concern to the Society as a body. Thus, although *Legal Studies* principally publishes works of legal scholarship reflecting basic research on substantive and adjectival law, it also welcomes scholarly contributions on how law is learnt and taught.[30]

The Editor's report to the Society's Executive Committee in 1996 illustrates the approach of the new Editor. In the second year of his tenure of that post, Professor Bell was pleased to report a healthy flow of articles for the journal, noting that an attempt was made to cover a wide variety of fields, and that published authors came from 12 different universities, and only 3 (including one joint author) held professorial rank. 'Diversity of universities and the opportunity for less senior staff to find outlets for publication continue to be part of the editorial approach.'[31]

Professor Bell was succeeded as Editor in 1999 by Professor Derek Morgan and Professor Celia Wells (both of Cardiff). Their appointment marked a departure for the Society's journal in a number of ways, as they pointed out in their introductory Editorial:

> As editors (the first time, incidentally, that the editorship has passed not only from single to joint responsibility but also involved a woman at the desk), we are the first whose

---

[27] 'Legal Studies—A New Editor' *SPTL Reporter* No 6 Spring 1993, 9.
[28] J Andrews, 'Editorial' (1993) 13 *Legal Studies* ix.
[29] Ibid, x.
[30] J Bell, 'Editorial' (1994) 14 *Legal Studies* x.
[31] J Bell, 'Legal Studies Report' (1996).

primary legal education was not delivered at Oxford or Cambridge. This is a note not for criticism, but for celebration of those inspirational teachers and scholars of the universities of Kent and of Warwick where we respectively learned something of whatever elements of craft we now bring to this task[32]

It was a further sign of the changes that had taken place since the relaunch of the Society's journal in 1980 that the new Editors could confidently acknowledge their good fortune in inheriting a journal 'with an established intellectual pedigree'; there was no doubt now that *Legal Studies* had reached maturity as an academic journal. [33] Noting the steady development that had taken place under their predecessors, the new Editors recognised that 'Legal Studies remains the journal of its members: we are merely temporary stewards for an interval.'[34] However, their appointment was not entirely without controversy. At the Annual General Meeting of the Society that year, the Vice-President, Professor Thomson (Glasgow), expressed concern that the Editorial in which the new editors had introduced themselves suggested that those undertaking doctrinal scholarship would not be published in future issues of the journal.[35] Some other members stated that they and their constituencies shared Professor Thomson's views. However, the President (and outgoing Editor), Professor Bell, was able to tell the meeting that he had spoken to the Editors (who were at that time in Australia): '[T]hey had assured him that they had not intended to cause offence. They had meant that a broader range of subjects would be treated in the future than had been the case previously.'[36]

Scotland and Ireland

Although membership of the Society had always been open to legal academics teaching in Scottish universities, one of Peter Birks' initiatives was to suggest in 1992 that the Society seemed a little Anglo-centric, and that perhaps this could be remedied by the creation of a Scottish co-ordinator, a suggestion which bore fruit with the appointment of a Convenor for Scotland, the first appointee being Professor Joseph Thomson (Glasgow).[37] It was some time later that the Society turned its attention to Ireland, but in 1996 discussions which had been going on for some time culminated in a proposal to make the necessary change in the Rules.[38] Once this was effected, the Assistant Honorary Secretary, Conor Gearty,

---

[32] D Morgan and C Wells, 'Editorial' (1999) 19 *Legal Studies* 4.
[33] Ibid.
[34] Ibid.
[35] SPTL Annual General Meeting 1999 Minutes, Minute 10.
[36] Ibid.
[37] 'Honorary Secretary's Report' *SPTL Reporter* No 4 Spring 1992, 2; for the appointment of the first Convenor for Scotland, see letter dated 19 August 1998 from P Niven (SPTL Administrator) to C Weston (Hon Treasurer).
[38] SPTL Council Agenda 8 March 1996; SPTL Council Minutes 8 March 1996, Minute C11/96.

took steps to raise the profile of the SPTL in Ireland, drawing attention to the changes, which had given the same status of membership to Irish colleagues as those in the UK, and mentioning items of interest both in the seminars and at the Annual Conference which would be of particular interest to legal academics in Ireland.[39] Another move to acknowledge all the jurisdictions covered by the Society was taken when the SPTL Seminars for 1998–2000 took as their theme 'Strengths and Weaknesses of the [English/Welsh, Scottish or Irish] Law of . . .'[40]

Socio-Legal Studies

The major change experienced in relation to socio-legal studies during this decade was the establishment of a new learned society specifically catering for scholars in this area. The first issue of *The Reporter* carried an advertisement for the newly formed Socio-Legal Studies Association (SLSA). Although it was such a new organisation, it offered its members a newsletter, seminars for policy-makers and postgraduates, an annual conference and discounts on some academic journals. It was also planning to compile a research directory and a directory of postgraduate courses.[41] Two years later, *The Reporter* carried an article describing the current activities of the SLSA, which by this time included, in addition to the items mentioned above, a conference on socio-legal research in Scotland and a Research Study Day to provide training in socio-legal research methods for those with limited experience of empirical research. The SLSA had also built up regular contacts with research funders and was publishing, in conjunction with Oxford University Press, a series of socio-legal readers.[42]

Relations with the Professions

Relations with the legal professions were temporarily improved at the beginning of the 1990s, as a result of negotiations which somewhat redressed the balance of power between the professions and legal academics, as compared with the situation in the 1980s. In his Presidential Address in 1990 Professor John Wilson noted that the professional bodies had moved away from their previous stance of

---

[39] SPTL AGM 1996 Minutes, Minute 7. Letter from C Gearty to person(s) unknown (undated, but with internal evidence that it was written in 1997).

[40] Letter (undated) from Prof D Hayton to person(s) unknown 'Re Four SPTL Annual Seminars'.

[41] *SPTL Reporter* No 1, Summer 1990, 7.

[42] 'The Socio-Legal Studies Association: Current Activities', *SPTL Reporter* no 5 Winter 1992, 15.

insisting on providing detailed syllabi for the core subjects, along with minimum teaching hours and seeking to exert control over the methods of assessment:

> Happily these restrictions have been considerably relaxed as the result of an accord recently reached between representatives of law teachers and of the two professional bodies. . . . In future the profession will merely indicate outline requirements for the teaching of core subjects.[43]

In his column in *The Reporter* Professor Birks attributes this success largely to the interventions at the Lord Chancellor's Advisory Committee on Legal Education of an SPTL member, Professor Graham Zellick (Queen Mary and Westfield), who did not sit on the Committee as an SPTL representative, but nevertheless, as a former legal academic 'was . . . largely responsible for the new and more liberal regime for core subjects'.[44] The SPTL as an association could not claim that it had overcome the resistance from the profession that it had experienced in the 1980s, but its members were the beneficiaries of astute action by Professor Zellick (and presumably others) who sat on the Lord Chancellor's Advisory Committee. *The Reporter* carried the full joint announcement from the professional bodies, confirming that prescribed syllabuses would be replaced by 'course outlines', and that the only requirement as far as assessment was concerned was that 'each subject should be properly assessed'. The tone of the announcement was much more conciliatory than those of the 1980s:

> [W]e do not wish to impede the proper teaching of law at the first degree level and we recognise the variety of valid approaches to any subject—whether comparative, jurisprudential, historical; emphasising policy and reform; contextual teaching; or inter-disciplinary (for example, economic analysis of contract or tort)—to take some examples.[45]

Professor Wilson also noted other reasons for improved relations between academia and the professions: law degrees had become the normal route for entry to the professions, and now that the professional bodies had a 'more relaxed' monitoring process for degree courses, he was of the view that law schools could continue to provide the academic stage of vocational training 'without seriously compromising the basic obligation of law schools to provide a liberal education'.[46] He also drew attention to the recent phenomenon of various forms of sponsorship provided by law firms and barristers which had resulted in the creation of new academic posts, as well as increased library resources.[47] Although Wilson was positive about the introduction of sponsorship to law schools, this

---

[43] J Wilson, 'The Role and Responsibilities of the Modern Law School', *SPTL Reporter* No 2 Winter 1991, 11.

[44] 'Honorary Secretary's Report', *SPTL Reporter* No 1 Summer 1990, 2.

[45] 'Qualifying Law Degrees and Core Subjects', *SPTL Reporter* No 3 Autumn 1991, 24.

[46] Ibid, 15.

[47] J Wilson, 'The Role and Responsibilities of the Modern Law School', *SPTL Reporter* No 2 Winter 1991, 15.

was not an uncontroversial matter, with commentators warning of the ethical dangers involved; they also pointed out that sponsorship was not evenly spread across the sector, with prestigious universities taking the lion's share.[48]

Further evidence of the growing co-operation between legal academics and the professional bodies was provided in 1991 when the Bar agreed that experienced academic lawyers 'with publications to their name . . . can now expect to be called to the Bar with dispensation from the [Inns of Court School of Law] course'.[49] A slight hiccup occurred when this new approach was introduced, causing an irritated academic to publish a letter in *The Reporter* indicating that there appeared to be a rule that only academics of more than 15 years standing could apply for this route.[50] The problem appeared to be quickly resolved in theory, as a statement by Richard Southwell QC also published in *The Reporter* made clear.[51] However, the following issue of *The Reporter* carried a short report, indicating that things might still not be progressing smoothly:

> The news which filters back about the operation of this scheme suggests that it is falling far short of original hopes. The fifteen-year rule may have been formally removed . . . but in practice only the very grand seem to be being accepted.[52]

This exchange illustrates that despite such attempts to forge more positive links, relations between legal academics and the professions remained somewhat fragile.

The SPTL's response to the Law Society's consultation on 'Training Tomorrow's Solicitors' in 1990 noted that about 60 per cent of law graduates at that time entered the legal profession, but made the point that 'law is not like medicine, a wholly vocational degree subject'.[53] Commenting that most university law teachers found the imposition of 'core subjects' tolerable, because they would probably be compulsory subjects in most law schools, the response suggested that 'the professions fund some more scientific research as to whether the core subjects actually relate to any genuine educational need of law students', in the light of the Society's view that

> the primary educational needs of law students are to acquire a feel for the structure of the subject and to develop facility in the handling of complex case klaw and statutory material together with the ability to relate this material to the social and economic context in which it should be placed. . . . These skills could be developed by studying a wide range of legal subjects which include, but certainly not exclusively so, the core subjects.[54]

---

[48] See A. Bradney, 'Ivory Towers and Satanic Mills: Choices for University Law Schools' (1992) 17(3) *Studies in Higher Education* 5; S Bright and M Sunkin, 'What Price Sponsorship?' (1991) 18(4) *Journal of Law and Society* 475; A Bradney, 'Paying the Piper' (1990) 24 *The Law Teacher* 137.

[49] *SPTL Reporter* No 3 Autumn 1991, 2.

[50] Letter from J de Lacey, *SPTL Reporter* No 4 Spring 1992, 31.

[51] R Southwell, 'The Academic Route to the Bar' *SPTL Reporter* No 4 Spring 1992, 30.

[52] 'The Academic Route to the Bar' *SPTL Reporter* No 5 Winter 1992, 14.

[53] 'Professional Legal Education' *SPTL Reporter* No 1, Summer 1990, 6.

[54] Ibid.

The response was critical of the fact that intending solicitors continued to study substantive legal subjects after graduating from university: '[I]t makes no sense at all to have a fourth year of study which consists of learning new material off by heart. Our view is that the systematic study of substantive law should, in principle, be undertaken exclusively in universities.' The response was also clear that the professions should not envisage any decrease in the length of law degrees, since England already had one of the shortest training periods for lawyers, and there was some support within the Society for the introduction of four-year degrees, if it were to become possible to charge the necessary fees.[55]

Some aspects of the Society's relationship with the professions remained decidedly tense. The Society continued to express concern about entry to the Inns of Court School of Law (ICSL), where the Bar was intending to reduce the number of available places and consequently introduce a selection procedure, pointing out that the selection criteria would need to be made clear to undergraduates. It was also concerned about the effect on international students of a proposal to defer Call to the Bar until the end of the first six months of pupillage, a matter that was to cause concern for some time.[56] Meanwhile, the lack of places on courses leading to the Law Society's Finals, leading to huge numbers of students being unable to embark on their vocational training, also came in for criticism.[57] The position in relation to the Bar training course remained difficult, with transitional arrangements put in place for 1993–94 giving precedence to the most academically highly qualified candidates.[58] The critical views expressed in *The Reporter* caused the last Chairman of the former Lord Chancellor's Advisory Committee on Legal Education, Sir Frederick Lawton, to write an article in defence of the Bar, although he made it clear that he did not himself support the new Bar admissions procedures.[59]

But the most acrimonious exchanges took place on the subject of the Common Professional Examination (CPE), introduced as an intensive one-year course to allow non-law graduates to cover the 'core' law subjects, and if successful, to move on to the vocational stage of training in the same way as law graduates. The Society issued a discussion document on the CPE, and followed this up with a seminar attended by representatives of the professions as well as by legal academics.[60] The Society's Education Committee then produced a report on the CPE. Noting the increasing popularity of the course, and the high success rates it enjoyed, the Committee commented that:

---

[55] Ibid, 7.

[56] 'Honorary Secretary's Report', *SPTL Reporter* No 3 Autumn 1991, 2; see also SPTL Executive Committee Minutes 6 June 1996, Minute E25.2.

[57] Ibid, 3.

[58] 'The Admission Procedure for the Bar Vocational Course 1993/94', *SPTL Reporter* No 5 Winter 1992, 2–4.

[59] F Lawton, 'May The Bar Be Right?' *SPTL Reporter* No 6 Spring 1993, 45.

[60] 'CPE Review: The Education Committee Reports' *SPTL Reporter* No 5 Winter 1992, 17.

> In recent times, the view seems to have become widespread that CPE graduates perform better than law graduates in the vocational course. After a careful study of the evidence, the Education Committee concludes that basically there is no difference between CPE and law graduates.[61]

Arguing that a proper assessment the impact of the CPE would require long-term monitoring, the Committee canvassed a number of solicitors for their views, and found general satisfaction; the view of the Committee was that 'one reason for this satisfaction had little to do with [CPE students'] legal knowledge, but is because of their maturity as compared with the average law graduate'.[62] Commenting that it was very impressed by the quality of CPE teachers and their students, the Committee nevertheless expressed grave reservations about the course.

> In broad terms, the Education Committee takes the view that the law is a highly complex body of knowledge and principles and that understanding it can be gained only after a lengthy period. Application of that knowledge and those principles involves skills of a high order. It does not accept that a sufficient knowledge of the law and of the skills needed for its application can generally be imparted through a one-year CPE course.[63]

Conceding that length was not the only relevant issue, the Committee nevertheless expressed concern at the brevity of legal training to which it contributed, and was firmly of the view that 'the law degree should be the normal avenue of entry to the legal profession and that the CPE should be for a small number'.[64] The Society's view of the CPE was less than positive.

The Society's Honorary Secretary had made no secret of his concerns about the CPE. In 1993 Professor Birks published an article in *The Times* (which was reprinted in shortened form in *The Reporter*), urging the Lord Chancellor's Advisory Committee to 'look hard at the question whether our legal system can tolerate a path to recruitment which entails so many risks and grievances'.[65] He followed this up with another article in the following issue of *The Reporter* entitled 'To Be Built on Sand: The Future Form of the CPE', which made the case against the CPE, beginning:

> It is a serious charge, not to be lightly made. But the evidence suggests that those who represent the professions in the laying down of rules fundamental to our legal education either do not care about the practicability of their requirements or do not know enough law to allow them to recognize a prescription which is essentially self-defeating.[66]

---

[61] Ibid.
[62] Ibid.
[63] Ibid, 18
[64] Ibid.
[65] P Birks, 'The Rise and Rise of the non-Law Graduate', *SPTL Reporter* No 7 Winter 1993, 4.
[66] P Birks, 'To Be Built on Sand: The Future Form of the CPE', *SPTL Reporter* No 8 Spring 1994, 1.

Professor Birks' differences of opinion with the professional bodies took a dramatic turn when he published an article in the next edition of *The Reporter* entitled 'The Consolation of Cassandra', subtitled 'There can never have been such an example of professional contempt for the work and experience of the universities'.[67] The particular object of his ire was the Bar's system of selecting candidates for admission to the ICSL, which, he argued, had produced 'a crop of injustices' just at the time when the students involved were sitting their final degree examinations, leaving them to cope with 'shattered career prospects, the shock of unfair rejection . . . and the search for avenues of complaint and redress'.[68] There was a great sense of injustice and 'many university lawyers gave up huge quantities of time both to fight the battles of the rejected students and to minimise the danger that injustice would be compounded as . . . the attendant upset knocked on into underperformance in Finals'.[69] Admitting that the situation was to some extent mitigated by the Bar's decision, in the light of many complaints, to admit extra candidates, and to approve a 'more sensible' system for the future, as well as ending the monopoly of the Council of Legal Education, Professor Birks went on to argue that the professional bodies needed to come up with a common system of training, in particular to overcome the Law Society's 'grotesque attempt to perpetuate central control while preaching devolution' and the disadvantages of its training system, which he described as 'inimical to good educational practice and indefensibly expensive'.[70] His article concluded:

> Nothing is gained by delivering universities with their depth of experience into the hands of Stalinist commissars whose only experience is in the skills and jargon of educational bureaucracy. And nothing will be more short-sighted or less welcome than one set of commissars for the solicitors and another for the barristers. All this seems obvious. Many things seemed obvious to the daughter of King Priam.[71]

His article was followed by a short postscript, telling readers that a recent decision by the Visitors to the Inns of Court had held that the Council of Legal Education had not behaved unfairly or irrationally in setting or applying the criteria of selection. Professor Birks' reaction to this was that he begged to differ:

> A body which selects for a post-university course, but refuses to take account of the university performance must be excluding criteria which it ought to take into consideration (there is some concession on this point, though the unfairness is said to have been cured by the subsequent decision to take these matters into consideration in giving the additional places); a body which sets an A-level threshold without declaring it must be acting unfairly, certainly to those who could have been saved the time, anxiety and expense of a competition they could not win . . . nobody is doubting the Council's good faith, but if this does not add up to perversity, nothing ever will.[72]

[67] P Birks, 'The Consolation of Cassandra', *SPTL Reporter* No 9 Winter 1994, 28–9.
[68] Ibid, 28.
[69] Ibid.
[70] Ibid, 29.
[71] Ibid.
[72] Ibid.

The response of the Law Society was to write to the Editor of *The Reporter* seeking an apology and retraction of the article, and failing that, to give notice that it would institute proceedings for defamation in respect of the article.[73] The Editor replied that an apology would not be appropriate, and the best course of action would be for the Law Society to reply in the pages of *The Reporter*.[74] Discussing the matter at the Executive Committee, Professor Birks explained that he had given serious thought to the matter of an apology, but had decided against it:

> [I]t was impossible to do it because, even supposing that the language of the article was exaggerated, it could not be right to acquiesce in an attempt to inhibit a vigorous debate. Certain people who had been to Redditch since the publication had assured him that nobody was genuinely upset by what had been said, that people were indeed joking about it, which if true tended strongly to confirm that the threat of proceedings was nthing but an attempt to curb the vigour of the opposition. It would be wrong to allow it to be curbed, whichever side was in the right.
>
> In reply to a question, the Hon Sec admitted that the sums of money which might be in issue, even if only by way of legal costs, must of course be worrying for the families of the individuals most obviously under threat, but he for his part was prepared to take the risk. If any court held the article to be defamatory, that would be a disaster much worse than the financial consequences which it would entail. If free speech could be suppressed in this way, and by, of all instruments, the Law Society, there would be no point in remaining a public teacher of our law. It was particularly important, therefore, whatever happened to these proceedings, that the next issues of *The Reporter* did not inhibit the freedom of their criticism, though there was of course no cause to seek out skirmishes by which to prove that its spirit remained unbroken. It happened that the next issue would carry vigorous criticism of the new joint announcement on compulsory subjects.[75]

When the next issue of *The Reporter* appeared, under the headline 'The Empire Strikes Back', the leading article summarised the dispute, remarking that 'we now have first-hand experience of the use of the tort of defamation as a technique for shutting people up'.[76] The Law Society had, in the end, agreed to withdraw their threat to sue, and an article by Nigel Bastin, a member of the CPE Board, putting the professions' views on the CPE, was published in *The Reporter*.[77] This incident serves to highlight that although in some ways the relationship between the professions and legal academics had appeared to improve at the beginning of the decade, fundamentally there was not much love lost between the two sides. The Society's Minutes contain numerous other examples of continuing friction over nearly all aspects of legal education.

---

[73] SPTL Executive Committee Minutes 10 February 1995, Minute E8/95 (1.4).
[74] Ibid.
[75] Ibid.
[76] 'The Empire Strikes Back', *SPTL Reporter* No 10 Spring 1995, 1.
[77] N Bastin, 'The CPE Route into the Profession', *SPTL Reporter* No 10 Spring 1995, 35.

The Advisory Committee on Legal Education and Conduct

In his Presidential Address in 1990 Professor John Wilson (Southampton) had expressed some concern about the demise of the Lord Chancellor's Advisory Committee on Legal Education due to the introduction of the Courts and Legal Services Bill. The new Advisory Committee would contain a majority of lay members and a remit covering professional conduct as well as legal education and training. Its members were to include only two academic lawyers, and four legal practitioners. Professor Wilson foresaw that it would be more difficult to maintain a dialogue between the professions and legal academics.[78]

Following the demise of the Lord Chancellor's Advisory Committee, the Society was quick to meet with Lord Griffiths, the Chairman of the new Advisory Committee on Legal Education and Conduct (ACLEC).[79] He was reported as being sympathetic to the Society's anxieties and very aware of the need to establish good lines of communication between the Committee and legal academics. To facilitate this, he proposed to establish the Standing Conference on Legal Education, which was to involve representatives of all the constituencies which had been represented on the former Advisory Committee., and would meet every six months. The SPTL agreed to supply the secretariat for this body, at least until it was firmly established.[80] An article written by the secretary to ACLEC appeared in *The Reporter* in Autumn 1991, keeping members informed about the initial progress of the Committee and informing them that it planned to undertake a general review of legal education in due course. When this occurred in 1995 the Society submitted a 16-page response to ACLEC's review of the academic stage of legal education, beginning by making a strong case, on educational grounds, for the introduction of four-year law degrees:

> We accept that there would be great difficulty in securing public funding for students taking the fourth year of a four year course, and that problems of access would be exacerbated if we were to insist upon such a rule in the absence of such funding. We would accept that such practical objections might lead the Committee to reject our plea for four year courses but this would not affect the nature or quality either of those objections or our arguments—any more than it would mitigate the loss that would in our view flow from that rejection.[81]

In addition to providing some context on the financial constraints under which law schools operated, the response also took the opportunity to emphasise the Society's view of law as a liberal education:

---

[78] J Wilson, 'The Role and Responsibilities of the Modern Law School', *SPTL Reporter* No 2 Winter 1991, 15.
[79] 'Honorary Secretary's Report', *SPTL Reporter* No 3 Autumn 1991, 1.
[80] Ibid, 1.
[81] 'The Advisory Committee on Legal Education and Conduct: the SPTL Response', 1. Note that the text of the response was published in full in the *SPTL Reporter* No 10 Spring 1995, 19.

> We do not always find it easy to discern the thinking of the Committee in its report, since there is a persistent tendency to talk with two voices. One voice talks about the law degree course as being the initial stage for prospective practitioners, the other speaks of law as providing a liberal education which prepares its pupils for a wide range of careers. . . . Our view is that, in so far as these two voices may speak differently, the university stage of lawyer's education must both inevitably and rightly be concerned with education rather than training and with the acquisition of understanding rather than with the amassing of factual knowledge. . . . We invite the Committee to share our view of law as a valuable education in its own right.[82]

The Society also argued that ACLEC should show 'a broad willingness to trust the universities' in relation not only to the substantive content of the 'core subjects', but also in matters of quality control, pointing out that universities were already subject to a complex regime of quality assurance.[83] It also takes the opportunity to reiterate the Society's misgivings about the CPE:

> The position of the SPTL is and long has been that one year conversion courses are not a satisfactory substitute for a law degree. The professions overturned Ormrod in allowing conversion courses to be completed in one year (27 weeks' study, now said to be rising to 36 weeks). We regard the one year conversion course as inadequate in both quantum and time.[84]

The confident tone of this response is a clear illustration of how far the Society had come since the days in the 1980s when it struggled to find a collective voice.

When the ACLEC Report was published, the Society speedily organised a special session at the Annual Conference to discuss it, followed by a one-day conference a few weeks later with both academic and practitioner speakers.[85] The following issue of *The Reporter* was a special issue on the ACLEC Report; it carried five articles examining different aspects of the Report, including one written by Professor Bob Hepple, a member of ACLEC as well as of the Society.[86] The Society could not be accused, on this occasion, of failing to take a lead in matters of legal education. Although the Society was not uncritical of some aspects of ACLEC's Report, in general it supported the approach taken, and was able to welcome the Report 'wholeheartedly', especially some of its major themes, including the recognition of law as a general education, the need for all lawyers, whether taking a first degree in law, or a CPE, to have the opportunity for in-depth study of law involving intellectual rigour, and the freedom for law schools to adopt a diversity of approaches, without being tied to a particular syllabus laid down by the professions.[87]

---

[82] Ibid, 4.

[83] Ibid, 5 and 13.

[84] Ibid, 11.

[85] 'Lord Chancellor's Advisory Committee on Legal Education and Conduct: First Report on Legal Education and Training; SPTL Preliminary Response'; Lord Chancellor's Advisory Committee's First Report on Legal Education, conference flier.

[86] *SPTL Reporter* No 13 Winter 1996.

[87] 'Lord Chancellor's Advisory Committee on Legal Education and Conduct: First Report on Legal Education and Training; SPTL Preliminary Response', 1.

Given the general approach which ACLEC had adopted towards academic law, and its apparently liberalising influence on the professional bodies, it was therefore a matter of great concern to the Society when in 1997 ACLEC was abolished. Before that took place, the Society had co-operated with ALT and CHULS in making clear to the Lord Chancellor's Department and the professional bodies their support for ACLEC and their view that any successor body should have legal education as one of its responsibilities.[88] Working together with other law associations in this way is a good example of the extent to which the changes taking place within the Society in the 1990s had brought about a change of culture in the way it operated. The Society continued its dialogue with the Lord Chancellor's Department about legal education, and by the end of the decade, faced with numerous proposals for change in the bodies advising the Lord Chancellor on legal education, had lobbied successfully for any new body to be chaired by a senior judge, rather than the civil servant originally proposed.[89] Reporting this to Council, the President said:

> [Our] letter was sent, and seems to have had a positive effect since we had heard just prior to the meeting that it had been agreed to ask Potter LJ to remain as Chairman of the Standing Conference as well as the replacement body for ACLEC.[90]

This incident provides another indication of the Society's increasing effectiveness in the field of legal education.

The Joint Announcement

The professional bodies decided that their Joint Announcement on qualifying law degrees should be reviewed in the light of ACLEC's report, and so issued an invitation in 1996 to members of CHULS, ALT and SPTL to put forward their views 'on what any student should know and be able to do at the end of a qualifying law degree'.[91] A long period of negotiation followed, during which various versions of a proposed new Announcement were discussed.[92] The Announcement which followed, and the commentary that accompanied it, reflected the influence of ACLEC, as well as the increasing ability of the academic associations to emphasise the role of a law degree as a general education in law, rather than merely the academic stage of legal professional training.[93] In their commentary on the proposed new Joint Announcement, the professional bodies stated:

---

[88] Letter dated 8 April 1997 from S Bailey (CHULS) to Mr C Beatty (Law Society).

[89] SPTL Council Minutes 10 December 1999, Minute C144/99.

[90] Ibid.

[91] Memorandum from N Bastin, Bar Council, dated 5 August 1998: 'Revision of the Joint Announcement on Qualifying Law Degrees'.

[92] 'Application by the Law Society of England and Wales and the General Council of the Bar to the Lord Chancellor'.

[93] Ibid.

The Report recommended that the law degree 'should stand as an independent liberal education in the discipline of law, not tied to any specific vocation'. . . . This reflects a widely-held view and is based, *inter alia* on the fact that only a quarter of the total number of law graduates will qualify as a solicitor or barrister. The Report also recommended 'that the law schools should be left to decide for themselves, in the light of their own objectives, which areas of law will bestudied in depth, which only in outline, which (if any) should be compulsory, and which optional, provided that the broad aims of the undergraduate law degree were satisfied'. . . .

The professional bodies have given careful consideration to these recommendations and do not want to prescribe the content of law degrees generally, or to inhibit the development of the law curriculum. The professional bodies have no wish to extend their regulatory control beyond those areas which are of direct concern to them. . . . This is clearly reflected in this . . . Statement.[94]

The Statement itself was based on seven 'Foundations of Legal Knowledge', which merely listed the substantive areas of law to be included, together with brief statements regarding areas of legal knowledge and skills expressed in very broad terms.[95] The Society's President, Professor Margot Brazier, commented in her report to Council at the AGM in 1998: 'While the final version is a compromise, the subject associations have obtained a reduction in the prescription of the content of legal subjects, and an alignment of the Announcement with Benchmark standards'.[96] This new Statement represented a real shift in the balance of power between the professions and academic lawyers, moving away from the professions' view of law degrees as reflecting the needs of practising lawyers, and towards the subject associations' view of the law degree as offering a liberal education. The Society had played its full part in achieving this shift.

Other Outside Bodies

Law Commission

Annual meetings with the Law Commission continued to take place. The Commission was clearly anxious to consult as many members of the Society as possible, and at the 1990 meeting, discussions took place about the need to improve communications, since Commissioners did not necessarily know to whom invitations to comment on proposals and initiatives. The Society agreed to try and appoint contact persons to liaise with the Law Commission and advise them about members who might be interested in a particular topic.[97] A full report of the annual meeting in *The Reporter* in 1991 included a note of discussion about

[94] Ibid.
[95] Ibid.
[96] 'President's Annual Report 1998–1999'.
[97] *SPTL Reporter* No 1, Summer 1990, 5.

the ways in which legal experts could be involved in the Commission's work, either on secondment or as consultants, with the SPTL representatives offering to publicise opportunities among members. A Law Commission advertisement about consultancy appointments appeared in the same issue of *The Reporter*, suggesting that this offer had been accepted immediately.[98] The meeting took a new form in 1995, when subject sections were invited to raise specific matters for discussion, supported by short written papers. The Subject Sections Convenor, Professor Rose, reported that this had resulted in a 'more useful and business-like meeting'.[99] The Law Commission also indicated that it was pleased with the new system. It wished to emphasise that even short responses to its consultation papers were very useful.[100]

By 1997 the Society was sharing its annual meetings with the SLSA, reflecting the growing maturity of that association, as well as of the SPTL, which was increasingly willing to work with it, another sign of change, as the Society actively pursued a less isolationist policy.[101] The Law Commission, on its part, showed an increasing interest in academic matters, with its Chair, Mrs Justice Arden, asking whether assisting the Law Commission counted for the purposes of the RAE and if not, whether there was anything the Commission could do about that. She was also keen to ask the academic organisations how Commissioners might become more aware of empirical legal research in areas relevant to their work.[102] The number of suggestions made by different subject sections for these meetings suggests that the Society's relationship with the Commission continued to be a close one, with considerable interaction taking place, both with the Society as a whole and with some of its individual members.

Lord Chancellor's Department

The Society continued to meet annually with representatives of the Lord Chancellor's Department. It was fortunate that for much of the decade that the Permanent Secretary at the Department was Sir Thomas Legg QC, who was sufficiently favourably disposed to the Society that he attended the meetings in person.[103] The meetings provided an opportunity for the Society to hear about matters raised by the Department, such as Lord Woolf's Inquiry into Civil Justice, or the reorganisation of the Court Service, and also to raise matters about which it was concerned, such as the under-representation of legal academics on the

[98] 'The Law Commission' *SPTL Reporter* No 3 Autumn 1991, 14 and 16.

[99] SPTL Council Minutes 13 September 1995, Minute C19/95.

[100] Ibid.

[101] Minutes of Annual Meeting Between the Society of Public Teachers of Law and the Law Commission 5 June 1997; see also Annual Meeting with the Lord Chancellor's Department, 25 June 1998.

[102] Minutes of Annual Meeting Between the Society of Public Teachers of Law and the Law Commission 5 June 1997.

[103] See eg 'SPTL Meeting With The LCD', *SPTL Reporter* No 4 Spring 1992, 4; Minutes of a Meeting with the Society of Public Teachers of Law, 1 February 1996.

Lord Chancellor's Advisory Committee, or the effects on overseas students of deferral of call to the Bar. [104] In 1997 the agenda notes for SPTL representatives reveal that the Society raised its concerns about the

> worsening tension between (a) increasing access to higher education and (b) maintaining and improving quality in view of pressures on resources affecting premises, class sizes, library, information technology, reflective time for staff, recruitment and retention of high calibre staff . . . especially when Research Assessment Exercise is designed to increase the difference in resources between the higher graded and lower graded law schools. [105]

At this meeting the Society also criticised the operation of PACH (a new system for allocating pupillages) and gave an enthusiastic response to the First Report of the ACLEC, especially 'what amounts to a qualifying law degree without the need for "core" or "foundation" subject syllabuses', although it regretted that financial constraints prevented ACLEC from recommending more extensive periods of study for non-law graduates. [106] A note from the Society's Honorary Secretary in 1998 comments that 'Much of the time each side is making the other not only better informed but wiser, so that helpful comment or advice may be given in a general way and so that influence may be exerted in other quarters.' [107] This comment reflected the Society's increasing ability to try and promote the political/public influence of academic lawyers.

Legal Education

Another indication of the more proactive approach that the Society began to adopt during the 1990s was the decision in 1991 to establish a joint SPTL–Committee of Heads of Law Schools (CHULS) Committee to consider the provision of resources for legal education. It was chaired by Professor John Wilson (Southampton), the Society's Past President, who had been a member of the Ormrod Committee, as well as being responsible for carrying out the periodic surveys of law schools that had begun in 1966. [108] The Committee carried out a survey of all law schools, and received answers from all but one institution, giving it a firm empirical basis for its Report, which was duly published in *The Reporter*

---

[104] 'SPTL Meeting with the LCD', *SPTL Reporter* No 4 Spring 1992, 4; Minutes of a Meeting with the Society of Public Teachers of Law, 1 February 1996.

[105] Agenda for Meeting with Lord Chancellor's Department, 6 February 1997.

[106] Ibid.

[107] Annual Meeting with the Lord Chancellor's Department, 25 June 1998.

[108] J Wilson, 'A First Survey of Legal Education in the United Kingdom' (1966) 9(NS) *JSPTL* 1; J Wilson and S Marsh, 'A Second Survey of Legal Education in the United Kingdom' (1975) 13(NS) *JSPTL* 239; J Wilson and S Marsh, 'A Second Survey: Supplement No 1' (London, Institute of Advanced Legal Studies, 1978); J Wilson and S Marsh, 'A Second Survey: Supplement No 2' (London, Institute of Advanced Legal Studies, 1981); J Wilson, 'A Third Survey of Legal Education in the United Kingdom' (1993)13 *Legal Studies* 143.

in 1992.[109] The Committee constructed models of four representative types of law schools, using the data it had gathered to show how seriously law was under-funded, particularly in relation to the provision of IT and library resources, but also in relation to the need for enlarged premises in which to house the rapidly growing numbers of law students.[110]

The Society continued to reflect an interest in the use of technology in teaching, publishing in 1992 the Executive Summary of the Bileta Inquiry into the Provision of Information Technology in UK Law Schools, which pointed to the need for investment in computing equipment and software, and in staff support and development, all of which would require increased resources. In addition to making recommendations about the ratio of computers to students, and the need for 'a dedicated legal technology computing laboratory' to facilitate teaching specialised legal information retrieval skills, the report indicated that support staff were 'an essential part of any serious IT program' and that significant involvement of law library staff was also needed. The report concluded that 'The success of an IT program depends upon the presence of a core of committed staff, and upon provision of staff development at all levels.'[111] The appearance of the Bileta item in *The Reporter* was followed by an article on the Law Technology Centre (LTC) at Warwick University, which aimed to promote and co-ordinate the development of information technology and computer-based learning in legal education. Noting that 'despite rapid development, legal education technology has yet to reach maturity', the article provided information about the LTC's resource pool, its information services and its intention to develop more fully its computer-assisted learning materials.[112]

The Society maintained its interest in legal education throughout the decade, supporting in 1996 the creation of a National Centre for Legal Education at Warwick University, whose object was to 'promote innovative teaching and learning by bringing together academics throughout the country for the development and dissemination of good practice'.[113] The Centre maintained its links with the Society by asking for a representative of the Society to sit on its Steering Group.[114] The Society also played its part in national debates on higher education, submitting a response to the National Committee of Inquiry into Higher Education (the Dearing Committee) in 1996 and to the QAA's consultation on accreditation and teaching in 1998.[115] In the latter case, the Society begins its response by expressing concern about the lack of previous consultation with

[109] 'Law School Resources', *SPTL Reporter* No 5 Winter 1992, 25.

[110] Ibid, 25–9.

[111] 'Executive Summary from the Bileta Inquiry into the Provision of Information Technology in UK Law Schools', *SPTL Reporter* No 4 Spring 1992, 18–20.

[112] A Paliwala, 'The Law Technology Centre', *SPTL Reporter* No 4 Spring 1992, 20–21.

[113] A Paliwala, 'National Centre for Legal Education (NCLE)' (1996).

[114] Letter dated 13 March 1997 from R Burridge to Prof D Hayton.

[115] National Committee of Inquiry into Higher Education: Response of the Society of Public Teachers of Law'; Consultation Paper on Accreditation and Teaching in Higher Education: Response of the Society of Public Teachers of Law.

subject associations on this matter, particularly as the proposals involved would directly affect its members and stressing the importance of subject-specific input into the initial and continuing education of university teachers.[116] The Society had come a long way since the somewhat apologetic responses of the early 1980s.

Quality Assurance Agency

The introduction of quality assurance processes as required by the Further and Higher Education Act 1992 was to have immediate impact upon members of the Society. The first audit of teaching was known as TQA, and it involved visits to departments to observe teaching, as well as examination of documentation.[117] An insight was given into some of the difficult issues posed by the introduction of TQA when Michael Allen (Newcastle) resigned as an assessor, and published an article in *The Reporter* explaining why he took that decision. He found the exercise to be one 'which had been conceived in haste and which was going to be performed come what may with no regard for the quality of the ultimate product'.[118] He criticised the lack of training for assessors, finding that little thought had been given to the very concept of 'high quality educational provision', and that comparability between assessments of different institutions was weak.[119] He felt that he could not continue to give legitimacy to the exercise by continuing to act as an assessor, and urged others to consider their position. When the Society wrote to HEFCE expressing unease about Mr Allen's resignation it received assurances that the matters he had raised would be addressed.[120] In fact Michael Allen was expressing at an early stage many of the criticisms that were later to be widely voiced by others. When HEFCE later commissioned an evaluation of the process, the resulting report strongly supported calls that had been made for a greater degree of transparency.[121]

Benchmarking

The assessment of teaching remained controversial. One of the projects that the QAA embarked on was to produce 'benchmarks' for academic disciplines, which were statements setting out expectations about standards of degrees, and defining what could be expected of a graduate in terms of the abilities and skills needed to develop understanding or competence in the subject. A 'benchmarking group'

---

[116] Consultation Paper on Accreditation and Teaching in Higher Education: Response of the Society of Public Teachers of Law.

[117] M Allen, 'Teaching Quality Assessment Exercise', *SPTL Reporter* No 7 Winter 1993, 25.

[118] Ibid.

[119] Ibid.

[120] SPTL Council Minutes 11 March 1994, Minute 7.3.

[121] R Barnett et al, *Assessment of the Quality of Higher Education: Report for HEFCE and HEFCW* (London, Centre for Higher Education Studies, Institute of Education, University of London, 1994).

was appointed for each discipline. The Society had some concerns about the process involved; in his editorial in *The Reporter* in Winter 1998, Tony Bradney summed up the situation when he wrote:

> Acting on the premise that there was widespread public concern about quality in universities, a premise for which it adduced no evidence, the Quality Assurance Agency asked not, was that concern justified, but, what could universities do to meet that concern. After a number of fanciful and far-fetched suggestions the latest proposal is the idea of benchmark standards for law schools. . . . There will be some in law schools who see merit in the proposals, some who are wholly against such an imposition on the autonomy of individual universities and some who have problems with particular parts of the suggested benchmark. What everyone, outside the Agency, will be concerned about is the speed with which the whole matter is being pushed through. Before law schools had been consulted about the proposals, assessors were being appointed and trained. Before law schools have agreed to the idea itself, let alone agreed the details of the proposal, the matter is being implemented. This is not the fault of those academics who have agreed to draft the standards or those who have agreed to act as assessors. It is, rather, a serious error on the part of those within the Agency who have managed the timetable for implementation. A concern with quality control normally involves a rigorous process of checking and counter-checking systems; for those in charge of the Quality Assurance Agency quality control betokens a frantic rush into a system no-one fully understands with implications that no-one has yet had the time fully to think through.[122]

The President, Professor Brazier, wrote to the Chief Executive of the QAA to express the Society's concerns:

> I am writing to express some disquiet about the progress of establishing the benchmarking group for Law. I understand that members have now been appointed and that the committee will meet for the first time only on 25 June. Academic reviewers will subsequently be appointed and trained in the autumn with a view to piloting the process in eight law schools (four in Scotland) very soon afterwards. I am concerned that haste in implementing the new quality assurance process should not impair the quality of the process itself.
>
> May I put a number of issues to you? If the benchmarking group only meets in June, is there sufficient time for debate and promulgation of standards by that group as a whole? Will it be possible to identify and appoint academic reviewers of the requisite standard who will be free to undergo training and act at such short notice? An especial worry for the SPTL is the need to ensure procedures appropriate for our very distinguished Scottish law schools. . . . Do the proposed standards adequately serve Scotland? I am told that SHEFCE has some reservations about the implementation of quality assurance procedures in Scotland.
>
> I am aware of the importance of the task before the QAA. I hope you will understand that my primary objective is that the system works as it should to all our benefit.[123]

---

[122] T Bradney, 'Quality or Cant?' *SPTL Reporter* No 17 Winter 1998, 1–2.
[123] Letter dated 5 June 1998 from Prof M Brazier to J Randall, CEO, QAA.

The Society consulted widely about the QAA consultation paper on benchmarking, circulating the relevant documents and encouraging Council representatives to send in their views.[124] The approach it took to these matters was another reflection of its increasing willingness to be proactive in matters affecting legal education.

Higher Education Funding Council for England

Towards the end of the decade, the Society became increasingly concerned about the pressures on resources for law schools. In 1998, the President raised this informally with one of the Society's Past Presidents, Professor Ross Cranston, who had just been elected as an Member of Parliament and was shortly to become Solicitor General.[125] In the following year the Society continued to press for improved resources for law when it was represented at a meeting which took place between the Chief Executive of HEFCE, Sir Brian Fender, and a number of those represented at the Standing Conference on Legal Education (SPTL, CHULS and the professional bodies).[126] Matters raised at the meeting included the particular importance of libraries to the discipline of law, the difficulties of meeting, on the basis of present resources, the broad range of outcomes contained in the professional bodies' Joint Announcement.[127] Sir Brian's response was that 'libraries were funded as part of the block grant and it was the job of local management to determine how it was spent . . . the funding formula could not easily be adjusted to deal with the genuine concerns raised'.[128] However, Sir Brian also indicated that there might be room for regional collaboration in relation to libraries, which the President, Professor John Bell, undertook to pursue with HEFCE.[129]

Research Matters

Supporting Research

The Society made a number of efforts to promote legal research during this decade. In 1992 Butterworths agreed to provide an annual sum for the subsequent four years to fund travel scholarships to enable SPTL members to travel to European law schools and research institutions or to enable law schools to pay

---

[124] Letter dated 10 July 1998 from P Niven to Council Representatives.
[125] Letter dated 5 June 1998 from Prof M Brazier to R Cranston MP.
[126] Meeting of the Standing Conference Delegation with Sir Brian Fender of HEFCE, 20 July 1999.
[127] Meeting with Sir Brian Fender of HEFCE 20 July 1999.
[128] Ibid.
[129] Meeting of the Standing Conference Delegation with Sir Brian Fender of HEFCE, 20 July 1999.

the travel costs of scholars from overseas whom they wished to invite to the UK.[130] During the same year, the SPTL, in partnership with the Foreign and Commonwealth Office, invited five colleagues from Czechoslovakia to visit law faculties in England. They visited for a fortnight and divided their time between Oxford, Warwick and Southampton.[131] The Annual Conference in 1992 adopted as its theme 'The European Law School' and involved distinguished scholars from other European law schools, as well as judges of the European Court of Justice.[132] During his Presidency, in 1996, Professor Hugh Beale (Warwick) sought to widen the membership of the Society by offering institutional membership to overseas law schools, hoping particularly that this would appeal to colleagues in Europe, who were otherwise not well represented within the Society's membership. He tied this in with a conference theme of 'Legal Change and Legal Scholarship Across Europe', aiming to encourage legal scholarship in this area.[133]

The Reporter regularly published information about the Society's Academic Purposes Fund, which continued to make annual awards. Generally, the Fund operated smoothly, although in 1996 the then Chair of the relevant Committee, Susan Bright, raised the continuing problem of ensuring that beneficiaries of awards reported back to the Society. (Should non-submitters be named and shamed? Should they give a presentation at the Annual Conference?) The Executive Committee was quick to take up her preferred solution, namely that award-holders should be required to submit a brief report for publication in *The Reporter*, with any non-reporters also listed.[134]

The Society made a further effort to encourage legal research with the establishment in 1992 of the SPTL prizes for outstanding legal scholarship. These were open to all members of the Society aged under 40, and would be awarded to scholars who, in the opinion of the judges, had written the most outstanding legal books published in the preceding academic year.[135]

SPTL Seminars

When Professor Peter Birks was elected as the Society's Honorary Secretary in 1989, one of his first initiatives was to establish a series of SPTL seminars, with the title 'Examining the Law Syllabus'. Announced in the first issue of *The Reporter*, they were 'open to all teachers, whether or not they belong to the SPTL'. Each seminar was to be devoted to one area of law, and the aim was 'to examine the problems encountered designing and delivering the syllabus in that area'. Three

---

[130] 'Increased Support from Law Publishers', *SPTL Reporter* No 5 Winter 1992, 13.

[131] 'Honorary Secretary's Report', *SPTL Reporter* No 4 Spring 1992, 2.

[132] Advertisement for Society's Annual Conference, *SPTL Reporter* No 4 Spring 1992, 5.

[133] Letter dated 28 February 1996 from Prof H Beale to Prof J Bridge. His suggestion was approved by council and confirmed at the 1996 AGM: SPTL AGM 1996, Minute 7.1.

[134] Letter dated 13 September 1996 from S Bright to Prof H Beale; SPTL Executive Committee Minutes 8 November 1996.

[135] 'Honorary Secretary's Report', *SPTL Reporter* No 4 Spring 1992, 4.

short papers would be delivered by the leader of the seminar and two invited speakers, followed by informal discussion. The first three topics to be announced were the law of property, public law and criminal law.[136] Compared with the somewhat inward-looking approach of the 1980s, this attempt to reach out beyond the confines of the Society was a breath of fresh air.

The seminars continued throughout the 1990s. The legal education theme which started them off was followed by other very varied topics. In 1992–93 a series of eight seminars on the theme of 'The Frontiers of Liability' was supported by the trustees of the Hamlyn Trust. Chaired by a distinguished academic or judge, they all involved leading academics in the relevant area, and covered topics ranging from 'The Limits of Judicial Review' and 'The Vienna Convention on the Sale of Goods' to 'Parents and Children: Rights and Protection'.[137] Other seminars in the 1990s included an extended series entitled 'Pressing Problems in the Law', which covered a wide range of subjects, from freedom of speech and professional negligence to insolvency and privacy,[138] while towards the end of the decade there was a series of 'The Strengths and Weaknesses of the Law of . . .' ; several of the sets of seminar papers were published as edited collections of essays.[139] Writing to his successor at the end of his term as Honorary Secretary, Professor Birks enclosed a letter from Lord Justice Brooke, saying:

> This is from Brooke LJ, and I enclose it because it is one in a long line of letters from judges which have said essentially that if they knew in advance and the time and place were not too awkward they would be eager to attend our seminars. I have a feeling that, at KCL, you will be exceptionally well-placed to capitalize on what is, I think, a quite strong desire to keep up with and in with the university law schools.
>
> The immediate cause of the letter was the publication by OUP of *Wrongs and Remedies*, which included four essays which he had chaired.[140]

It appears that the seminars were successful not only in promoting academic debate, but also in raising the profile of the Society.

Library Matters

The Society's Libraries Committee benefited during the 1990s from the Chairmanship of Professor Terence Daintith (IALS). During this decade, a wholesale revision of the Statement of Minimum holdings was undertaken. A Consultative Group was established in 1993, consisting of the members of the Society's Libraries Committee together with co-opted members from other interested parties, including the British and Irish Association of Law Librarians, the ALT,

---

[136] Ibid, 1.

[137] 'SPTL Seminars 1992–1993', *SPTL Reporter* No 4 Spring 1992, 28–9.

[138] SPTL Programme for 1994–95; SPTL Programme for 1995–96.

[139] See undated letter from Prof D Hayton 'Re Four SPTL Seminars'. For publication of seminar papers, see eg SPTL Executive Committee Minutes 9 June 1994, Minute E20/94.

[140] Letter dated 3 August 1996 from Prof P Birks to Prof D Hayton.

the Law Society and the ACLEC.[141] The Group also appointed a Principal Researcher, Dr Peter Clinch, law librarian at University of Wales College of Cardiff.[142] The ACLEC provided substantial funding for research on the forms and levels of provision in university law libraries, which enabled a variety of statistics to be produced, informing the Group's work.[143] The new 'Statement of Standards for University Law Library Provision in England and Wales' was published in 1995.[144]

The major change that the new document introduced was a move from a minimum holdings list to a comprehensive set of standards for all relevant aspects of library provision. To assist law schools and librarians in interpreting the standards, each one was accompanied by comments illustrating its application and relating it, where appropriate, to actual levels of provision as reported by law schools and libraries.[145] The Introduction to the new 'Statement of Standards for University Law Library Provision in England and Wales' includes a masterly survey of developments in legal education since the publication of the first version of the minimum holdings document in 1958, including the introduction of EU law, increased numbers of students studying for a wider range of qualifications, diverse styles of teaching, and an emphasis on the learning of skills, particularly research skills, which provided particular challenges for law libraries.[146] Together, these developments meant that a statement of minimum holdings was no longer appropriate, nor in keeping with best practice in information science. As the Working Group noted:

> Changes in law teaching challenge the very idea of a 'holdings list' which represents a common view of adequate and appropriate knowledge. Changes in the environment of law teaching require that the Statement be reviewed critically in the light of new functions—as a support for external assessment and monitoring—that it may consequently be called on to perform. And changes—especially technological changes—in law materials again invite reconsideration not only of the content of the Statement, but also its design.[147]

There were a number of key factors in the new Statement, which sought to address all these changes. First was the importance of defining effective library provision in such a way that it could readily be used by external bodies for monitoring and assessment purposes, ie as a set of standards.[148] The electronic revolution experienced since the Statement was first drafted in 1958 meant that

---

[141] *Report of the Consultative Group for the Review of the SPTL Statement of Minimum Holdings for Law Libraries in England and Wales*, 2.

[142] Ibid, 3.

[143] Ibid.

[144] *A Library for the Modern Law School: A Statement of Standards for University Law Library Provision in England and Wales* SPTL, September 1995.

[145] Ibid.

[146] *A Library for the Modern Law School: A Statement of Standards for University Law Library Provision in England and Wales* SPTL, September 1995, paras 5–10.

[147] Ibid, para 11.

[148] Ibid, para 13.

electronic material needed to be included.[149] It was also important to cover a whole range of factors relating to the quality and level of service offered to users.[150] Finally, in line with current thinking on these matters, the new Statement was expressed in terms of 'propositions about what a law school's library should enable its academic users to do'.[151] Overall, the new Statement was a major achievement by the Society, enhancing its continuing contribution to the basic research structure of the discipline of law. Having undertaken such a radical revision of the Statement, the Working Group was keen that regular revisions should take place, especially so that all the statistical data could be kept up to date. The Society funded a revision in 1997, and then concluded an agreement with the British and Irish Association of Law Librarians (BIALL) that the two organisations would alternately fund the necessary surveys.[152]

Subject Sections

In terms of legal scholarship, it had become increasingly obvious that the specialist groups lay at the heart of the Society. They attracted a great deal of participation from members and non-members alike, and provided the opportunity for discussion and debate of a vast range of legal research topics. However, their links to the Society were far from uniform, and there was little uniformity in the way they were organised. This was far from ideal. As Professor Birks wrote in his column in *The Reporter*:

> The Society exists above all to promote the study of law. Hence it was not a matter for pride that the arrangements for helping particular subjects had become somewhat confused. Some subjects were covered by official committees, others by unofficial interest groups. Council has now set up a new system of subject sections. Each subject section has a panel and a convenor, and anyone (whether a member of the Society or not) may join a section simply by asking the convenor to add his or her name to the list.[153]

Bringing them firmly into the Society's administrative structure signalled that the Society was acknowledging their importance. Dr Francis Rose (Cambridge), who had already been co-ordinating the specialist groups, now became the Society's first Subject Sections Convenor, and published a set of guidelines in *The Reporter* covering the objects, membership, finance and meetings of the subject sections. He also encouraged members interested in starting new sections to contact him.[154] Reports from subject section convenors about the activities of their

---

[149] Ibid, para 14.
[150] Ibid, para 4.
[151] Ibid, para 15.
[152] SPTL Libraries Committee Minutes 22 October 1997, Minute 3.2; SPTL Libraries Committee Minutes 24 April 1998, Minute 3.
[153] 'Honorary Secretary's Report *SPTL Reporter* No 3 Autumn 1991, 2.
[154] FD Rose, 'Subject Sections', *SPTL Reporter* No 4 Spring 1992, 21–3.

groups began to appear in *The Reporter*, revealing that some groups were very active, organising their own specialist conferences in addition to putting on a programme of papers at the Annual Conference.[155] Some subject sections also produced their own newsletters; copies of those for the public law section and the property and trust section exist in the archive and reveal that their convenors were keen to encourage participation by members. In his 'Sort of Newsletter' for the public law section in 1996, in addition to providing information about the annual meeting with the Law Commission and sessions at the Annual Conference, Professor David Feldman (Birmingham), welcomed 'news, views, offers of help and other communications to distract me from examining and to make future Section events (even) more exciting'. He canvassed a range of topics upon which members might want to comment:

> For example, do let me know what is happening in the public law field at your institu-
> tion. In relation to teaching, fellow public law teachers would be interested to know
> about new courses, and about experiences in teaching initiatives. Have you used soft-
> ware such as that produced by the Law Courseware Consortium? How might new
> teaching methods and new developments change the public law curriculum in coming
> years? . . . [I]f we have a change of government in the coming months, how might con-
> stitutional reforms necessitate a change of syllabus? . . . On the research front, are there
> are exciting projects that you would like people to know about? Please feel free to send
> me material on these or other subjects to make colleagues' lives more vibrant and
> exciting.[156]

In addition to the subject sections, the Society continued to have a close relation-ship with the United Kingdom National Committee of Comparative Law (UKNCCL), which had for many years held its annual meeting immediately prior to the society's Annual Conference. This pattern was to continue after the formation of the subject sections, for the UKNCCL was a constitutionally sepa-rate body, although drawing its membership from largely the same constituency as the SPTL, and keen to continue its close relationship with the Society.[157]

The Research Assessment Exercise

The other area in which the Society sought to support the research interests of its members was by its continuing involvement in consultations about the RAE. The Society's response to the UFC's consultation about the 1992 exercise expressed concern that periodic RAEs were damaging to 'the prosecution of major projects of real importance', and that there appeared to be no clear assurance that quality, rather than quantity, of research would be assessed. An assurance was sought that the names of people on the assessment panels would be published and that

---

[155] 'Convenors' Reports', *SPTL Reporter* No 4 Spring 1992, 23–4.
[156] D Feldman, 'SPTL Public Law Section: A Sort of Newsletter', *SPTL Reporte* No 3 June 1996, 1.
[157] I Fletcher, 'The United Kingdom National Committee of Comparative Law', *SPTL Reporter* No 4 Spring 1992, 26.

panels would give reasons for their gradings. Criticism was directed towards the suggestion that research should be of industrial or commercial relevance, noting that 'all forms of legal research in one way or another serve the public interest in achieving a better understanding of our law and legal system'. Particular concern was expressed about the assessment of interdisciplinary work, (perhaps reflecting the fact that the Society did not perceive itself as solely interested in traditional doctrinal research).[158]

When the panel was announced for the 1992 RAE, the Society was pleased to find that the names of the assessors were indeed published, and although reasoned decisions would not be given for decisions made, it appeared that there would be some informal feedback.[159] The Society was less than happy about the UFC's attitude to the problem of 'major projects'—its reply on that topic was that it would not wish to encourage short-term work, but that 'it thought there was no danger of that happening, since those engaged on large projects . . . could expect to make a positive report in every second assessment', thus entirely missing the point, as far as the Society was concerned. 'This answer was evidently unaware of the pressure on people not to be nil-returners in any round.'[160]

The Society was equally involved in the 1996 RAE, having a meeting with members of the law panel, along with representatives of the SLSA and the ALT.[161] The Society ensured that it consulted widely with its members about the operation of the RAE; an 'extremely useful' exercise, as one head of department described it.[162] The main points made by the Society when it wrote to the Chief Executive of HEFCE were that the criteria for grading departments should be made known much earlier in the relevant period than they had been in 1992, that the panel should contain a wide spread of expertise, that due recognition should be given to multidisciplinary research (and research written in languages other than English) and that attention should be paid to the particular position of early-career scholars.[163] In making these points, the Society was expressing widely held misgivings about the RAE process, as reflected in the academic literature on the subject.[164]

By the time of the 1996 Exercise, the RAE was firmly established within the Society's activities. It liaised with CHULS on its nominations for members of the panel, and agreed to work with all the subject associations in responding to consultations, hoping to develop a common approach.[165] After the 1996 Exercise

---

[158] 'Universities Funding Council', *SPTL Reporter* No 4 Spring 1992, 17–8.

[159] 'The Research Assessment Exercise', *SPTL Reporter* No 5 Winter 1992, 16.

[160] Ibid.

[161] Letter dated 15 August1995 from J Newman (Panel Secretary for Law RAE Panel) to Prof J Wylie.

[162] Response to SPTL RAE Consultation 1996.

[163] Letter dated 18 December 1996 from Prof D Hayton to Prof B Fender, HEFCE.

[164] See eg A Talib, 'The Continuing Behavioural Modification of Academics since the 1992 Research Assessment Exercise' (2001) 33(3) *Higher Education Review* 30; for law in particular, see D Vick et al, 'The Perceptions of Academic Lawyers Concerning the Effects of the United Kingdom Research Assessment Exercise' (1998) 25 *Journal of Law and Society* 536.

[165] SPTL Executive Committee Minutes 10 February 1995, Minute 2; SPTL Executive Committee Minutes 12 December 1997, Minute 44.1.

was over, the Society was immediately concerned with its response to consultations over the next exercise, making the point that measuring research using the RAE as a mechanism was very costly, both in terms of staff time preparing submissions and panel members in evaluating them.[166] 'Given the rather crude nature of the present exercise and the confusion of its objectives, as well as the evidence that it encourages gamesmanship as much as research, we would suggest that the Funding Council look at a simpler system which is less burdensome.'[167] The response concluded with the Society's strong views about equal opportunities:

> On equal opportunities grounds, we consider it essential that the panels should be required to give due allowance for career breaks due to maternity leave, illness or other such reasons which justify a lower volume of output.[168]

The Society's continuing involvement in the successive RAEs which took place during the 1990s was one of the ways in which it demonstrated its commitment to legal research and scholarship.

Conferences

In 1992 the then President, Professor Roy Goode (Oxford), introduced a number of changes to the format of the Annual Conference. He had indicated in the strategy document he published during his Presidential year that he thought it was important to involve the membership of the Society more fully in its activities and that the Conference needed to be better developed:

> The Annual Conference should be seen as the major event of the Society's calendar but will only attract the full support of members if its academic content is substantially strengthened and the meetings of the subject sections treated as an integral part of the programme, not as an external event latched on to the conference.[169]

For the Annual Conference in 1992 he duly ensured that the subject section meetings were fully incorporated into the main conference, writing in the pre-conference publicity:

> The former Special Interest Groups, reconstituted as SPTL Subject Sections, will be an important component of the Conference as a whole, instead of being detached as separate events as hitherto.[170]

---

[166] Research Assessment Consultation Paper 2/97: Response by the Society of Public Teachers of Law.

[167] Ibid.

[168] Ibid.

[169] Goode, above n 8, 13.

[170] Advertisement for Society's Annual Conference, *SPTL Reporter* No 4 Spring 1992, 5.

This innovation signalled that the Society wished to actively involve as many members as possible in its conference, rather than finding that many participants left before the 'main conference' took place.[171] In addition, Professor Goode stressed the academic content of the programme:

> The academic content of the programme has been substantially enlarged, with the incorporation of the meetings of the subject sections into the programme as a whole and no fewer than seven plenary sessions.[172]

This was a clear indication of his wish to emphasise that the Conference was a meeting of a learned society, which took intellectual matters seriously. These changes to the Annual Conference, though significant, took some time to become firmly embedded in the Society's culture. For the next few years, the subject sections still tend to be on the first two days of the conference, followed by two days of plenary sessions.[173] However, from 1997 onwards, the subject section meetings were interspersed between the plenary sessions, and the change was fully implemented.[174] Other aspects of the Annual Conference were slower to change: at the beginning of the decade, the conference programme still featured 'excursions', though these appear to have faded out in the middle of the decade, and do not appear from 1996 onwards.[175] Few menus for the Annual Dinner survive, but those which do indicate that a toast to the Queen was given at the Dinner in 1993. Nevertheless, the Conference had undoubtedly changed greatly by the time the decade ended, when it was a much more intellectual event than had formerly been the case.

Women

While the 1990s saw the election of the Society's first two female Presidents, Professor Margot Brazier (Manchester) in 1997 and Professor Hazel Genn (UCL) in 1999, it was still the case that in some aspects the masculine ethos of the Society continued. For example, the convenors of the first group of the Society's seminars, on 'Examining the Law Syllabus', were all male, except for Nicola Lacey, who convened the third seminar, on criminal law, and, with the exception of the two female Presidents, the Society's Officers continued to be exclusively male.[176] The continuing dominance of the stereotypical middle-class white male did not

---

[171] Ibid.
[172] Ibid.
[173] See SPTL Annual Conference programmes 1993, 1994 and 1996.
[174] See SPTL Annual Conference programmes 1997 and 1998.
[175] See SPTL Annual Conference programmes 1996, 1997 and 1998.
[176] 'SPTL Seminars Examining the Law Syllabus', *SPTL Reporter* No 1 Summer 1990, 1.

go unnoticed in this era of change. In his Strategy Document Professor Goode raised the question of equality of opportunity, commenting that:

> The Society is dedicated to equal opportunities, and there is little recent evidence to indicate the existence of barriers to entry to law teaching, or to promotion, on grounds of race or sex. Yet it remains the case that the number of senior posts held by women and by ethnic minorities is small. Is this not an issue which the Society should examine?[177]

However, more women were participating in the Society's activities than ever before. The delegate list for the 1999 Annual Conference shows that 37 per cent of the delegates were female, and of these, 11 (13 per cent) were professors. Of the men attending, 35 per cent were professors.[178] While not appearing to take a strongly proactive role in matters of equality, the Society showed that it was willing to help address such issues when in 1999 it supported, together with the ALT, a workshop run by the Women Law Professors' Network, 'The Cat-Flap in the Glass Ceiling' on gender issues in the law teacher's career.[179]

Conclusion

As the end of the decade approached, the Society began to contemplate another set of major changes when the then President, Professor Margot Brazier, held a special meeting of the Society's Executive Committee in July 1998 to consider 'The SPTL at 90'. Her purpose in doing so was to encourage members of the Committee to think strategically about the role of the Society.[180] In doing so, she was consciously building on the work of her predecessors; Professor Roy Goode's 'Strategy Document' was one of the background papers considered at the special meeting.[181] A paper written by the Society's Honorary Treasurer, Clive Weston, summed up the Society's position as he saw it:

> Until quite recently, the SPTL was rather an amateurish, friendly, ineffectual organisation which had almost as much a social as a professional and lobbying purpose. A big change came with Peter Birks' tenure of the Secretaryship (1989–96), when a number of academic initiatives were taken (such as the beefing up of the sections and inauguration of the Seminars): this enlarged the SPTL's claim to be a learned society, and it became a much heavier hitter intellectually. Additionally, the Society was taken by the scruff of the neck by Roy Goode (President 1991–92) who taught it to think big in

---

[177] Goode, above n 8, 15.

[178] SPTL Conference 1999 Delegate List.

[179] Email dated 14 July 1999 from C Wells to P Niven 'The Cat-Flap in the Glass Ceiling'; see also C Wells, 'Working With Women Workshop: The Cat-Flap in the Glass Ceiling', *SPTL Reporter* No 19 Winter 1999, 6.

[180] CA Weston, 'Response to President for Special Meeting of Executive Committee on July 4th 1998'.

[181] 'Strategy Document', version 2.

terms of influence and contacts. Professor Goode's strategy document of October 1991 remains a major statement of the many concerns, academic and professional, which the society faces or should be facing.[182]

In the discussion paper which she circulated before the meeting, Professor Brazier identified some key issues that she saw the Society facing as it approached its centenary.[183] These included the need to clarify its role as a professional representative body of law teachers, both in relation to the professional bodies and in relation to a changing system of higher education, especially given that the SPTL was not the sole body representing law teachers. As a learned society, the SPTL should be representing academic lawyers within the world of scholarship: did it have strong enough links with funding bodies to do this effectively? Professor Brazier was especially aware of the progress made by the SLSA in this regard: 'Once again, we are not the only players in the field. The SLSA has established a reputation (especially among younger scholars) as the intellectually lively body.'[184] Were there internal matters, to do with the organisation of the Society, which could be improved? Some critics had suggested that 'The SPTL is rather "dead". It lacks excitement and does not prompt a desire for future involvement.'[185] Would an enlarged Executive Committee be a good idea? Should the Society rethink its committee structure?

The minutes of the meeting record the general view that the Society was perceived as the 'older statesman' among similar bodies concerned with legal education, and that, while it had significant strengths, in terms of its subject sections, the SLSA, in particular, was seen as more dynamic.[186] The Society had a role to play in relation to both scholarship and to educating both its own members and the outside world on a range of issues; it needed to co-operate more closely with the other law subject associations to present a united front when appropriate. The development of the Society's scholarship role and the drawing-in of younger academics were very important. Consideration should also be given to internal matters, such as the role of Council—there was currently a perception that it was a dull forum.[187]

In carrying out this review, the President sought to involve the whole Society. After preliminary discussion by the Executive Committee, the matter was discussed at Council at the Annual Conference in 1998 and a substantial article appeared in *The Reporter*, setting out the issues for consideration and telling members 'Your views are very much sought.'[188] Among the issues Professor Brazier drew to members' attention were whether the Society could do more in its role as a learned society, perhaps by holding seminars in different parts of the

---

[182] Weston, above n 180.
[183] M.Brazier, 'SPTL: Issues for Our Future' (1998).
[184] Ibid.
[185] Ibid.
[186] Note—Special Meeting of the Executive Committee.
[187] Ibid.
[188] M Brazier, 'The SPTL at 90', *SPTL Reporter* No 17 Winter 1998, 4.

country, by using the Annual Conference to better effect, and especially by ensuring that a greater proportion of papers resulted from the call for papers, since: 'The conference needs to belong to its members as much as to the President in office.'[189] Perhaps more funds to support research could be made available by the Society, especially for younger scholars. In thinking about the organisation of the Society, Professor Brazier noted that the Executive were making several suggestions about this, including that the Executive Committee should be enlarged and made more representative of the membership, and that greater use should be made of Working Parties, to allow greater involvement of members in the Society's activities.[190] Finally, she suggested that consideration should be given to the question of the Society's name. '[F]or myself', she wrote, 'I would regret abandoning our historic nomenclature. The Society must, however, address its profile.'[191]

In the event, the Society was to take on board many of the changes envisaged in this consultation, which was part of the continuing change experienced during this decade. One immediate change was that the Executive Committee was enlarged, to include nine members of the Society, of whom three were to be 'recent' (fewer than eight years' standing); in appointing such members, in so far as it was practicable, Council was to take into account factors such as gender, ethnicity, regional representation, type of institution and subject section representation.[192] Other organisational changes included the establishment of two Working Groups, one on research (to deal with all matters relating to legal research, as opposed to legal education) and the other on nominations (to deal with requests to the President to nominate to various bodies or for honours in the Honours Lists).[193] It was quickly decided to make these groups a permanent part of the Society, by constituting them as sub-Committees, and to do the same with the Legal Education Committee.[194]

In the final year of the decade, the Society began to move towards one of its most radical changes—a change of name. This had first been mooted as part of the examination of 'The Society at 90'. At the Annual General Meeting in 1998, it had been agreed that a Working Party would investigate the possibility of obtaining a Royal Charter for the Society (which would also involve a change of name).[195] The reasons behind this decision were set out in a Discussion Paper drawn up for the Working Party.

> First, the present name does not accurately describe the membership. Under rule 3 membership of the society is broadly available only to those people teaching law at degree level. There are many people in schools and colleges who, in the ordinary sense

[189] Ibid.
[190] Ibid, 5.
[191] Ibid.
[192] SPTL Council Minutes 5 March 1999, Minute 105/99; SPTL AGM 1999, Minute 4.
[193] SPTL Council Minutes 10 December 1999, Minutes C 141/99 and C142/99.
[194] SPTL Council Minutes 10 December 1999, Minutes C141/99, C 142/99 and C140/99.
[195] SPTL AGM 1998 Minutes, Minute 7.

of the phrase, are public teachers of law but who are not eligible for membership of the Society because of the level at which they teach law. Secondly, the present name of the Society is not one that gives a sense of an academic discipline with the same stature as other similar bodies in other academic areas.[196]

The Working Party, chaired by Professor Hazel Genn, duly balloted the membership by email to ascertain whether there was support for a change of name, if so, to what, and whether the new title should include the word 'Royal'.[197] The ballot paper canvassed three possibilities: the Society of Legal Scholars, the Society of Academic Lawyers and the Society of Jurists.[198] Guided by the results of the ballot, the Working Party decided that it should propose the Society of Legal Scholars as being the name which best reflected the activities and aspirations of the Society.[199] Having got that far, the Society decided to go ahead with investigating the possibility of obtaining a Royal Charter. Commenting on this move, the Administrative Secretary, Peter Niven, had notified Professor Genn that:

> It should be noted that there were some strident voices against this proposal when it was raised. Some members have threatened to resign. . . . However, it is felt in the Council and the WP that royal status will give the Society an edge when it comes to negotiations with the Law Commission, government departments and other outside bodies.[200]

The Society's Executive Committee decided that the Royal prefix should be sought, as it would enable 'the President to speak with the same apparent weight and authority as the President of revered long-standing Societies like The Royal Society, The Royal Geographical Society'.[201] As required by the Society's rules, the proposed name change was duly approved at a Special General Meeting of the Society in December 1999, and subsequently confirmed by postal ballot of all the members.[202] This was how things stood at the end of the decade.

The 1990s had been a period of significant change for the Society. Not only had it taken steps towards being a more serious learned society, reorganising the subject sections and integrating them fully into the Annual Conference, as well as abandoning the practice of having conference 'excursions' and providing increased opportunities for academic debate. It had also reformed its committees, bringing in early-career academics, and taking on board the need to promote gender equality, at least in its internal structures. Throughout the decade the Society had participated to an increasing extent in national debates about legal education, and had often played a leading role in interchanges with the legal professions. It was a very different Society from that of the previous decades.

---

[196] Sub-Committee on Royal Charter/Name Change 'Discussion Paper'.
[197] Notes from Working Party on Change of Name, 26 April 1999.
[198] SPTL Change of Name Ballot Paper.
[199] 'Reasons for Resolution'.
[200] Notes from Working Party on Change of Name, 26 April 1999.
[201] 'Reasons for Resolution'.
[202] See SPTL General Meeting 2 March 2001.

11

The New Millennium:
2000 and Beyond

> The Society can be proud of its standing as a learned society, a standing it did
> not always have.
>
> (Professor Richard Card, Presidential Address 2002, 'The Legal Scholar')

Introduction

Our approach throughout this book has been to try to allow those involved in the
Society's history to speak for themselves through the documents we have
unearthed. However, we should like to draw the attention of readers to the fact
that from 1990 onwards, the Society's archives are not yet open to the general
public. We were granted access to records from that date onwards by the Society
on the understanding that we would use our discretion in what we made public.
In relation to the most recent past, from 2000 onwards, we have, as with the
material relating to the 1990s, omitted material not otherwise publicly available
which, were it to have been included, would have constituted a breach of privacy
relating to living individuals. Our treatment of the years from 2000 to the present
day has been necessarily more superficial than that which went before, as it is not
possible, without the benefit of some distance of time, to properly evaluate events
so close to our own time, quite apart from the Society's need to keep confidential
some recent documents which relate to matters still under negotiation or discussion with various third parties. Despite those limitations, we hope that what
follows is sufficient to give readers an accurate picture of the Society's most
recent past.

Readers should also note that all documents in the archives relating to the
2000s are uncatalogued, so have no reference numbers attached.

Research Matters

This decade saw a continuing determination on the part of the Society to increase its profile as a learned society. One consequence of this policy was its decision to celebrate the new millennium by commissioning a volume of essays discussing likely developments in different areas of the law over the next 20 years. The book, published by Hart Publishing under the title *Law's Future(s)*, covered both different areas of law and different approaches to legal study, in an attempt to reflect the plurality of work being carried out by members of the Society.[1]

The Society's focus on research led it to continue its support of members' research activities in a number of ways. It has funded jointly with the British and Irish Association of Law Librarians (BIALL) an annual survey of academic law libraries in the UK and Ireland so that the 'Statement of Standards' could be regularly revised.[2] The Society's stewardship of the Statement led to another major revision in 2009, when a small working group was established to accomplish this, with the Honorary Secretary, Professor Stephen Bailey (Nottingham) and the Chair of the Society's Libraries Committee, Dr Jules Winterton (IALS), as co-chairs. Dr Peter Clinch (Cardiff), whose expertise had been very valuable when previous versions of the Statement were produced, was appointed as specialist advisor to the Working Group.[3]

The Society's annual seminars, which, as the website says, it regards as 'one of its flagship events' have provided a varied offering of topics, including 'Commercial Law and Commercial Practice' (2002), 'The Law of the Sea' (2005) and 'Redefining Sovereignty: An International Debate on Sovereignty and International Economic Law' (2006).[4] Meanwhile, the Society has continued to respond to an ever-increasing number of consultation papers relating to research, as well as keeping its members informed about research-related matters by publishing relevant items in *The Reporter*, such as an explanation of the evolution of the Arts and Humanities Research Board into the Arts and Humanities Research Council, making known concerns about possible changes to the research library at the IALS and reporting on the Nuffield Inquiry into empirical legal research.[5]

---

[1] 'Law's Future(s)' *SPTL Reporter* No 21 Winter 2000, 6; D.Hayton (ed) *Law's Future(s)* (Oxford, Hart Publishing, 2000).

[2] SLS Libraries Committee 2002–2003 Annual Report.

[3] 'Report from Executive Committee to Council 11 March 2009', Council Document C04/09/A, para 5.

[4] 'Society of Legal Scholars Annual Seminar Series 2005 Invitation to Submit Proposals' *The Reporter* No 27 Winter 2003, 5; R Barnes, 'The 2005 Society of Legal Scholars Annual Seminar' *The Reporter* No 31 Winter 2005, 13; 'The Society of Legal Scholars Symposium 2006' *The Reporter* No 33 Autumn 2006, 22.

[5] S Worthington, 'The AHRB's Plans for its Future Role as the Arts and Humanities Research Council' *The Reporter* No 26 Spring 2003, 5; 'The Roberts Report on the RAE' *The Reporter* No 27 Winter 2003, 7; H Genn (2007) 'Law in the Real World: Building Capacity in Empirical Legal Research' *The Reporter* No 34 Spring 2007, 4–6.

The Research Assessment Exercise

The external audit of research has become firmly established as a major part of the culture of the academy, and the Society has made increasing efforts to keep its members informed about the whole process, beginning with the 2001 Exercise, when *The Reporter* published the general report produced by the law RAE panel, ensuring that all members were fully aware of the panel's views.[6] The Society's response to the Roberts Review of the management of the RAE was published in full on the Society's website in 2003.[7] It argued strongly for the retention of assessment by peer review, noting that it was the Society's firmly held view that 'only an autonomous Law panel will have the ability to review very different types of work across the whole spectrum of legal scholarship'.[8] It also made the point that assessment of research should not take place at intervals of less than six years, to allow researchers to engage in longer-term projects.[9] In 2005 the RAE manager for the 2008 exercise was present at Council, where he gave a PowerPoint presentation about the process and answered questions.[10] Members were kept up to date with information about the exercise by regular items in *The Reporter* as well as on the Society's website, starting in 2004 with an article by the Honorary Secretary on 'Preparations for the Next RAE and Law Panel Membership'.[11] This was followed in the next edition of *The Reporter* by a substantial article explaining the process by which the Society had arrived at its nominations for RAE panel membership, setting out the names of all those who had been nominated.[12] There is copious correspondence about the RAE in the archives, suggesting that the Society has taken its role as a learned society seriously in this regard, ensuring that it plays its part in keeping its members fully informed about developments concerning the RAE. Successive Chairs of RAE panels have given presentations to members of the Society, and this is an occasion when the Society has worked closely with the other academic law associations to plan such events, as well as seeking to reach as much consensus as possible with them about matters such as nominations to the panel.[13]

Research and the Society

Overall, research plays a much more important part in the Society's life than it has done previously. In part, this is because the Society has reflected changes in

---

[6] 'RAE 2001: Law Panel: General Overview' *The Reporter* No 24 Spring 2002, 6.
[7] 'The Roberts Report on the RAE' *The Reporter* No 27 Winter 2003, 7.
[8] 'Review of Research Assessment 2003: SLS Response' , 2.
[9] Ibid, 3.
[10] SLS Council Minutes 8 September 2005, Minute C18/05.
[11] *The Reporter* No 28 Spring 2004, 12.
[12] Ibid.
[13] See www.legalscholars.ac.uk/research/rae/index.cfm; N Wikeley, 'Preparations for the Next RAE and Law Panel Membership' *The Reporter* No 28 Spring 2004, 12.

the nature of legal academia. As Professor John Bell said, in his Presidential Address in 2000:

> Compared with the era of my first two Leeds predecessors as Presidents of the SPTL, research is now a major activity in legal academic life. Neither Professor Phillips (President 1914) nor Professor Hughes (President 1931) wrote anything significant. For them, the subjects on which they wrote were hobbies, as much as fishing at his home in North Wales was a hobby for Professor Hughes. . . . Rightly things have changed. Research in law has become a more professional activity[14]

However, the Society's increasing involvement over the years is not just a reaction to changes in academic life. It also springs out of conscious decisions, such as those arising out of Professor Brazier's review of 'The Society at 90', to respond to the increasing interest in legal research displayed by its members, and to ensure that the Society continues to grow in its role as a learned society, as well as in its role representing the interests of university law teachers.

Legal Studies

The Society's journal is one of the main reflections of its interest in research. This decade saw some major changes for *Legal Studies*. In 2001, the long-standing book reviews editor, Professor Richard Kidner, stood down from his post. He had taken over from the previous book reviews editor, Professor Richard Card, in 1984, so had held his post for the best part of 20 years. Reporting this to Council, the Editors of *Legal Studies* wrote:

> A previous editor, John Andrews, wrote of Dick Kidner's predecessor that he had pursued the task with great vigour and dedication, while noting that 'it is not always easy to persuade academics to write a major scholarly review of a new work' ((1984) 4 *LS* 1). That Dick Kidner has distinguished the role of review Editor for nearly 20 years is in itself a major achievement. That he has persuaded reluctant academics to continue to write scholarly considerations of new material in significant numbers is astonishing. That he has maintained the Society's learned publication with a regular, timely, varied and challenging library of reviews is a matter both of signal achievement and intellectual celebration. Successive editors and the Society as a whole are indebted to Dick for this contribution, and this note can be but small acknowledgement of it.[15]

The new book reviews editor was Professor Tony Prosser (Bristol), who continued Professor Kidner's policy of attracting substantial reviews of a wide range of different titles.

In 2003 *Legal Studies* experienced another change when it became available online for the first time, through Hein Online.[16] Change continued when in 2006

---

[14] J Bell, 'Research and the Law Teacher' *SPTL Reporter* No 20 Spring 2000, 5.
[15] 'Legal Studies Editors' Report 2000–2001', SPTL Council Document C44.1/01/A.
[16] 'Executive Committee Report to Council' *The Reporter* No 27 Winter 2003, 6.

Professor Derek Morgan and Professor Celia Wells stepped down as Editors. The Editorship was duly advertised in *The Reporter* and a new editorial team was appointed, composed of Professor Rob Merkin, Ms Jenny Steele and Professor Nick Wikeley at Southampton University, with Professor Jill Poole (UWE) taking over from Professor Prosser as Book Reviews Editor.[17] Paying tribute to their predecessors, the new team were particularly grateful for the smooth transition of the journal, carried out in somewhat difficult circumstances when it was 'between publishers'.[18] The new Editors were able to reaffirm the contribution made by the Society's journal to legal research, noting that 'as a result of the commitment and flair of successive editors, *Legal Studies* is now recognised as one of the leading generalist law journals in the UK'.[19] In addition to their aspiration to maintain the high standards and general interest of the journal, the new Editors explained that they would also continue to encourage early-career academics to publish in *Legal Studies* since '[t]he journal has never been, and should not become, the preserve of a select few, but keeps its doors open to high quality scholarship from all sources'.[20] The editorial team also explained the background to another change which was taking place with regard to the journal, which was a change of publisher. Butterworths (now LexisNexis UK) had published the journal for the whole of its first 25 years, but following that company's decision to focus their efforts on the practitioner market, the relationship with the journal had ended. The new publishers, Blackwell, would introduce a number of innovations, including a greater online presence, which would help the journal to capitalise on its growing international readership.[21]

The Reporter

The Society's newsletter also plays its part in bringing to members' attention developments in higher education policy and in legal education which affect research. During discussions about its change of name, the Society briefly considered whether to change the name of *The SPTL Reporter* to 'The Legal Scholar', but decided instead to make the less radical change to *The Reporter*.[22] Under the editorship of Professor Tony Bradney (Keele) the policy of including a mixture of

---

[17] 'Editorship of Legal Studies' *The Reporter* No 30 Spring 2005, 17; 'Editorial' (2006) 26(1) *Legal Studies* 1.

[18] 'Editorial', ibid, 2.

[19] Ibid, 1.

[20] Ibid, 2.

[21] More changes to the editorial team followed in 2008 when Professor Wikeley resigned from the editorial team on his appointment as a Judge of the Upper Tribunal (Administrative Appeals Chamber) and was replaced by Professor Poole. SLS Council Minutes 11 March 2009, Minute C03/09. Note that in 2007 Professor Poole moved to Aston University, and in 2008 Professor Steele took up a Chair at York University.

[22] SPTL Council Minutes 14. December 2001, Minute C44.2/01.

news and legal education items (including those relating to research) continued. His editorials continued to offer a whimsical take on academic life, combined with serious analysis of legal education issues. The first editorial of the decade, entitled 'This Brave New World' offered readers a mock 'multiple choice exam paper' on academic life.[23] Readers were invited to circle the correct answers to questions including:

2. A Head of department is

a. A psychotic whose absurd decisions are a result of their complete inadequacy as a human being

b. a harmless drudge whose responsibilities far exceed the powers given to them by the university.

c. A largely mythical figure best contacted via a ouija board.

3. 'With great respect' means

a. Even an intellectually challenged, lower order form of life could not believe what you just said.

b. You have clearly been taking illegal chemical substances which you have obtained from a supplier who adulterates their goods.

c. With great respect.

5. Senior Lecturers are

a. Expected to do everything that a professor does but are paid less.

b. envied by lecturers and scorned by professors.

c. Members of a department's lecturing staff.

Two issues later, the Editor was asking readers to think about assessment; concluding an article entitled 'Law Schools and the Egg Marketing Board' based on the premise that academics were in danger of over-assessing their students (a process that he likened to grading eggs), Professor Bradney wrote:

> Assessment matters. Thinking of different ways of trying to assess more and more accurately the knowledge and skills of our students is a vital part of the educational process. We need to do a lot more research into what kinds of assessment work well. But anyone who thinks that the focus of a student's learning should be the assessment is suffering from an advanced form of CJD. Education is about a personal transformation that never stops and can never be wholly measured. Yet, what are we teaching students when we assess them, formally and informally, as frequently as we now do throughout each year of their courses? We are teaching them that what matters is the examination, not that which is being examined. Why are we doing this? Because frequent assessment gives us an easy response to those who want to measure what we do as teachers. Because we lack the courage to say that a university law school is not the Egg Marketing Board and we are not in the business of grading eggs.[24]

---

[23] T Bradney (2000) 'This Brave New World' *SPTL Reporter* No 20, 1.
[24] T Bradney (2001) 'Law Schools and the Egg Marketing Board' *SPTL Reporter* No 22, 2.

After a satirical look at the departmental meeting—

> The [Research] Committee has been looking at the problems that some people have in being able to find time to produce high-quality research. The problem seems to rest mainly with those senior people who are so heavily involved in lunchtime meetings in the Senior Common Room that they simply don't have time to spend long hours writing, or reading, or indeed thinking[25]

—Professor Bradney turned his attention to the notion of academic freedom, offering an editorial in quite a different tone, concluding that academic freedom needs to be protected not only from 'those outside the university who would seek to use the university for their own means' but also from

> those academics whose enthusiasm for a vision about what they would like to do in the law school topples over into a plan for what everybody else in the law school should do. Academic freedom means the freedom for us to do our work. It also means allowing other academics the freedom to do their work. [26]

Other editorials in *The Reporter* addressed 'Academic Duty' (speaking truth to power[27]), appraisal ('your student questionnaires for those funny little legal theory courses you run . . . all come out with the majority of students expressing themselves as "extremely satisfied". That's worrying, isn't it? We're not here to mollycoddle the students'[28]) and the need for individuals to give their active support to organisations such as the SLS:

> We need them so we can exchange ideas. We need them to negotiate with other organisations. . . . We need them so that our individual fight for autonomy is made easier . . .our organisations need nurturing if our community is to thrive. However, that nurturing frequently seems to be someone else's job.[29]

Over the decade, *The Reporter* has encouraged members of the Society to reflect on almost every aspect of legal academic life, and occasionally to smile while doing so.

Outreach

The Society has continued to develop its relationships with all the relevant research funders, attending meetings arranged by them for learned societies, and publicising opportunities to members.[30] It has also responded to an increasing

---

[25] T Bradney (2002) 'Welcome' *The Reporter* No 25 Winter 2002, 1.
[26] T Bradney (2003) 'On Academic Freedom' *The Reporter* No 26 Spring 2003, 1–2.
[27] T Bradney (2004) 'Academic Duty' *The Reporter* No 28 Spring 2004, 1.
[28] T Bradney (2005) 'Your Appraisal' *The Reporter* No 30 Spring 2005, 1.
[29] T Bradney (2006) 'On War and Politics' *The Reporter* No 32, 1–2.
[30] See eg R Card (2003) 'Report on AHRB Research Strategy Seminar on Research and Research Resources' and letter dated 5 March 2003 from N Wikeley, 'AHRB Peer Review College'.

number of consultation papers, about legal education, for example responding to the Law Society's Training Framework Review, about matters generally concerning higher education, such as the response to the HEFCE review of research funding in 2003, and about matters concerning the legal profession, including responses related to constitutional reform—'A New Way of Appointing Judges' and 'The Future of Queen's Counsel'.[31] The Society was pleased to find its responses to those consultations quoted extensively in summaries of the consultation processes issued in January 2004.[32]

The annual meetings with the Law Commission have continued throughout the decade, although since 2001 these meetings have changed in format, from large meetings with a number of subject section convenors attending, to a smaller meeting whose purpose is to discuss strategic policy issues, such as how members of the Society and SLSA can best help in the work of the Commission, and to identify future items for the Commission's programme.[33] The nature of this meeting is a frequent topic of discussion among the participants (who now include a representative of the ALT) who are all convinced of the need to get together and exchange views, but who are constantly looking for the best format to achieve this.[34]

As part of the programme of outreach that it undertook at the beginning of the decade, the Society held a series of receptions in different locations, beginning in Dublin in 2003. A similar reception took place in Edinburgh in 2004 and one in Belfast in 2006.[35] The receptions were designed as equivalents of the annual President's Reception, with the aim both of raising the profile of the Society and serving as a focus for encouraging new members to join the Society.[36] Further outreach occurred as a result of the Society's realisation that it had a growing membership throughout Ireland.[37] Recognising the importance of proper representation for this group of members, in 2005 Dr Eoin O'Dell was elected as the first Convenor for Ireland.[38]

The annual President's Reception in London is an occasion when the Society aims to raise its profile by inviting representatives of research funders and other academic bodies, of the legal profession (particularly those concerned with legal

[31] See file on 'Training Framework Review'; RAE correspondence in file entitled 'SLS Research Committee'; email dated 30 September 2003, 'HEFCE Review of Research Funding'; 'SLS Response to Consultation Paper CP08/03: Constitutional Reform: The Future of Queen's Counsel'; SLS Response to Consultation Paper CP10/03: Constitutional Reform: A New Way of Appointing Judges'.

[32] Report from Executive Committee SLS Council Minutes 25 February 2004, Minute C04/04/A Para 11.

[33] 'SPTL Law Commission Etc' SPTL Council Document C39.3/01/A.

[34] Email dated 10 February 2009 'Re Law Commission Meetings With Law Subject Associations' from Prof E Cooke (Law Commissioner) to Prof F Cownie

[35] Report from Executive Committee, SLS Council Minutes 25 February 2004 Document C04/04/A; 'Report from Executive Committee to Council' SLS Council Meeting 8 March 2006 Minute C04/06 refers; para 4.2.

[36] Report from Executive Committee to Council, SLS Council Meeting 8 March 2006, Minute C04/06 refers; para 4.2.

[37] SLS Council Minutes 23 February 2005, Minute C04/05.4.

[38] SLS Council Minutes 8 March 2006, Minute C04.1/06

education), and members of the senior judiciary who are Honorary Members of the Society to meet members of Council and of the Society's Executive Committee. For many years it had been held in one of the Inns of Court, but in 2000, during the Presidency of Professor Genn (UCL), it moved to a more academic location at the British Academy.[39] This was another symbol of the Society's aim to establish itself firmly as a learned society.

Relations with the Legal Profession

The Society has continued to communicate the views of its members in response to consultation papers and other documents issued by the professions. Much of that task has been undertaken by the Legal Education Committee.[40] It has also fallen to the Legal Education Committee to take the lead in the Society's negotiations about the Joint Announcement with the professional bodies. In 2001 there was concern that the professional bodies wished to undertake a comprehensive overhaul of the Joint Announcement. When the matter was discussed at Council, it was agreed that 'We need to have confidence in what we teach in the LLB degree.'[41] This was another occasion on which the Society urged all the Law subject associations to work together, contacting CHULS to ensure that it would be represented at crucial meetings.[42] In the event, matters were settled to the satisfaction of the subject associations, who were able to point to the imminent introduction of a new quality assurance regime for universities which would, it was hoped, meet many of the professions' concerns.[43] This was also the case in 2003, when there was further concern over proposals made in relation to the Joint Announcement and quality assurance. The Society convened a special meeting of Council to consider a proposal by the Bar Council to amend the Joint Announcement, to formulate the Society's response and to provide a mandate for the Society's negotiators.[44] However these proposals eventually turned out to be unproblematic for law schools, as the changes did not materialise in their original proposed form.[45] Similarly, although there was initial alarm over proposals contained in the Law Society's Training Framework Review, and the Society sent in detailed responses to a number of consultation papers, the changes did not, in the end, materialise.[46] However, in all these cases, the Society had to take the professions' moves seriously, and respond accordingly. In the light of the increasing

[39] Invitation to President's Reception 2000.
[40] See eg SPTL Council Minutes 10 September 2001, Minute 22/2.
[41] SPTL Council Meeting 2 March 2001, Minute C08.2/01.
[42] Ibid.
[43] 'Report on Meeting with Representatives of the Bar and Law Society about the Academic Stage of Training held on 23rd March 2001', SPTL Council Document C22.2A.
[44] SPTL Council Agenda: Special Meeting of Council 3 May 2002.
[45] SLS Council Minutes 17 September 2003, Minute C21/03.
[46] Report from Executive Committee to Council 2006 C06/06/A para 5.1.

importance of the Legal Education Committee in contributing to many of the responses drafted on behalf of the Society, both with regard to legal education and higher education generally, the Society decided in 2006 that the Chair of the Legal Education Committee should automatically sit on the Executive Committee; Professor Fiona Cownie thus became the first person to sit on the Society's Executive in that capacity.[47]

The Developing Society

In 2001 Professor David Hayton was succeeded as the Society's Honorary Secretary by Professor Nick Wikeley (Southampton). In carrying out his role as Honorary Secretary, Professor Wikeley was assisted by Mrs Sally Thomson, who succeeded Peter Niven as the Society's Administrator in 2001.[48] One of Professor Wikeley's first tasks was to oversee the Society's change of name. This proved to be more complicated than had been anticipated. The Society's informal applications to obtain a royal charter and royal status had not been favourably received, mainly because the SPTL was not the only relevant body of legal scholars or teachers, so the decision was taken not to pursue this further.[49] However, it was decided to proceed with a change of name. The President, Professor Thomson (Glasgow) expressed the view that 'it is vital to change from being a society of *Public Teachers* of law since many people do not understand what the SPTL is about and do not understand what a public teacher of law is'.[50]

At a Special General Meeting of the Society held on 2 March 2001 Council agreed unanimously that the name of the Society be changed to 'The Society of Legal Scholars in the United Kingdom and Ireland'; this had to be confirmed by a postal ballot of all the members.[51] The Rules of the Society also had to be changed to reflect its new name, which required a further ballot.[52] As far as the Society was concerned, the name-change was finally effected in 2002, and a new logo was also approved.[53] However, although the Society took all the steps it thought necessary to effect the relevant changes, the Charity Commission then decided that in its view the Society had not been acting within its constitution so that another change of Rules would be necessary.[54] Having considered all the issues, and taken the advice of the Charity Commission, the saga finally ended when a Special General Meeting of the Society agreed to rescind the old Rules of

---

[47] SLS Council Minutes 6 September 2006, Minute C17/06.
[48] SPTL Council Minutes 10 September 2001, Minute C20/01.
[49] SPTL Council Minutes 15 December 2000, Minute C40/00.
[50] Ibid.
[51] SPTL Council Minutes 2 March 2001, Minute C04.2/01.
[52] R Card and N. Wikeley, 'Ballot on New Rules: Explanatory Note' *The Reporter* No 23 Winter 2001, 5.
[53] SPTL Council Minutes 1 March 2002, Minutes C04.1/02 and C04.2/02.
[54] SLS Council 17 September 2003, Minute C16.8/03.

the Society and adopt in their place, as from 1 October 2004 a new set of Rules containing all the amendments consequential on the name change.[55] The title of the article in *The Reporter* explaining the situation to members 'Why Is There Yet Another General Meeting and Ballot on the New Rules?' reflected the length and complexity of the story of the Society's change of name.[56]

When Professor Richard Card (De Montfort) became President of the Society in 2002, he became the first person to hold that office while working in a 'new university', and to date has remained the only person to do so, although other legal academics working in new universities have been centrally involved in the Society's activities, including the Society's webmaster, Richard Edwards (UWE) , the current Chair of the Legal Education Committee Professor Richard Taylor (UCLAN) and the current Subject Sections Convenor, Professor Lucy Vickers (Oxford Brookes). The conference over which Professor Card presided was the first one held under the Society's new name. In his Presidential address he noted that:

> Legal scholarship has not always been at the heart of the Society's mission. Indeed, until the Society's rules were changed earlier this year, the Society's object was expressed by rule 2 simply to be the advancement of legal education. A glance, for example, at the Presidential Addresses of the past, certainly up to the 1980s, shows that considerable attention was given to legal education and the role of the law teacher, and little to legal scholarship.[57]

Professor Card went on to note the Society's increasing interest, over the previous 20 or 30 years, in legal scholarship, and the increasing number of activities it had undertaken in that area, concluding that now it had reached the stage where it could be proud of its standing as a learned society 'a standing which it did not always have'.[58]

Finance

Clive Weston (Birmingham) retired as the Society's Honorary Treasurer in 2000, having held the post for 17 years.[59] During his term of office the Society and its activities had grown hugely, and the new Treasurer, Professor Stanton (Bristol), took the opportunity to introduce new systems of organisation using modern technology both for financial affairs and membership, creating a Membership Database for the Society, which provided a single authoritative source of infor-

---

[55] J Birds and N Wikeley, 'Why Is There Yet Another General Meeting and Ballot on the New Rules?' *The Reporter* No 28 Spring 2004, 5–6.

[56] Ibid.

[57] R Card, 'Presidential Address 2002: The Legal Scholar' *The Reporter* No 25 Winter 2002, 12.

[58] Ibid.

[59] 'Clive Weston' *SPTL Reporter* No 21 Winter 2000, 4.

mation about its members.[60] In addition to assisting in the financial management of the Society, this also assisted with the preparation of the *Directory of Members* (for which the Honorary Treasurer also took over responsibility). Recognising the increasing burden of work falling on the Honorary Treasurer, the Executive Committee agreed that Professor Stanton should have a paid part-time assistant, so the Society acquired its second paid employee, Sara Bladon.[61] When Professor Stanton stepped down in 2005, to be succeeded by Professor David Miers (Cardiff), the Executive Committee recorded its appreciation for the 'major and enduring improvements to the Society's financial arrangements' that he had brought about.[62]

Professor Miers's first task on taking office was to complete a financial review of the Society, which had already been suggested by Professor Stanton.[63] In his report to Council in March 2006 he confirmed Professor Stanton's view that the Society was facing a deficit on its income and expenditure account, which would have to be met from capital reserves.[64] Clearly this was not sustainable, and Professor Miers recommended doubling the subscription rates, with the exception of the postgraduate rate, which would merely see a small increase. In making this recommendation, Professor Miers not only drew attention to the traditional benefits of membership, such as the receipt of *Legal Studies* and *The Reporter*, but he also emphasised the increased level of activities that the Society was now undertaking:

> The factors that Keith identified that point to the need to increase subscription levels remain valid; indeed, they have become more acute. There has been a significant expansion in membership and activities over recent years. Membership now stands at 2,640, compared to around 2,200 (a figure which included many non-payers) when the last fee increase was implemented in 2000. In terms of the Society's academic health this expansion is to be welcomed, but it inevitably increases the burden on the Society's officers who, to a great extent have carried that burden as a matter of public service. In recent years the officers' lobbying role (particularly the President) in representing the legal academic community and lobbying government departments, the professional bodies, the funding council and others has become increasingly demanding as consultation papers and proposals for change proliferate. The Society also relies on a small number of paid employees, but it is inevitable that we will need to seek a greater amount of employed support to assist the officers' work. It may be noted that some other learned societies of comparable size employ their own full-time administrative staff.[65]

---

[61] See SPTL Council Minutes 2 March 2001, Minute C05/01 and 'Report from Executive Committee to Council' SLS Council Meeting 8 March 2006, para 2.

[62] K Stanton 'Current Personnel', May 2003.

[62] Report from Executive Committee to Council, SLS Council Meeting 8 March 2006, Minute C04/06 refers; para 2.

[63] KStanton, 'Subscriptions' *The Reporter* no 30 Spring 2005, 18; 'Increases in Subscription Levels' SPTL Council Minutes 8 March 2006, Doc C/09/06/A.

[64] Ibid.

[65] Ibid.

The increase in the subscription was also needed to allow the Society to continue to develop, and to undertake new initiatives. When the matter was put to Council in September 2006, the subscription increases were unanimously agreed.[66]

New Technology

It became apparent during the early part of the decade that the Society's website was going to be increasingly important. The Society first had a page on the website of the United Kingdom Centre for Legal Education (UKCLE), which was overseen by Edward Phillips (Greenwich), a member of the Executive Committee.[67] Following his retirement from the Committee, website management was taken over by Richard Edwards (UWE), who had a great deal of relevant expertise; he was elected to the Society's Executive Committee in 2002. During that year, the website migrated from the UKCLE site to its own site.[68] The following year Richard Edwards carried out a wholesale reconstruction of the website.[69] Commenting on the developments which had taken place, which included the ability to make membership applications and credit card payments through the website, the Honorary Treasurer was able to describe it as 'a very slick professional operation'.[70] The website had expanded greatly from its original size of only eight pages; it had also acquired a new address: www.legalscholars.ac.uk.[71] It has continued to grow, both in size and importance during this decade, and has often featured in discussions at Council and the Executive Committee, where the society has frequently expressed its gratitude to Richard Edwards for the work he has undertaken.[72] In recognition of the growing amount of work involved in the maintenance of the website, Mel Scott was employed to assist Richard Edwards, thus giving the Society another paid part-time worker.

Email

During this decade, email became much more prominent as a method of communication between the Society and its members. In 2001 there was extensive discussion at Council of the best way to organise email communications and the Society took a straw poll of members' views which indicated that a large

[66] SLS Council Minutes 6 September 2006, Minute C19/06.
[67] SPTL Council Minutes 14 December 2001, Minute C37.3.
[68] 'Your Questions Answered' *The Reporter* No 25 Winter 2002, 4.
[69] Letter dated 11 December 2002 from N Wikeley to R Edwards; K Stanton 'Current Personnel', May 2003; SLS Council Minutes 13 December 2002, Minute C43/02.2.
[70] K Stanton, 'Current Personnel', May 2003.
[71] 'Website Issues' Document E18.6/02; R Edwards, 'Society of Legal Scholars Website—An Update' *The Reporter* No 26 Spring 2003, 18.
[72] See eg SLS Council Minutes 25 February 2004, Minute C07/04.

majority favoured direct email communications from the Society.[73] As the system has settled down, the Honorary Secretary sends round regular email bulletins, so that members are not swamped with too many individual emails.[74] The ease of communication allows the Society to circulate not only Society news and events, but also to pass on information sent to it by other organisations and individuals that may be of interest to members.

Peter Birks

In July 2004, the Society was saddened to learn of the death from cancer of Professor Peter Birks. His obituary in *The Reporter*, written by his successor as President of the Society, Professor John Birds (Sheffield), paid tribute to Peter Birks' great service to the Society:

> The Society owes as great a debt to Peter as I think it does to anyone in living memory...without his tireless devotion and unfailing courtesy and concern, the Society would be a much less interesting and influential organisation. [75]

Similar comments were made in the obituary which appeared in *The Times*, where it was said that in his role as Honorary Secretary of the Society Professor Birks 'was the person primarily responsible for transforming it, through root and branch reform, into today's thriving learned society'.[76] At the memorial service held in Peter Birks' memory at the University Church in Oxford, Professor Andrew Burrows spoke of the former teacher and colleague whom he had known for more than thirty years:

> Tutorials in Brasenose with Peter engendered . . . feelings of excitement tinged with fright. Peter was so passionate about the subjects he was teaching and so anxious for his students to share in the enterprise of constructing clear and elegant pictures of the law. But it could be nerve-wracking because he would sometimes come up with fiendishly difficult questions and expect us to come up with acceptable answers.[77]

Later, when Professor Burrows taught alongside Professor Birks, he found that:

> For Peter, research and teaching complemented each other so that it was natural for him to continue to use the Restitution seminars to develop his published views. Those seminars constituted the most rewarding experiences as a teacher that I have ever had. And it was all down to Peter . . . at times the depth of [his] knowledge was simply breathtaking.[78]

[73] 'Straw Poll re Circulation of SPTL News' SPTL Executive Committee Document E04.9/02/B. See also SPTL Council Document C37.4/01/A and 'Communication With Members', SPTL Council document C05.3/02/A.

[74] See www.legalscholars.ac.uk/email-circulars/index.cfm

[75] Obituary—Peter Birks *The Reporter* Winter 2004, 1.

[76] 'Professor Peter Birks' *The Times* 9 July 2004, 59.

[77] A Burrows, address at Peter Birks' Memorial Service, University Church of St Mary the Virgin, Oxford, 20 November 2004.

[78] Ibid.

Speaking of the more public man and his scholarship, at the same memorial service, Lord Rodgers drew attention to Professor Birks' contribution to the increased status of academic lawyers:

> Perhaps, of all things, his role in that development would have pleased Peter, the immediate Past President of the Society of Legal Scholars. It has rightly been said that the Society owes a greater debt to him than to anyone in living memory. During his time as Secretary of the Society of Public Teachers of Law between 1989 and 1996, he not only embarked on a root and branch reform of its structures, but somehow found time to organise a remarkable series of Saturday seminars in All Souls which attracted senior judges, practitioners and academics from around the world. The whole point of these occasions was that everyone took part on an equal footing and that they all learned from one another. That was Peter's vision of how our understanding of the law would grow.[79]

In 2004, the Society's Book Prize was renamed the Peter Birks Prize for Outstanding Legal Scholarship, in commemoration of the Society's former President and Honorary Secretary.[80] Writing about this decision, Professor Birks' widow, Dr Jacqueline Birks, wrote:

> I think that the renaming of the book prize as a memorial to Peter is quite wonderful. He would have said that it is amazing, not at all deserved, and that you should think again. He would have liked it very much though. . . . He was devoted to the SLS, he held it in high esteem and considered it of immense importance. I can remember his many years as Secretary. He had no assistance but refused to learn more efficient ways of carrying out the endless administrative tasks. 'Takes too much time' he would say as he addressed letters by hand. Theodore knows all the colleges in Oxford because he and his father delivered all the SPTL mail in Oxford by bicycle. . . . I think the book prize is a perfect memorial. . . . Later in the month I shall take a peep at the SLS website to see the results.[81]

The Society owed a great debt to Peter Birks, and the decision to rename the book prize provided a fitting memorial to the time, thought and energy which he had devoted to its service. The Prize underwent a further development in 2006 when the then President, Professor Tony Dugdale (Keele), decided to invite the winner of the previous year's prize to give a presentation about the winning book. Dr Joshua Getzler, a Fellow at St Hugh's College, Oxford, thus became the first prize-winner to do this, making a presentation about his book 'A History of Water Rights at Common Law'.[82] The idea proved to be a success, and has become a regular feature at the Annual Conference.[83]

---

[79] Lord Rodgers, address at Peter Birks' Memorial Service, University Church of St Mary the Virgin, Oxford, 20 November 2004.

[80] 'Peter Birks Book Prizes for Outstanding Legal Scholarship' *The Reporter* Spring 2005, 24; letter dated 4 October 2005 from Prof A Paterson to Dr J Birks.

[81] Letter dated 8 September 2005 from Dr J Birks to Prof A Paterson.

[82] SLS Conference Programme, Keele 2006.

[83] See SLS Annual Conference Programmes 2007, 2008, 2009.

Conferences

The increasing complexity of academic life has led Presidents of the Society to begin to rely on professional conference managers to assist with the organisation of the Annual Conference.[84] In order to ensure that experience gained by one President as regards conference management and organisation was passed on to others in their turn in 2002 the Society established an Annual Conference Advisory Committee.[85] This committee was much assisted by the contribution made to its work by Mrs Rachel Card, a former academic, and wife of the President in 2001–02, who was responsible for the Conference when it was held for the first time at a new university (De Montfort). She passed on detailed notes and checklists to her successors, which formed the basis of a new version of the conference 'bible', which is updated each year by the current President.[86]

The work of the Society's Subject Sections Convenor has grown considerably during the decade. Professor Peter Sparkes (Southampton), Convenor from 1999 to 2006, played a major role in co-ordinating the academic programme for the Annual Conference, working closely with the Society's webmaster, Richard Edwards, to develop a more efficient system for assembling the programme.[87] He also oversaw a change in the nature of the Subject Sections, opening up their membership to all members of the Society. Explaining the change to members in *The Reporter* in 2001, Professor Sparkes wrote:

> For several years the various committees of the Society have been discussing the future of panels. When they were originally set up, it made sense to have a core membership committed to attend conference and to respond to consultation papers. But most convenors now feel that it makes more sense to accept offers of help from wherever they come. Especially since the email revolution has made it so much easier to keep in touch with a large nationwide membership. So it is now proposed to move to smaller core groups—perhaps one or two deputies assisting the convenor—with direct lines of communication with the wider membership.[88]

The Subject Sections have remained at the centre of the Annual Conference, and during this decade an annual meeting of all the Subject Section convenors has become a regular event, allowing them to pass on directly to the President and Subject Sections Convenor feedback about conference organisation and other matters which concern their members. It also gives the Society an opportunity to consult the convenors about any initiatives it is contemplating.[89] When Professor Sparkes stood down in 2006 he was succeeded by Professor Lucy Vickers (Oxford

---

[84] See eg Conference Management File 2009.

[85] SPTL Council Minutes 1 March 2002, Minute C04.6/02. See also eg Agenda for Conference Advisory Sub-Committee Meeting 4 November 2005.

[86] See Conference Management File.

[87] SLS Council Minutes 25 February 2004, Minute C08/04.

[88] P Sparkes, 'Subject Sections' *SPTL Reporter* No 22 Spring 2001, 5.

[89] See eg SLS Annual Calendar 2004.

Brookes); one of the new activities she has co-ordinated has been the establishment of the Society's 'Best Paper Prize'.[90]

During this decade, the Annual Conference has provided the Society with an opportunity to inform its members about the activities of several of the bodies it corresponds with more formally on other occasions, inviting them to make presentations at the conference, including the City Solicitors' Educational Trust, and the Authors' Licensing and Collecting Society, which hosted receptions at the 2006 conference organised by Professor Tony Dugdale (Keele).[91] In 2004 a new 'open' section was created, to allow the presentation of papers for which there was no obvious home otherwise, and to act as an 'overspill' for sections whose programme was full, as well as permitting new subjects to try out sessions without creating a full-blown subject-section.[92] The new section was eventually christened 'Gibraltar' (in the sense that the Bishop of Gibraltar has jurisdiction over all of continental Europe that is not within a specific diocese).[93] Dr Augur Pearce (Cardiff) gave the first paper in the new section, appropriately entitled 'Extraterritoriality, Colonialism and National Church: English Ecclesiastical Jurisdiction in Continental Europe'.[94]

As a result of changes to the Rules of the Society in 2002, postgraduate research students became eligible for membership of the Society.[95] The Honorary Treasurer was able to report the following year that there had been a healthy growth of membership amongst eligible postgraduates.[96] The Society decided that it should develop its activities in relation to postgraduates; one immediate step was to offer its postgraduate members subsidised registration rates for attendance at the Annual Conference.[97] Professor Alan Paterson also organised a special session for postgraduates at the Annual Conference at Strathclyde University in 2005.[98]

Although the Annual Conference retains much the same form as that developed in the 1990s, with the subject section sessions forming the heart of the programme, there have been some innovations in keeping with contemporary trends. One of these is an increasing awareness of environmental concerns. The development of the Society's website has allowed bookings for the Annual Conference to be made online since 2006 and the amount of hard copy related to the Conference has decreased significantly.[99] Professor Celia Wells introduced 'eco' conference bags at the conference in Durham in 2007, a trend followed by

[90] www.legalscholars.ac.uk/conference/best-paper-prize.cfm

[91] SLS Annual Conference, Keele 2006, Programme.

[92] 'Executive Committee Report to Council' *The Reporter* No 27 Winter 2003, 6; see also SLS Council Minutes 15 September 2004, Minute C19/04.4.

[93] Ibid.

[94] SLS Annual Conference, Sheffield 2004, Programme.

[95] 'The Society and Postgraduate Research Students', SPTL Council Document C05/03/A.

[96] Ibid.

[97] Academic Purposes Fund Minutes 20 March 2003, Minute A06/03.

[98] SLS Annual Conference, Glasgow 2005, Programme.

[99] K Stanton 'Current Personnel', May 2003; postcard advertising SLS Annual Conference, Keele 2009.

her successors, Professor Sarah Worthington and Professor Fiona Cownie. Another innovation was Professor Card's introduction of an 'Early Career' reception at the conference in 2002. Introducing this idea to members in *The Reporter*, Professor Card explained that a panel discussion on matters of particular relevance to those in the early stages of their careers, such as writing for publication and obtaining research funding, would be followed by a reception giving an opportunity for informal contacts to be made with others in a similar position. The early career event has become a regular part of the programme, and remains an indication of the Society's commitment to its members at all stages of academic life.[100]

Delivering his Presidential Address at the Society's Annual Conference in Glasgow in 2001, Professor Joe Thomson drew attention to some of the ways in which the Society had developed since he first attended one of its annual conferences in Edinburgh in 1970.[101]

> There were no subject groups in 1970 and the papers which were delivered were less specialised, in other words most of us could understand what most of us were trying to do in our research. . . . The point was that even a young lecturer had the opportunity to hear and meet the leading scholars in her discipline which in those days was simply called law.[102]

The Annual Conference has changed in many ways, but above all, it is still a place where legal scholars can met each other and discuss aspects of their subject which matter to them.

Conclusion

In the century since its first Annual General Meeting in 1909, the Society of Legal Scholars (then the Society of Public Teachers of Law) has grown and changed out of all recognition from its modest beginnings. It enters its second century as a full-blown learned society, catering not just for teachers of law, but for legal researchers as well. It has learnt to work with the other law subject associations to represent more effectively the interests of legal academics, and it undertakes a great number of activities. Long gone are the days when the Annual Conference was the only event which members could attend, and that just as passive auditors. Members of the Society are now at the centre of the Conference through their active participation in the Subject Sections, delivering a growing number of papers every year. The Society's Seminar and the Peter Birks Book Prize are established as annual events, together with the President's Reception and meetings with the Law Commission, Ministry of Justice and the other law subject

---

[100] See conference programmes for SLS Annual Conferences 2002, 2006, 2007, 2008, 2009.
[101] J Thomson, 'Presidential Address 2001' *SPTL Reporter* Winter 2001, 7.
[102] Ibid.

associations. The Society is an active member of the Academy of Social Sciences, and it regularly meets with funding bodies, government departments and other organisations whose activities affect legal academics. Over the years, the Society has established a journal, a substantial newsletter and it has embraced new technology so as to communicate more effectively with its members, with an extensive website and regular emailings. It has restructured its internal system so as to include a much greater diversity of members on its committees, and women have come to take their proper place within the Society; their eligibility for membership was long delayed, but now the Society has had five female Presidents since 1997, three of them in succession from 2006 to the present day.[103]

The Society decided to celebrate its centenary by commissioning this history, but also by holding the first of a series of Centenary Lectures, to be held in different locations in forthcoming years.[104] The first Centenary Lecture was delivered by Professor William Twining, Emeritus Quain Professor of Jurisprudence at University College London, and a Past President of the Society who held office in 1979–80.[105] The title of the lecture, 'Punching Our Weight? Academic Law and Public Understanding' allowed Professor Twining, while congratulating the Society on its achievements to date, to urge it on to greater things in the future, especially in the public arena, where, he argued, moves to increase public understanding of law are lagging behind those to increase understanding of other disciplines, especially science.[106] As a fitting centenary project, the Society also agreed to fund further work on its archives, which are only part-catalogued.[107]

As the Society looks forward, despite its unquestionable achievements, there is always more to be done. It still has a low profile among the general public, and is less well known among members of the legal profession than it might wish, given the importance of its relationships with the professional bodies, especially with regards to the Joint Announcement. There are international links to be made as well; there are other similar organisations with whom sporadic links have been made, such as the Association of American Law Schools and the Canadian Association of Law Teachers, but much more could be done.[108] In terms of giving a lead in matters of legal education, the Society could provide more activities for its members specifically related to the teaching of law, as well as more research-related activities.

But although the Society must always seek to improve, and to do more for its members, the centenary of its foundation provides an opportunity to look back on the efforts of all those who, over the years, have contribute towards making it

---

[103] Female Presidents of the Society have been: Professor Margot Brazier (Manchester) 1997–98; Professor Hazel Genn (UCL) 1999–2000; Professor Celia Wells (Durham) 2006–07; Professor Sarah Worthington (LSE) 2007–08; Professor Fiona Cownie (Keele) 2008–09.

[104] See www.legalscholars.ac.uk/centenary-lecture/

[105] Ibid.

[106] Ibid.

[107] 'President's Report to Council 11th March 2009', private papers of Prof F Cownie, in SLS archive.

[108] For links with international organisations, see *The Reporter* No 32 Spring 2006, 2 and 5.

the organisation it is today—not just the former Presidents and Honorary Secretaries, the Honorary Treasurers and Subject Sections Convenors, the editors of all the Society's publications, the paid staff and all those who have served on Executive and other Committees, but also the thousands of members who have contributed to the Society's development, and whose efforts may allow the Society's members today to echo the words of its first President, Henry Goudy. 'We are teachers of Law—a great and noble occupation!'[109]

---

[109] Prof Goudy, first President of the Society of Public Teachers of Law, in his 'Introductory Address to the Society of Public Teachers of Law in England and Wales', delivered at the First Annual General Meeting, 1909.

INDEX

Academic Purpose Fund
  research initiatives, 179, 180, 203, 233
Academy of Social Sciences, 263
Administrative Law Group (SPTL), 182
Advisory Committee on Legal Education
  academic/practitioner divisions, 131
  core subjects, 133, 134
  disappointment, 131–4
  entry to legal profession, 133
  establishment, 131
  European Community Law, 145, 177
    see also **European Community Law**
  first report, 131
  legal research, 176
  second report, 133
  SPTL
    continuing support, 169
    Note of Dissent, 133, 134
    relationship, 217, 223
    representation, 133, 176
    response, 133, 134
    review, 132
Advisory Committee on Legal Education and Conduct, 223–5
Anderson (J N D), 93, 103, 108
Andrews (JA), 164, 201–3, 205, 208, 214
Annual Conferences (SPTL)
  1908–1909
    Annual General Meeting, 4, 5, 14, 15
    Constituent Committee, 3
    elections, 5
    initial attendance, 5
  1910–1918
    annual dinners, 17, 19, 33
    Annual General Meetings, 29, 31–4, 80
  1919–1930
    annual dinners, 39
    Annual General Meetings, 38, 39, 46
  1930–1939
    annual dinners, 56, 57
    Annual General Meetings, 49, 54, 56, 57
  1940–1960
    annual meetings, 60, 70, 72
  1960s
    annual dinners, 103, 104
    conference attendance, 100, 101
    conference programme, 101
    location, 102, 103
    social programme, 101, 102, 119
    speakers, 102

  sponsorship, 101, 104
  1970s
    academic content, 153
    annual dinners, 153, 154
    conference programme, 151
    group discussions/working groups, 151
    improvements, 155
    participation levels, 152
    specialist groups, 151
    visitors, 154, 155
    Young Members Group influence, 155
  1980s
    annual dinners, 196, 197, 199
    conference programme, 204
    financial pressures, 196
    location, 198
    publishing exhibition, 197, 198
    speakers, 196
    specialist groups, 198, 203
    sponsorship, 196, 197
    Sweet & Maxwell Prize, 197
  1990s
    academic contact, 240
    changes, 239
    conference programme, 240
    participation, 240
    SPTL Subject Sections, 239
Association of American Law Schools, 150, 263
Association of Law Students and Apprentices, 75
Association of Law Teachers (ALT)
  establishment, 110, 111, 122
  SPTL relationship, 110, 111, 193, 194
Association of University Teachers (AUT), 90, 92
Atiyah (PS), 160, 179
Austin (J), 6, 7

Bar
  Bar Council, 173
  entry requirements, 170–2, 176, 218, 219
  examinations, 8, 115, 116
  Messes, 13, 20, 23
  self-regulation, 13
  social acceptability 13
  structure, 12, 13
  tenancies, 174
Batt (R), 68, 69
Beale (HG), 233
Bell (JS), 214, 215, 248

Bevan (HK), 181, 201
Birds (JR), 258
Birks (PBH), 14, 208, 209, 213, 215, 217, 220–2,
    233, 236, 258–9, 262
Bleak House, 7
Boards of Legal Studies
    funding, 26
    public organisations, 26
    Sussex Board, 26
    Yorkshire Board, 11, 26
Bowers (AD), 3, 4, 17, 59, 191, 192
Bradney (A), 212, 213, 231, 249–51
Brazier (M), 226, 231, 240–3, 248
Bridge (JW), 144
British and Irish Association of Law Librarians
    (BIALL), 157, 234, 236, 246
Britton (PA), 186
Brown (LN), 205
Bryce (J), 9, 10
Burrows (AS), 258

Cairns (MB), 74, 82
Canadian Association of Law Teachers (CALT),
    112, 194, 263
Card (RIE), 248, 255, 262
Casson (DB), 166
Centenary celebrations
    Centenary Lectures, 263
    publication, 263
Centre for Socio-Legal Studies, 139, 183
    see also Socio-legal studies
Chapman (A), 2
Chorley (T), 40, 71, 72, 74, 75, 82, 83
Civil Service Commission
    Civil Service Examinations, 55
    legal analysis, 55
College of Law
    admission procedures, 173
    SPTL contact, 173
    vocational training 135
    York Branch, 173
Committee of Heads of University Law Schools
    (CHULS), 166, 167, 228, 229, 232, 238
Committee of Vice-Chancellors and Principals
    (CVCP), 85
Committee on Legal Education
    establishment, 50
    examination/teaching requirements, 51, 53
    function, 50, 81
Committee on Social Services and Law, 139,
    140
    see also Socio-legal studies
Common Professional Examination (CPE),
    219, 220, 222, 224
Commonwealth Law Conference, 113, 149
Commonwealth Legal Association, 149, 150,
    195
Consumer Law Group (SPTL), 178, 181
Contract Law Group (SPTL), 181

Copinger (W), 1, 2,5
Copyright
    Copyright Licensing Agency (CLA), 189
    Crown Copyright, 191
    law publishing issues, 157
    legislative reform, 191, 204
    primary legal materials, 189
    SPTL Libraries Committee, 189
    Whitford Committee, 189
Council of Legal Education, 27, 29, 59, 63, 64,
    115, 116, 134, 135, 170–2, 221
Coutts (JA), 98
Cownie (F), 254, 262
Cozens-Hardy (H), 28
Crane (FR), 66, 118, 136, 146
Cranston (RF), 232
Criminal Law Group (SPTL), 182
Cross (R), 121, 150

Daintith (TC), 234
de Zulueta (F), 50
Dennis (IH), 182
Diamond (AL), 140, 141, 190
Dicey (AV), 3, 41
Directory of Members (SPTL), 125
Dowdall (HC), 4
Dugdale (AM), 259, 261

Eastwood (RA), 57, 81
Economic and Social Research Council (ESRC),
    185, 186, 204
European Community Law
    Advisory Committee on Legal Education, 145
    Fédération Internationale de Droit Européen
        (FIDE), 144
    SPTL Committee, 144
    UK Association for European Law, 144
    UK/EC membership, 144
    Young Members Group interest, 144
European Law Teachers, 65, 66

Fédération Internationale de Droit Européen
    (FIDE), 144
Financial stringency (SPTL/1980s)
    Committee of Heads of University Law
        Schools (CHULS), 166, 167
    financial cut backs, 166, 167
    Research Assessment Exercise (RAE), 167
    secretarial assistance, 167
    SPTL concerns, 166, 167
    student numbers, 166
    Swinnerton-Dyer letter, 166
    two year degrees, 166
    university finances, 165, 166
    University Grants Committee (UGC), 166,
        167
First fifty years (SPTL)
    capital donations, 80
    economies of scale, 80

First World War 80
law teachers
    professional role, 81
    staffing levels, 81
legal education
    common law studies, 81, 82
    humanities, 82
    legal history 80
    library resources, 80
    Scottish initiatives, 82
    sociology, 82
    statute law teaching, 82
membership, 80, 82
Oxford/Cambridge influences, 79
post-war period
    academic conservatism, 81, 82
    admission of women, 82
    increase in membership, 82
    more active role, 83
recognition issues, 79
relationship with legal profession, 79–81, 83
resources, 80
structural weaknesses, 80
student numbers, 81
First World War
    Germanophiles, 33
    Honorary Members (SPTL), 32–5
    influences/effects, 32–5, 80
Fitzgerald (PJ), 108
Fletcher (IF), 127, 190

Geldart (WM), 38, 41
Genn (H), 240, 244, 253
Glazebrook (PR), 182
Goode (RM), 209, 210, 239–41
Goodhart (AL), 93
Goudy (H), 4, 5, 15–17, 18, 20, 33, 37, 38, 80, 264
Gower (LCB), 71, 77, 134, 141
Graveson (RH), 124
Griew (EJ), 182
Griffiths (JAG), 109
Griswold (E), 76
Grodecki (JK), 166, 176, 184, 185, 198, 200
Gutteridge (HC), 49

Hamlyn Trust, 234
Harris (DR), 183, 184
Harvey (BW), 150
Hayton (DJ), 210, 254
Hepple (BA), 224
Heyworth Committee on the Future of Social Studies, 89, 106, 107
Higher education
    see also **Robbins Committee**
    aims, 86
    Committee of Vice-Chancellors and Principals (CVCP), 85
    expansion, 86, 87, 89, 119, 142, 143
    funding councils

        Higher Education Funding Council for England, 208, 232
        Higher Education Funding Council for Scotland, 208
        Higher Education Funding Council for Wales, 208
    quality assurance, 208
    quality audit, 208
law schools
    applications, 87
    comprehensive survey, 87
    expansion, 87
    provincial universities, 87
long-term planning, 85
'new universities', 207
'old universities', 207
pressure for change, 85
Quality Assurance Agency (QAA), 208
reforms, 85, 207
social policy, 85
Teaching Quality Assessments (TQAs), 208
University Grants Committee (UGC), 85, 87, 135, 142, 143
Holborn College of Law, 91
Holdsworth (WS), 45
Hopkinson (A), 5, 18, 25, 26
Howard League of Penal Reform, 56
Hughes (JDI), 45, 53, 81
Hughes Parry (D), 52
Human rights law
    British Institute of Human Rights 145
    European Convention on Human Rights (ECHR), 145
    teaching, 145

Imperial School of Law, 9, 37, 38
Incorporated Council of Law Reporting, 40
Information technology
    Joint Academic Network, 190
    legal education, 186
    Lexis/Butterworths 190, 204
    on-line library access, 190
Inns of Court
    Council of Legal Education, 27, 29, 59, 63, 64, 115, 116, 134, 135, 170–2, 221
    legal education, 7–10
    professional organisation, 12
    recognition of degrees 8
    reforms 13
    School of Law 7, 30, 171, 172, 176, 219, 221
    social influence 13
Institute of Advanced Legal Studies (IALS)
    archives, 1
    comparative law, 51
    establishment, 51, 52, 67
    interdisciplinary studies, 108
    legal research, 67
Institute of Criminology, 106
Institute of Legal Research, 51

International relationships (SPTL)
  1908–1909
    Imperial Law School, 9
    India, 7
  1910–1918
    Australian contacts, 30
  1919–1930
    corporate contacts, 47
  1940–1960
    Australian contacts, 66
    US contacts, 66, 76, 77
  1960s
    academic contacts, 112
    African contacts, 112, 113
    American Society on International Law, 113
    Australian Universities Law Schools Association, 113
    British Council, 113
    Canadian Association of Law Teachers (CALT), 112
    Commonwealth Law Conference, 113
    Denning Report on the Legal Education of African Students, 112
    Leverhulme Trust, 113
    mooting competitions, 113
  1970s
    American Association of Law Schools, 150
    Australian contacts, 150
    Australian Universities Law Schools Association, 149
    Commonwealth Law Conference, 149
    Commonwealth Legal Association, 149, 150
    South African issues, 149
    University of Singapore, 150
  1980s
    Australian contacts, 194, 195
    Canadian Association of Law Teachers (CALT), 194
    Commonwealth Legal Association, 195
    EU-related matters, 195, 196
    Jean Monnet Fellowships, 195
    travelling scholarships, 195

Jacob (JIH), 111, 175
Jacobs (FG), 111, 144
James (PS), 90, 124, 144
Jenks (E), 1–5, 11, 12, 14, 17, 18, 23, 24, 27, 30, 37–40, 55, 73, 79, 81, 83
Jolowicz (JA), 125, 163, 164, 175, 179, 194
Jolowicz (HF), 43
Journal of the Society (JSPTL)
  book reviews, 126
  changes (1970s), 125
  changes (1980s), 203
  continental initiatives, 66
  contributions (1970s), 125, 126
  Directory of Members (SPTL), 125
    editorial content, 43, 44
    editorial policy, 163, 164
    expansion, 72
    final issue, 163
    influence, 80
    information sharing, 45
    Jolowicz (JA), 125
    law teaching, 48
    legal culture, 46
    legal education matters
      educational progress, 45
      educational provision, 45
      research, 45
    origins, 42, 43
    publication, 43, 80, 125
    purchase, 43
    twice yearly publication, 72, 73
    wartime suspension, 59

Kay (M), 150
Keeton (GW), 90
Kidner (R), 248

Landon (PA), 70
Laski (H), 50
Law Commission
  Law Commissioners, 136
  Law reform, 118, 119
  SPTL members
    contacts, 136, 226, 227
    research leave, 136
  Society of Legal Scholars contacts, 252, 262
Law libraries
  BIALL, 157, 234, 236, 246
  electronic material, 236
  library resources, 71, 80, 105, 114, 146, 229
  minimum holdings, 234, 235
  on-line library access, 190
  SPTL Libraries Committee, 189
  Statement of Standards, 235, 236, 246
Law publishing
  Australian experience, 157
  BIALL cooperation, 157
  book prices, 158, 159
  commercial publishing, 156, 159
  copyright, 157
  legal journals, 158, 159
  market forces, 156, 159
  monograph publishing, 156, 158, 160
  production quality, 159
  publishing function, 156
  publishing opportunities, 156, 157
  rising costs, 155, 158, 159
  scholarly writing, 156
  small jurisdictions, 157, 159, 160
  small publishers, 159
  socio-legal subjects, 160
  SPTL
    concerns, 155

Law Series, 160, 178, 179, 203
    publication fund, 160
    Publishing Committee, 160
    Publishing Working Party, 138, 156–60
US experience, 157
Working Papers, 159
Law reform
codification
    contract law, 118
    criminal law, 119
family law, 119
Law Commission, 118, 119, 136
    see also **Law Commission**
Law Reform Coordinating Committee, 118
SPTL activity, 118, 136
Law Reform Committee, 53
Law Revision Committee
establishment, 52
function, 52
reports, 52, 53
Law Society
creation, 7
educational initiatives, 10, 11
Legal Education Committee, 135
professional conduct, 12
provincial developments, 11, 12
SPTL relationship, 218, 222
Society of Legal Scholars relationship, 253, 254
Law teachers
1910–1918
    adequate teaching, 34
    duties, 15, 16, 34
    legal skills, 34
    original work, 34
    'public' role, 16, 20, 21
    remuneration, 15, 24
1919–1930
    duties, 37, 44
    life insurance, 40
    professional expectations, 47
    research, 45
    teaching methods, 39
1930–1939
    administrative responsibilities, 49
    examination duties, 49
    legal culture, 53
    professional expectations, 53
    professional links, 53
    professional practice, 49
    provincial universities, 54
    recruitment, 50
    research activities, 49
    teaching opportunities, 49
1940–1960
    European law teachers, 65, 66
    exploitation concerns, 72
    part-time teachers, 66, 72
    'public' teachers of law, 65
    remuneration, 72
    staff levels, 66
    staff/student ratio, 66, 67
1960s
    academic qualifications, 94
    competing professions, 91
    international experience, 94
    lectures, 94
    part-time teachers, 94
    professional qualifications, 94
    research facilities, 94, 95
    remuneration levels, 90–2, 94, 119
    self-confidence, 98
    teacher training courses, 98
    teaching facilities, 95
    teaching loads, 94
    teaching techniques, 97
    tutorials, 94
    unfilled posts, 90
1970s
    career appointments, 147, 148
    contribution to public life, 147
    job satisfaction, 147
    legal research, 147–9
    legal scholarship, 148, 149
    non-expository approach, 149
    remuneration, 14
Law Technology Centre (LTC), 229
Lawson (FH), 75, 76, 96, 101, 114
Legal Action Group (LAG), 139
Legal education
    see also **Legal profession relationship**
1908–1909
    common law subjects 6
    comparative studies 7
    English law 8
    influences 6, 7
    international law 6
    judicial support 14
    Roman law 6
    missed opportunities 6, 7
    origins 6, 7
    Oxford/Cambridge 6, 8, 12
    Parliamentary Select Committee, 7
    professional subjects 7
    reforms 7–10
1910–1918
    case-method, 31, 34
    degree courses, 25
    duties, 15, 16
    legal publications, 30, 31
    Oxford/Cambridge 16
    range of subjects, 25–8
    reforms, 25–8
    Roman law, 25
    Royal Commission on University Education, 27–9, 31
    student numbers, 25, 28, 29

Legal education – *continued*
  1919–1930
    case books, 38, 40, 42
    development, 44, 45
    intellectual engagement, 44
    legal history, 41–3
    local initiatives, 38
    professional cooperation, 44
    reforms, 37–9, 46
    research, 45
    teaching in schools, 46
    teaching methods, 39
    Year Book Project, 41
  1930–1939
    administrative law, 55
    cultural/vocational divide, 53, 54
    enlargement, 55
    legal history, 55
    local government law, 55
    'practical' education, 53
    student numbers, 55
    unified system, 53
  1940–1960
    academic conservatism, 68–71, 81, 82
    active debate, 76, 77
    common law studies, 68, 70, 81, 82
    curriculum, 75
    educational conservatism, 68–71, 81, 82
    humanities, 74, 82
    intrinsic value, 76
    jurisprudence, 69
    legal history, 68, 69
    legal profession relationship, 74, 75
    liberal education, 74–6
    library resources, 71
    preparation for legal practice, 69
    Roman law, 69
    Scottish initiatives, 75, 76, 82
    social sciences, 74, 75
    sociology 70, 71, 82
    statute law teaching, 69, 71, 82
  1960s
    compulsory courses, 93
    core subjects, 93
    examinations, 97, 98
    expansion, 86, 87, 89, 119
    lectures, 94, 97
    legal system courses, 93
    optional subjects, 94
    research facilities, 94, 95
    Roman law, 93
    SPTL Survey, 92–6, 119
    staff/student ratio, 94
    standards of scholarship, 96, 97
    student numbers, 9
    teacher training courses, 98
    teaching techniques, 97
    tutorials, 94
    university admissions, 99, 100

    vocational training, 99
  1970s
    administrative law, 135
    core subjects, 133, 134
    European Community law, 144, 145
    expansion, 142, 143
    human rights law, 145
    legal research, 140, 141
    library resources, 146
    pedagogy, 146, 147
  1980s
    audio-visual aids, 187
    changes assessed, 204
    clinical legal education, 187, 188
    information technology, 186
    Law Schools Admission Test (LSAT), 188
    socio-legal studies, 187
  1990s
    accreditation and teaching, 229
    benchmarking, 230–2
    Committee of Heads of University Law
        Schools (CHULS), 228–9, 232
    Dearing Committee, 229
    Higher Education Funding Council, 232
    information technology, 229
    Law Technology Centre (LTC), 229
    library resources, 229
    National Centre for Legal Education, 229
    Quality Assurance Agency (QAA), 230
Legal Education Authority, 10
Legal profession relationship
  1908–1909 (SPTL)
    academic relationship, 8, 9, 12–14
    legal education reforms, 8–10
    professional influence, 13
    recognition of degrees, 8–10
    responsibility, 8, 15
  1910–1918 (SPTL)
    academic relationship, 32
    professional education, 25
    professional qualification, 25
  1919–1930 (SPTL)
    professional cooperation, 44
    professional education, 40, 43
  1940–1960 (SPTL
    academic influence, 73
    academic relationship, 67, 73–5, 79
    professional training, 74
  1960s (SPTL)
    Bar examinations, 115, 116
    Council of Legal Education, 115, 116
    law-making function, 114, 115
    Law Society, 115, 116
    solicitors' training, 115
  1970s (SPTL)
    academic relationship, 134, 135
    administrative law teaching, 135
    core legal subjects, 133, 134
    solicitors' training, 135, 136

1980s (SPTL)
  Bar Council, 173
  Bar entry requirements, 170–2, 176
  College of Law, 173
  consultation processes, 171, 172
  core subjects, 171, 173
  Council of Legal Education, 170–2
  Inns of Court School of Law, 171, 172, 176
  Law Society examinations, 170
  Marre Committee, 172, 173
  Northern Ireland, 172
1990s (SPTL)
  Advisory Committee on Legal Education,
      217, 223
  Advisory Committee on Legal Education
      and Conduct, 223–5
  Common Professional Examination
      (CPE), 219, 220, 222, 224
  core subjects, 217
  Council of Legal Education, 221
  entry to the Bar, 218, 219
  improvements, 216, 217
  Inns of Court School of Law, 219, 221
  Joint Announcement, 225–6
  law school sponsorship, 217, 218
  Law Society, 218, 222
  solicitors' training, 218, 219
  Society of Legal Scholars
  Joint Announcement, 253, 263
  Law Society contacts, 253, 254
  Legal Education Committee contacts, 253,
      254
  World War II, 63
  see also **World War II**
Legal Studies
  editorial development, 215
  editorial policy, 178, 214, 215
  Editors 248, 249
  international readership, 249
  publication, 163, 165, 203
  publishers, 249
  socio-legal studies, 183, 184
  success, of, 165

Macdonell (J), 29, 30
Marre Committee, 172, 173
Marshall (R), 100
Mcauslan (JPWB), 170
Megarry (RE), 63, 66, 97, 98
Membership issues (SPTL)
  1910–1918
    academic appointment, 21, 22
    academic qualifications, 20–2
    active teaching members, 22
    discrimination, 22
    exclusions, 21, 22
    Honorary Members, 32–5
    legal qualifications, 22, 24
    Northern Ireland, 32, 35

Scotland, 32, 35
    women members, 21, 22
  1919–1930
    Honorary Members, 39
    social status, 39
  1930–1939
    academic qualification, 56
    active members, 55
    associate members, 56
    corresponding members, 55
    emeritus members, 56
    formerly active, 55
    Honorary Members, 55
    Northern Ireland, 54
    Scotland, 54
    women members, 57, 58
  1940–1960
    active members, 64
    increased membership, 73
    teaching qualification, 64
    women members, 67–9, 82
  1960s
    ALT relationship, 110, 111
    divided opinions, 109, 110, 119
    eligibility 109–11
    federal structure, 110
    institutional membership, 110
  1970s
    eligibility, 161
    women members, 161
  1980s
    ALT relationship, 193, 194
    eligibility, 193, 205
  1990s
    eligibility, 210, 211
    equality of opportunity, 241
    Irish initiatives, 215, 216
    Scottish initiatives, 215
    women members, 241
Merkin (R), 249
Miers (D), 256
Ministry of Justice
  legal education and conduct issues, 177
  research work, 177
  SPTL cooperation, 177
Mitchell (J), 144
Montrose (JL), 70, 71, 74, 75, 82, 87, 92, 95, 106,
      112, 116
Morgan (D), 214, 249
Murison (AF), 34

National Board for Prices and Incomes, 92
National Centre for Legal Education, 229
National Incomes Commission (NIC)
  establishment, 90
  law teaching profession, 90
  SPTL submission, 90–2
  university staff remuneration, 90–2

National Service
effect, of, 59
Newsletter
Constituency News, 192
Editors
Mary Hayes, 191, 194
Nigel Gravells, 191
Young Members Group influence, 191

Odgers (B), 27, 29, 33
Ormrod Committee on Legal Education
academic law teaching, 117
academic/professional lawyer relationship,
129, 130
ALT/SPTL joint submission, 111
comparative views
Canadian perspective, 130
US experience, 130
core subjects, 131
effects, 161
entry into the profession, 129, 132, 137
implementation, 129
inter-disciplinary approach, 117
law school freedom, 129
practitioner law teachers, 129, 130
recognition of law degrees, 129, 132, 137
report, 129
scholarship/research, 117, 118
SPTL
concerns, 117
criticisms, 131–3
representation, 116
submission, 116, 117
terms of reference, 116
vocational training, 135

Parker (CF), 99, 126, 133, 152
Pedagogy
assessment methods, 146, 147
audio-visual aids, 146
coursework, 147
examinations
multiple choice, 146
open book, 146, 147
legal information retrieval systems, 146
practice of teaching, 146
Peter Birks Book Prize, 259, 262
Pettit (PH), 4, 185
Pollock (F), 8, 33
Poole (J), 249
Prisoners of war
wartime correspondence courses, 61
Prosser (JAW), 248, 249

Quality Assurance Agency (QAA), 208, 212,
213, 230

Relationship with the profession
see **Legal profession relationship**

Renton Committee
SPTL submission, 126
Research Assessment Exercise (RAE)
assessment panels, 237, 238
Committee of Heads of University Law
Schools (CHULS), 238
cost centres, 180
criticisms, 238
effective performance indicators, 180
external audit, 247
frequency, 247
lack of transparency, 180
preparations, 247
research funding, 180
Roberts Review, 247
SPTL involvement, 180, 181, 204, 237–9
teaching resources, 167
Research matters
see also **Research Assessment Exercise (RAE)**
1930–1939
importance, 49
Institute of Legal Research 51–3
research provision, 49, 51
1960s (SPTL)
Institute of Advanced Legal Studies, 93
research facilities, 95
research pressures, 94, 95
1970s (SPTL)
empirical research, 140, 141
expository tradition, 148
financial difficulties, 140
library resources, 146
research degrees, 148
research leave, 148
SPTL Survey, 140
1980s (SPTL)
Academic Purpose Fund, 179, 180
comparative law, 178
computers and law, 178
family law, 178
product liability, 178
property law, 178
reproductive medicine, 178
specialist conference activity, 178
SPTL activity, 178
SSRC programme, 178
tortious liability, 178
1990s (SPTL)
Academic Purpose Fund, 233
library matters, 234–6
Specialist Subject Groups 236, 237
SPTL prizes, 233
SPTL seminars, 233, 234
support, 232
travel scholarships, 232, 233
UK National Committee of Comparative
Law, 237
2000 and beyond
annual seminars, 246

BIALL cooperation, 246
consultation papers, 246
importance, 247, 248
library resources, 246
publications, 246
Robbins Committee
establishment, 85
influence, 86
responses, 86
Robbins Principle, 86
SPTL submission
Chairs in law, 89
Commonwealth relations, 89
conditions of service, 89
curriculum, 88
importance of law teaching, 88
legal sociology, 88
liberal educational values, 88
need for resources, 88
professional training, 88
remuneration issues, 89
significance, 89
staff recruitment, 89
terms of reference, 86
Royal Commission on Legal Services
entry to legal profession, 137
SPTL submission, 137
Royal Commission on University Education,
27–9, 31

Selden Society, 56
Smith (FE), 79
Smith (JC), 87, 128, 161, 182, 194, 199, 200
Smith (TB), 153
Social Science Research Council (SSRC)
allocation of resources, 139, 176
socio-legal studies, 139–41, 185
Society of Legal Scholars
change/choice of name, 244, 254
conferences
Advisory Committee, 260
conference management, 260
format, 261
postgraduate members, 261
subject sections, 262
Subject Sections Convenor, 260
finance
financial management, 256
financial review, 256
membership database, 255, 256
modernisation, 255
subscription increases, 257
new technology
email, 257, 258
Society's website, 257
outreach
Academy of Social Sciences, 263
Association of American Law Schools, 263
Canadian Association of Law Teachers, 263

consultation papers, 252
international links, 263
Irish membership, 252
Law Commission contacts, 252, 262
Ministry of Justice, 262
President's Reception, 252, 253, 262
profile raising, 252
research funds, 251, 252
relationship with the legal profession
Joint Announcement, 253, 263
Law Society, 253, 254
Legal Education Committee, 253, 254
Royal Charter, 244, 254
rules, 254, 255, 261
Society of Public Teachers of Law (SPTL)
see also **Law teachers**; **Legal education**
1908–1909
Annual General Meeting, 4, 5, 14, 15
finances, 1
formation, 3
historical context, 6
initial support 1, 2
intellectual justification 14
judicial support, 14
meetings, 2, 3
membership, 3, 4
structure, 2
1910–1918
administrative structure, 17
Annual Dinner, 17
Annual General Meeting, 23
annual subscription, 17
collegiality, 19
constituent meeting 17, 20
finances 18
membership issues, 20
officers, 17–19
permanent base, 18
public role, 27
purposes, 20
records, 18, 19
1919–1930
change of name, 46
provincial representation, 42
social expectations, 46
1930–1939
annual subscription, 56, 59
regional meetings, 54
social life, 56, 57
wine fund, 56
1940–1960
academic conservatism, 68–71, 81, 82
administrative work, 64
Australian contacts, 66
European contacts, 66
exchange visits, 66
influence, 72, 73
intellectual regeneration, 77

SPTL 1940–1960 – *continued*
  relationship with legal profession, 67, 73,
    70
  transatlantic contacts, 66
  1960s
    Council of Legal Education contact, 115,
     116
    international relationships, 112, 113
    law reform, 118
    Law Society contact, 115, 116
    relationship with legal profession, 114–16
  1970s
    administrative structure, 124
    amendment to rules, 124
    decision-making processes, 124
    European Community Law, 144
    increased costs, 126
    law reform, 136
    obstacles, 127
    relationship with legal profession, 134, 135
    subscription increases, 125
    Young Members Group influence, 124,
     125, 127, 161
  1980s
    Advisory Committee on Legal Education,
     176
    College of Law contact, 173
    Law Commission contacts, 174–6
    Ministry of Justice contacts, 177
    relationship with legal profession, 170–4,
     176, 204
    Research Assessment Exercise (RAE), 180,
     181, 204
    research matters (generally), 178
    specialist groups, 181, 182, 203
    structural reform, 205, 206
  1990s
    academic interchange/scholarly debate,
     209
    Advisory Committee on Legal Education,
     217, 223
    Advisory Committee on Legal Education
     and Conduct, 223–5
    changes/initiatives, 208–10, 242
    Common Professional Examination
     (CPE), 219, 220, 222, 224
    core subjects, 217
    Council of Legal Education, 221
    international outlook, 209
    Joint Announcement, 225, 226
    Law Commission contacts, 226, 227
    law school funding, 209, 217, 218
    Law Society contacts, 218, 222
    legal education, 209
    legal scholarship, 242
    library matters, 234–6
    Lord Chancellor's Department (contacts),
     227
    name change, 243, 244

  relationship with legal profession, 216–26
  representational role, 242
  research matters, 232–7
  Royal Charter request, 243, 244
  Socio-Legal Studies Association (SLSA),
   242
  strategic role, 241–3
Annual Conferences (SPTL)
  see **Annual Conferences (SPTL)**
assessment (first fifty years)
  see **First fifty years (SPTL)**@INDEX-S =
collective voice (1980s)
  consultation papers, 168, 169
  controversial issues, 168
  core subjects, 169
  Government Green Papers, 168
  legal education, 169, 170
  legal profession reforms, 168, 169
  press contact, 168
  relationship with legal profession, 205
  student numbers, 169
  university funding, 169
Consumer Law Group, 178
financial stringency
  see **Financial stringency (SPTL/1980s)**
international relationships
  see **International relationships (SPTL)**
law publishing
  see **Law publishing**
membership issues
  see **Membership issues (SPTL)**
Presidential Addresses
  publication, 199
  subject-matter, 199–203
Robbins Committee
  see **Robbins Committee**
research matters
  see **Research matters**
rules
  amendment (1970s), 124
  American example 20
  initial drafts, 20
specialist subject groups
  Administrative Law Group, 182
  Consumer Law Group, 178, 181
  Contract Law Group, 181
  Criminal Law Group, 182
  Criminal Law Reform Sub-Committee,
   182
  expansion, 181, 182
  participation, 236
  Public Law Reform Sub-Committee, 182
  publications, 237
  Socio-Legal Group, 137, 138
  Special Committees, 182
  Subject Sections Convenor, 236
  Tort Group, 181
World War II
  see also **World War II**

annual meeting, 59
correspondence courses, 60, 61
emergency measures, 59
period of office, 59
Young Members Group (YMG)
see **Young Members Group (YMG)**
Socio-Legal Group (SPTL), 137, 138
Socio-legal studies
Academy of Social Sciences, 184
Association of Learned Societies in the Social
Sciences, 184
Centre for Socio-Legal Studies, 139, 183
Committee on Social Services and Law, 139,
140
development, 183
doctrinal/socio-legal debate, 138
Economic and Social Research Council
(ESRC), 185, 186, 204
emergence, 105
Heyworth Committee on the Future of Social
Studies, 89, 106, 107
Institute of Advanced Legal Studies, 108
Legal Action Group (LAG), 139
library resources, 105
publications, 183, 184, 216
research, 139–41, 216
social economic environment, 141
Social Science Research Council (SSRC),
139–41, 185
Socio-Legal Studies Association (SLSA), 216,
242
SPTL
Socio-Legal Group, 137, 138
views, 184, 186
Young Members Group (YMG), 107
see also **Young Members Group (YMG)**
Sparkes (P), 260
Stallybrass (WT), 69
Stanton (K), 256
Steele (J), 249
Stein (PG), 184, 193
Street (H), 101, 147

Tapper (CFH), 101, 105
Teaching Quality Assessments (TQAs), 208, 230
The Reporter
Constituency News, 211, 213
editorial policy, 249
editorials, 250, 251
Editors
Anthony Bradney, 212, 213, 231, 249–51
William Swaddling, 211–13
legal education matters, 209, 212
publication, 211
Quality Assurance Agency (QAA), 212, 213
Research Assessment Exercise (RAE), 212, 213
subject matter, 211–13
Thomas (P), 183
Thomson (JM), 215, 262

Tort Group (SPTL), 181
Trevelyan (E), 33
Twining (WL), 107, 112, 128, 129, 138, 148, 149,
156, 157, 160–2, 164, 263

Uglow (J), 159, 160
**UK National Committee of Comparative Law
(UKNCCL)**, 237
**Universities Central Council on Admissions
(UCCA)**, 99, 100
University admissions (1960s period)
career implications, 99
clearing house system, 100
gender differences, 99
London University, 99
Oxbridge entry, 99
Universities Central Council on Admissions
(UCCA), 99, 100
University Grants Committee (UGC), 85, 87,
135, 142, 143, 166, 167

Vickers (L), 260
Vocational training
College of Law, 135
costs, 135
Council of Legal Education, 135
Ormrod Committee on Legal Education, 135
polytechnic/university law schools, 135, 136
solicitor's training, 135, 136
University Grants Commission (UGC), 135

Wade (ECS), 46
Walker (DM), 75, 76, 82
Wallington (PT), 171
Webb (S), 28
Wedderburn (KW), 108, 109
Wells (C), 214, 249, 261
Wikely (N), 249
Williams (G), 75, 146, 153
Wilson (G), 130, 132, 133, 139, 140
Wilson (J F), 93, 95, 119, 133, 216, 217, 223, 228
Winfield (PH), 49
Women
entry into the legal profession, 44, 57, 58
equality of opportunity, 241
gender issues, 241
SPTL
membership, 21, 22, 57, 58, 67–9, 82, 161
participation, 241
university admissions, 99
World War II
correspondence courses, 60, 61, 81
Council of Legal Education, 63, 64
destruction of buildings, 62
examinations
onboard HM Ships, 63
overseas examinations, 63
fire-watchers, 62
prisoners of war, 61

World War II – *continued*
  professional legal education, 63
  refresher courses, 63
  staff numbers, 63
  staff/student casualties, 62
  student numbers, 63
  university conditions, 61–3
Worthington (S), 262
Wortley (BA), 67, 107

Year Book Project, 41
Young Members Group (YMG)
  annual meetings, 127
  assessment, 192, 193
  calls for reform, 121–5, 127
  constituency representatives, 127
  establishment, 104, 119
  European Community Law, 144
    see also **European Community Law**

first meeting, 104, 105
importance, 105
influence, 155, 161, 191
law reform issues, 122
legal education issues, 122, 123
membership issues, 122
newsletters, 123–5
publishing initiatives, 122
relationship with legal profession, 123
significance, 119
socio-legal studies, 107
    see also **Socio-legal studies**
specialist legal groups, 122, 127, 128
teaching techniques, 128, 129
trade union activities, 122
workshops, 122

Zellick (G), 217